BIG EIGHT FOOTBALL

Books by John D. McCallum

Ivy League Football: Since 1872

Big Ten Football: Since 1895

We Remember Rockne

College Football, U.S.A.

This Was Football (with Walter Heffelfinger)

Getting Into Pro Football

College Basketball, U.S.A.

The World Heavyweight Boxing Championship

The Encyclopedia of World Boxing Champions

Dumb Dan

Crime Doctor

Dave Beck

Ty Cobb

The Tiger Wore Spikes

Everest Diary

That Kelly Family

Six Roads From Abilene

Going Their Way

BIG EIGHT FOOTBALL

John D. McCallum

CHARLES SCRIBNER'S SONS / NEW YORK

Big Eight Football
is a registered trademark
and is used with the permission of
the Big Eight Conference.

Copyright © 1979 John McCallum

Library of Congress Cataloging in Publication Data

McCallum, John Dennis, 1924–
Big Eight football.

1. Big Eight Conference—History. 2. Football.
I. Title.
GV958.5.B3M29   796.33′263′0973   79-15394
ISBN 0-684-16316-0

1 3 5 7 9 11 13 15 17 19 M/C 20 18 16 14 12 10 8 6 4 2

To

Wayne Cody

One who has

brought much

joy to the

sports fans

of the

Pacific Northwest

Contents

BIG EIGHT FOOTBALL

Prologue

have said this before: get two old-time football players together, who bridge the gap and know the old days, and the talk will go back down the years. Let younger athletes sit in on it, and they will listen respectfully for a while before they become convinced that the talk is a pack of damned lies.

And in an era of super specialists and platoon football, how can they think otherwise? Listen, do football players play for 60 minutes a game anymore? How many of them tackle as well as block? The answer, of course, is obvious: not many.

I had heard and read so much about some of those old geezers that, until I actually started meeting some of them, after World War II, I was sure they never really existed. There was Pudge Heffelfinger, for example. Pudge played football at Yale in 1889, when Walter C. Camp was coach. A three-time All-American, he was the first guard ever to pull out of the line and run interference for the ball carrier. In 1953, shortly before he died, Pudge and I wrote *This Was Football* together. But until I actually met him in the flesh, I was certain that he was only a literary invention of some science-fiction writer, very likely one of Gargantua's rowdy companions. Say, wasn't he the big old boy so huge that when he trotted onto the field the mere weight of him caused tidal waves as far away as the Red Sea? Didn't it take an ant eight hours just to walk across one of his knees? Wasn't he the guy who once ripped up Yale Field by the roots and threw it halfway across Connecticut? Wasn't that Pudge Heffelfinger, against Harvard, who sent all of his teammates to the bench and then beat the Crimson by himself, 150–6? Didn't he once pick up a Princeton halfback in the palm of his hand and squeeze the very life out of him?

Bald-faced exaggerations, of course. But you get the picture. William Walter ("Pudge") Heffelfinger (always known as Walter or Pudge) was unique. He was only nine days short of his sixty-sixth birthday when he played his last football game. Actually, he was not a giant at all (at least not by present standards). He stood 6 feet 3 inches and weighed only 198 pounds, but to pick an argument with him on a football field with anything less than a Gatling gun was a sure form of suicide. His peculiar talent was mashing ball carriers into funny shapes and sizes. He was the original Attila the Hun of football linemen.

Because of people like Heffelfinger, college football is more than a national madness—it is part of our folklore. Its personalities have grown in the public consciousness from ordinary human beings into heroes and demigods. A vast body of legend has accumulated about the game. It is, on the whole, a glittering romantic legend, and its stories are as many and various as the tales recounted in the age of fable.

Down the years, football has been a game of changes in systems, techniques, and philosophies, which occur about once a decade, usually as part of a cycle. The spread punt, for instance, was abandoned in the early part of the twentieth century and returned to popularity forty years later. The four-point offensive stance for linemen disappeared with the discontinuation of power football and returned in the 1950s with Woody Hayes's "three yards and a cloud of dust" philosophy. The T formation disappeared from the scene in 1900 until it was resurrected by Clark Shaughnessy at Stanford in 1940, and it has dominated football ever since.

Generally, there is nothing much new in offense or defense. An impression of newness is created when a series, formation, or defense is successfully employed by a team and becomes nationally recognized. The successful action is then adopted by other coaches. Like an old suit, a football idea will return to fashion if one waits long enough. The cycle of offense from one year to another is often determined by the trend in defense throughout the country and the technique employed during the previous season. In a restricted sense, a team's offense will differ from week to week, depending on what is expected from the defense. Packed defenses force teams to use their flank games almost exclusively and to throw the ball, even though they have a mediocre passing attack.

During the late 1940s and early 1950s ball-control football, with little passing and a minimum of different running plays, was the vogue. The great success of Army and Ohio State on land with this grind-'em-out, small-chunk offense started a trend toward this type of offensive football. During this period many people in the coaching profession and the press believed that the success of so many teams with control football was forcing the passing game to a point where it was about to become as extinct as the dodo bird.

There was considerable concern about the necessity of doing something with the playing rules before this kind of offense completely upset the balance between the team with the ball and the defense. Some felt that the abolition of the unrestricted, or free, substitutions rule in 1953 did much to place this emphasis on the running game. In reality, the power offense with emphasis on ball control was nothing more than a return to the caveman type of football played in the 1890s. Coaches soon flocked to this offensive idea because a successful offense or defense can be copied without fear of patent infringement. Trends develop when coaches assume that what is successful for one team will be successful for another.

The surest thing about football is that somewhere a coach will come up with a different frill, a unique twist, or a new look to give the game added color. This has been true for more than a hundred years because football is a dynamic game that reaches new heights of drama and perfection with the arrival of each autumn.

There was a time in college football when hardness, courage, great enthusiasm, and reckless abandon were the ingredients of winning defensive football. Today, it takes a great deal more in the way of speed and savvy beyond these basic fundamentals to play excellent defense. Football defense is like pitching in baseball—it can be responsible for between 60 and 80 percent of the victories.

If a 1979 offensive football team played the best 1940 defensive team, there is every reason to believe that the scores would be astronomical. If you don't think so, just look at some of the present-day scores. Turning back time, there was virtually no pass defense in 1940, and a contest between 1979 and 1940 teams would be a version of Notre Dame versus the "Little Sisters of the Poor." Today, the defensive geniuses must defend against the sprint outs, drop backs, roll outs, bootlegs, and wide receivers who can all run the 100-yard dash in 9.6 or 9.7 seconds. In addition, they still have all the problems they had in the 1940s and 1950s.

College football has never been better. The collegians now average 40 percent more plays than the professionals, and this is mainly because the pros use 26 of the 30 seconds permitted to get the ball in play. The college teams are using 15 of the 30 seconds allowed by rule, and in the last three weeks of the season it is usually reduced to 13 seconds. In 1958, 20 seconds was the average time taken to put the ball in play. The Sunday spectator spends 10 minutes of his afternoon watching the pros standing in the huddle or walking out to the ball. The slowest pro team gets off fifty-seven plays and the fastest college team runs off ninety-seven.

The Football Code, which prefaces the College Rules of the Game, states, "Traditionally, football is the game of the schools and colleges." It is the game of the colleges because almost all segments of the game originated on the campuses. Deep in this vein, there was much speculation in 1978 when St. Louis Cardinals owner Bill Bidwill hired sixty-two-year-old Charles ("Bud") Wilkinson as head coach. Wilkinson had been out of coaching since 1963, when he walked away from the head coaching job at Oklahoma a living legend.

Tom Banks, the Cardinal center, called the Wilkinson hiring "one of the weirdest things I've ever seen."

"What has Bidwill gotten us into?" asked wide receiver Mel Gray.

Added linebacker Eric Williams, in his second season at St. Louis: "Wow! That dude is *old.*"

Even more disturbing was the assessment of Ralph Neely, the Dallas Cowboy guard who played his college football under Wilkinson at Oklahoma in 1962–1963: "I personally think the odds are against him. The game has changed so much in the last fifteen years."

But Wilkinson was not intimidated. He said he didn't think there were any changes in football he couldn't learn. After all, weren't the 1978 Cardinals using the popular 3–4 defense for the first time?

"And, shucks," Bud Wilkinson pointed out, "all the 3–4 is is a variation on the *Oklahoma defense* that I invented thirty years ago."

Touché.

Nebraska vs. Iowa State,
November 6, 1971

Colorado vs. Missouri,
October 25, 1969

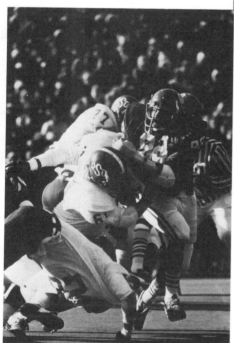

Oklahoma vs. Oklahoma State,
November 30, 1974

Kansas vs. Kansas State,
October 13, 1973

This Is Foot ball Count. y

F orget all that stuff about Princeton and Rutgers and the first college game in 1869. In the land of the pickup truck and cream gravy for breakfast—down there in the old dirt-kicking Big Eight territory—the natives think *they* invented football. And they believe with a passion that their big ol' boys play tackle better than anywhere else in the world. Why, football out there is bigger than cowboy boots and the Stetson hat—it's bigger than country music—bigger even than girls.

It wasn't always so, of course. A reporter's account of an early-day, local football game at Lawrence, Kansas, read as follows:

A little nonsense now and then is relished by the wisest men. Truly was this proverb exemplified last Saturday when a goodly crowd assembled to see a group of local prominent business men throw aside their conventional dignity in a rollicking game of football. The score was 76 to 42 in favor of the home team. Capt. Fry acted as umpire and referee, and what he said was final. Elmer Pratt, quarterback for the home team, while making a long dash downfield, stopped to tie his shoe and lost the ball. Elmer said, "Kings ex," but not soon enough to prevent the opposing right guard from falling on him. Cyrus Hornbeck, president of the local bank, watched the game for a few moments and then left in disgust. "There's no fool like an old fool," he said. He then announced he was raising the rent on the home of J. Milton Brown, the home team's 126-pound right guard.

Time marches on. Old grouch Hornbeck is long forgotten, and football today is a geographical, historical, and social event. Ever since Nebraska started playing Notre Dame, in 1915 (Cornhuskers 20, Fighting Irish 19), everyone who follows the Big Eight has had *somebody* he especially likes to see beaten. During the week of their game, Nebraska feels about Oklahoma the way Yale feels about Harvard. Beneath the breast of every Kansas bass drummer lies a hatred for Missouri. Whirl a Colorado man around several times and he'll stagger straight to Lincoln, Nebraska, with a couple of buckets of silver and gold paint, if the cardinal and gold of Iowa State hasn't already beaten him there. Give an Oklahoma State supporter a few drinks, and he'll bet all the beef on the hoof he's got that the OSU Cowboys will whip the Sooners.

Tradition and rivalry are words that belong almost exclusively to the vernacular of college football. Old as the two words are, they are irreplaceable, for it is what they suggest that specifically separates the college game from that of the professionals. Sophisticates with their double drag-outs and their post-and-gos may not like it, but college football *is* Nebraska playing Missouri with the Big Eight championship hinging on the outcome. It is also a street brawl in downtown Dallas the night before Oklahoma plays Texas, and Colorado students stealing the Kansas mascot.

This will give you an idea of football's status in Lincoln: The Cornhuskers opened the 1976–1977 basketball season by winning ten of their first eleven games. One of the local newspapers then ran the headline "NEBRASKA NOW 10–1," and 12,000 fans booked flights to the Orange Bowl.

What is Big Eight football? It is Kansas State rooters pelting the visiting Kansas University players with banana peels to get even for a game the year before, when KU fans showered hot dogs all over K State's star player.

Big Eight football is Jim Dickey being hired as head coach at Kansas State. "The Wildcats haven't won a conference championship in forty years," he said as he signed his new contract. "Well, if I don't win a championship in that same length of time, I'll resign."

Big Eight football is Washington State playing Nebraska at Lincoln in 1977. Both teams wore the same color combinations—scarlet for the Cornhuskers, and crimson for the Cougars. Adding to the confusion, the teams even warmed up identically. One of the Washington State players came out of the locker room quite late, and he had to pass through the NU squad, busily engaged in their stretching exercises. In fact, at that precise moment they were doing the same warm-up drills as WSU. What the hell—why not? So the Washington State player jumped in with the Nebraska players and did his exercises with them. No one caught on either—until one of the WSU coaches finally came over and escorted his boy to the right side.

Big Eight football? Well, it's Alex Karras recalling a dry, hot summer day in Norman, Oklahoma, when he was playing an exhibition game with the Detroit Lions against the Philadelphia Eagles. It seems that Alex has always had a phobia about bugs and mice and such:

Bugs especially. I just go crazy with that stuff. Well, there we were, in Norman, Oklahoma, where the Oklahoma Sooners have made so much history. Have you ever been in Norman, Oklahoma, in August? It must have been 200,000 degrees hot. I started sweating my pants off as soon as we arrived there. But even worse than the heat were the bugs. *I'll never forget the bugs. The playing field in Norman looks nice and fresh and green, but when you*

hit the ground on a tackle or a block, it comes alive—z-z-z-z-z—these bugs coming out of there. Sweat bugs, I think they are. You get terribly tired playing in that awful heat in Norman, but you don't relax lying around on the ground, no sir! The bugs will get you. If you get hit to the ground, you jump up fast as you can. God's truth! You hardly ever see anyone lying on the ground in Norman, Oklahoma.

Though the Texas Longhorns do not belong to the Big Eight, their annual football ferocity with Oklahoma is strictly *M*A*S*H* for players and fans alike. It is one of the maddest spectacles of sport. The game is played in the Cotton Bowl, with 76,000 seats of the stadium crammed with the loudest, most animated partisans in college football, evenly divided between Texans and Oklahomans. Regardless of the team records, the excitement is there each year. Just before the game's kickoff a few years ago, fullback Harold Philipp of Texas, talking about the Texas boys playing for Oklahoma, compared the Texas defectors to American soldiers playing for Germany during World War II. During the contest an immense roar wafts up from the stadium on every play, and the two large bands play "Boomer Sooner," the Oklahoma fight song, and "Texas Fight," the Longhorns' song, over and over again, always to the accompaniment of a cheering, jeering mob of singers. More often than not, the action in the stands matches the fighting on the field.

In some ways, these Texas–Oklahoma games are a bit much. When he was still coaching, Darrell Royal called them "old-fashioned, country, jaw-to-jaw, knucks-down gut checks." Knucks down? "Yeah," he explained, "like when you shot marbles as a kid and then you started playing for 'keeps,' and everybody got knucks down. You hoped that

Folsom Field, University of Colorado, Boulder.   Capacity: 52,005.

ISU Stadium, Iowa State University, Ames.   Capacity: 50,000.

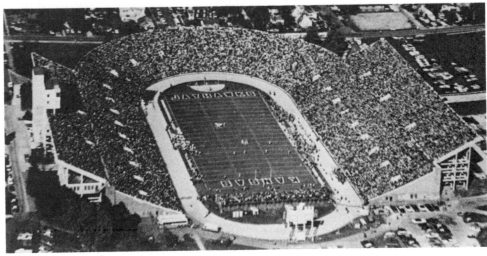

Memorial Stadium, University of Kansas, Lawrence.   Capacity: 51,500.

other guy's hand would quiver, and if it didn't, then you knew you were all covered up with trouble. When Texas plays Oklahoma, we're often all covered up with trouble."

Friday night before the Texas–Oklahoma game has become the biggest gut check of all, at least for the fans. For blocks, in the heart of Dallas, in the hours leading up to and just after midnight, the fans play something that could be called World War III. Sirens ring out as the city comes under the siege of drunks, wanderers, shouters, pranksters, rooters, and tone-deaf music makers. The all-time record for arrests tops 800.

Bob Greene, the syndicated columnist out of Chicago, said that he has a friend who attended the University of Oklahoma. Shortly before the 1978 Texas game, this friend learned that he would be unable to pick up the game on any television or radio station in the town where he lived. So he did the only obvious thing. He put on his Oklahoma jersey, got out his Boomer Sooner doll (when you pull the string in the doll's neck, it sings "Boomer Sooner" and squawks "Beat Texas" and "Go Big Red"), and called his father in Little Rock, Arkansas. Then he had his father put the telephone next to the radio for the entire second half, and thus was able to hear the play-by-play, live as it happened.

Down through the years, the Big Eight has played some of the best college football in the country. Out in the corn belt they grow them bigger, stronger, and tougher. In his Civil War memoirs, General William T. Sherman pointed out that though the Southerners usually beat the Easterners on the battlefield, it was the hard-bitten farm boys from what is today Big Eight territory who broke the back of the Confederacy. "Our corn belt pioneers had not forgotten how to use their legs," General Sherman said. "They could really march."

The motorcar age hasn't seemed to atrophy those legs, either, as witness the number of top ten teams, All-Americans, professional prospects, and Heisman Trophy winners that have come out of the Big Eight.

When All-Pro defensive halfback Don Paul was playing for the world champion Cleveland Browns some years ago, the consensus around the NFL was that the best players came out of the Big Eight. Paul recalled:

The people who made the big plays seemed to come from those schools. They had a winning way about them. When the going got tough, they got tougher. In my college career at Washington State we'd lose to the big California powers—USC, Stanford, UCLA, Cal—but from the standpoint of physical punishment, it was like a honeymoon compared to playing those muscled-up bullies from the Big Eight. They really socked you. I remember something Coach Paul Brown once said to me. He said that when he got ready to build his Browns, he invariably scouted the Big Eight Conference first.

Typical of the hard-nosed football played in the league was the Oklahoma–Nebraska game of 1971, played on Thanksgiving Day at Norman. Whenever those two teams meet it always seems to be the "game of the century," or a grand final summit meeting to decide who's No. 1 in the polls. Actually, there was nothing "typical" about this encounter. It was something special. It would be virtually impossible to thumb through the pages of Big Eight history and find a matchup in which *both* sides played so admirably, so tenaciously, for an entire 60 minutes of football. Some of the more cerebral types who will keep replaying the game in years to come put it right up there alongside the greatest collegiate football battles ever. Maybe so, consider-

KSU Stadium, Kansas State University, Manhattan. Capacity: 42,000.

Faurot Field, University of Missouri, Columbia. Capacity: 60,931.

Memorial Stadium, University of Nebraska, Lincoln. Capacity: 76,015.

ing the tense conditions that existed.

The contest brimmed with quality. Both teams appeared positively unbeatable. They had been steamrolling everybody, week after week. The Sooners had averaged an awesome 563 yards and 45 points per game against nine straight opponents, three of whom were among the nation's best teams: USC (33–20), Texas (48–27), and Colorado (45–17). The Oklahoma statistics not only led the country in 1971, they were destined to become national records. Offense was the name of the OU game, and Jack Mildren, Greg Pruitt, Joe Wylie, Jon Harrison, and Tom Brahaney, operating from a fashionable wishbone T, were what made it go. Mildren was in the process of becoming the first quarterback within memory to gain over 1,000 yards rushing—but he could also throw. And in halfback Pruitt, later a pro star, Mildren had the fastest breakaway runner in college football. Pruitt's favorite play was to take a wide pitchout from Mildren off the wishbone's triple option; it had a lot to do with the 1,423 yards Pruitt had already gained.

Speed was everywhere in the Oklahoma backfield. Joe Wylie and Roy Bell were almost as fleet as Pruitt. So was Jon Harrison, the sure-handed flanker who was Mildren's favorite target.

Nebraska's numbers were almost as imposing as Oklahoma's. The Cornhuskers had demolished ten straight opponents for an average of 38 points a game; in total offense, they were gaining 441 yards a game. More important, they had allowed a mere 6.4 points a game, tops in the country.

Nebraska was a complete team, coupling a balanced attack of passing and running with a stubborn defense. Arrayed with such All-Americans as Johnny Rodgers, Jerry Tagge, Jeff Kinney, Rich Glover, Willie Harper, and Larry Jacobsen, the Cornhuskers reflected the

personality of Coach Bob Devaney. They probed and hammered, ran and passed, working toward field position, and holding that line. They thought of themselves as a team without stars, but stars had emerged. Quarterback Jerry Tagge, big, strong, and intelligent, was a star. He could throw, run, read defenses, and lead. He was the boss. In the huddle once, Jeff Kinney, the powerful running back, said to Tagge, "I'm tired, Tag." And Tagge scowled and said, "Shut up, I'll tell you when you're tired."

Then there was Johnny Rodgers, halfback and flanker. He could beat you catching, running, returning punts, or simply by going in motion. He was a game breaker, a constant threat.

Everyone who had played both teams during the season was asked to make a comparison.

"Oklahoma has a more devastating attack," said Vince Gibson, whose Kansas State Wildcats were demolished by the Sooners, 75–28. "Their backs are flashy and swift. They only want the football so they can score again. Chuck Fairbanks's theory is that his team will simply outpoint you."

Perhaps Fred Casotti, the Colorado assistant athletic director, said it best: "It depends on how you want to die. Oklahoma kills you quick, like a dagger in the heart. Nebraska slowly gives you cancer."

This was how it was when 63,385 ticket holders and a national TV audience of millions watched the two giants line up for the kickoff that Thanksgiving Day in 1971. Briefly, everything ultimately balanced out, according to the scouting reports, even the crucial few mistakes. The Sooners fumbled the ball three times, Nebraska once. The only penalty in the game was a costly Nebraska offsides. Both teams packed crushing fury on offense, which more or less pushed the de-

Owen Field, University of Oklahoma, Norman.   Capacity: 71,827.

Lewis Stadium, Oklahoma State University, Stillwater.   Capacity: 49,991.

fenses around. But then, as coaches Fairbanks and Devaney agreed afterward, you can't stop every weapon. Both sides stopped the maneuvers they feared most, but in so doing they opened the floodgates to virtually everything else. From the Oklahoma wishbone, Nebraska stopped the wide pitch to Pruitt, but gave up Mildren's keepers, Leon Crosswhite's fullback jabs into the line, and most of all Mildren's passes to Jon Harrison. To stop Pruitt, the Cornhuskers were forced to cover Harrison one on one, which was an impossibility. He caught four vital passes, two for touchdowns, as Mildren dropped back and calmly drilled the ball smack on target. From Nebraska's powerful I-spread and I-slot attack, Oklahoma took away the passing game, smothering Rodgers with double and triple coverage, rushing Tagge unendingly. But the Sooners had to sacrifice their power running, and that was where Kinney became a hero.

In this way the two rivals exchanged touchdowns evenly from scrimmage, four for four, and Oklahoma added a field goal, which kept looming up as possibly the real difference as the teams fought on. But there always lingered the one factor they had not traded—a pearl of a punt return by Rodgers in the game's first 3½ minutes. It was one of those sudden, shocking, insanely thrilling plays in which an athlete, seized by the moment, "twisted, whirled, slipped, held his balance, spun, darted, curved and fled all the way to the goal line," as author Dan Jenkins so aptly put it afterward. The play was good for 72 yards. When Rodgers got back to the Nebraska bench, dead with exhaustion, he did what most everybody in the Oklahoma stadium probably wanted to do. He threw up.

What the punt return accomplished was monumental to the Nebraska cause. It gave the Cornhuskers an 11-point lead twice during the game, at 14–3 in the second quarter and

28–17 late in the third quarter. It forced the Sooners to play catch-up football all afternoon. And when that marvelous magician, Mildren, overcame the Nebraska lead twice, back bounced Tagge and the Cornhuskers to recapture it with a single drive.

With just 7 minutes left to play, Mildren had done all he could. He had dashed for two touchdowns and passed for two more. He had wishboned 467 yards against the best defense in collegiate football. And he had given his team a 31–28 lead in a game that had left everybody talking to themselves. Both teams had just about run out of heroics.

But Nebraska still had Tagge and Rodgers and Kinney, and the Nebraska attack was gearing up for one last barrage. On the sideline, Coach Devaney remained calm. He had lost control of himself only once earlier in the game, when he turned to his defensive platoon on the bench and grumbled sarcastically, "Why in hell don't some of you guys give Glover some help once in a while?" Rich Glover, the All-America quick middle guard, had been making most of the tackles.

But Devaney was calm again now, and when the Cornhuskers jacked up for a final drive of 74 yards, he was willing to let Tagge run the show. The Oklahoma defense was worn to a frazzle, and Tagge knew it. The Nebraska ground game had taken its toll, especially on Kinney, who had banged his way to 174 yards and three touchdowns.

In the huddle, none of the Cornhuskers said a word to Tagge. Nobody had to remind them what had to be done. They *knew* what had to be done. "We never doubted we were going to win the game, one way or another," Tagge remembered later.

The drive ate up 6 minutes on the clock and required a dozen plays. Tagge would break out of the huddle, walk up to the line, and frequently call an audible. While Oklahoma waited for a pass, he would key on the Sooner safety and run to the opposite side. Kinney broke loose for two thrashing runs of 17 yards and 13 yards. He broke tackles, he ground defenders into the turf. His jersey was in shreds.

For the Cornhuskers, there was one moment of plain hell. They had come up to a third down and 8 at the Oklahoma 46, 3 points behind, the clock running, and Oklahoma fighting desperately for a fumble. Tagge called a pass right there, and Oklahoma had a rush on, forcing the Nebraska quarterback to flee for his life. He darted to his right, angling, looking for a receiver, desperate. Out of the corner of his eye, he could see Ray Hamilton, Oklahoma's best defensive end, bearing down on him. He also saw Johnny Rodgers squirming between two defenders, and at the last second he drilled the ball to Rodgers on the Oklahoma 35. Somehow Rodgers caught it for a first down. The Nebraska drive was still alive.

Two minutes later, Nebraska had driven to the Oklahoma 6. With second down and goal to go, Tagge glanced up at the clock and suddenly called time. He wanted a little reassurance from Coach Devaney. He trotted over to the sideline, and they chatted.

Devaney told Tagge to go for the touchdown. "No field goals, no ties," Devaney said.

"Don't worry, coach," Tagge told him. "I'll take us in."

"What's your best play?" Devaney asked.

"I think it's the off-tackle with Jeff," Tagge said.

"Okay, let's run it without any mistakes," Devaney said. "Remember, we're going for the touchdown."

"We'll get it," Tagge said.

Tagge gave the ball to Jeff Kinney on the off-tackle power play, and Jeff banged ahead for 4 yards, down to the 2. Tagge called for Kinney to run the same play. This time Jeff barged over for the touchdown, making the final score 35–31, Nebraska.

Upstairs in the press box, journalists from Malibu to Boston were calling it the greatest college game ever played. Up there also, Nebraska's Don Bryant and Oklahoma's Johnny Keith, the sports-information directors of the two schools, had been sweating out the game together, trying to make light of the game, trying to enjoy it, trying not to act very involved.

"We gave 'em a show, didn't we, Don?" said Keith.

"I think we wrote 'em a pretty good script," Bryant said.

"If I had to see one of these damn things every week, I'd drown myself in a bucket of cream gravy," said Keith.

"Wait till I get my hat and I'll go with you," Bryant said.

It was that kind of game.

In 1978 the two rivals staged another game of the century to decide who was No. 1 in the nation. Nebraska won this one, too, and its fans went around with their index fingers in the air, shouting, "We're No. 1." A Nebraska manufacturer, caught up in the thrill of victory, quickly rushed out an order for 10,000 drinking mugs with the score printed across the front: "Nebraska 17, Oklahoma 14." Before the order could be delivered, however, Missouri popped up and upset the Cornhuskers, 35–31, in the final league contest of the season.

The 10,000 mugs? The order was cancelled. That's the way it goes in the Big Eight all the time.

"We're No. 1!"

There are two major college football polls, one published by Associated Press, the other by United Press International, and they appear in the sports sections of the daily newspapers every Monday evening or Tuesday morning for four months during each football season. Their purpose is to rank the top twenty teams in the nation. Based on ignorance, prejudice, and politicking, it would be easy to dismiss them as a waste of time except for one thing. They ultimately determine which college football team is No. 1 in the country.

The AP poll, which was started in 1936, is compiled from the votes of sixty-nine newspaper writers and television and radio reporters; the UPI, fourteen years younger, reflects the opinions of forty-two head coaches.

The poll business had its origin in 1925. As you might have guessed, good old Knute Rockne of Notre Dame had a big hand in it. What actually occurred was this. A teacher of economics at the University of Illinois named Frank G. Dickinson was a football buff who privately enjoyed rating all the teams in the country by his own mathematical formula. He happened to mention this in the classroom one day, and a student in the back row who was sports editor of the *Daily Illini* wrote a story about it. The story came to the attention of a Chicago clothing manufacturer named Jack Rissman, another buff, who decided he would like to use Dickinson's ratings to select the top team in the Western Conference each year (they didn't all play each other), so that he could present a trophy to the winner. When Rockne heard about this, he invited both Dickinson and Rissman to lunch at South Bend and said, "Why don't you make it a *na-*

tional trophy that Notre Dame will have a chance to win?" Never one to miss out on a good thing, Rock also persuaded Dickinson and Rissman to predate the trophy so that the 1924 "Four Horsemen, Seven Mules" Notre Dame team could be the first genuinely "official" national champion. And so that was how football polls began, and how the Fighting Irish won their first national crown—at lunch!

Professor Dickinson's system was quite simple. Once the season was over, he divided all teams into two categories: those that won more games than they lost, and those that didn't. Then he gave points for wins over teams in the first division and fewer points for wins over teams in the second division. Quality of schedule was not a factor, but the number of games played was, except for postseason bowls. Still, the Dickinson rating system was accepted by fans as the most authoritative until the AP started its poll in 1936.

Everything considered, a solid case can be built around the Big Eight as the most skilled, the best-balanced conference in the country. Since 1936, when Nebraska ranked ninth in the voting, the league has failed to place at least one of its members in the top ten only seven times: 1937, the war years of 1942–1944, 1946, 1947, and 1959. On nine occasions at least two of its teams have made the top ten; and in 1971 Nebraska, Oklahoma, and Colorado finished first, second, and third in the final AP poll. Through 1978 the Sooners finished in the AP's top ten no less than twenty-three times, and Nebraska fifteen. Oklahoma has won the national championship five times, the Cornhuskers twice. Furthermore, the Big Eight has produced four Heisman Trophy winners: Oklahoma's Billy

At the start of the 1978 season, Oklahoma Coach Barry Switzer surprised opponents by revising his powerful wishbone offense and installing an I formation with a tailback position. He did it to take advantage of speedy Billy Ray Sims—and Sims responded by winning the Heisman Trophy.

Vessels (1952) and Steve Owens (1969), and Johnny Rodgers (1972) and Billy Sims (1978) from Nebraska.

Balance? In 1978, for example, the Big Eight season was evenly split between title contenders (Oklahoma, Nebraska, Iowa State, and Missouri) and also-rans (Colorado, Kansas, Kansas State, and Oklahoma State). In the preseason polls, Oklahoma ranked No. 4, Nebraska No. 10, and Iowa State No. 20. For the postseason bowl games, Oklahoma, Nebraska, Missouri, and Iowa State all received invitations.

For much of the season, Nebraska ranked No. 2 in the nation. Typical of the manner in which they shook up opponents, they knocked the bejeebers out of Kansas, 63–21, in Lawrence. The Huskers had a Big Eight–record 799 yards in total offense (516 rushing, 283 passing), the most since they took up football in 1890. Craig Johnson, a third-stringer, rushed ten times for 192 yards and scored on runs of 64 and 60 yards and on a 78-yard pass play. Around Lincoln, Nebraska, the cry was "We're No. 1." After losing to Nebraska, 69–17, Indiana coach Lee Corso said, "I was beaten 69–19 while I coached at Louisville and threw in the towel. Today I couldn't even find a towel to throw in." The 69 points were the most ever scored against an Indiana squad since the school took up football in 1885. Nebraska ran for 415 yards and passed for 198. Leading the way was I. M. Hipp, who scored four touchdowns inside the 10-yard line while piling up 123 yards.

Despite his team's undefeated status and lofty ranking in the national polls, Nebraska coach Tom Osborne was guarded in his comments to the press. Looming up ahead was the dark cloud of Oklahoma, undefeated and definitely in the hunt to be national champion. Nebraska had not beaten the Sooners in five

years. Make no mistake, Coach Barry Switzer had another powerhouse.

Switzer had a ground attack based on speed and a defense braced with strength. In senior Thomas Lott, he had what he called "the best wishbone quarterback ever to play at Oklahoma." Lott, the team's leading rusher in 1977 with a 5.5-yard average, directed a breakaway backfield whose attack point was over right guard Greg Roberts, a top NFL prospect. Elvis Peacock was gone, but Switzer still had an experienced backfield, with speedsters Billy Ray Sims, Freddie Nixon, Jimmy Rogers, Kenny King, and David Overstreet.

Before the season, Switzer said that the obvious threats to his hopes for an unbeaten season were Texas and Nebraska. He need not have worried. Going into the Texas game, his five-and-a-half-year record at Oklahoma was 55–5–2; afterward, it was 56–5–2. He had never finished lower than first in the Big Eight, and twice his Sooners were national champions.

Switzer had a suspicion his 1978 Oklahoma team was loaded, especially on offense, and in the Cotton Bowl against the Longhorns they proved it, 31–10. They played lights-out football. Click, click, and it was 14–0 less than 3 minutes into the second quarter. When the startled Texans finally plodded off the field, they knew they had been rounded up and branded with a big OU. Halfback Billy Sims played like a bull in a corral. He hammered and rushed his way to 131 yards in twenty-five carries, scored two touchdowns, and threw the block that enabled David Overstreet to get across the goal line. "Sims is a great, great back," Switzer said. "Before the game, I don't think people knew that. Now they do." Sims was averaging 7.4 yards per carry.

The Sooners were No. 1 in the national polls by the time they arrived in Lincoln for the Nebraska showdown. The Cornhuskers

After closing out his playing career with the Washington Redskins and San Francisco 49ers, Tom Osborne joined Nebraska Coach Bob Devaney's staff in 1962 and became head coach in 1973.

ranked No. 4. Though they were described as "a good but not great football team," one that hadn't beaten Oklahoma since winning the national championship in 1971, now was an excellent time for them to win the conference title outright for the first time since 1972, go to the Orange Bowl, and possibly earn even another national championship. Nebraska, 8–1, had lost only to No. 3 Alabama in the opening game of the season.

The Nebraska fans smelled blood. They couldn't contain themselves. For several nights before the game, their behavior was raucous, even riotous. At a pep rally, the atmosphere was so rowdy that Coach Osborne and some of his players took leave. Osborne said he could appreciate their enthusiasm, "but, well, it can be frightening."

The Saturday of the big game was cold, gray, and windy. The weather, however, did not discourage 76,015 people from using their tickets. They celebrated the ninety-ninth straight sellout in Memorial Stadium by pitching oranges on the field and at one another.

Deep in their hearts, the Sooners were confident they would win. "We have the psychological edge," one of them said. "We win each year because we have better players." They also had a big, fast wishbone backfield of Sims, King, Overstreet, and Lott, which was almost certain to sweep Nebraska dizzy. Even Lance Van Zandt, the Cornhuskers' defensive coordinator, feared as much. He admitted that his secondary was probably not big enough or fast enough to plug any holes in the Nebraska trenches. Van Zandt wished the rules allowed him to use twelve players on the field; maybe that would do it. "They do everything but throw the kitchen sink at you," said Osborne. "And they keep it up until you finally screw up."

As for Switzer, he said his biggest worry

Few teams enjoy a more loyal following than Nebraska. This aerial view of the 1978 Nebraska–

Oklahoma game at Lincoln shows the ninety-ninth straight sellout (76,015) in Memorial Stadium.

was fumbles. "Funny how a big game like this builds tension and affects so many people," he said. "Nebraska is as big as us and has no respect for our defense. None. They run right at you. We must have poise. We must keep our poise, no mistakes. We must remember who we are."

At first, Oklahoma remembered. With 8:09 to go in the first quarter, Sims tore loose on a twisting, turning 44-yard touchdown run. Then, still in the same period, Rick Berns, who gained 113 yards in 25 carries, committed the only blot on an otherwise brilliant day. He fumbled on his own 13-yard line and Oklahoma recovered. But three plays later Lott fumbled on the Nebraska 8—the first of four turnovers charged to the Oklahoma quarterback—and the Huskers had the ball back.

Early in the second quarter, after a 26-yard Nebraska punt, Lott lost the ball again, this time on the Nebraska 38. With a 20-mile-per-hour wind at his back, quarterback Tom Sorley marched his team straight down to the Oklahoma 10, where, moments later, Berns crashed into the end zone to tie the score 7–7. That's the way the half ended. Although Switzer said he wasn't concerned about his sagging charges, he wasn't smiling when he joined them in the locker room.

That old affliction, butterfingers, continued to plague the Sooners in the second half. Now it was Overstreet's turn to demonstrate. He fumbled the ball at midfield, and Sorley again marched his team across the goal line, with I. M. Hipp, the onetime walk-on and now the second-leading rusher in the Big Eight, running three times in a row and finally scoring. The kick was good and Nebraska had the lead, 14–7, the first time in nine games that Oklahoma had trailed. But not for long. Midway through the quarter, the Huskers pounced on another fumble by Lott, but then had to give it back because they were ruled offsides at their own 35. Sims then tied the score again on a 30-yard touchdown run.

Early in the last period, Nebraska drove to the Oklahoma 13, first down. But that's as far as they got. Four plays later they had to settle for a 24-yard field goal by Billy Todd. That was all the scoring for the day (17–14), but not the action.

On the following kickoff runback, the ball went to Oklahoma's Kelly Phelps. John Ruud tackled him so hard that he fumbled on the Nebraska 11 and Nebraska fell on it. The Husker fans went wild, then riotous, for the officials wrongly ruled that the ball was dead before the fumble. It was a dreadful call. Osborne protested loudly, but to no avail. Hurriedly, he called his unhappy players around him and told them, "They aren't going to cheat us out of a victory. Now go out there and get that ball back and cram it down their throats."

Now it was Sims's turn to be the goat. The nation's leading rusher, with 1,397 yards going into the game, had kept the score close with 153 yards on the ground as he scored both Oklahoma touchdowns. But now he quickly went from hero to goat. He lost the ball twice. With 8:10 left to play, the Sooners down on the Nebraska 22, he lost the ball the first time. Then came the crusher. Sims's second fumble came with only 3:27 left on the clock, after a twisting, tackle-breaking gallop of 17 yards around his right end. Jeff Hansen and Andy Means smashed into him at the 3, forcing the ball to pop out of his grasp, and Jim Pillen saved the day for Nebraska. This was the same Jim Pillen who had intercepted two Alabama passes in the fourth quarter to preserve a 31–24 Nebraska win in 1977.

Billy Sims accepted his fate philosophically.

"I just fumbled," he said after the game. "It was carelessness. We beat ourselves. Nobody beat us. When you make mistakes like we did, anybody can beat you."

Barry Switzer leaped to the defense of his Heisman candidate. "Billy's a great football player," he said. And then to stress his point, he added, "Who else has rushed for 1,550 yards or has tied an NCAA record by putting together three 200-yard games in a row this season?" He was referring to Sims's 231 yards against Iowa State, 202 against Kansas, and 221 against Colorado.

Still, the consequences of those fourth-quarter fumbles were inescapable. Had Sims hung onto the ball, Oklahoma probably would have won, and almost certainly would have assured his school its sixth straight Big Eight title and with it another national championship. But the Sooners were now going to need a lot of outside help if they were going to win anything.

And that was precisely what they got on the last Saturday of the regular season. The script went like this. No. 2 Nebraska was poised to stomp all over visiting Missouri and thereby lure No. 1 Pennsylvania State to the Orange Bowl in Miami for a one-on-one clash for the national championship.

On the first play from scrimmage, Rick Berns rumbled 82 yards for a touchdown, and the Huskers seemed on their way to a date with destiny. But Missouri, which had stunned defending national champion Notre Dame, 3–0, on a 33-yard field goal by Jeff Brockhaus to open the season, was bent on playing the role of spoiler, and in the third quarter went ahead, 28–24, on a 4-yard run by James Wilder. Then Tim Hager reclaimed the lead for Nebraska, 31–28, on a 4-yard burst of his own. Then back came the Tigers, only to fumble the ball away at the Nebraska 4. But they wouldn't quit. With 3:42 left, they drove 74 yards for the winning touchdown on Wilder's 7-yard run. Like the pivotal Ne-

In 1978 a 6-foot, 205-pound, 4.5-second sprinter in the 40-yard dash, Billy Ray Sims, became only the sixth junior in forty-four years to win the Heisman Trophy, and the third Oklahoma player to win it. En route to the award, he averaged 7.6 yards per carry, rushing for 1,762 yards in eleven games.

braska victory over Oklahoma in 1971, this game wound up 35–31, except that this time the Cornhuskers were on the short end of the score.

While all this was going on, a Cotton Bowl representative had called a press conference to announce that Oklahoma would play in Dallas, but at the last minute the Sooners decided they wanted to try to avenge the previous week's loss to Nebraska by meeting the Cornhuskers in the first-ever all–Big Eight Orange Bowl. Nebraska was furious. "We beat them once and shouldn't have to do it again," grumped Tom Osborne. "A raw deal." Added athletic director Bob Devaney, "It's not fair to our team." By losing to Missouri, the Huskers had nobody but themselves to blame. The loss made it possible for Oklahoma to tie them for the conference championship—and now there was to be a rematch. Still, it was the best possible game the Orange Bowl could get. These were the nation's top offensive teams (Nebraska, 501.4 yards per game) and the top scoring teams (Oklahoma, 40 points per game), with second spot in each category going to the other team.

Few disputed that Oklahoma was the best rushing team in the country. In its final regular-season appearance, it amassed 692 yards in total offense while crushing Oklahoma State, 62–7, as the sensational Heisman Trophy winner, Billy Sims, ran for 209 yards and scored on runs of 1, 35, 2, and 9 yards. That gave him 20 touchdowns and a Big Eight single-season rushing record of 1,762 yards, 82 more than Terry Miller had for Oklahoma State in 1977. Clearing the way for Sims was the winner of the Outland Award, offensive guard Greg Roberts. They were two good reasons why the professional odds makers were making Nebraska as much as 10-point underdogs. Jerry Moore, the assistant coach at Nebraska, was philosophical about his team's

fate. "How many seasons do you get a chance to beat Oklahoma twice?" he asked. Perhaps Moore was thinking about the monster Oklahoma had created for itself in 1976 and 1977—*fumbles.* Twice in those two seasons, just when the Sooners were on the verge of national championships, the "monster" fumbled away its chances. On New Year's night of 1978, in the Orange Bowl, heavily favored Oklahoma coughed up the ball three times and tumbled, 31–6, to Arkansas, while in their recent loss to Nebraska the Sooners fumbled six times.

Well, Oklahoma avenged its only defeat by beating Nebraska in the Orange Bowl, but the victory only seemed to add to the Sooners' frustration. They ran up a 31–10 lead, then held off the Huskers for a 31–24 triumph in what was being called the Rematch Bowl. The Sooners were convinced that they had let the national title slip through their fingers when they had lost six of nine fumbles during the earlier Nebraska game at Lincoln. Quarterback Tom Lott summed up his teammates' feelings after the Orange Bowl:

There's no way this second game replaces the first one. There's no way to make up for losing the national championship. How can you forget losing to the Huskers? Something like that affects your life so much—and we can't blame nobody but ourselves. I doubt if we can ever make up for that loss at Lincoln. We'll be remembered as the team that lost the national championship by 3 yards. Without that fumble [by Sims], we'd have been playing Penn State in the Orange Bowl for the national title.

In Miami, Billy Sims was determined to prove he could hold onto the football, and he did. But he was still thinking about the time he didn't. "I think I showed that I'm capable of holding onto the ball," he said after the game. He scored two touchdowns and gained 134 yards rushing. "Definitely they were trying to strip the ball away from me. They knew that if they caused a lot of turnovers, they had another shot at beating us. They were looking at me the whole game. They were always calling my name when we came up to the line."

Rick Berns, who ran for 99 yards for Nebraska, was asked what the rematch meant. "I don't think it proved anything," he said. But it did. It proved that a Big Eight team wasn't going to be national champion. That honor went to Alabama (AP) and Southern California (UPI). Oklahoma finished third in the polls, Nebraska eighth.

Weeks after the Orange Bowl, Tom Osborne was still bemoaning the fact that two teams from the same conference fought again in a bowl game. He said, "I was disappointed that someone from our league didn't step up and say, 'This isn't right.' We've got enough trouble in our conference knocking each other off without knocking each other off in a bowl."

As Osborne reflected on what the loss meant to him, he said he was aware of the taunts that he couldn't win the big one and that his record against Oklahoma was now 1–5. He also knew that a bad year around Lincoln was 9–3. But he was not petrified about losing his job, and he was not unemployable. The perfunctory, low-key, scholarly Osborne —he has a doctorate in educational psychology—started at Nebraska as an unpaid graduate assistant to Bob Devaney in 1962. It was Devaney, now athletic director and legendary coach, who made Nebraska football great. And Osborne, demonstrating that education was not wasted on him, was reluctant to be the first to follow Devaney as coach. But in 1969, after Nebraska had struggled by Kansas State, 10–7, the two men were on the team bus returning to Lincoln when Devaney blurted, "Would you be interested in taking over when I quit?" Osborne said he probably would. In 1973 he did, and he has survived. And he'll go on surviving. But, he agrees, a few more victories over Oklahoma would help him to survive better.

Roots

No one has ever been able to figure out how old the sport of football is, except that its origin has been traced as far back as 478 B.C. Some claim that it all started when Julius Caesar came upon Teutonic tribesmen kicking and throwing and running with an oval-shaped object in what vaguely resembled a game of football. Closer inspection revealed, however, that it wasn't a ball at all they were tossing around; rather, it was the freshly severed head of an enemy soldier. History is not clear on the question, but you might say it was the first time anyone had lost his head over the game of football.

Years later, here in the United States, in 1869, there was a good road between Nassau Hall and New Brunswick, just twenty New Jersey miles to the north, and one afternoon twenty-five students from Old Nassau (the name was changed to Princeton in 1896) stormed into town to play a similar number of undergraduates from Rutgers. They all wore one-piece leather uniforms, no helmets, and ran with the dazzling speed of tree trunks. What occurred that day had some of the elements of rugger, bearbaiting, and an Indian massacre—all over the possession of a fat leather ball. Improbable as it seemed, fall Saturday afternoons in America were done for. College football was born.

Of course, it took more minds than just those at the two New Jersey schools to develop college football into the slightly paranoid religion it has become: a game watched by paying millions who worship a Heisman winner one season and fire his coach the next. Harvard and Yale had much to do with its early sophistication. Without them we might never have had the scoring we know, the snapback, eleven men to a side, or tailgate picnics out-side the stadium before a game.

Knute Rockne was once asked where his highly maneuverable Notre Dame shift came from. Without hesitation he snapped, "Yale. *All* football comes from Yale."

When Harry Mehre, the old Notre Dame star, was coaching at Georgia, he said, "I'd rather beat any team in the country than Yale. For to me and most of us, Yale means American football." Fielding H. Yost, who coached at Nebraska (1898) and Kansas (1899) before going on to lasting fame at Michigan, echoed Mehre's sentiments. "Walter Camp and Yale *are* football," he said. "Yale was the first to have the true feel of the game, a game which means spirit, body contact, and team play, all the finest elements of competition. Of course, many others have come along since, but it was Yale that set the earlier pace." It was not to-tally unexpected, then, that a Yale man, Wal-ter C. Camp, would go down in history as the father of modern football.

Intercollegiate football won something of a stamp of approval on December 1, 1883, when the Rev. Henry Ward Beecher, the noted Brooklyn preacher, stood in the pulpit of his Congregational Church and told his parish-ioners: "I stood yesterday to see Yale and Princeton at football. I always did hate Prince-ton, but I took notice there was not a coward on either side, although I thank God that Yale beat." The Elis did "beat," winning 6–0 in the mud at the Polo Grounds in New York.

Only fourteen years had elapsed since Princeton and Rutgers had started the football rolling. The Reverend Beecher's ecclesiastical endorsement proved convincingly that the relatively new sport had already become a powerful social influence in an America then emerging from rural status to industrial ma-

Before he went on to become one of the greatest coaches in the history of college football, at Oklahoma, Phi Beta Kappa Charles ("Bud") Wilkinson was an All-America guard and then a quarterback on Minnesota's national championship teams in 1934, 1935, and 1936.

Called the father of American football, Walter C. Camp was a member of the Intercollegiate Football Rules Committee for forty-eight years. He changed the game from rugby to American football, creating the scrimmage line, eleven-man team, signal calling, and the quarterback position. This photo was taken in 1924, the year before he died.

Few coaches in all history took football more seriously than Fielding H. ("Hurry Up") Yost. He was usually seen on campus with a football under his arm. Yost was head coach at Nebraska in 1898 and at Kansas in 1899, then went on to lasting fame at Michigan.

Edward North Robinson coached Nebraska in 1896 and 1897 before going on to an illustrious career at Brown and a place in the coaches' National Football Hall of Fame. His two-year record at Lincoln was 11–4–1.

turity. Within the first twenty-five years after the first crude kicks at New Brunswick, consider what had happened.

A crowd of more than 40,000 people paid to see Princeton play Yale at New York's Manhattan Field.

Football moved out of the Northeast, beyond the Allegheny Mountains, across the Mississippi, and all the way to the Pacific Ocean.

Alumni interest crystallized on whether or not "the football team" succeeded in the short schedule in autumn.

All-America selections had become a fact.

Most important, football had become a game that ladies could attend with propriety. It was rough and nasty, so rough and nasty that Harvard called off its 1885 schedule, but since it was collegiate the ladies could attend to wave their little pennants and threaten to swoon at proper moments.

Artists and writers glorified the sport, including the moments when expertly placed punches bloodied noses. Frederic Remington, the artist who later won immortality by depicting cowboys and the western plains, drew a huge portfolio of football pictures that *Harper's Weekly* featured over a five-year period in the 1880s.

Richard Harding Davis, the renowned writer and war correspondent who died in France during World War I, played football at Lehigh and during the late 1880s poured out profuse prose on the glories of football and the giants it nurtured.

Remington, Davis, and others perpetuated the legend that football was a heroic, rugged man's game, but unlike horse racing, the other big spectator sport, where only males and females of ill repute dared to be seen, football was also fitting for ladies. In other words, football was *in.* It was respected. It was fashionable. It was fun.

Football was still in its primitive state when it finally moved westward. In what is now the Big Eight Conference, Missouri, Kansas, Colorado, and Nebraska were the first to begin playing it. They all started in 1890. The Cornhuskers beat Omaha YMCA, 10–0, in their first football game of record; Missouri walloped a pickup team, 22–6; Kansas lost to Baker, 22–9, and Denver Athletic Club shut out Colorado, 20–0.

Next to take up the game was Iowa State, in 1892, when the Cyclones tied State Center, 6–6. Then came Oklahoma, in 1895, losing to Oklahoma City, 34–0. A year later, Kansas State lost to Fort Riley, 14–0, in its first game. Oklahoma State was a loser in its initial effort, too—a 12–0 defeat at the hands of Kingfisher, in 1901.

There was none of this platoon business. In those early days, players had to go both ways. They carried only a handful of substitutes, even though the teams sometimes scheduled games two or three days apart. Football was truly a game for iron men. Once the game started, a man could not leave unless he was hurt, but a team quickly learned how to get around this rule: the captain simply whispered to one of his teammates, "Get your arm hurt, or something," whenever he wanted to bring in a fresh player. Once, when John W. Heisman, for whom the trophy is named, was playing for Pennsylvania in 1888, his captain turned to him between scrimmages and said, "Get your neck broke, Heisman!"

Vernon Parrington, who coached at Oklahoma (1897–1900, won 9, lost 2, tied 1), recalled that the teams wore jerseys and shorts of a wide variety. "But we wore no helmets or pads," he said. "As a matter of fact, a player who dared turn up in homemade armor was considered a sissy. Long hair was the only head protection we had, and as part of the preseason preparation the players would begin letting their hair grow in June. Some of the players, particularly the medical and divinity students among them, also let their beards grow, earning the nickname 'Gorillas.' "

Coach Parrington said there was also a shortage of sweaters back in football's Stone Age, so they all wore snug-fitting canvas jackets over their game jerseys. That's where the appellation "canvasbacks" came from. Tackling was ragged—a wild, haphazard, clutching, above-the-waist sort of tackling.

"When opposing runners wore loose garments they were often stopped by a tackler grabbing a handful of loose clothing," Parrington recalled. "Some players wore pants, or jackets, or black horsehair, so when a pursuer made a fumbling grab at a runner, he lost his fingernails."

There were frequent arguments over the referee's decisions. The entire team took part, too, so that much of the time the ref scarcely knew who was captain. Every player was allowed to argue as much as he pleased.

One of the biggest problems was the fact that there was no neutral zone between the two scrimmage lines. There was only an imaginary scrimmage line drawn through the center of the ball. Naturally, the rush line players of both teams were constantly striving to crowd this imaginary hairline, in order to get the jump on their opponents. This is what caused so much of the wrangling between teams and officials. There were so many charges and countercharges, and pushing and wrestling, that it frequently took the quarterback a full minute to get the ball back in play.

The name of Vernon Parrington brings a quaint footnote to football history. After leaving Emporia College in Kansas, he went to Harvard, and he hated and feared it in ways that shaped him as much as his home had done. He went back to Emporia, taught for

three years, then moved to the University of Oklahoma, where he was the English department and football coach. But when it was learned he had been to Harvard, of all places, he was fired. Apparently, those who fired him hated and feared Harvard as much as he did.

Football games of the pre–World War I period, like the wars of that age, were fierce struggles of youthful courage and strength waged over small pieces of ground. Force drove headlong against force. Gains came in feet and often just in inches. Players were trained to block on offense, tackle on defense, and to give and take it all the time. The idea was simple enough: sock it to 'em until something gave. It was a game that hurt, a game of pads slapped against unprotected faces, of two stalwarts charging point-blank into an opponent and knocking him to his knees, and of crashing blocks as a wave of interference rolled a man out of the play. It was a tough game played by a hardy breed of young men. It was raw-meat football. It was the kind of football they were, by now, playing at such colleges as Kansas, Missouri, Nebraska, Iowa, and Washington University of St. Louis— charter members of what was originally known as the Missouri Valley Intercollegiate Athletic Association, founded on January 12, 1907. Iowa State, then known as Ames College, and Drake were added in 1908.

Historically, the facts behind the Big Eight are these.

Starting in the Missouri Valley Conference, Iowa dropped out in 1911 to join the Big Ten. Kansas State, then known as Kansas State College of Applied Science and Agriculture, was admitted in 1913 to make it a seven-school league again. Then Grinnell came in in 1919 and Oklahoma a year later. In 1925 the conference grew to ten teams when Oklahoma A. & M. withdrew from the Southwest Conference.

In his only season at Missouri (1909), Hall of Fame coach William W. Roper never lost a game (7–0–1). He then went north to Princeton. While other coaches are remembered for tricky systems and won-lost records, Roper is remembered for his locker-room oratory, come-from-behind victories, and heart-stopping upsets. He convinced his Missouri players that if they wore black and gold and their opponents didn't, they were a cinch to win.

That's the way they stood until 1928: Kansas, Missouri, Nebraska, Washington University, Iowa State, Drake, Kansas State, Grinnell, Oklahoma, and Oklahoma A. & M. Then, on May 19, 1928, in a meeting at Lincoln, Nebraska, six of the seven state schools (Oklahoma A. & M. was the exception) formally organized what they called the Big Six Conference. On December 1, 1947, it was changed to the Big Seven, with the addition of the University of Colorado from the old Skyline Conference, and finally to the Big Eight, on June 1, 1957, when Oklahoma State University came back.

The formal purposes of the Big Eight are "to control and manage intercollegiate athletics in the institutions of the association"; "to establish standards and promote scholarship and high ideals in sportsmanship"; and "to formulate principles and disseminate information regarding the proper place of athletics in schools and colleges."

The affairs of the Big Eight are conducted through faculty control, to retain for intercollegiate athletics its rightful role as an integral part of the overall educational process and the student-athlete as an integral part of the student body. Faculty representatives (persons of professional rank who do not receive pay, primarily for services rendered in connection with athletics or physical education) serve as the policy-directing group of the conference; directors of athletics serve as the operating body or administrative agency.

Generally unrecognized, Oklahoma played a considerable role in popularizing the forward pass. Having lost all their regulars following a 6–2–0 record in 1913, the Sooners decided to pin their hopes on an aerial circus the next season. Coach Bennie Owen adopted what was described as "a wide-open, reckless

All-America fullback Claude Reeds (1913) still holds the distance punting record at Oklahoma—a 102-yarder against Texas in 1911, when the rules called for a 110-yard field. He booted himself right into the National Football Hall of Fame.

attack," and it paid off handsomely. Oklahoma scored the most points (435) of any major team in the nation on the way to nine wins, one loss, one tie:

67	Central Normal	0
67	Kingfisher College	0
96	Ada Normal	6
13	Missouri	0
7	Texas	32
16	Kansas	16
23	Oklahoma Aggies	6
52	Kansas Aggies	10
35	Arkansas	7
33	Haskell Indians	12
26	Henry Kendall	7

Before his retirement, Oklahoma sports publicist Harold Keith wrote *Oklahoma Kickoff,* a fascinating history of OU football. In it he pointed out:

In many ways the 1914 team stands as Bennie Owen's finest coaching job of all time. Never before had it been necessary for him to use so many untried men in frontline positions, or to alter so radically the style of play. Without his all-out emphasis of the forward pass, the Sooners probably would have lost half of their games. Because of the comparative isolation of the Southwest, the Sooners' bright aerial achievements passed totally unnoticed everywhere except in the Valley. Eastern authorities couldn't see the forward pass as anything but a foolish gamble.

Parke Davis, a football historian of the day, reported that there was only a small number of forward passes, and that "for every forward pass that went through for a touchdown in 1914, two forward passes were intercepted and run back for a touchdown." And this from Walter Camp in 1914: "No team has as yet suc-

ceeded in combining both forward passing and running with proper skill."

Unbeknownst to Camp, the game's chief architect, his running-passing equation was being solved down in cowboy country, at Norman, Oklahoma. "There the Sooners' forward passing had related itself to the Oklahoma offense as naturally as dancing relates itself to music," wrote Harold Keith. "With Geyer throwing a ball that, compared to the modern streamlined pigskin, looked like a squash, Oklahoma in 1914 completed one mile of forward passes, actually scoring 25 touchdowns with the play besides employing it several additional times to convoy the ball to within a few yards of the goal. But as far as the East was concerned, the feat might just as well have occurred on the planet Mars."

It was not as though football was forsaking the grand old hip feint and the stiff-arm, or the dipsy-doodle and the pad thump, or all of the things that had helped to make the game so colorful, but the forward pass was here to stay. Averaging thirty to thirty-five passes a game, the 1915 Sooners snuffed out ten straight opponents:

67	Kingfisher College	0
55	Weatherford Normal	0
102	Alva Normal	0
24	Missouri	0
14	Texas	13
23	Kansas	14
14	Henry Kendall	13
24	Arkansas	0
21	Kansas Aggies	7
26	Oklahoma Aggies	7

The 1915 Sooners were convincing proof that aerial machinations could be made a major part of the offense, and it was not unusual for the passing yardage to surpass the running yardage, game after game. This was the premise adopted with the new streamlined ball in the mid-1930s by Texas Christian, Arkansas, and Tulsa. But Bennie Owen of the 1914–1915 Oklahomans was one of the pioneers. Harold Keith said:

The 1915 Oklahoma team was in many ways the most singular team Owen ever developed. Its experience, aerial pyrotechnics, poise, and fighting spirit concealed feebleness in other departments that ordinarily might have proved fatal. It had to come from behind in five of its major games. It was peculiarly handicapped because of its frailness, its mediocre defense, its undistinguished punting, and because it didn't have much running attack from the 10-yard line to the goal, owing to Forest (Spot) Geyer's inability to buck. Consequently, it was compelled to place an abnormal emphasis upon offense. With its passer and best receivers returning intact from 1914, its aerial game was its ace in the hole, despite the fact that every opponent plotted painstakingly to stop it, rushing Geyer hard, and often assigning two men on end Homer Montgomery.

After Oklahoma's victory over Texas, Captain Berry, the UT tackle, said, "The forward pass beat us. That was our specialty, but we acknowledge Oklahoma's superiority." And Texas coach Dave Allerdice added: "It was the most thrilling exhibition of forward passing ever seen in the West."

Oklahoma featured what it called "our teasing optional pass sequence." It worked to perfection in blanking Missouri, 24–0. On the Sooners' second touchdown, the Tigers' defensive halfback was sucked in. Rayburn Foster whipped the ball over his head to Montford ("Hap") Johnson, who caught it for a 20-yard gain. When the Missouri halfback dropped back on the next play, anticipating another pass, Foster faked the pitch and, with his

Coach Bennie Owen's 122–54–16 record at Norman made him an Oklahoma legend.

Hall of Fame end Guy Chamberlain of Nebraska made All-American in 1914 and 1915. From prep school to the Cornhuskers and through his first five seasons as a professional, Chamberlain did not play in a losing game.

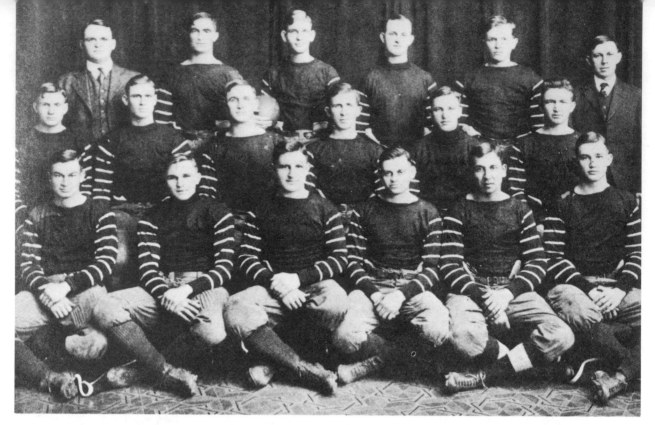

Coach Bennie Owen and his all-conquering Oklahoma Sooners team of 1915 (10–0–0). Along the way they stomped Alva Normal, 102–0. *Front row:* Elmer ("Trim") Capshaw, Charles Swatek, Rayburn Foster, Montford ("Hap") Johnson, Jess Fields, Prentice Lively. *Middle row:* Clifford ("Dutch") Meyer, Howard McCasland, Willis Hott, Oliver Hott, Frank McCain, Homer Montgomery. *Back row:* Assistant Coach Ed Meacham, George Anderson, Captain Forest ("Spot") Geyer, Curry Bell, Leon Phillips, Coach Bennie Owen.

The nationally ranked, undefeated Nebraska Cornhuskers (8–0–0), whose 20–19 upset of Notre Dame stunned the country in 1915. *In front:* Joe Caley, P. W. Proctor. *Front row:* Ted Riddell, Edson Shaw, E. L. Abbott, Dick Rutherford, Paul Shields, Harold T. Corey, Guy Chamberlain. *Second row:* Guy Reed, John Cook, John Rasmussen, Coach E. O. Stiehm, Hugo Otoupalik, Lum Doyle. *Back row:* Herbert Reese, Jimmy Gardner, Paul Halbersleben, Ellsworth Moser, Ed Kositzky.

blockers paving the way, swept his strong side to score.

The years 1911 through 1915 were glory days for Oklahoma. Sure, they had had their football heroes from the late 1890s—Fred Roberts, Ralph Campbell, and Willard Douglas—but Bennie Owen, one-armed coach from 1905 through 1926, hit the jackpot during those five seasons with thirty-eight wins, seven losses, and one tie.

At the same time that Oklahoma was forging into the national football picture, Nebraska was also compiling a noteworthy record. In 1915 the Huskers completed the most successful era in their football history up to that time—five triumphant years under Ewald ("Jumbo") Stiehm. Stiehm, only a few years out of Wisconsin, arrived at Lincoln in 1911. For the next five years, Nebraska won thirty-five games, lost two (both to Minnesota), and tied three. They won the Missouri Valley Conference championship four times in a row.

The Cornhuskers' glory was complete in 1915. Notre Dame, which had catapulted to national prominence in 1913 with its famous upset over vaunted Army, was among Nebraska's victims. It beat the Irish with the forward pass. On the first Nebraska touchdown, Guy Chamberlain passed to Ted Riddell for 37 yards and then raced around end to score on the next play. After Notre Dame blocked a punt to take the lead again, 13–7, Nebraska came smashing back in the second half. Joe Caley hit Chamberlain for 20 yards; Chamberlain passed to Caley for 19 more, and then scored on a sweep. The try for the extra point was missed, and that's the way the score stood, 13–13, until late in the fourth quarter. Then the Huskers forged ahead, 20–13, on passes of 17 and 35 yards by Chamberlain to Herbert Reese and Ted Riddell. Notre Dame charged back on a touchdown by Dutch Bergman, but

the extra point was wide of its mark and Nebraska had its victory, 20–19.

"With the win over Notre Dame," wrote the *New York Times,* "Nebraska definitely has come of age. It must be ranked with the major powers."

Guy Chamberlain lived up to his nickname. He was, indeed, "The Champ." Both the United Press and Walter Eckersall, sportswriter for the *Chicago Tribune,* named him on their All-America teams.

Nebraska and Notre Dame became established rivals. Under coach Fred Dawson, the Cornhuskers were the biggest stumbling block for Knute Rockne's touted teams of the 1920s.

	Notre Dame	Nebraska
1915	19	20
1916	20	0
1917	0	7
1918	0	0
1919	14	9
1920	16	7
1921	7	0
1922	6	14
1923	7	14
1924	34	6
1925	0	17

Dan Young, a Notre Dame man, was close to Rockne and the Irish players in the 1920s, and he once recalled the nonchalance exhibited by George Gipp, Notre Dame's Mr. Legend, toward the 1920 Nebraska game. Young said:

By this time the Notre Dame–Nebraska game had bloomed into one of the hottest rivalries in football. Whenever we played them in Lincoln, the Husker fans really let us have it. They lampooned us with cries like "Fish eaters! Fish eaters! Fish eaters!" Our players didn't feel very welcome. The 1920 game was played at Lincoln on the third Saturday of the season, and Nebraska officials had neglected putting benches on our side of the field. Instead, they placed stacks of straw along the sidelines for our substitutes to sit on. Despite these subtle aggravations, Gipp had a great afternoon on the field, leading us to victory. He ran his lungs out, until he was totally pooped. Yet Rockne refused to give him a rest. I can see Gipp, hands on hips and tongue drooping, sidling up near the Notre Dame side of the field, and begging Rock to take him out of the game. Unsympathetically, Rock merely turned his head and walked away. He was teaching the Gipper a lesson, of course. Gipp was not exactly a stickler for training habits.

Gipp got even with his coach, however. Several times, with the ball resting between the Notre Dame 20- and 30-yard lines, quarterback Joe Brandy called for Gipp to punt. But instead of punting, Gipp dropkicked. I think that's where Rock lost most of his hair. Gipp once dropkicked a 68-yard field goal, but there against Nebraska he was trying for 70 and 80 yards. Each time he dropped back to kick, he'd dropkick. Rock got the message. He finally sent in a substitute for Gipp. Gipp dragged himself off the field, plopped to his knees totally exhausted on a pile of straw, and then crawled over behind where Rockne was standing and grabbed a cigarette out of a spectator's hand, took several drags, and handed it back. Suddenly it dawned on me. While Rockne had been trying to work Gipp into condition, all Gipp had on his mind was getting out of the game so he could have a fast smoke.

On the subject of Rockne and George Gipp, Young set the record straight. According to

Notre Dame's legendary George ("Win One for the Gipper") Gipp on the day of the big Nebraska game in 1920 at Lincoln. The Irish won, 16–7.

common belief, Rockne gave his legendary "win one for the Gipper" speech just before Notre Dame played Army in 1928. But, as Young said:

That's not true. He first gave it in Indianapolis, on October 29, 1921, minutes before the Indiana game. Rockne asked our kids to "win this one for the Gipper," because the Hoosiers had bragged how they were the ones who got Gipp the previous season, when he suffered a broken collarbone. After Rockne had finished, the Irish nearly tore down the door rushing out of the locker room. Final score: Notre Dame 28, Indiana 7. That marked the first time that the ghost of George Gipp, who had died in his prime the previous winter, came back to haunt a Notre Dame opponent.

Sports pages and alumni too often rank football coaches according to the number of games their teams win, a meaningless yardstick. A far more accurate measure of Knute Rockne would be provided if you took into account the deep influence he had over his players. He used football as an instrument of human relations, as a furnace of team combat for forging the indissoluble bonds of comradeship and tolerance and understanding. He also gave his athletes a sense of humor.

For instance, Notre Dame was playing Nebraska at South Bend, on November 15, 1924, and the Irish had the ball on the Husker 2-yard line, second down and only inches to go for a first down. That was the team starring Notre Dame's fabled "Four Horsemen" backfield. Against Rockne's better judgment, quarterback Harry Stuhldreher decided to give fullback Elmer Layden and halfback Don Miller a breather and take a chance on Jimmy Crowley, the other halfback, making the first down. So Stuhldreher called Crowley's signal for a run off tackle. Crowley described it this way:

As I got the ball and started, a Nebraska tackle crashed through our defense. He was the biggest, ugliest, and meanest tackle I'd ever seen. His eyes were as big as saucers and they blazed with a wild, savage glare. He had his mouth wide open and his two teeth gleamed like fangs of a saber-toothed tiger. My friend Elmer, thin and frail, was leading me into the line. He took in the situation at a glance, and never hesitated. Gritting his teeth, shutting his eyes, he hurled his fragile body into the tackle's path, cutting the monster down with a tremendous crash. Well, you can imagine my feelings, the gratitude stirred by my friend's unselfish devotion. I tell you, that was more than fifty years ago and not a day has passed since but I have thanked Elmer in my heart for that deed of sacrifice. To his dying day, there was a bond between us that time could not wither.

Of course, there's a postscript to that story. In the same Nebraska game, we had the ball deep in our own territory, fourth down and 9. Stuhldreher made the orthodox decision for such a situation. He called the signal for Layden to carry through the line. As Elmer got the ball and started, the other Nebraska tackle came through. He was bigger and uglier and meaner than the first. His eyes were as big as dinner plates and they blazed with a cannibalistic light. His mouth was wide open and he had only one tooth, which gleamed like the tusk of a maddened boar. He bore down on Elmer hungrily, grinning evilly. I was leading Elmer into the line this time. In the winking of an eye, I sized up the situation. I knew everything depended on me. I thought of the earlier play and how Elmer had saved me at a frightful cost to himself, and a hot wave of gratitude swept over me. Gritting my teeth against the grinding shock, shutting my eyes —I turned away! I couldn't bear to look.

Well, when they finally peeled off the tackle and scraped Elmer up, he spoke in a thin, reedy voice. "Oh, Jimmy," Elmer said to me. "Oh, how I wish Rock would play Harry O'Boyle at left half." Mind you, Harry O'Boyle wasn't even a regular on our team, yet all their adult lives there was an indestructible bond between Elmer and Harry, a friendship that football created and nothing could destroy.

Manning the Notre Dame trenches that afternoon was Edgar E. ("Rip") Miller, the hard-nosed right tackle on both offense and defense. Rip became the first of Notre Dame's famous 1924 "Mules" (linemen) to be elected to the National Football Hall of Fame. Against the Huskers, he opened up gaping holes at his position for the Horsemen to gallop through for large gains. He was tenacious and tough enough to manhandle one side of the Nebraska line by himself, and repeatedly thwarted All-America Ed Weir's bulldozer rushes. Playing alongside Rip was end Ed Hunsinger, who kept shouting at him when he sensed a Nebraska play coming their way: "Here they come, Rip—give me some help." All-America Rip Miller was no dummy. "Take care of your own position, Hunsinger! I've got all I can do protecting myself." For the rest of the season, that became the byword of the Four Horsemen and Seven Mules.

The way Steve Owen, coach of football's New York Giants for many years, used to tell it, he was riding his cow pony down a road in Oklahoma. He pulled up at the side of a school field where some boys were playing a strange game. Having looked on for a while, he said to the coach, "What are they playing?"

"Football," the coach said. "Would you like to try it?"

Steve, stout and quick, got off his pony.

"What do I do?" he asked.

"Try to run with the ball through that team. See if you can get as far as the goal posts down there at the other end of the field."

The team kicked off and Steve, catching the ball, started down the field. Ten yards . . . fifteen . . . twenty. Dodging, twisting, turning, lunging. Tacklers who dove at him reeled away from contact with him. At a full gallop and all alone, he crossed the goal line.

"What do I do now?" he asked the coach.

"Try it again," the coach said. "This time without your spurs."

Well, it probably wasn't that way at all. But it might have been. For Steve Owen, as big as a barn, was a cowhand in his youth in Enid, Oklahoma, and it wasn't far from the range that he played in his first game of football. He grew up in the pre–World War I years and learned about the game from newspaper accounts of the Oklahoma Sooners, Texas Longhorns, and Kansas Jayhawks. He once told me:

In those days the image folks had of any kid football player from the Southwest was that he was big and had muscles, chawed on a big plug of tobacco, and walked around wearing a sombrero, a loud flannel shirt, chaps, boots, and spurs. Tell anyone in New York you were from Oklahoma and he immediately thought of cowboys and Injuns. Brute strength and ignorance—Southwestern athletes were stuck with that image in the old days.

I remember when Nebraska played Army at West Point in 1928. The Cornhuskers were tough. They ran through the Big Six, which was just starting out, and came up to the Army game undefeated. They'd shut out Iowa State, Kansas, Kansas State, Missouri, and Pittsburgh, and held Oklahoma to one touch-

Tackle Ed Weir, a member of the National Football Hall of Fame, twice played on Nebraska teams that beat the great Knute Rockne's Notre Dame Fighting Irish—the only losses for Rockne during 1923 and 1925. Rockne picked Weir as "the best tackle I have ever seen," and in 1969 Weir was named to the All-Time All-America Team.

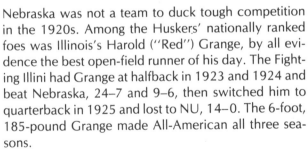

Nebraska was not a team to duck tough competition in the 1920s. Among the Huskers' nationally ranked foes was Illinois's Harold ("Red") Grange, by all evidence the best open-field runner of his day. The Fighting Illini had Grange at halfback in 1923 and 1924 and beat Nebraska, 24–7 and 9–6, then switched him to quarterback in 1925 and lost to NU, 14–0. The 6-foot, 185-pound Grange made All-American all three seasons.

The power in Kansas's first Big Six championship season (1930) was 210-pound fullback Jim Bausch. A member of the National Football Hall of Fame, he also won the decathlon title in the 1932 Olympic Games at Los Angeles.

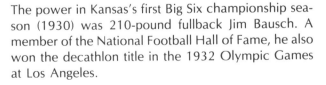

down. They were big, fast, and confident. Their fans felt they were No. 1 in the country. Ernie Bearg, in his fourth season at Lincoln, didn't play helter-skelter football; he favored a sound, balanced game, molding his defense as a base and building on it. From end to end he had a line that was massive and rough and tough.

Biff Jones was the Army coach, the same Biff Jones who later coached at Oklahoma and Nebraska. In 1928, he had some surprises for the Huskers, and by the time it was over Nebraska was all black and blue and licking its wounds. The score was 13–3, Army, and the champions of the new Big Six were branded as "big and dumb." Back home the Nebraska fans were so disgruntled that Bearg was fired and Dana X. Bible took his place.

The game itself was as baffling as a Rube Goldberg cartoon. Everything seemed to backfire for Nebraska. Reb Russell, the Huskers' great fullback, and Bearg were at each other's throats all afternoon. Clair Sloan, the halfback, ran 60 yards for a touchdown, only to have it called back by what Nebraska writers claimed was an extremely biased referee.

The best Nebraska could do was a field goal by Sloan. Red Cagle, the great Army triple-threat back, burst through the Nebraska line to score first for the Cadets. Then Army scored again in the final minutes on a pass when Nebraska claimed it was so dark they couldn't see the passer or the receiver.

That ended the muscle era at Nebraska. The fans demanded that their teams be able to do something besides flex their biceps. They wanted players with more brains, less brawn. Dana X. Bible brought them exactly what they wanted.

During the years 1929 through 1936, before he went to Texas, Coach Bible won the Big Six championship six times. In those eight years he lost only three league games. His overall record at Nebraska was 50–15–7.

Dana Xenophon Bible, better known as D. X., was a bald, lip-smacking, scripture-quoting son of a Latin and Greek scholar whose unspectacular coaching techniques brought solid, fundamental football to Lincoln. He frowned on fancy football. His basic formations were the punt, the Minnesota shift, the single wingback, and the double wingback. His pet maneuver was a fake-punt-and-run play on third down. In his book *Championship Football* he gave the perfect exposition of how to mold a winning team. His chapter on scouting spelled out in infinite detail the lengths he went to to get a good rundown on a future opponent. He made his scouts answer forty-two mimeographed pages of questions on each game and fill out eight more pages of comments and diagrams. The book supplied a sample of this scouting form, broken down into such logical divisions as defensive formation, offensive formations, forward passing attack, and so on. Under the heading "kickoff," the scout was required to record the direction, height, and distance of each kick, the lineup of the kicking team, the players who were downfield first under the kick, the players who were down last, and the player (if any) who acted as the safety man, plus such additional data as whether the kick was made from the center of the field, whether a deliberately short kick was ever tried, whether the ends went straight downfield or cut toward the ball, and, finally, which players were the most consistent tacklers.

From start to finish, Bible was at all times boss on the field. He mentally divided the gridiron into six general areas, and he laid down the law to his quarterbacks: "First, from your own goal to the 20-yard line, get the ball out as quickly and safely as possible. Two, from your own 20 to your 40, a run or kick will do the

National Football Hall of Fame coach Dana X. Bible, hired by Nebraska in 1929, lost only three Big Six Conference games in eight seasons.

Cigar-smoking, rotund Lynn O. ("Pappy") Waldorf started coaching football at Oklahoma A. & M. (1929–1933) and compiled a 34–10–7 record. He went to Kansas State in 1934 and won the Big Six title (5–0–0), and later took California to three straight Rose Bowls, 1949, 1950, and 1951 (but all were defeats).

George Sauer remains one of the great names in football history, both as a fullback at Nebraska and as head coach at Kansas, where his Jayhawks shared the Big Six Conference championship in 1946 and 1947 with Oklahoma.

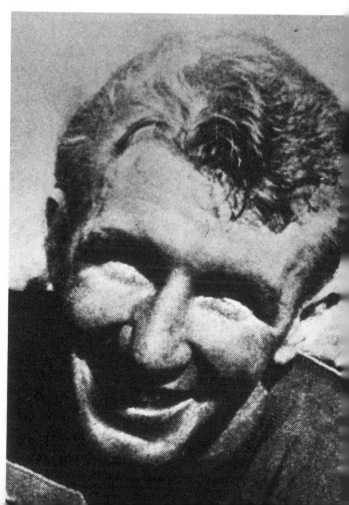

trick. Three, from your own 40 to their 40, run, pass, or kick. Four, from their 40 to 20, pass. Five, from their 20- to 5-yard line, use special plays, backward and lateral passes, double reverses, fake-run-and-pass plays. Six, from their 5 to the goal line, this is the scoring zone, so give the ball to the best ball carrier."

On the bench during a game, Bible was—well, seldom on the bench. Space was reserved for him there, but he almost never occupied it. The players not in the starting lineup always stood up, close to the sideline, at the kickoff, and D. X. stood with them. But when they sat down, he remained on his feet. The chances were that if you had put a pedometer on him, you would have found that he covered more ground than any of his halfbacks in the course of a game, and this is not knocking the young men who played halfback for him. Remember, they were in and out of the game, while Coach Bible "played" 60 minutes every Saturday. He roamed up and down the sideline, watching the players, the officials, occasionally yelling at them all, darting back to the bench to talk to a player going into the game, striding out to meet a player he was removing, consulting with his assistants.

The players sitting on the bench were supposed to watch the game closely. There were times, however, when a couple of them could not see what was happening because the coach was standing in front of them. None of his players would have been too surprised had he ripped off his coat and torn right into the ball game. They knew that the temptation to be out there was strong upon him sometimes.

Bible failed to win the Big Six conference title only in 1930 and 1934. His stars at Nebraska were headed by fullbacks George Sauer (elected to the National Football Hall of Fame in 1954) and Sam Francis, and tackles Ray Richards and Hugh Rhea.

On the negative side, Bible lost four out of four games to Minnesota, coached by Bernie Bierman, and the best he could get out of eight games with Jock Sutherland's Pittsburgh teams was scoreless ties in 1930 and 1932. This, however, did not detract from his stature very much, because the Gophers and Panthers were top national powers and the Huskers usually pushed them to the limit.

Even though Nebraska lost to Minnesota, 7–0, and to Pitt, 19–6, in 1936, the Cornhuskers ranked No. 9 in the national polls. The Gophers finished No. 1, the Panthers No. 3. The loss to Minnesota rates among the historic heartbreakers, for there were only 59 seconds left when Andy Uram, taking a lateral from quarterback Bud Wilkinson on a punt return, raced 75 yards for a touchdown.

The aftermath emphasized Bible's ability as a practical psychologist, even though he was, in effect, again calling on character. The next game was with Indiana, and the Hoosiers led the Cornhuskers, 9–0, at the half in great measure because UN was still "down" from its effort against Minnesota. The halftime scene in the Nebraska dressing room was something to remember. D. X. just threw away technical details and concentrated on psychology. He challenged his players' desire to win, their courage to fight back. He offered starting positions to the first eleven men who wanted badly enough to beat the rest of the team to the exit. They lit out for the door. Bible beat them to it. Then he stood blocking the way, insisting they weren't ready. A genuine mob scene developed. Normally affable players knocked each other down fighting to get out. Some squared off and fought. The pandemonium was terrifying. And it worked. Nebraska came back to win the game, 13–9; and they played the second half with only eleven men.

"Coach Bible was a forceful leader," said one of his Huskers years ago. "He had courage

Lawrence ("Biff") Jones, a West Point graduate, was head coach at Oklahoma in 1935–1936 and at Nebraska from 1937 to 1941. In his last year at Nebraska, he led the Cornhuskers to the Rose Bowl against Stanford, but lost 21–13.

to match any situation. No matter the problem, he could take charge. He had the ability to organize a team into a loyal and spirited group. He demanded discipline and respect, and he got it."

When Dana X. Bible left Nebraska for Texas in 1937, he negotiated one of the best contracts in the history of college coaching. The Longhorns wanted him so badly that they gave him a twenty-year contract, the first ten years as coach and athletic director, the second ten years as athletic director, at $15,000 a year. Before they could agree to the deal, the Texas legislature pondered and debated. Fifteen grand meant that Bible would be getting more than the college president. The legislature resolved the impasse by raising the president's salary.

Bible said it would take him five years to build a championship team at Texas. He missed by one; it took him six years.

Bible's successor at Lincoln was Lawrence McCeney ("Biff") Jones, the old Army coach. His four-year record at West Point was 30–8–2 during the years of halfback Christian Keener (Red) Cagle, Old No. 12, a legend in the annals of football. An escape artist, Red Cagle delivered the hysteria that brought the mobs swarming to Yale Bowl and Yankee Stadium and Chicago's Soldier Field whenever the Cadets played there.

Actually, Biff Jones coached for two seasons at Oklahoma before moving to Nebraska. Still an officer in the army, he led the Sooners in 1935 and 1936 to records of 6–3 and 3–3–3. He built a firm foundation at Norman on which Tom Stidham, his line coach, who succeeded him, fashioned an Orange Bowl team in 1938. Harold Keith, director of Oklahoma sports publicity then and during the later dynasty of Bud Wilkinson, said, "Biff Jones gave us our first real organization." And Karey Fuqua, who played for Biff at Oklahoma, said of him:

"My one-year experience with him was during the fall of 1935, from which time I did not see him until the winter of 1941. He was coaching one of the teams for the East–West game, which because of Pearl Harbor had been moved from San Francisco to New Orleans. His team was housed at Louisiana State, where I dropped in to say hello. He never forgot a face. He immediately said, 'Hello, Karey,' and sat down and visited with me for a while."

For more than a decade, Biff Jones coached football and remained in the army. In 1937 he retired with the rank of major and signed with Nebraska. His five-year record with the Cornhuskers was 28–14–4. He delivered Big Six championships in 1937 and 1940. He developed Charlie Brock, center; Fred Shirey and Forrest Behm, tackles; and Warren Alfson, guard, into All-America linemen. His 1937 team was the first Huskers to beat Minnesota (14–9) since 1913, and the 1939 team was the first to beat Pittsburgh (14–13) since 1921.

The author Bill Gulick (*Hallelujah Trail, They Came to a Valley)* attended the University of Oklahoma in 1935–1937 and played frosh football. He remembers Biff Jones as "a stern disciplinarian, typical West Point. You knew who was boss. Biff stressed football fundamentals. His teams were always well prepared."

Gulick enrolled in the best professional writing school in the country, headed by Foster Harris and Rhodes scholar Walter F. Campbell, who wrote under the name of Stanley Vestal. In those days, the University of Oklahoma was more noted for the famous writers it graduated than for its football program. Gulick roomed with a member of the football varsity whose job, as part of his athletic scholarship, was to "guard" the football stadium one night a week for eight dollars.

"He *guarded* the stadium?" I asked Gulick.

"No lie," Bill said. "That's how our athletes got through school. They guarded the stadium. That was about the extent of the free rides around Norman in those days."

"What about grades? Did they make the players crack the books?"

"If they passed, they got to play."

"Were the courses stiff?"

"They took such mindbenders as the Theory of Golf, the Theory of Volleyball, and the Theory of Basket Weaving."

"What was the enrollment at Oklahoma then?"

"Between six thousand and seven thousand."

"Did the Sooners draw well?"

"Football attendance was only a few thousand a game."

Life in the Big Six Conference improved marvelously for Biff Jones at Nebraska. His 1940 team, after losing its opener to Minnesota, 13–7, won its eight other regular-season games and became the first Cornhusker team to play in a bowl. They were invited to oppose Stanford in the Rose Bowl. Coached by Clark Shaughnessy, the Cardinals used the T formation with man-in-motion and flankers, the forerunner of all modern offensive sets. More important, Stanford fielded an exceptional backfield of Frankie Albert at quarter, Pete Kmetovic and Hugh Gallarneau at the halves, and Norm Standlee at fullback. Shaughnessy rated his backfield "one of the twelve greatest backfields of all time. They were the perfect combination."

Shaughnessy, voted Coach of the Year in 1940, was the first coach in college football to stake his career and reputation on the revolutionary T formation.

"A lesser man would have been afraid to present a formation so startling as the T," commented Frankie Albert recently. "Clark alone deserves credit for creating many formations from the basic T while an assistant to the Chicago Bears' George Halas."

There were skeptics, of course. Pop Warner, for one, was sure Shaughnessy had lost his mind when he initiated the pro-type T at Stanford. "If Stanford wins a single game with that crazy formation, you can throw all the football I ever knew into the Pacific Ocean," Warner said. "What Clark is doing is positively ridiculous." But Shaughnessy had his reasons:

Always in the past, the offense tried to coil up power in the ball, then explode it, splitting the defense. The effort was made to stretch the defense thin, then penetrate it. That was the basic idea of Pop Warner's single wing and Knute Rockne's Notre Dame shift. Our approach at Stanford was different. We coiled up the defense in as small an area as possible, then ran around it or threw over it. We shuttled tackles and ends back and forth along the line laterally, shifting the guards sometimes in an unbalanced line and sometimes in a balanced line. Shuttling tackles and ends, shifting guards, and setting a man in motion—away from the play—forced the defense out of a set position. It made old set defenses obsolete.

Hugh Gallarneau, at the outset, confessed he didn't know what to think of the T. "We were skeptical," he said later. "At our first meeting, Shaughnessy reminded us that his name wasn't Shag and told us to call him coach or mister. He sounded like a professor. But he had enthusiasm. He'd diagram a play and say, 'This play will score fifty touchdowns.' That sounded great to me, but when he said we would be going into the line without blockers, I thought he was crazy."

The old fundamentalists of the power game —Bob Neyland of Tennessee, Bernie Bierman of Minnesota, and others—scoffed at the brush blocking, the deception, the flankers. But after Shaughnessy took a Stanford team of much the same personnel that had won only one game in 1939 (14–3 over Dartmouth) and led it into the Rose Bowl against Nebraska, the rush to the T formation was on. By 1950 there were only a half-dozen schools still using the single wing, Notre Dame box, or anything else. And as the defense began to catch up with the Shaughnessy T, the offense evolved into the split T, on to the wing T, the slot T, and so forth.

In the Rose Bowl, Nebraska took a 7–0 lead over Stanford on a seven-play, 53-yard march built around Vike Francis, its spinning fullback. Stanford tied it, 7–7, but the Huskers again gained the lead after Allen Zikmund recovered a Kmetovic fumble of Herman Rohrig's 56-yard quick kick. Rohrig then passed to Zikmund for the touchdown, but the extra point was blocked.

A 40-yard pass from Albert to Kmetovic and a 39-yard punt return by Kmetovic behind a series of outstanding blocks gave Stanford two touchdowns and the game, 21–13.

Nebraska took a special pride in that Rose Bowl team, because thirty-eight of the thirty-nine players on the traveling roster were home grown. When the invitation from the Pasadena Tournament of Roses committee came, the city of Lincoln, and the state, went wild. "It was the greatest thing that happened to Nebraska since William Jennings Bryan ran for the presidency," said Nebraska newspaperman Gregg McBride. The demand for tickets in Lincoln was so intense that businessmen formed what they called the "Last Man Club." The idea was for every native to be sent to Pasadena except one, the last man, who would be left behind to guard the bank.

Although Colorado was more than a decade away from joining the conference, there was verbiage aplenty spewed forth in behalf of Byron R. ("Whizzer") White, one of the most intellectual athletes ever to play football. A future Rhodes scholar, the Colorado quarterback did amazing things in heroic fashion. His dominant presence included all the weapons: run, pass, kick, and think. He led the nation in scoring in 1937, completed twenty-one of forty-three passes for 475 yards, punted with pinpoint accuracy, and led the Buffaloes to the Cotton Bowl against Rice.

"Go it, Whizzer!" was the Colorado battle cry of the day, and the bang-bang, ubiquitous White seldom let his fans down. He could strike suddenly and from any point of the field. Against Denver in 1936, he scuttled 102 yards to score, and gained 97 yards against Utah. He was a one-man gang in Colorado's 17–7 victory over Utah the following season. Fighting to maintain their unbeaten status, the Buffs trailed the Redskins, 7–0, when the Whizzer got on his horse and took over. In the final 20 minutes of the contest, he kicked a field goal, scored twice on touchdown runs of 95 and 57 yards, and kicked both extra points —in short, he personally accounted for all of the Colorado points. His first touchdown was typical of him. After he took a high punt on his own 5-yard line, six Utah tacklers had him pinned in a corner. But they couldn't keep him there. Twisting, squirming, ducking, and dodging, he eluded them and took off down the sideline. Once in the clear he put on a full head of steam and simply outran his pursuers.

As a senior, an All-American, White was the country's leading rusher, with 1,121 yards on 181 carries in 8 games. Scoring 248 points to 26, the Buffaloes were undefeated during the regular season.

Considering the manner in which Whizzer White cheated defeat with game-saving, last-ditch touchdown runs, opponents could be excused for thinking there was no justice.

Colorado halfback (and later Supreme Court justice) Byron ("Whizzer") White was the toast of college football. In 1937, prior to accepting a Rhodes scholarship, he led the nation in rushing, scoring, and total offense. His exploits earned him a place in the National Football Hall of Fame.

An All-America guard in 1938 at Iowa State and National Football Hall of Famer, 210-pound Ed Bock started every game during his college career and played a full 60 minutes in many of them.

Missouri Coach Don Faurot (*right*) father of the split T, talks strategy on the practice field with the quarterback who made it work, 1939 All-American Paul Christman. The Tigers were Big Six champions that season, and both men are in the National Football Hall of Fame. Two seasons later, Faurot developed another All-American destined for the Hall of Fame, center Darold Jenkins.

Whizzer White proved them wrong. Today, he is a U.S. Supreme Court Justice—and a member of the National Football Hall of Fame.

While Whizzer White was doing his thing at Colorado, Ike Hayes was attracting attention at Iowa State University as a 162-pound football guard. He was All-Conference in 1934–1935, and even received All-America mention. When he graduated he became a prominent veterinarian. Ike had a brother and sister. His sister, Mary Hayes, became an actress and took a shot at Broadway, where she made it big. She starred in several road-company shows and then got into radio. And what about Ike and Mary's brother? Oh, he became a football coach—Wayne Woodrow ("Woody") Hayes. You may have heard of him.

To call Missouri the "pits" in Big Six football in the early 1930s would be an understatement. Frank Carideo, an All-America quarterback of Knute Rockne's last two national championship teams at Notre Dame, had been brought to Columbia in 1932 to juice up a sagging program, but the best he could muster was two wins in three years. Sorrowfully, Carideo's overall record was a demoralizing 2–23–2. On the field, the Tigers had become an embarrassment to the conference.

Don Faurot was offered the job at a starting salary of $4,500. He saw it as an opportunity of a lifetime.

Donald Burrows Faurot was something of an old-fashioned fellow with modern ideas about how to win football games. A nonsmoking, nondrinking conservative, he frowned on high-pressured recruiting practices. In 1948, for example, when Missouri played in the Gator Bowl, all of the forty-eight Tigers on the squad were natives. In that sense, then, Faurot was old-fashioned, binding himself with the strictest recruiting limitations.

On the other hand, Faurot's coaching techniques were ultramodern and inventive. He originated the most powerful single post–World War II football system—the split T formation. In 1950 it took him only three weeks to write the book *Secrets of the Split-T Formation,* the accepted bible of the system. As head coach at Missouri (1935–1942, 1946–1956, with ninety-six wins, sixty-four losses, nine ties), Faurot earned the reputation of doing more with less than any coach in America.

"Not one of Don's players could make my team," chastized a Big Ten coach whose team had just beaten Missouri. And yet Faurot led the Tigers to the Orange, Sugar, Cotton, and Gator (twice) bowls. He stressed spirit and toughness in his players. What inspired him to invent the split T? Faurot said:

I lost my star passer, Paul Christman, in 1941. But I still had two fast halfbacks, Harry Ice and Bob Steuber. I had watched the Chicago Bear T formation, and I was enamored with the short pitchout. So I started from there. By setting the quarterback in motion for a wider pitchout to our fast backs, I figured we could get them away better than from the single wing or straight T. The split T had every element of deception and all the machinery for power runs and surprise runs or passes—all in the hands of the sliding quarterback and disposable by him at will. Besides, it required only average personnel, no great passer, and the one-on-one blocking in the line was relatively simple. We did just fine with it. We won the Big Six title in 1942, led the country in net rushing with 307 yards a game, and went to the Sugar Bowl.

Paul Christman was a legend in his own time at Missouri. Now only the legend remains—he was only fifty-one when he died of heart seizure in 1970. After he won All-America honors as a quarterback, he was part of the Dream Backfield of the old Chicago Cardinals when they captured the NFL championship in 1947.

Christman passed Missouri into national prominence in an era (1938–1940) when it was more fashionable to run with the ball, and he did it with such finesse and accuracy that it took twenty-nine years to erase his college records (by Terry McMillan in 1969).

A St. Louis boy, Paul quit Purdue to enroll at Missouri in 1938. Coach Faurot saw that Christman was slow and poor defensively, but he took a shine to Paul's passing. Paul was out of place in the double wing, which required something of a dancing master in the deep position. Faurot did some thinking. He decided to switch to the short punt formation, slot Christman deep, and wound up winning twenty of twenty-eight games over the next three seasons.

Christman said he knew he was awkward:

Coach Faurot knew I had to be able to run to make my passing effective. So I spent hours in the off-season, working with Coach Faurot on my quick starts and short sprints. I actually improved my speed. It didn't end there, however. He also helped me in other ways. We came up to the 1939 Oklahoma game with the conference championship at stake. The Sooners were telling reporters that they had not one but two *passers better than I. Coach Faurot said nothing. He just pasted clippings of the insults all over the bulletin board in our fieldhouse. We got the message. We won the game, 7 to 6—and we were the underdogs.*

Elected to the National Football Hall of Fame in 1956, Paul Christman became a famous football commentator on TV in the 1960s and was noted for his terse, knowledgeable analyses of college and pro games on all three major networks. His formula for TV success: "Never insult the intelligence of your viewer. If you have nothing to say, shut up."

But that is not what Missouri fans will remember their old quarterback for. They will always remember him for his dry sense of humor, his leadership, and his knack for coming up with the big play.

Two-time All-America quarterback Paul Christman passed, ran, and inspired his Missouri Tigers right into the Orange Bowl. He still holds Missouri's record for total offense: 4,151 yards.

Missouri's striking one-two TD punch—halfback Bob Steuber (*left*) and fullback Don Reece—powered the Tigers to the Big Six championship in 1941 and 1942. Both were named All-Conference, and, in 1971, Steuber was elected to the National Football Hall of Fame.

August 16, 1961

Dear Friend:

Thank you very much for remembering me. At 99, one looks like this -- and writes like this.

Gratefully,

Amos Alonzo Stagg

Amos Alonzo Stagg didn't invent football—it just seemed that way. His impact upon the sport was felt from Yale all the way down to the Big Six Conference and beyond. Stagg's numerous innovations included the huddle, direct pass from center, wind sprints, man-in-motion, unbalanced offensive line, backfield shift, numbering players, cross-blocking, 6-2-1-2 defense, and double flanker with twin backs and blocking back. Old "Double A" still showed his sense of humor at age ninety-nine, when he sent this card to all those who remembered him on his birthday—he lived to 105.

Time Out for War

Young men who were playing college football in the fall of 1938 faced a singular experience: a new period of history took shape more visibly for them than for any previous college generation. Virtually overnight, they moved from the campuses into the demands of war and international responsibility.

The dividing line was obvious.

At precisely one o'clock on Saturday morning, October 1, 1938, the Munich crisis reached its climax when six hundred gray-clad German soldiers crossed the border to begin the occupation of Czechoslovakia. In a few frightful hours, the world came to the realization that World War II was not only a possibility but was imminent. In the United States, the handwriting was on the wall: no more could the country remain detached from world affairs. But for the athletes who were college seniors, the drama came down to a finer point of crisis. They were on the gridirons the day the story broke, and for many of them the world passed from one period to another almost between the opening kickoff and the final whistle of their football games.

At first, Americans appeared indifferent to the world situation. To a lot of them, Great Britain, Germany, and Poland seemed light-years away. They were still concerned with winning football games, getting good grades, trying to keep alive financially. Life went on as usual. The movies were crowded: the Marx Brothers in *Room Service,* and the first full-length cartoon, *Snow White and the Seven Dwarfs.* Two new Broadway shows had just opened, both hits: Olsen and Johnson's *Hellzapoppin'* and Clare Boothe Luce's *Kiss the Boys Goodbye.* The sports news even offered a laugh in keeping with the times—the misadventures of Jack Doyle, the Irish heavyweight. In a fight with Billy Phillips that week, he missed with a powerful right, spun completely around, slipped, crashed through the ring ropes, landed on his head—and knocked himself out. Seen against preoccupations like these, the Nazi occupation of Czechoslovakia was indeed remote.

Whatever role the United States plays in world affairs in the future, it is not likely that the same sense of unreality about the international scene will exist ever again. During World War II, American ideals and character were tested as never before.

Once the United States entered the war, it caused perplexing problems for college football. Whole teams were wiped out by the draft. Many schools dropped the sport for the duration. Some made freshmen eligible for varsity competition in order to keep their teams alive. Platoon football and tough academic standards made it difficult for most schools to remain competitive. Columbia's coach Lou Little summed up the situation in 1942:

Football is experiencing many changes. Equipment is less plentiful. In the face of wartime priorities, last season's equipment will have to do in most cases and it may become somewhat threadbare before long. But who cares? Veteran players are fewer. Hundreds of players who had looked forward to their senior season are now in combat, flying fighter planes, manning machine guns, or walking the decks of the navy's fighting craft. Football crowds are smaller. It is harder now to reach the games which are played in the small, secluded college towns, heretofore so easily reached by unhampered motors. Gas rationing is now a fact—but these problems do not matter. Football is still being played; harder, in fact, than ever before. We have become an offensively minded people. Defense bonds have become war bonds. The bombers and the ships they buy are weapons of attack, not defense. We've got to strike, not parry.

With the 1940s came a major development: a new style of offensive football called the T formation. Clark Shaughnessy at Stanford took the oldest formation in football, the original T, and joined it with the man-in-motion. This combining of the flanker and man-in-motion with a hard-hitting, quick-opening attack made for an offense of ever-changing structure. It placed a big burden on the defense with the wide variety of its patterns. Those coaches who did not jump on the bandwagon felt compelled to add new features to their attacks for greater deception.

Missouri was the best of the Big Six in 1941 and 1942..Writing in *Football* Magazine, Frederick Ware gave some details:

The Tigers are generally blessed with youthful regulars and high-test sophomores. There will be slight, if any, deterioration in the calibre of their team in 1942. Last season, Missouri was only two points away from T-totalism and greatness. Until they met Fordham in the rain-drenched Sugar Bowl their terrific running attack and rugged defense more than offset the lack of a dependable passer and punter. Fordham blocked a kick, and the safety stood up for the only scoring of the game, 2–0. Despite a parade of his athletes to war, Coach Don Faurot figures to win the Big Six championship again. Carrying the load will be halfbacks Bob Steuber, who will call the plays, and Freddy Kling, center Jeff Davis, ends Bert Ekern and Marshall Shurnas, tackles Leo Milla and Ed Hodges, and guards Jack Keith and Mike Fitzgerald. The strength of Missouri is reinforced by a No. 2 lineup, mostly lettermen, so doughty that only a couple of the most talented first-year kids have managed to win positions on it.

The Tigers went on to make Ware a genuine expert, though not by much. Oklahoma tied them, 6–6, but then had to settle for second place in league standings after losing to Nebraska, 7–0. That left Missouri with a 4–0–1 record, while the Sooners finished 3–1–1.

The year 1943 went down as the Great Mystery Year. That is, it was no longer a question of who would win the starting fullback job at Mammoth U. The problem now was which college would play what college, if any, and when and where and how. In other words, football was on the ration list, and the fans simply had to adjust. Nearly every schedule was scrambled by travel restrictions. The conversion of the colleges to essential warfare had shoved spectator sports far down to the bottom of national priorities. Varying regulations for army and navy campus trainees created a situation in which the navy schools were the fat "haves," and the army schools were the haggard "no-gots." The Selective Service Act continued to take its toll. Freshmen classes got smaller, and younger, than ever before. In many cases, freshmen comprised the total manpower supply of football.

A coach's program was also subject to the vagaries of service transfers. No enlisted trainee knew how long he would stay put, or where, and this factor would cause team strength to fluctuate from week to week. And then there was the coaching situation. Most of the younger coaches and most of the big-name career men were in officers' uniforms by now. Essentially, it was "service football" under collegiate auspices.

The Big Six played under emergency regulations in 1943. Practically anyone who was enrolled in school was eligible—freshmen, servicemen, and even former professionals, if they were accredited trainees. Unlimited summer practice was approved, together with a September opening for fall practice.

All scouting was eliminated. As a substitute, coaches agreed to exchange offensive formations at least a week prior to each game. "Of course," Oklahoma's Dewey Luster said, "some of the players may not line up exactly the way they're supposed to. They may surprise their own coach as much as the opponents."

Coach Luster found a solution for wartime, undermanned football: he taught his Sooners the assignments for two or three positions. During spring practice, he had a squad of thirty players. All but four of them had gone off to war by September. Yet Oklahoma won all its league games, and, overall, was 7–2–0 for the season. It lost only to Texas, 13–7, and Tulsa, 20–6.

"Football is the ideal sport for training youngsters to the mood of war," Dewey Luster said. "There's simply no acceptable substitute for the rugged give-and-take of free-wheeling body contact." He then came back in 1944 and won the conference championship again, and finished second to Missouri in 1945.

By now, a new mood of optimism was manifesting itself around the country. Grantland Rice summed it up for everybody when he wrote:

We talk of our Golden Age of Sport, the Fabulous Twenties when our champions of champions flourished—the man-eating Dempsey, the peerless Earl Sande, the transcendental Tilden, the grand-slamming Bobby Jones, the incredible Babe Ruth, the magnificent Grange—and when will we see such figures again? The curious answer is that they are here. We are in those times now. We are on the threshold, yes. The war is over, the skies are clear, the sun rides high, the wind blows fresh and fair, and king football is on the brink of another great era.

The end of World War II was the beginning of a tremendous phase of football consciousness that was sweeping across America. The years just ahead were destined to be mostly golden, with cheering crowds and gallant heroes. Once more, college football would be dressing itself in spangles and tinsel. Everywhere you looked, it was boom, ballyhoo, and buildup for football. It was no longer just a college game. It was about to become a national industry—a magnificent pageant played in crisp, zippy air, the smell of burning autumn leaves, with pretty cheerleaders, marching bands in scarlet capes, brown footballs in the air, running and diving figures in pads, and gold in the fields. And a coincidence —postwar, halcyon days, money days, and a football-mad public hungry for action.

Memories: Another Year, Another Day

They were swapping yarns about Big Eight football—Bud Wilkinson, betraying no wear from his single season as head coach of the St. Louis Cardinals, fifteen years after departing Oklahoma; John McKay, his red hair gone silver during sixteen years of service with the University of Southern California Trojans and three with the Tampa Bay Buccaneers; Bob Newton and Ken Geddes, former Nebraska All-America linemen; Don James of the University of Washington, college football's Coach of the Year in 1977 and former assistant at Kansas and Colorado; Jim Walden, who both played and coached under the great Bob Devaney; Terry Beeson, the Seattle Seahawks' terrific One-Man Gang from the Kansas Jayhawks; Jim Owens, All-American and cocaptain under Wilkinson at Oklahoma and the man McKay credits with bringing respectability to West Coast football, when he coached Washington to back-to-back Rose Bowl triumphs over the Big Ten; and Earl Luebker, assistant to sports-information director Harold Keith at Oklahoma during Wilkinson's early years there.

The occasion was the Challenge Bowl—McKay's Pacific Ten senior All-Stars versus Wilkinson's Big Eight seniors—at Seattle's Kingdome in early January 1979. John Harvey McKay versus Charles Burnham Wilkinson. It would be difficult to find two men less alike in all respects but one: in briefly overlapping careers as coaches of college football, Wilkinson and McKay dominated the game. In the years 1947 through 1975, they won a combined total of 272 games, twenty-three conference championships, two Sugar Bowls, four Orange Bowls, five Rose Bowls, seven national championships with seven undefeated teams. And Wilkinson's masterpiece of forty-seven consecutive victories with Oklahoma has never been equaled, or seriously challenged.

It seems unbelievable, but throughout the interlocked reigns of Wilkinson and McKay, their teams met but once—in 1963, when the Trojans were defending national champions.

"We lucked out," said Wilkinson. "We beat 'em, 17–12. It was 104 degrees on the floor of the Los Angeles Coliseum. We were used to the heat, and they weren't."

That was Bud Wilkinson's last season at Oklahoma. McKay never got a chance to even the score as a college coach.

Speaking of the weather, Jim Owens recalled that he would just as soon forget the dog days in Norman:

Hot? It was so hot we'd get up at 5 A.M. and be on the field at 6 for two hours' practice before eating breakfast. In preseason, Bud held two-a-day workouts, and there was nothing we could do about those afternoon drills. If you survived the heat, you knew you were in great condition. We lost a lot of weight. In those days, 1947–1949, the coaches didn't think it was a good idea to have much liquid on the field. They'd give us an orange peel to chew on, but no water, no Gator-Aid, no iced tea. We lost tremendous amounts of weight during practice, then tried to make it up with lots of liquid at the end of the day.

Owens let out a sustained groan. All this talk about late summer heat in Norman, Oklahoma, made him think about the Oklahoma Drill. Oklahoma Drill? "Yes," Owens said. "It's an invention of Bud's, adapted from a play called the Oklahoma Dive—a drill exercise in which a pair of tackling dummies are set up about six feet apart and between them,

Versatile All-American Ray Evans, halfback for Kansas, passed, punted, and ran his way into the National Football Hall of Fame.

facing each other, two linemen square away just as they would on the line of scrimmage."

Behind the offensive player, five or six yards back, Owens said, a running back is poised, and at a coach's signal "hut!" he receives a handoff and runs full-tilt forward, hopefully over or past the defensive man, who is wrestling with the player opposite. The back's running room is restricted by the two tackling dummies, and the trick is to read which way the offensive lineman is playing the defensive man opposite and to make one's cut accordingly.

"It is a brutal exercise for all three players," Owens said. "It's especially brutal for the defensive player, who must fend off the blocks of his opposite number and also try to make the tackle on the running back."

Jim Owens, a regular big buster of a guy in his early fifties, still looks back on Wilkinson's Oklahoma Drill ruefully. The barbaric nature of football is never more graphically evident to him than when the action between several linemen is isolated—the grunts, the self-goading cries that erupt from within the plastic helmets—with their teammates standing around as if they were watching bull mastiffs in a blood pit.

Ever since 1963, when he walked away from college coaching, Bud Wilkinson has remained a part of the American scene. His collegiate coaching record of 145–29–4 included three national championships and the longest winning streak in college football history. Then came an unsuccessful run for the U.S. Senate—"it seemed like the thing to do," Wilkinson said—and three years of advisory service to President Richard M. Nixon. More visibly, he was ABC's college football color commentator for ten years, the strong, soothing voice of reason above the din.

Ever since he started writing publicity for the Sooners in 1947, Earl Luebker, now a

sports columnist for the *Tacoma News Tribune,* has been a Wilkinson watcher.

At Oklahoma, Bud treated his players like gentlemen and expected the same from them. He's a great manipulator. He can make people do things they don't really want to do, then make it seem like it was their idea. He is a very articulate man. At Oklahoma, when he got through talking to you, he had you convinced you could run through a brick wall. He looked only at the bottom line, and that was winning.

The bottom line at Oklahoma showed fourteen conference championships in seventeen years, four undefeated seasons, and two Sugar Bowl and four Orange Bowl trophies. Wilkinson was so successful that in 1957 three Texas oilmen, avid University of Houston backers, offered to give Wilkinson two gushing oil wells and two yachts—one of them a 125-footer—if he would coach their team. Wilkinson declined.

As a member of the great national championship Minnesota teams of the mid-1930s, Wilkinson had a key role in what was probably the most spectacular single clinical play in Coach Bernie Bierman's dynasty. It was an extemporaneous lateral of a punt that brought victory when a scoreless tie seemed imminent. Bud was a hard-nosed guard for the Gophers in 1934 and 1935, but was shifted to quarterback in 1936, as a natural leader. As ball handler, he engineered the beginning of the game-winning play. Dick Cullum was there and described it this way in the *Minneapolis Times:*

There were 68 seconds to play. Nebraska had the ball on its 43-yard line. Sam Francis, the Cornhuskers' best kicker, had been

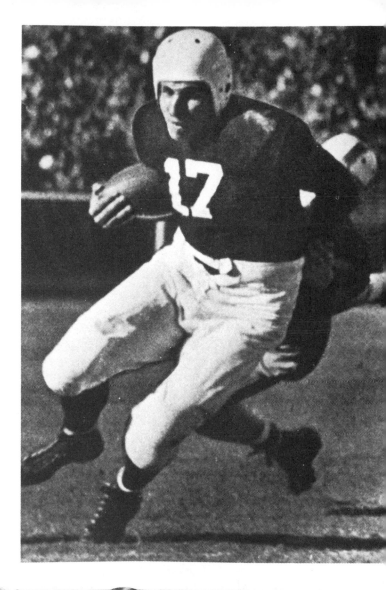

The Player of the Game in Stanford's victory over Nebraska in the 1941 Rose Bowl was the Stanford Cardinal halfback Pete Kmetovic.

Nebraska fullback Vike Francis (*arrow*) plunged over from the 3-yard line to give the Huskers a 7–0 first-quarter lead in the 1941 Rose Bowl, but Stanford fought back to win the game, 21–13.

removed in favor of Ron Douglas, a sophomore. Douglas punted a short, high one to Wilkinson on Minnesota's 28. Wilkinson caught the ball near the sideline, and took the first step to the inside and backwards, drawing all the tacklers toward him.

It was not until one of them had him by one leg that he let the ball go. Uram caught it on the 25-yard line and ran through a broken field 75 yards to a touchdown. It was unquestionably one of football's finest plays. Bierman called it the most perfectly executed spur-of-the-moment play he ever saw. He also insisted that every man used the maximum of good judgment in clearing the way for Uram, who himself used perfect judgment in setting his pace and choosing his course. At one stage, every Nebraska player was on his back. This phenomenal and brilliant play decided a very tough ball game, 7–0, in the last 60 seconds.

At the end of the 1936 season, Wilkinson was awarded the Big Ten Medal as the outstanding scholar-athlete. Otis Dypwick, who served thirty-one years as sports-information director at Minnesota, was Wilkinson's best man at his wedding. Otis told me:

It used to gripe the heck out of me in class. Bud, a super all-around athlete, would go on football or hockey trips and I'd take notes in class for him and he'd get an A in the subject while I got a C. Because his success as a football coach so overshadowed everything else he ever did, people forget that Bud was one of the greatest goalies in the history of college hockey. In school, he was a tall, handsome guy, plenty smart and very versatile. He could have lettered in three or four varsity sports: baseball, golf, football, and hockey. He was a running guard for Bierman, before moving to quarterback, when we ran out of quarterbacks in Bud's senior season. As quarterback,

all he did was lead us to the national championship in 1936, the first year of the AP poll.

Wilkinson told me that the switch from guard to quarterback was not too hard for him. "Minnesota ran from a single wing and the quarterback was the blocking back," Bud said. Even so, with just one season under his belt, he was named the College All-Stars' starting quarterback and led the collegians to their first victory over the Green Bay Packers, 7–0.

Later, as head coach at Oklahoma, Bud said he acquired most of his technical knowledge of football from Bierman. He also learned the importance of physical fitness in Bernie's ultraphysical methods. He explained:

The best way to attain superb physical condition is to punish yourself in practice after you are already dead tired. In other words, run those wind sprints, hit that dummy, again and again and again. There's nothing new about this concept. I learned it myself, the hard way, at Minnesota. I'll never forget it as long as I live. It was a cold, raw day and we were practicing in the field house. Coach Bierman had us running wind sprints. We'd run, then stop, then he'd have us run again, and again, and again. It was pure torture. But I have another clear memory, too. It was of the game on the very next Saturday. We beat Iowa, 52–6.

Bob Geigengack, Yale's magnificent track coach, was at Iowa Pre-Flight with Wilkinson in 1943. Bud was just one of a very large staff of famous sports names there, but Geigengack never forgot a remark by Moon Mullins, the former Notre Dame star under Knute Rockne, which Geigengack later found to be prophetic. Geigengack remembered:

In 1943 and 1944, at the height of World War II, Oklahoma did not lose a single conference game. Pictured here are the members of the youthful 1944 championship squad. Dewey Luster was the head coach.

We used to hold clinics at Iowa Pre-Flight. Going home from one of these one night, Moon said to me, "Bob, any time you are in a civilian capacity and an opportunity comes up to recommend that youngster, Bud Wilkinson, don't hesitate to do so, because I believe he will someday be established as the finest football brain in the United States." It certainly turned out that way, and I often wonder how Moon Mullins could have known so far in advance.

The year 1955 was one of Wilkinson's greatest seasons as a coach. The performance highlight was Oklahoma's extension of a victory string that reached thirty games with the sensational 20–6 stomping of previously unbeaten Maryland in the Orange Bowl. The Sooners injected a new dimension into football with their colorful "fast break" attack. Blitzing their opponents by sprinting out of the huddle and launching their plays with a breathless rush, Wilkinson's mighty men were unanimously named the nation's No. 1 team.

In the locker rooms at Oklahoma, huge red and white placards pounded home the words "Play Like a Champion." Yet if a boy didn't want to play at all, that was his privilege, too. Sounding much like A. Whitney Griswold, the Yale president who believed that college football had forgotten its main purpose, Coach Wilkinson said:

I don't see any reason why a boy should feel he has to be a football player, if it's against his personality. He'd be better off in some other line of endeavor. A lot of boys participate in football because their girls think it's nice or their parents want them to, but there's a tremendous number of young men who are blessed with an abundance of physical energy and truly combative spirit. They have to relieve themselves of that pressure and test their minds and bodies. Football fulfills that demand for total effort and teaches them fair play, discipline, teamwork, and loyalty.

I am totally of the opinion that because football is a morale game, because it is primarily a game of the heart, I believe you must first find a boy of character, a boy who first must be a good enough college student to do college work without undue difficulty, and to be able to graduate from college. If he doesn't have that much academic ability, he doesn't belong in college, that's all there is to it. I believe college athletics are for college students. Most people don't believe coaches feel that way. But they do.

In that vein, in 1952 I wrote an article for the Newspaper Enterprise Association in which I pointed out that college football was no longer a game of all brawn:

Next time you watch a college football game, don't discount the candlepower behind the horsepower that moves the ball. Chances are that All-America blocking back can tie you in knots—from Archimedes to Zanzibar. In today's hyped and complex game, football is no longer a Broadway for the scholastic jerk. "Football today is a game of chess at high speed," says Biggie Munn. "Dullards only mess up the works." Thirteen members of his Michigan State squad are B students. And Johnny Wilson, his defensive left halfback, is a Rhodes Scholarship candidate as a journalism undergraduate. Coach Bud Wilkinson has his share of blue-ribbon students, too. During the last four years, 92 percent of the football Sooners have earned diplomas. Forty percent graduated in Business School; 12 percent in Geology; 12 percent in Physical Education; and 4.8 percent in History, Arts and Sciences, Psychology and Mechanical Engineering. Letterman Bill Price . . . picked up 132 credits in Mathematics and Petroleum Engineering, of which 124 were straight A's, the rest B's.

The postwar football boom was on. With the federal government paying their way on the GI Bill—tuition, books, and sixty-five dollars a month—thousands of veterans returned to campus life from such places as North Africa, Guadalcanal, and the skies above Britain. They were older now, more mature, battle-wise, and bigger. Forget the Knute Rockne fight-talk psychology. The athletes were more sophisticated now. Subsequently, the season of 1946 promised some of the best football in college history.

With the new era came a major development: the T formation hit its stride. But one major coach who did not feel compelled to go along with the new T craze was Charley Caldwell of Princeton. After experimenting with it briefly, he junked it in favor of the bread-and-butter single wing. He smiled at self-styled experts who argued that the single wing was old hat, saying the T was the only way to go. To make his point, Caldwell then won thirty of thirty-one games. Caldwell told me:

It depends upon whose single wing or T it is. The single wing I use is a complex and elaborate system involving power, deception, perfect timing, and multiple threats from different sides. It has more variations than the T. Our basic off-tackle play on a direct pass and buck-lateral series has thirteen variations. Not the least asset of the single wing is that it lends itself to control of the ball. In one of our big games, there were 137 plays. We had the ball for 101. When our opponents came in pressing, to stop the steady attack, we went outside or passed them silly. When they drew back a little, we resumed the inside and reverse plays.

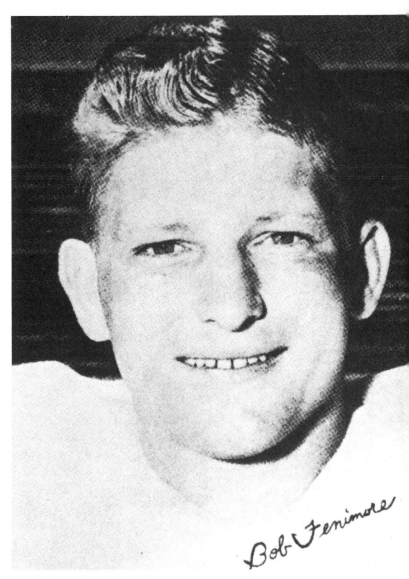

Oklahoma A. & M.'s all-around halfback Bob Fenimore was one of the biggest names in wartime college football and All-American in 1944 and 1945. He was the star of the Cowboys' Cotton Bowl victory over Texas Christian (34–0) on New Year's Day, 1945, and over St. Mary's (33–13) in the Sugar Bowl the following season. The key to Hall of Famer Fenimore was versatility—he completed 51 percent of his passes, was an excellent runner and fine punter, intercepted passes, and returned punts. His 5,099 yards is still a school career record for total offense.

Charles ("Bud") Wilkinson as he looked at thirty-one, the father of two sons and assistant to Coach Jim Tatum of Oklahoma's 1946 Big Six champions (shared with Kansas).

Coaches who tell you they use this system or that system because of the nature of their material is nonsense. If you have the material for the T, you have the material for the single wing. They're going to the T because they are afraid of the alumni, who insist on a more fan-pleasing, wide-open game. It's a case of economics. They have to sell tickets to fill those big stadiums.

Caldwell said he would take the single wing over the T when it came to passing tactics. He explained:

The T quarterback takes the ball from center, swings back faking a pitchout and runs back farther to pass. He gets little opportunity to spot anyone except the primary receiver. The single wing passer is always looking forward, watching developments, and spotting secondary receivers in case the primary one is covered. He doesn't commit himself to pass until the last second, and defending backs cannot give undivided attention to potential receivers until he does. Many times the play continues as a ground attack.

Listening to Charley Caldwell, I had to wonder why so many coaches were switching to the modern T with man-in-motion. "They had modern football at its best all the while," Charley told me. "All they had to do was embellish it."

Despite Caldwell's enthusiasm for the single wing, Jim Tatum, the new coach at Oklahoma, announced at a press conference that he would be using the T. The last time the Sooners used the T was in 1910, when Bennie Owen abandoned it for the single wing. With the new offense, Tatum hoped to improve on Dewey Luster's record of 27–18–3 (19–4–2 in the conference) during the war years at Norman. Although the squad ran almost entirely to good ol' Oklahoma boys or panhandle Texans, there was one exception. He was Jake McAlister, a 235-pound tackle who played with Alabama in the 1942 Rose Bowl. "He was captured, domesticated and signed citizenship papers on the spot," crowed Harold Keith, the Oklahoma publicist. On the first day of practice, sixty-five candidates showed up at Owen Field. Among them were the Andros brothers, Plato and Dee, Buddy Burris, George Brewer, Eddy Davis, Max Fischer, Warren Giese, Joe Golding, Myrle Greathouse, Ed Kreick, Norm McNabb, Jack Mitchell, Jim Owens, Darrell Royal, Jim Tyree, Wade Walker, and Dave Wallace.

Oklahoma's imposing array of war veterans notwithstanding, there was a fairly substantial feeling throughout the Big Six that Missouri would win its fifth title in eight years. Don Faurot had rounded up 150 players to choose from, and he admitted that his Tigers would be stronger than the 1945 championship team that made a clean sweep of its league games and lost a thriller in the Cotton Bowl to Texas, 40–27. But Faurot protested the No. 1 billing. "How can you single us out as the preseason favorite?" he asked. "Practically every team in the country is going to be better. Everybody has a good number of war veterans back and there's going to be fewer standout teams. It's a matter of who has picked up the most strength. In the Big Six, I say it's Kansas and Oklahoma."

The debate was on. Jim Tatum said the Sooners would do well to win half of their games:

The Big Six Conference is a strange land filled with people whose idea of prognosticating this year's race is to repeat the order in which the teams finished in 1945, then hurry down to the corner drugstore for a cup of

Triple-threat (a term you don't hear anymore) halfback Billy Dellastatious weighed only 168 pounds, but it was enough to help Missouri win all of its league games in 1945 and a spot in the Cotton Bowl.

coffee. Frankly, I have no idea who will win. Much of my coaching has been in North Carolina, on the southeastern coast. I've never seen a Big Six game. Besides, the football picture all over the country will be enormously complicated by the return in one season of a five-year accumulation of talent.

Oklahoma was playing its toughest nonconference schedule in history. The first opponent was merely Army, No. 1 in the nation and undefeated for two years. The Cadets had their one-two punch back—Felix ("Doc") Blanchard and Glenn Davis—and their triple-threat quarterback, Arnold Tucker. Fritz Crisler, the Michigan coach, said he had never seen two finer ball carriers in one backfield than "Mr. Inside" and "Mr. Outside." Crisler said:

Illinois had its Red Grange, Michigan had its Tom Harmon, Stanford had its Ernie Nevers, Notre Dame its George Gipp, but Army boasts two *super stars. In my book, Blanchard and Davis comprise the greatest one-two punch in football history. They whipsaw you to a frazzle. If the defense tightens up to stop Blanchard, Davis flits around the flank. If the defense widens to halt Glenn's flank raids, Doc tears your midriff wide open. It is impossible to rig a defense which can stop Blanchard and Davis simultaneously. Even if you can check both of them, Tucker and Ug Fuson might run you out of the ball park.*

Tatum and the Sooners had their hands full, all right. Blanchard, 6 feet and 206 pounds of raging fullback, won the James Sullivan Award, the Heisman Trophy, and the Robert Maxwell Cup as the outstanding athlete, football player, and amateur sportsman of 1945. He ran the 100-yard dash in 10 seconds flat. He grew up in the turpentine forests of South Carolina and got the pigskin fever

early. As a toddler of five, he used to practice placekicks while his fourteen-year-old aunt held the ball. Doc celebrated his sixth birthday by smoking a corncob pipe and setting the barn afire. Fourteen years later he was to set the nation's gridirons on fire.

The war caught Doc in his freshman year at the University of North Carolina. He was an infantry private when West Point talent scouts discovered him in a southern army camp. "Ideal officer material" was the official verdict. "A helluva football prospect," scribbled the scout in a report to West Point gridiron G.H.Q. Both estimates proved correct.

Billed as a second and faster edition of Minnesota's Bronko Nagurski, Blanchard lived up to advance publicity. Incredibly fast off the mark for so large a man, piano-legged Doc was made to order for quick-breaking T formation plays, in which a lightning getaway is essential. Once through the tiny openings made by "brush blocks," Blanchard ran his own interference, trampling over anybody who got in his path.

Blanchard's accomplice, Glenn "Junior" Davis, otherwise known as "Mister Outside," was a close-coupled, chunky chap, 5 feet 9 inches tall, 170 pounds in weight, who supplemented Blanchard perfectly, because Glenn had the meteoric speed to turn an enemy flank. Once he got outside the defensive triangle, he was gone with the wind. As a West Point cadet, he lettered in three varsity sports during his plebe year—football, baseball, and basketball. He could have added a fourth letter, had he chosen to go out for track. "Running doesn't interest me," he said, "unless it's linked up with some sort of team game."

In 1945, Davis smashed the all-time record for the U.S. Military Academy physical efficiency test, scoring 926½ points out of a possible 1,000. Nobody else had ever come near 900 points in this all-around program, which included such agility tests as wall climbing under full marching pack, rope scaling, digging trenches, push-ups, pull-ups, weight lifting, running, jumping, boxing, fencing, bayonet drill, and calisthenics.

"It's significant," commented Red Blaik, "that Davis, Blanchard, and Tucker finished one-two-three in this physical efficiency test for the entire Cadet Corps. The collective performance of this group speaks louder than adjectives, and helps explain why this particular trio was so effective in our backfield. They were all born athletes."

Davis was no fancy Dan sideline stepper. Unlike many football sprinters, he had the power and instinct to knife through needle-eye holes inside tackle. He could dodge a tackler or pivot out of his grasp with a leg drive that was simply amazing in a 170-pound halfback. He had what doctors call outstanding peripheral vision—the knack of sizing up at a mere glance the location of each approaching tackler even as he eluded the man directly in his path. The layman would say, "He's got eyes in the back of his head." It explains why Davis so often ran through half the enemy team for touchdowns.

Now we come to a flaxen-haired, chess-brained chap who masterminded the Army T formation of 1946, Arnold Tucker. Tucker handled the passing and ferreted out soft spots in the opposing defense. He stood 5 feet 10 inches, weighed 174 pounds. Notre Dame scouts called him the "perfect T formation quarterback."

Tucker, for some reason, didn't get the publicity he deserved. Coach Blaik said he was the most underrated player in America. "Arnold had the play-picking judgment of Harry Stuhldreher, who quarterbacked the Notre Dame Four Horsemen, and the limber passing arm of Sammy Baugh, yet the sportswriters hardly gave him a tumble," Blaik said. "I wish

we could have kept his ability a secret from enemy scouts."

On the Tuesday before the Oklahoma game, Army's dreams for a third straight undefeated season received a serious setback. Doc Blanchard was in the hospital. He had suffered a leg injury in the Cadets' 35–0 victory over Villanova the previous Saturday and sat out the last three quarters of the game. He was not expected back in uniform until Friday, and it was doubtful if he would play.

The New York press was mad at the West Point coaching staff for attempting to keep Blanchard's injury quiet. When Oscar Fraley, a United Press columnist, asked for details, he was told: "Nothing wrong. Just a heel bruise suffered in practice." Then Col. Harvey ("Jabbo") Jablonski, one of the Army line coaches, let the cat out of the bag. He confessed that Blanchard had suffered a leg muscle bruise against Villanova, which brought every doctor in the Hudson Valley running to the infirmary. Fraley wrote:

Without Blanchard the Army is just another ball club, as it showed when Glenn Davis, "Mr. Outside," was smothered because the Blanchard threat was removed from the middle. So the odds are that if Doc can stand, he'll play. Actually, when you get past the first team Army is just mediocre. Such nationally honored stars from last year's team as Dewitt Coulter, Al Nemetz, Dick Pitzer and Captain Johnny Green have graduated. And now without Blanchard to threaten the middle and tighten the secondary so Davis can run wide, it's just another ball club. If Blanchard sits it out, Oklahoma should win to the accompaniment of thundering cheers from coaches who have tasted Army's crushing cleats during the past two years. For Red Blaik has pulled no punches in his victory march, and many a coach is nursing a grudge. They make no secret of the fact that when they finally get Army down, they'll kick 'em. But as long as Blanchard and Davis combine for a one-two punch, they'll be tough to shave. As Herman Hickman, the Cadet line coach, put it when talking to Quarterback Arnold Tucker: "First run Blanchard into the middle. Then run Davis wide." And Tucker asked, "What then?" "Migawd!" roared Hickman, "isn't that enough?" It is. But without Blanchard you may be hearing about quite an upset come Saturday.

The headlines in Sunday's *New York Herald-Tribune* capsuled the outcome perfectly:

CADETS RALLY AFTER VISITORS SCORE FIRST

61-Yard Passing Drive Ties Count in Second Period Before 25,499

TRUMAN WITNESSES GAME AT WEST POINT

Blanchard on Sidelines as Teammates Halt Strong Sooner Eleven

Gene Ward, writing in the *New York Sunday News,* opened his story this way:

A man from Missouri—President Harry Truman—plus 25,499 other avid fans watched and waited to be shown Army's explosive brand of football yesterday—and the Cadets had the gosh-darndest time showing 'em. Their big, battering Blanchard was sweating

it out on the bench with an injury. Glenn Davis was getting smeared around. Their coach was jitter-bugging along the sidelines, jockeying his lineup. Finally, the Cadets had to resort to breaks and brains of their T-formation fuse, quarterback Arnold Tucker, to overcome Oklahoma's seven-point lead and win a 21–7 victory in Michie Stadium at West Point.

A two-touchdown rally in the second half at last cracked a 7–7 deadlock and won 'em their 20th consecutive triumph. But Harry Truman, as impartial commander-in-chief, can carry good news back to Navy. Army isn't so tough this year.

In fact, the Cadets, who crunched all comers in 1944 and 1945, haven't had so much trouble since they first started their victory streak. No team has come as close since Navy whipped 'em back at the tail end of the 1943 campaign. And, if it hadn't been for quarterback Tucker, the pigskin premises up the Hudson might have been a very sad place today.

Years later, Red Blaik talked about the game. He recalled that Blanchard's missing the game constituted a minor irony. He said that Doc had looked forward to it with special relish because the Sooners were coached by his second cousin, Jim Tatum:

However, Cousin Jim didn't know for sure that Cousin Felix wasn't going to play until the actual kickoff. Blanchard and Davis were cocaptains and Doc suited up and went out with Glenn for the toss of the coin. Our psychology was to keep Blanchard's playing a possibility as long as we could in the minds of the Sooners. They were already approaching the game with sufficient confidence and dedication.

Six of the players on that Oklahoma team

went on to become head coaches: halfback Darrell Royal (he was shifted to quarterback later that season) at Washington and Texas, quarterback Jack Mitchell at Kansas, tackle Wade Walker at Mississippi State, ends Jim Owens and Warren Giese at Washington and South Carolina, and Dee Andros at Oregon State. They went on to play for the early teams of the Bud Wilkinson regime. Bud was Tatum's assistant in 1946 and scouted our opening game against Villanova. Then when we played the Sooners he sat up in the press box spotting for Tatum.

Since this was the first year with the split T for most of the Oklahoma players, they were having normal growing pains with it, such as we had experienced three years before with the straight T. Nevertheless, they were plenty tough. We were able to resist their terrific bid for victory only through an intrepid team effort, highlighted by the full flowering of Arnold Tucker as a quarterback and the flair of Glenn Davis to murder you one way—this day as a pass receiver—if you stopped him another. It was Tucker, more than anybody else, who helped us beat Oklahoma.

After the game, I had to put in a command appearance at a cocktail party given by the superintendent, Major General Maxwell D. Taylor. President Truman was also there, and after a time he took me aside. "Red," he said, "what do you think about your chances with Navy?" With uncommon optimism, I said, "Reasonably good." "They've got to be better than that," said the President. "I have twenty dollars riding on that game and I don't want to lose to any Navy so-and-so."

The following Saturday, Dave Wallace and Darrell Royal teamed up to give Oklahoma its first victory of the postwar era. The opponent was Texas A. & M. and the game was played at Norman. After 58 minutes of fierce strug-

Oklahoma versus Texas has always been one of the most colorful rivalries in college football. In the 1946 contest at Dallas, 5-foot 6-inch scatback Johnny Alsup gained 6 yards for the Sooners on this reverse around left end, but the Longhorns won the game, 20–13.

Senior guard Buddy Burris captained Oklahoma in 1946 and earned All-America recognition.

gle, it appeared the two teams would settle for a 7–7 standoff. The Sooners piled up 376 total yards and several times drove to the Aggie goal line, but they couldn't break the tie. Then, with 2 minutes left, halfback Royal burst loose on a quick opening play. He boomed around left end, then swerved back to the west sideline, and after evading tacklers for 31 yards was finally bumped out of bounds on the A. & M. 6. Three smashes at the line gained only 2, and an offsides penalty pushed the Sooners back to the 9. Now there were only 40 seconds left on the clock.

Dave Wallace, the sophomore quarterback, turned to Royal in the huddle and said, "Okay, Darrell, you hold it and I'll kick it."

"Field goal!" screamed the grandstand quarterbacks. The angle was bad and a breeze blew in his face, but Wallace was game. He was confident.

Tension hung heavy over Owen Field. The ball would be kicked from Royal's hold on the 15-yard line. With the goal posts 10 yards beyond the goal line, the ball had to travel 25 yards to reach the uprights, and more than that to get over the crossbar.

"Has Wallace ever tried one of these before?" somebody up in the stands wanted to know.

"Oh, he's not going to kick it," he was told. "It's going to be a fake of some kind."

"That Tatum's a foxy one, all right."

"Sure. Watch for a pass. Wallace is a good passer."

While the fans were doping it all out, John Rapacz, 6 feet 3 inches, and 220 pounds, and the Oklahoma center from Kalamazoo, Michigan, leaned over the ball and prepared to hike it back in good shape to Royal, who would be teeing up the ball for his quarterback. Now the sideline strategists weren't so sure. Maybe the Sooners weren't bluffing. Maybe Wallace really was going to try to drive it through with his powerful right leg. But look at that poor angle.

The mostly partisan crowd of 28,000 was quiet now. Everybody was standing, their hearts pounding, as they watched Wallace calmly line up his kick. Slowly he took two steps back and, head down, faced the goal posts, waiting for Rapacz's snapback. His arms hung loosely at his sides. His crimson and cream jersey was covered with sweat and grime, a testimony to his hard playing. A long murmur ran around the stadium. The Oklahoma fans didn't know what to expect. You could almost hear the silent prayers, the pleas, encouraging him, helping him all they could. No one was sitting now.

Rapacz snapped the ball back to Royal. Royal set it up nice and pretty. Wallace stepped forward and dug his toe viciously into the ball. The ball tumbled high and true. It wavered for just an instant in the breeze, and then curved toward the middle of the goal posts. For a split second there was no signal from the referee, Ted O'Sullivan—and then, suddenly, he flung his hands upward.

The riot was on. Royal and Wallace had their arms around each other and were hugging the breath out of one another. Grown people were doing strange dances on the seats and kissing and whooping. And out on the field the Sooners swarmed all over Wallace. They poured from the bench and around him and all of them were shaking his hand and thumping him on the back, and you could tell by the wide grin on his face as he glanced up at the big scoreboard and saw the final numbers—Oklahoma 10, Texas A. & M. 7—that this was a supreme moment of his life.

"Bring on the Longhorns!" somebody shouted, in reference to Oklahoma's next opponent, Texas, No. 1 in the polls.

"Texas next!" came the chorus. "Texas! Texas! Texas!"

Walter Driskill scouted the Longhorns for Oklahoma in their 54–6 victory over Oklahoma A. & M., and what he had to tell Jim Tatum and his staff was not good. He reported on Monday morning:

Texas doesn't make any mistakes, offensively or defensively, and they do not beat themselves. Their quarterbacking is exceptional. They will check any play called in the huddle to take advantage of a defensive weakness. Bobby Layne calls their signals. Joe Magliolo, their blocking back, calls the plays when Layne is not in the game. Blair Cherry, the Texas backfield coach who next year will succeed Dana X. Bible as head coach, says Layne can thread a needle with his passes and that they have four receivers who can outrun our fastest back. Cherry believes the Texas passing attack would demoralize any team in the country. "We couldn't hold down the score if we wanted to," Cherry said.

Even in college, Bobby Layne, who later starred for the Detroit Lions, was a flamboyant cock-of-the-walk leader. Competitiveness glowed in him. He was a rough character, with brass. His methods were often hard-handed, but they worked with most of his teammates, because he was admired by the older players and held in awe by the younger ones, though the cussings-out he was likely to give embittered some of them, so that they'd go off in a corner and sulk. But how Layne could play football. When he played, no one ever watched anyone else on the field but him. He had that cocky walk when he came out of the huddle, almost a duck walk because of the little pot he had for a belly. And then you could see his face. He didn't wear a face bar, yet he had all his teeth. Then he wore a shrunken old-fashioned helmet that looked like he'd swiped it off the head of George Gipp, one of those old-timers. It sat up high on his head like an inverted flower pot, and you could—well, recognize him. You didn't have to look at his number and reach for your program to know that it was Bobby Layne. He had a face for you to look at. Then he had those thin little shoulder pads, not much more than a piece of cardboard they were, and he didn't bother about any of the other pads, so that when he was out there he looked like a person from this world. Next to him, everybody else looked like a bunch of space cadets.

Jim Owens, who played end on the 1946 Oklahoma team, made the following comments on Layne:

And then there was Bobby's confidence. He was the best leader there ever was with 2 minutes to go. That's when you've got to cut the mustard. When that was the situation, Layne could move the ball with a team of Pee Wee Leaguers. When we were preparing against him, we used to say that Bobby never really lost a game. We said that time just ran out on him a few times. That's not a bad guy to have around running the show for you.

As an All-America back, Bobby Layne was an institution who ranked next to Sam Houston in Texas. Even the cowboys came down off their horses long enough to follow his career. One of them said:

Mr. Bobby? Why, he's the biggest, baddest thing there is in Austin. When he dies, they should stuff him and set him up out on the main highway, just outside of town, with a sign hanging on him. People would come for miles around to look. Some sharp boy could make a heck of a lot of dough running a concession like that. 'Course I'll tell you something else, which is that Bobby Layne ain't never going to die off. He's one tough sumbitch.

The Longhorns came up to the Oklahoma game hotter than a sheriff's pistol. In addition to beating Oklahoma A. & M., the defending Sugar Bowl champions, they had also throttled Missouri, 42–0, and Colorado, 76–0. They were ranked No. 1 in the polls, while the Sooners were No. 22.

Boasted one Texas writer:

If Oklahoma holds Texas to 35–0, it will be a moral victory. The Sooners haven't beaten the Longhorns since 1939. Overall, the series stands 27–11–2, Texas. Although Oklahoma hopes to have a good, sound team by November, it is still struggling with its new split-T offense and lacks the unity it hopes to develop. And yet Coach D. X. Bible isn't taking Oklahoma lightly. He knows that it stopped Army's great Glenn Davis and it held Texas A. & M. to six yards. Bible says it will be Texas' speed vs. Oklahoma's power.

Details of the contest were summed up in this account by sports editor Jere R. Hayes, of the *Dallas Daily Times Herald:*

Dana Bible's supposedly superhuman Steers from Texas U., who bowled over Missouri, Colorado and Oklahoma A. & M. by top-heavy scores in chalking up an amazing total of 172 points that sent them to the top of the nation's football polls, came near being stymied in their march toward the national championship Saturday afternoon in the huge Cotton Bowl by a hard-socking, speedy squad of Sooners from Oklahoma. It was only after one of the toughest battles in the 46-year-old rivalry that the Longhorns managed to squeeze through with a 20-to-13 victory over Jim Tatum's boys, a contest that left the record-breaking crowd of 50,000 fans quivering from excitement.

But for the uncanny accuracy of their two passing stars, Bobby Layne and Frank Guess, the sturdy Steers would likely have bowed in defeat, for the Oklahomans outplayed them on the ground and turned in one of the most sparkling defensive games ever witnessed at the bowl. But Texas' superiority in the air was clearcut. Layne and Guess whipped shots to Bechtol, Ellsworth, Schwartzkopf and Canady for long, timely gains, and kept the Steers out in front all the way. A total of 240 yards was gained in the air by Texas. That tells the story of the Longhorn victory.

On the ground, the Sooners were poison, and their powerful line fought the huge Texas line to a standstill. Layne, Ellsworth, Canady and Guess were able to gain only spasmodically on running plays, but in the main the Sooners were able to stop them. In direct contrast, the Steers could not check the vicious ground thrusts of Joe Golding, Darrell Royal and Dave Wallace, who piled up a total of 142 yards running.

It was simply a case of one great ball club beating another great team. For both teams were great.

Despite the loss, Oklahoma moved up to No. 13 in the national polls. Army regained No. 1 with a 20–13 victory over Michigan, while Texas dropped to No. 3, behind Notre Dame. The Sooners, now 1–2, were the only Big Six Conference team to rank in the top twenty. "Probably no team ever has enhanced its reputation by defeats as has Oklahoma," pointed out the Associated Press in New York. "The Sooners gained more prestige by losing to Army and Texas than it could have by rolling over a dozen minor foes."

Ever since the Big Six was launched in 1928, the league was regarded as something of a Big Three, with Oklahoma, Nebraska, and Missouri capturing every championship but two. Now the picture was brightening at Kan-

Kansas halfback Ray Evans was always a threat and a big reason the 1946 and 1947 Jayhawks shared the Big Six Conference championship with Oklahoma. Evans also made All-American as a basketball guard in 1942 at KU.

sas. After seven weeks, the Jayhawks, a genuine dark horse in preseason polls, suddenly found themselves in a dogfight with Oklahoma as the two teams prepared to square off at Lawrence. Until then, no one had paid much attention to Coach George Sauer's light but fiery team. Kansas had no horde of behemoths such as those who used to represent the crimson and blue; in fact, it had one of the lightest teams in major college football, a varsity that listed only two men over 190 pounds. Wrote one scout: "What the Jayhawks lack in beef they make up for in spunk, intelligence, alertness. Quite often an opponent beats itself with a poor play, then the Jays jump down their throats." To date, Kansas had "jumped down the throats" of Denver (21–13), Wichita (14–7), Iowa State (24–8), and Oklahoma State (14–13). They tied Texas Christian (0–0), and lost to Nebraska (14–16) and Tulsa (0–56). Meanwhile, following its first three games, Oklahoma rolled over Kansas State (28–7), Iowa State (63–0), and Texas Christian (14–12).

"To beat Kansas," Jim Tatum said, "you must stop Ray Evans, their All-America left halfback. He runs, he passes—he can beat you so many different ways." Tatum spent a week drilling his Sooners on how to stop Ray Evans.

Going into the game, Oklahoma was 2–0 in the conference, Kansas 1–1. Outweighed 20 pounds per man, the Jayhawks were 14-point underdogs.

Writing in the *Oklahoma City Times,* John Cronley told what happened:

LAWRENCE, KANSAS.—Carve out a prominent niche for Kansas, high among the nation's giant killers.

Coach George Sauer's lively little fellers galloped through the mud to gridiron glory in a driving downpour when the embattled Jayhawks scored on a field goal from the 31-yard line in the last 75 seconds to throw the Big Six championship into a turmoil by upsetting Oklahoma, 16–13.

The battle, which couldn't have been soggier if played on the inside of a rainbarrel, was drifting along toward a tie when Paul Turner, reserve end who hadn't seen an iota of service up to that point, trotted into the gooey proceedings, his uniform spotless and gleaming as he huddled with his mud-splattered teammates.

When the Jays lined up and Ray Evans dropped back to hold the ball for Turner, not even the most rabid rooter among the 15,000 dripping Kansas partisans would have given the substitute better than a 100–1 chance of goaling from the gumbo.

The ball was over near the east sidelines, at an extremely difficult angle, when Turner methodically measured off his distance. A cross wind was puffing out of the northeast. But from the second that Turner's toe met the ball there was not the slightest doubt that it was good. It would have been a magnificent kick even under perfect conditions.

As in last week's equally startling one-point defeat of the Oklahoma Aggies, Kansas was given two chances to score, on opponents' mistakes, and the Jays, propelled along by Oklahoma fumbles, made the very best of both opportunities to twice shove OU behind one-touchdown deficits. But for some remarkable hot-footing it over the sloppy turf by Joe Golding, the Sooners never would have had a chance and would have suffered a severe beating rather than the tough three-point margin.

Golding scored both touchdowns for the Sooners. His best of the day as he made a runaway of the individual scrimmage race with a total of 130 yards gained was a brilliant 65-yard end sweep that wangled a 6-6 tie, early in the second quarter.

Oklahoma played a strong game in the face of the wretched weather, beating KU in every department except passing. Looking all the world like men from Mars in their blackened uniforms, OU outdowned, outrushed, and outkicked the Jays, but by outfumbling (3 to 1) this Cinderella team, they helped dig their own graves.

Kansas did Missouri a big favor. The Oklahoma loss elevated the Tigers to undisputed possession of first place in the Big Six. Oklahoma, Kansas and Nebraska share a three-way tie for runnerup.

While Kansas was shutting out Kansas State, 34–0, the following Saturday, Oklahoma was playing Missouri at Norman. For Jim Tatum and Don Faurot, the game represented a reunion. During the war, Tatum had served as Faurot's line coach at Iowa Pre-Flight. There had since been some question over who taught whom the split T formation. Then Tatum cleared the air. "Our T is basically the same as Don's," Jim said before the Missouri game. "I learned it from him when I was his assistant. Until then I had no confidence whatever in the T. I was strictly a single wingback and unbalanced line man. My T formation came from Faurot, just as my single wingback came from Carl Snavely, upon whose coaching staff I served at North Carolina and Cornell."

Taking advantage of two fumbles, a blocked punt and a 75-yard pass interception, the swashbuckling Sooners bowled over Missouri 27–6, before 33,000 homecoming fans. The victory threw the Big Six race into a four-way tie. Oklahoma's savage line knocked the Tigers loose from the ball six times in the first half—and OU recovered four of the fumbles and turned them into touchdowns. Oklahoma finished out the game with third- and fourth-stringers.

The following Monday Hal Middlesworth wrote:

If you didn't recognize that Missouri team as a Don Faurot team you aren't the only one. The Tigers disappointed a lot of people who remembered Faurot's crack, crisp outfits of prewar days and who expected a reasonable facsimile of same against the Sooners. But it wasn't there. Practically none of the tricky stuff through the quick-opening middle. Few of the fancy wide-sweeping laterals that gave Oklahoma so much trouble in previous years. It's easy to see why—fairly or not—the students at Missouri began groaning after the Tigers' 0–17 defeat by Southern Methodist earlier. Missouri isn't Missouri this season. Jim Tatum offered an explanation. He says coaches returning from the service haven't yet had time to whip their teams into their previous styles of play. By next season, he says, it will be a different story.

Kansas and Oklahoma finished in a tie for the Big Six championship, with victories over Missouri (20–19) and Nebraska (27–6), respectively, with 4–1–0 conference records. The Jayhawks were 7–2–1 overall, 23 percentage points better than Oklahoma, but in OU's final regular game of the season it flattened Oklahoma A. & M., 73–12, earning the Sooners a bid to the Gator Bowl, whereas Kansas stayed home.

Oklahoma's opponent at Jacksonville, Florida, was North Carolina State (8–2), coached by Beattie Feathers, former Tennessee All-America back. This was OU's second appearance in a bowl game, having lost to Tennessee, 17–0, in the 1939 Orange Bowl.

The Gator Bowl went pretty much the way the odds makers felt it would go. Reported Oklahoma City sports editor John Cronley:

Oklahoma fully lived up to its formidable football reputation. It battered North Carolina State, 34–13, in the second annual Gator

All-America end Otto Schnellbacher, 6 feet 3 inches and 180 pounds, was Ray Evans's favorite target in 1946 and 1947. Kansas historians list Schnellbacher as one of the ten top linemen ever to play at Kansas.

Bowl before 17,000 holiday fans. A flashy offense, which centered around line-ripping Eddy Davis, who scored three of the Sooner touchdowns with short line smashes, exploded in its full fury in the second quarter and three lightning scores left the Wolfpack reeling and in a state of shock from which they never recovered. Jim Tatum's boys ran the full gamut of their fancy repertoire to pull away from the Southerners and leave them standing there, flatfooted.

The 1946 season finished on a note of speculation for the Sooners. In his column, "Once Over Lightly," Cronley asked:

Is Bud Wilkinson, one of the outstanding members of Jim Tatum's coaching crew, leaving Oklahoma for Drake? It is no secret they want him. He has all the qualifications to step into a head coaching job. The decision by Wilkinson will be governed by two factors: (1) Whether he wishes to step into a head man's job at once, even at a smaller school, or (2) whether he elects to await more seasoning, one or two more successful seasons, and then a shot at one of the country's topflight posts. The betting is that Wilkinson will stay at Oklahoma.

The drama was building.

Here's Bud Wilkinson
MEET THE NEW OU COACH

On January 20, 1947, thirty-two-year-old Bud Wilkinson began one of the most successful careers in football history as Oklahoma's head coach. He is seen here strolling across the university campus after signing his contract to succeed Jim Tatum.

The Name Is Bud Wilkinson

In early January 1947, rumors were rampant. Jim Tatum said he couldn't imagine how they got started. According to an Associated Press dispatch from New York, where Tatum was attending a national football coaches' convention, he was going to quit his job at Oklahoma to take a lucrative offer from the University of Maryland. Tatum's present contract called for $8,000 in 1946, $9,000 in 1947, and $10,000 the following year.

When AP's Hugh Fullerton, Jr., asked Tatum if there was any truth to the story, the Oklahoma coach insisted it wasn't so. "I'm going back to Norman and look for a house," he said.

Shortly afterward, Maryland's athletic director Gearey Eppley was asked the same question. After a lengthy explanation as to Maryland's problems and various possible solutions to them, Eppley confessed, "I'm going to talk to Tatum."

That must have been some talk.

On January 18, the *Daily Oklahoman* broke the following story:

TATUM RESIGNS AT OU to TAKE MARYLAND OFFER

Jim Tatum, who brought Oklahoma a winning football team and a bowl game victory in his first year as head coach, has resigned to accept an offer from the University of Maryland and the Sooner post will be offered to Charles "Bud" Wilkinson, his first assistant.

Tatum's resignation, it was learned, was accepted Friday by the university's board of regents, although no official announcement was made. At the same time Wilkinson was tendered the job and he is expected to accept.

It was reported that Tatum will receive $12,000 a year for a five-year agreement to be head football coach and athletic director at Maryland. He was hired at Norman on a three-year contract totaling $27,000 but the board of regents last week offered him an increase which was reported to bring his salary to $12,000 a year for the remainder of his contract.

As Tatum's first assistant, Wilkinson's salary has been $6,800 a year.

Wilkinson said he planned few changes. "We will use the same style of offense we used last season," he said. "Of course, I will be adding some variations I've picked up from the other years I've coached."

Wilkinson's assistant coaches included Bill Jennings, Dutch Fehring, Gomer Jones, and Walter Hargesheimer. The latter resigned as head football and basketball coach at Massachusetts State to join Wilkinson, and Jones, who had been head line coach at Nebraska, became the first Husker ever to join the Sooners. Fair enough—in 1936, Oklahoma had lost Biff Jones, its coach and athletic director, to Nebraska shortly after he resigned at Norman to attend staff school at Fort Leavenworth.

What sort of coach was Bud Wilkinson? Jim Owens, his pass-catching All-America end, tells us:

Bud was a man who knew what his job was, knew how to do it surpassingly well, and went about it quietly. He was no shouter, no bully, but you knew where you stood with him. He was honest, he was fair. He said he expected more from us than football. As members of the

/ 77

team, he said he expected us to be well-groomed, well-dressed, well-spoken, well-thought-of in the community. Above all, he said, he expected us to work as diligently at our studies as at football. The reasoning for this was simple. He said it was important that the rest of the student body identify with young men who behaved like gentlemen off the field, who had some sartorial style. He said the fans needed to be reassured that the football team had class.

An honor student himself, Bud made us hit the books, he really did. He stressed it a lot. He made the other coaches aware of it, too. We even had study sessions. If some of the guys got in trouble academically, the other fellows would help tutor them. Bud felt very strongly about our classroom work, and was able to convince us how important our schoolwork was. Of course, you can't sell everybody, and we had a few fellows who didn't come up to standards, or didn't care that much about their futures, other than just the football part of it. But the majority of us did; having been in the war, we were primarily back in college for one reason: a degree. A lot of the fellows, older now, were already married with children, and they had responsibilities to think about. So Bud didn't have to do a lot of convincing.

Bud's credo was excellence. To be excellent was to be well-prepared, well-organized. He placed a great deal of emphasis on staff organization, on having our practices well-planned. He was able to get across to all the players what our approach to the game was going to be; I don't mean the game coming up, I mean the whole approach to football, offensively and defensively. He was very articulate. He told us why we were using the split T, its objectives, and how it best suited our particular talents. He was a master at being able to make himself understood by everybody.

This was a problem, I think, for some coaches after World War II. But Bud was able to have enough discipline to earn the players' respect. We had a lot of guys who'd been through hell, and after several years of bloody combat they weren't a bit interested in listening to anyone giving them a whole lot of discipline. Bud was intelligent enough to realize this. As a hangar deck first lieutenant on the aircraft carrier Enterprise, he'd been through it himself, at Iwo Jima, Tokyo, Kyushu, and Okinawa. I think Bud was as intelligent a man as there was in coaching—and more intelligent than most—and he exuded the same enthusiasm and drive he'd had as a top player at Minnesota—and it rubbed off on all of us.

Usually low-key, Bud could get emotional occasionally during a game. And then he'd get really excited. One story he tells about Darrell Royal is about the time Darrell was moved from right halfback to quarterback on our 1948 team. Darrell was having trouble adjusting to the split T. Bud worked with him and worked with him. "Dammit," Bud told him, "what you must do is key on the outside defensive lineman. Watch him. If he commits himself to you, pitch out; if he plays for the pitch out, cut inside." Darrell was just having a terrible time learning that. And then, all of a sudden, it clicked. He started doing everything perfectly. One day, after two years, Darrell walks up to Bud and says, "Gee, Coach, I've learned what to do." And Bud said, "Good, I've only been telling you for nearly three years how to do it."

The key to our success was preparation. Bud always had us well-prepared. We worked very hard. Bud wasn't a rough, tough, gruff, coarse-talking prototype like Lombardi, but he worked us hard. He demanded plenty from us. We won a lot of our games on conditioning and mental attitude. Without those, you don't win the tight games. We had grit, and Bud *could get it out of us. He had us mentally tough. He drove us hard, himself even harder. "Gentlemen," he'd tell us, "it's fun to be a winner." We'd hold team meetings on Sunday and review Saturday's game film, and discuss our game plan for the next game. Monday's, we'd loosen up, wear only sweats or shorts. But those who saw very little action on Saturday, Monday was their hardest day. That was when the younger players had a chance to get in a full afternoon's work, while the regulars relaxed. The tempo stepped up on Tuesday, rose to a peak on Wednesday, and then tapered off again. Thursday, we'd work on special plays, polish the kicking game, and maybe even a few bursts of sharp hitting, just enough to hone our edge. Fridays were reserved for travel, if we were playing out of town, or, if the game was at home, the workout was light and short. That was a typical Wilkinson week.*

You hear a lot about the Oklahoma–Texas rivalry. It had a special meaning to us. We wanted to beat Texas something fierce. They were right up there with Nebraska and Missouri on our hate list. We always played the Longhorns in Dallas, a neutral site. While Texas and Oklahoma have been playing since 1900, and while the game has been a special attraction of the State Fair of Texas since 1915, it is only since the end of World War II that the rivalry has become intense. Take the 1947 game, which Texas won behind Bobby Layne, 34–14. It was raw, it was rugged. It featured some of the most aggressive hitting in football—both on and off the field. A near riot broke out. A referee's decision caused thousands of booze bottles to be hurled down onto the playing field [and the state fair has sold beer and soft drinks in paper cups ever since]. One minute all was under control and the next more than 50,000 maniacs, pretty evenly divided between Oklahomans and Texans, were standing and screeching. This was fairly

amazing, for most of the crowd was awfully hung over from Friday night when they just turned downtown Dallas into World War II, a No Man's Land.

A freakish situation just prior to halftime —when Texas ran a play and scored after the clock had run out—so aroused our side that Bud Wilkinson and his assistants charged across the field to protest to the officials. That started it. The game was halted to clear the field of bottles and cushions which were chucked from the fans. At the end of the game, with hundreds of angry people milling around the field and fist fights breaking out all over the place, here came a police car at top speed to escort the officials from midfield. The cops literally fought their way out of the stadium.

Well, that just about ended the Texas–Oklahoma series. The Oklahoma alumni wanted the series culminated—period. No ifs, ands, or buts about it. The trouble was, we were subject to a $5,000 forfeit fee if we failed to show up in Dallas in 1948. The Dallas sportswriters had a lot of fun with that one. "Go on and stay home," they shouted at us in print. "We'd be better off without you, anyway." Fortunately, school officials worked out their differences and the series went on unbroken. But Oklahoma–Texas has always been that kind of game, where, as Darrell Royal once said, you have to screw your navel to the ground. You have to scratch, bite, and spit at the other guy all day long or he'd have your head. Playing the Longhorns in Dallas was our idea of the lions versus the Christians. It has always been one of the maddest spectacles of sport. Always a sellout, the Cotton Bowl is crammed with the throatiest, most enthusiastic partisans in football, evenly divided between Texans and Oklahomans. Regardless of the team records, the excitement is there each year; the game matches state *against state, school against school, fraternity against fraternity, tradition against tradition.*

The Texas game was very important, very prestigious to us. Texas, the state, is so much bigger than Oklahoma. They have so many more athletes to draw from. They overwhelm you. But we fought 'em. In my four years at Norman, we beat 'em twice, lost twice. They won the first two, but we got even in 1948 and 1949, both by scores of 20–14. Until then, it was mostly Texas. We got damn sick of "Texas Fight," their fight song, and "Hook 'em Horns," which they were always jeering at us.

Darrell Royal? We were teammates, of course. He could play any position. Wilkinson played him at halfback and quarterback. He could run, pass, punt, catch passes, play defense.

He never forgot the first time he visited Norman. He was still just a kid and he saw those big red helmets with the white "O" on 'em, and those big shoulder pads, and he knew it was going to be Oklahoma for him. "Why," he said, "I knew I couldn't go anywhere else." He went back to Hollis, his home town, and got his radio and put it out there on the porch on Saturdays so he could listen to the Oklahoma games and make believe like he had on one of those red helmets as he ran around dodging trees and stiff-arming rose bushes.

Looking back, you just knew that Darrell was something special. I mean, he had that look of a leader. He was competent, intelligent, combative. The quarterback was the key to our T system, and Darrell made it go. It didn't take a genius to see that he was destined to be a great coach.

As a team, we were very close. We had pride, unity. It began with our very first game, I think. That was the 1946 Army game. We traveled back to West Point unheralded, just a bunch of country boys back from the war.

Army hadn't lost in twenty games, and they were calling Blanchard and Davis the Touchdown Twins. The bettors didn't give us much of a chance, four- and five-touchdown underdogs; maybe they knew something we didn't. We had been together for only three weeks. But we had determination. We weren't about to roll over and play dead—not in front of President Truman, not in front of all those generals, not in front of the New York press. Suddenly there we were, knocking heads with all those wartime All-Americans, guys we'd been reading about during World War II. We fought 'em right to the eyeballs; we even led for a time, we played magnificently. We almost beat 'em, too, which would have been the upset of the decade. I think that's when our team started to jell. I think if you had to put your finger on it, that's when Oklahoma's dominance of college football really began.

While the 1947 Sooners played under the rules of two-platoon football, Bud Wilkinson and his coaching staff favored the concept of having a first unit and a second unit for both offense and defense. Jim Owens said:

We played both ways. You blocked as well as tackled. Bud substituted by units. Usually, midway through the first quarter, the second team came in to relieve the starters. I'm old-fashioned. I think football players should be taught to play both ways. At Oklahoma, by keeping our troops fresh, we were able to keep the ball longer and thus wear down the defense. We often had the ball 45 minutes out of the 60 minutes. That's a big advantage; a ball-control offense is hard to beat. Fortunately, we had the personnel to make it work.

The experts picked Oklahoma and Kansas as cofavorites in the Big Six in 1947. Floyd Olds, the resident genius, said no. "Skip that

After World War II, newspaper headlines on the sports pages were dominated by Oklahoma football. The Bud Wilkinson era was a fact.

SOONERS SWING FROM HEELS, FLATTEN MIZZOU, 41-7, BEFORE RECORD THRONG

SOONERS *Smash* CORNHUSKERS, 27-6

OU Clinches Tie For Big Six Title

Husking Bee-utiful—Aggies Revived

SOONERS SMASH NEBRASKA, 41-14

Huskers Gain Only 22 Yards Rushing

By JOHN CRONLEY
(Oklahoma City Times Sports Editor)

NORMAN, Nov. 13—After watching Nebraska boom into an early 7-0 lead here Saturday afternoon the Sooners stirred up another strong dose of their Missouri medicine, whipping across three scores in 4½ minutes of the second quarter as the Cornhuskers were cleanly shucked, 41-14.

Although it was another lightning attack which flattened the Huskers for their worst defeat in the 29-year history of this series, Oklahoma was far off form at the outset but it shaped up nicely after doing about everything wrong in the opening quarter.

The 28,000 onlookers suffered through unofficial "Flagday" here at Owen field as ragged play on the part of both teams found the officials doing yeoman work with their mournful whistles and monotonous red handkerchiefs.

The articlers peeled off a total of 228 yards while the rivals were being punished with 29 penalties. Many others were declined as OU was stuck 17 times, for 153 yards.

So versatile was the Sooner offense that six different men contributed

Sooners Are Second on National Ballot

Irish Are Far Ahead; Cadets Drop 2 Rungs

Sooners Remain Third

Broncos Next For Oklahoma

Army, Still Second on List, Will Close Out Season Against Navy; OU Has 2 More Games

Roundy Says He'll Take Royal For All-America Quarterback

SOONERS RIP LSU, 35-0; RECORDS FALL

85,000 See Heath In 86-Yard Sprint

Sugar Bowl Play-By-Play

JAYHAWKS STUMP SOONERS, 16 TO 13

Reserve End Boots Field Goal In Fading Seconds for Kansas

WILKINSON NAMED COACH OF YEAR

Young Sooner Is Nominated By Colleagues

44.7 Average Gives Furman

On the Level

TEXAS CRUSHES SOONERS. 34-14

47,000 See Near Riot as Fumbles, Penalties Sink OU

Texas Typhoon

Jack Mitchell Is Player of the Year; Five Sooners on All-Oklahoma Team

Tulsa Places Three Men, Aggies Two, Chiefs One on 1947 State Selection

By HAL MIDDLESWORTH

JACK MITCHELL, the University of Oklahoma's crazy-legged runner who is probably the first man in T formation history to make a major offense out of a quarterback sneak, Monday was named The Daily Oklahoman's "Player of the Year" as the fifth annual all-Oklahoma football team was selected.

Oklahoma's co-champions of the Big Six conference, dominated the all-star eleven for the second straight year with five men on the squad. Tulsa's Golden Hurricane landed three spots, the Oklahoma Aggies two and Oklahoma City University one.

Here are the players, picked upon their season-long performances:

ENDS—Bobby Goad, Oklahoma, and Russell Frizzell, Tulsa. TACKLES—Wade Walker, Oklahoma, and Nelson Greene, Tulsa. GUARDS—Darrell Meierenheimer, Oklahoma A&M, and Buddy Burris, Oklahoma.

CENTER—John Rapacz, Oklahoma.

BACKS—Jack Mitchell, Oklahoma; Hardy Brown, Tulsa; Jim Spavital, Oklahoma A&M, and Carl Allen, Oklahoma City University.

Mitchell, a 22-year-old junior who stands 6 feet and weighs 180 pounds, is one of the most unusual backs in football. Not particularly fast and an average passer, he nevertheless piled up nearly 600 yards by rushing this season—a figure probably never approached by a T-formation quarterback.

HIS success lay in his ability to smell out a hole in the Sooners' quick-opening T, then whirl around the blockers into the open.

He turned out to be a good pass catcher, snaring one -ong one for a touchdown against Kansas, and an excellent punt returner. Leader of the nation in that department last season, he lugged a punt back 89 yards to pace against Detroit in the Oklahoma '47 opener and was favored by many kickers all season.

His signal calling has been far above average and one of his most valuable assets has been his teammates' confidence in his ability to send them on the right assignments.

After the Sooners' 26-14 victory over Texas A&M in September, when Mitchell scored two touchdowns and passed to two others, Homer Norton, the

On the Level

Called "The Ghost" by teammates, Allen played a season at Ouachita college, Arkadelphia, Ark., before entering the airforce. A pilot with 31 months of service, he played two years on AAF teams before enrolling at OCU.

Frizzell and Goad personal decided contrasts as the all-Oklahoma ends. Frizzell, 240-pound Tulsa sophomore, was moved to end from tackle at mid-season and immediately gave the Hurricane the lift it needed to win some vital games. Goad, on the other hand, weighs only 168 pounds and appears too frail to hold his own in the rough going. He is, however, one of the most vicious blockers in the Big Six.

Walker Is Captain

Walker has been co-captain of the Sooners since a mid-season election by the squad and is one of the greatest blocking tackles of Oklahoma history. Weighing 210, he has been an all-Big Six choice two straight years. Greene, the 235-pound giant who is the all-Oklahoma team's other tackle, winds up his career at Tulsa this year with a series of outstanding performances. His home is in Shawnee and he is a former marine.

Burris, 213-pound smashing Sooner guard from Muskogee, does his job well offensively and defensively and closed his amazing Sooner career with a sensational performance against the Oklahoma Aggies. The nation's scouts picked him for their "all-American" team last year and he is every bit as good this season.

Meierenheimer, the young Aggie who gets the other guard assignment, was one of the season's surprises. He is a 180-pound freshman from Attica, Kan., who didn't figure prominently in Cowboy plans when the season started. But he showed so much speed and blocking ability that he won himself a starting spot after three games and was the talk of the stands when the season ended. He's

cochamp bunk," he said. "It's Oklahoma all the way. From tackle to tackle, they boast one of the most devastating lines in college football. In any event, this is the last dance for the Big Six." (In 1948, the conference was expanding to seven teams. Colorado would join the league in round-robin play.)

Bud Wilkinson was asked if he agreed with the experts' assessment of the 1947 race. "No. Kansas is the team to beat. Didn't they beat us last year? And doesn't George Sauer have every man jack of his starting lineup back?"

One of those veterans was Ray Evans, a Hall of Fame candidate. He had the credentials: he had a strong arm, ran the ball from scrimmage, returned punts, punted, and played defense. He was what Jim Owens called a 60-minute player. Grantland Rice, the Associated Press, and the *New York Sun* labeled the Kansas halfback as a can't-miss All-American. In 1942, before he went into the service, Evans led the nation in passing (over 1,100 yards) and became the second player in history to complete more than 100 passes in a season. He also placed fifth in total offense among the country's ball carriers. In 1946 he led the Jays in passing, rushing, scoring, and total offense, earning All–Big Six and All-America honors. Off the field, he was senior-class president and scholastic honor man.

For once, the experts could take a bow. The conference championship did come down to the Oklahoma–Kansas game. After four weeks, the league standings fleshed out like this:

	All Games			League Games		
	W	L	T	W	L	T
Kansas	3	0	1	1	0	0
Oklahoma	2	1	0	0	0	0
Missouri	2	2	0	0	0	0
Nebraska	1	2	0	1	0	0
Iowa State	1	3	0	0	2	0
Kansas State	0	4	0	0	0	0

Kansas opened the season against Texas Christian with a scoreless tie, then blitzed Denver, 9–0; Iowa State, 27–7; and South Dakota State, 86–6. Oklahoma was coming off a 34–14 loss to Texas after beating Detroit, 24–20, and Texas A. & M., 26–14. Losing to the Longhorns was a humiliation the Sooners would have to live with for 364 days. Bud Wilkinson knew his team would have to play lights-out football if they hoped to stay in the race to be champion of the Big Six, where victories, no less titles, tended to be hard-scrabble.

History was on the side of Kansas coach George Sauer. As a player and coach, he had never lost a game to Oklahoma. Sauer was a fullback at Nebraska during the Dana X. Bible reign. In 1931 the Sooners had traveled to Lincoln and for three quarters held the Huskers scoreless. Then, in the last period, Sauer began flexing his muscles. Breaking off tackle, he slid around a linebacker and rushed 47 yards for the first touchdown of the game. A moment later he intercepted an Oklahoma pass and returned it 70 yards for a score. That was Nebraska's margin, 13–0. The next year, at Norman, Sauer stuffed OU like a sausage. He kept the Sooners back on their heels with his booming punts, he linebacked savagely, and he riddled the defense constantly with his headlong plunges. Final score: Nebraska 5, Oklahoma 0. As a senior, in 1933, Sauer played his way into the National Football Hall of Fame. He was methodically devastating. In a 16–7 victory over Oklahoma at Lincoln, he led the Huskers on a 72-yard touchdown drive, kicked a field goal, and was all over the field making tackles. Oklahoma heaved a sigh of relief when Sauer graduated and fervently hoped they had seen the last of him. They hadn't. In 1946 he replaced Henry Shenk as head football coach at Kansas.

No one had to remind Sauer and Wilkinson

The 1947 Kansas Jayhawks, starring the All-Americans Ray Evans, Otto Schnellbacher, and Don Fambrough, shared the Big Six title with Oklahoma, earning an invitation to the Orange Bowl, where they lost to Georgia Tech, 20–14. The Jays lost their chance to win the game in the final minute by fumbling the ball on the 2-foot line.

that the winner of their game would be in a good position for all the Big Six marbles. This was stressed in their pregame pep talks. Wilkinson told his players:

I don't have to tell you about the importance of this game. You know as well as I do that Kansas is tough, and that no one can beat 'em but you. For you to do it, though, is going to require a top team effort. You know the attitude with which they are coming in here. You know they beat you last year, and you know they think they can do it again today. That's why I know it's going to take your best effort.

The professional gamblers had made Oklahoma a 13-point favorite. George Sauer told his players: "The experts think Oklahoma has played a tougher schedule. They're saying the Sooners will walk all over you. Well, I think you can win. But to do it you're going to have to run harder and tackle harder and block harder. It's going to take a great effort, so let's have it. Let's go!"

"Let's go!" shouted the Jayhawks, and they brought their hands together in unison. "Let's go! Go!"

There was the roar of 34,700 throats (a new attendance record at Norman) as the starting teams took their positions out on the field. The public-address announcer ran down the starting rosters:

Kansas	Position	Oklahoma
Small	LE	Tyree
Ettinger	LT	Paine
Fambrough	LG	Burris
D. Monroe	C	Rapacz
Tomlinson	RG	Andros
Johnson	RT	Walker
Schnellbacher	RE	Goad
McNutt	QB	Mitchell
Evans	LH	Jones
Bertuzzi	RH	Thomas
Pattee	FB	Davis

Details of the contest were given banner-line treatment in the Sunday editions. Hal Middlesworth of the *Daily Oklahoman* likened it to a prizefight:

Oklahoma and Kansas threw knockout punches at each other all afternoon in a brilliant display of football offense and wound up with both of them on the gridiron "canvas" in a 13–13 double kayo. The large crowd saw the two highly-geared running teams trade it out toe-to-toe in a match which Kansas deadlocked late in the third quarter.

The Jayhawks, who knocked the Sooners into a Big Six title tie last season with a last-minute field goal for a 16–13 victory, kept UO in check by stopping cold Jack Mitchell, Oklahoma's crazy-legged quarterback. Mitchell, who had been second among the country's running backs with a pregame average of 115 yards, was choked off to a net of 24 yards as Kansas ends charged in to chop him down at the line of scrimmage. The Sooners, on the other hand, wrecked Kansas' outstanding defensive record as they continued to roll along the ground with a total of 227 yards. Until Saturday, Kansas had given up only 54 yards a game on rushing.

Out-downed, out-rushed and out-passed, the Jayhawkers achieved what amounted to an upset by taking advantage of their chances while the Sooner line leaked at inopportune times. It was touch-and-go all the way, with Kansas first taking the lead, then the Sooners jumping ahead with two touchdowns and appearing heading for a rout in the second half, then the Jayhawkers finally tying it up just before the end of the third quarter. At that, the Sooners might have worked in one more touchdown except for the fact that the clock ran out on them as they reached the Kansas 16-yard line.

Mostly it was bone-crushing ground action which produced the touchdowns, with Frank Pattee going over from the 3-yard line and

Forrest Griffith from the 4 for Kansas. For the Sooners, Darrell Royal scored one TD from a yard out but the other touchdown was a real thriller, with Mitchell catching a long pass from Charley Sarratt for a 49-yard payoff gain.

Ray Evans, the Jays' All-American halfback, fired up an 80-yard drive to help put Kansas on the scoreboard first. Twice he fell back as if to pass, then suddenly burst for good gains. Then he passed to Otto Schnellbacher to the Oklahoma 18, where he and Bud French moved it down to the 3-yard line just as the first quarter ended. A penalty pushed Kansas back but Evans regained the lost yardage and then Pattee skidded through untouched for the first TD of the day. Don Fambrough's kick was wide.

In the last quarter, an 11-yard punt by Darrell Royal and fumbles by George Thomas and Charley Sarratt stalled the Sooners twice in the final period as both teams remained bogged down in midfield, but Royal finally lofted a punt 65 yards to shove Kansas back to the 26 and give Oklahoma its last chance. There was 1:45 minutes left to play when the Sooners finally got the ball. They made the most of their time with a passing flurry which might have counted had it started earlier. They rolled down to the Kansas 16 before they were twice penalized for delaying the game and Royal's last-second desperation pass was intercepted by Evans on the goal line as the game ended.

After that, the league schedule seemed to favor Kansas. "Oklahoma must play tough Missouri at Columbia and Nebraska at Lincoln," speculated Skipper Patrick of the Associated Press. "The Jays, on the other hand, travel to Nebraska, but get Missouri at Lawrence in the season finale."

For the rest of the regular season, Kansas did not lose again:

55	Kansas State	0
13	Nebraska	7
13	Oklahoma State	7
20	Missouri	14
54	Arizona	28

Following their tie with Kansas, the Sooners lost to Texas Christian, 20–7, the very next week, then won the rest of their league games: Iowa State, 27–9; Kansas State, 27–13; Missouri, 21–12; Nebraska, 14–13; and Oklahoma Aggies, 21–13. The final standings left Kansas and Oklahoma tied at 4–0–1 for the championship, but the Orange Bowl selection committee chose the Jays to play Georgia Tech in Miami because their overall 8–0–2 record surpassed Oklahoma's 7–2–1.

On New Year's Day, Kansas was on the slippery end of what has been called "the most famous fumble in Orange Bowl history." Whatever its evaluation, the muffed ball cost UK a bowl game. Facing second and goal at the Georgia Tech 1-yard line with less than 2 minutes to play, Lynn McNutt, the Kansas signal caller, attempted a quarterback sneak. But he dropped the ball on the snap from center, it rolled loose, and Rollo Phillips, an alert Tech guard, fell on it. The Jays never got another chance, as the Engineers ran out the clock.

At that, Kansas had fought back gamely in the last quarter. Red Hogan had hit Ray Evans with a 12-yard pass to bring the score up to 13–20. Don Fambrough kicked the extra point. Soon after, center Dick Monroe recovered a Tech fumble on the latter's 42. Two successful passes, Hogan to Otto Schnellbacher, carried the ball to the 10. Then Evans put his head down and rammed the ball to the 1, where the lights went out for Kansas on the next play.

There's a postscript to the 1947 season. It involved Doak Walker, perhaps the greatest all-around football player ever. For three years—1947, 1948, 1949—he did everything at Southern Methodist. If you wanted a 70-yard quick kick, Doak kicked it. If you wanted a 30-yard field goal, he kicked that, too. He would rise up and complete a pass on one play, then leap up and catch one from somebody else. He ran, he passed, he caught passes, he blocked, he kicked field goals and extra points, he punted. He also played defense. Throughout most of his career, in the era of one-platoon football, he was a 60-minute man. He was a safety and he made tackles all over the field. He intercepted passes and he was a one-man demolition derby in the SMU secondary.

As a sophomore, in 1947, Walker guided the Mustangs to a Southwest Conference championship, then to a 13–13 tie with Penn State in the Cotton Bowl. He scored one touchdown on a run and threw a 53-yard pass for the other. He won the Maxwell Trophy that year as college football's greatest player and was third in the Heisman balloting, which he won the following season.

Among the Mustangs' victims in 1947 was Missouri, 35–19. Don Faurot said he would never forget Walker. "He was a remarkable athlete. He stood 5 feet 11 inches and weighed about 170, but he was built like a rock and he would not be beaten. That was the best of it—his competitiveness, his terrific desire to win. He was always demonstrating that overwhelming quality."

His best college game ever probably came in 1947 against traditional rival Texas Christian University, which had beaten Oklahoma, 20–7. During the game, Doak had broken loose for runs of 80, 61, and 56 yards. He had completed ten of fourteen passes for 136 yards. He had returned three kickoffs for 163 yards, and three punts for 53. He had scored two touchdowns and kicked one extra point. All in all, he had gained 471 yards that afternoon. The Mustangs led, 13–12, with 90 seconds to play, but TCU then blitzed 80 yards on three plays to take what appeared to be an insurmountable lead. Following the touchdown, a TCU lineman taunted Walker, "Well, Doak, what are you going to do now?"

Walker said, "We're going to score again."

The kickoff came to Doak on the 3-yard line. He started toward the right sidelines, faked a reverse, kept the ball and accelerated. He was stopped, finally, on the TCU 35-yard line. Two plays later the SMU passer, Gil Johnson, lofted a pass to Walker, and Doak made an impossible catch on the TCU 10-yard line. On the next play, with time running out, three defenders surrounded Walker, and Johnson found another receiver all alone on the goal line. So SMU pulled out a tie.

"Doak always seemed to be capable of the impossible," Don Faurot said. "In a pinch, he was always ready."

Missouri scheduled the Mustangs three times during the Walker years. After losing in 1947, the Tigers bounced back to snuff out SMU the next year, 20–14, but fell again in 1949 as one-man-gang Walker's gluttony went uncurbed, 28–27.

So great was Doak Walker's reputation that one young man, Ron Meyer, now the SMU football coach, named his dog after the Mustang star.

Boomer Sooners

Bud Wilkinson's picture came out at you from the magazines in the late 1940s and you didn't have to know very much about him to tell that he was something special. He was boyishly handsome, he was articulate yet appealingly modest, and his deeds matched his appearance. And he came to flower when the nation was still full of idealism. We had just won a great war, we still respected the old-fashioned virtues, and we danced to the lyrics of "Isn't It Romantic?" and believed that life *was* romantic. In those years, college football fed our romantic notions. College football had vitality. The joy was in the stadium and we could all smell the chrysanthemums. Bud Wilkinson was the right man in the right place at the right time.

In his early years at Norman, Wilkinson was the incarnation of everything that was good about football. He packed tremendous influence. He would visit high schools and tell boys that they should eat green vegetables, drink milk, and get at least 8 hours of sleep a night, if they expected to grow up to play football at Oklahoma. The thing was, Bud Wilkinson believed what he was selling. He believed in the Sooners and he believed in himself. Dr. George Cross, president of OU, was also a believer. Dr. Cross, who had once played guard at South Dakota State, had never lost his enthusiasm for football. In 1949 he was widely quoted in newspapers from coast to coast for telling a frosh assembly at the University of Oklahoma, "We want a freshman class here that our football team can be proud of."

By 1963, when Wilkinson walked away from the head coaching job at Oklahoma, his collegiate coaching record of 145–29–4 included 3 national championships and 47 consecutive victories, which remains the longest winning streak in college football history. He had truly become a legendary figure. His place in history was secure.

During the winter of 1947–1948 a half-dozen major universities tried to wean Wilkinson away from Oklahoma. The headlines on the sports pages of the day told the story. The *Daily Oklahoman* ran the following:

WILKINSON CALLED TO NAVY JOB TALK
Sooner Coach Leaves Today For Annapolis Conference; Yale Overtures Also Bared

---

Bud Wilkinson, the University of Oklahoma's 32-year-old football coach, will leave Monday for Annapolis to confer with United States Naval Academy officials about Navy's head coaching job, *The Daily Oklahoman* learned Sunday.

It also was learned that Yale University, which recently lost Howie Odell to the University of Washington, also has made overtures to Wilkinson.

The Navy job has been open since January 12 when Capt. Tom Hamilton resigned as football coach to accept appointment as athletic director. At that time it was announced the Navy would break with tradition and hire a civilian coach for the first time in history. Army started a similar practice in 1941. Jim Tatum and Don Faurot have also been mentioned for the Navy job. All three men served in Hamilton's physical fitness Navy program during the war.

Dr. George L. Cross, president of UO, said he will "do everything possible to keep Wilkinson because I am convinced that he is among the few really outstanding young coaches in America today."

Two days later, the *Daily Oklahoman* reported:

WILKINSON IS SILENT AFTER THREE-HOUR PARLEY WITH NAVY

ANNAPOLIS.—Charles Bud Wilkinson got acquainted Tuesday with the Navy football scene, which might be his own stamping ground in a month or so.

Wilkinson huddled with the Naval Academy's athletic executive committee for nearly three hours, then looked over the big "yard" at Annapolis with an eye particularly on the football plant.

The Oklahoma coach remarked only that he had had "an interesting talk" Tuesday morning. Otherwise there was no suggestion as to how much ground had been covered.

George Sauer, who guided his Kansas eleven into the Orange Bowl last season, was due Wednesday for a similar meeting with the Navy braid.

It took Wilkinson only three days to make a decision after the job was offered to him. This from the *Daily Oklahoman:*

WILKINSON CHOOSES SOONERS OVER NAVY

Bud Wilkinson will remain as the University of Oklahoma's football coach. Dr. George L. Cross confirmed at Norman today that Wilkinson had withdrawn his name at Annapolis and would continue at UO on the terms of his present contract. He still has three years left of a contract calling for $10,000 annually. In addition to continuing as head football coach, he will remain in the position of "acting athletic director."

Dr. Cross said Wilkinson has not asked for any concessions to stay at Norman. "He decided he just wanted to stay here," Dr. Cross said.

Oklahoma's gain was Kansas's loss. That is, once Wilkinson took himself out of the picture at Annapolis, George Sauer was hired to coach the midshipmen. The Jayhawks then replaced Sauer with J. V. Sikes.

The game of musical chairs was not over. Next, Yale University approached Wilkinson. The *Daily Oklahoman* again:

WILKINSON TO DECIDE TODAY ON LUCRATIVE OFFER BY YALE

Yale University will offer a five-year contract to Bud Wilkinson if he wants the job at the eastern school, it was learned Wednesday.

Yale has followed Harvard and Navy in requesting the young Oklahoma coach to go east for a "talk." He was approached Wednesday by an official of the Yale alumni board, who told him: "If you want the job, it's yours. We will recommend you to the school and the recommendation will be accepted."

Once more, Dr. George L. Cross, UO president, said he hoped Wilkinson will decide to remain at Oklahoma. "Bud has an unusual combination of talent in that he wins football games, builds character and makes many friends. I know he could have gone to Harvard or Navy if he wished. I don't blame the other schools for wanting him, but I do wish they wouldn't pick on us just now."

Twenty-four hours later, Wilkinson officially rejected the Yale offer. "I am very happy at Oklahoma and do not intend to break my contract here," he told a news conference. President Cross added:

Bud has been very decent about this. At a time when it is fashionable for coaches all over the country to walk out on their contracts, Bud made his decision to stay without requesting any financial change, or any change, in the conditions of his present contract. His contract remains unchanged. At no time has he tried to use any prospect of a better financial offer as a lever to better his salary situation at the University of Oklahoma. He made his decision to stay with us on the premise that he had a contract at Oklahoma, and didn't wish to break it. In view of recent precedent everywhere else, I think this makes his action an exemplary one, as well as unique.

That did not end the bidding for Wilkinson's services, however. Syracuse, where he was an assistant coach before the war, wanted him, and so did the Wisconsin Badgers, who made a serious offer.

The old conference was growing. With Colorado coming in, the Big Six was now the Big Seven. On the coaching front, the emphasis was on youth. Don Faurot was the only coach in the league with more than a year's experience—and only he, Wilkinson, and Iowa State's Abe Stuber were holdovers. The new head coaches included Potsy Clark at Nebraska, Ralph Graham at Kansas State, J. V. Sikes at Kansas, and Dallas Ward at Colorado.

An unofficial poll of the coaches picked Missouri to win the 1948 league championship. In a nutshell, they lined up the teams this way:

MISSOURI: The Tigers lost fewer key men than any other contender; were greatly im-

proved at end; had the backs to make Faurot's baffling mixture of passes, laterals, and end sweeps work.

OKLAHOMA: Graduated a full team of starters and near-starters; line not quite up to 1947; but backfield as strong if Jack Mitchell and Darrell Royal came through; Missouri game could decide title.

NEBRASKA: The league's dark horse; Potsy Clark teams known for developing tremendous momentum late in season, which was when the Huskers played both Oklahoma and Missouri.

KANSAS: Crippled too badly by graduation and eligibility ruling to figure prominently.

IOWA STATE: Smartly coached by Abe Stuber in 1947, Cyclones had one of the fanciest offenses in league; figured to give several teams trouble.

KANSAS STATE: New coach Ralph Graham faced man-killing challenge of rebuilding.

COLORADO: Dallas Ward, in his first year as coach, said he would be trying to convince someone the Buffs wouldn't finish last; scheduled to play all league teams except Oklahoma.

Bud Wilkinson said that, yes, the Sooners were going to have a "pretty good football team, but so is everyone else." Frankly, he said, he didn't think his 1947 edition was as good as most people thought it was:

We were behind at one time or another in eight of the ten games we played. Sure, we won seven of them, but we never were able to control the game. We had too many games like 24–20 over Detroit. When you win a game by one point or one touchdown that's not enough. You're not being very impressive then.

In 1948 at Norman, Nebraska drew first blood against Oklahoma. On third down, Husker fullback Frank Callopy rifled a 37-yard pass to end Howard Fletcher on the Sooner 10. OU's Pete Tillman and Ed Lisak went up for the ball with Fletcher, who tipped it away from the defenders and took it on the run, scooting past Darrell Royal to score. Oklahoma struck back to win, however, 41–14.

This year? We've lost a lot of good men. If we expect to win anything this year, we must have some passing. We have good receivers in Jim Owens, Bobby Goad, and Reece McGee. It's up to us to find a passer—not a thrower. The difference comes when you're under fire. You're an open target when you stretch out your arm and a couple of big linemen bang through and smack you. If you can take that and get the ball away, well, then you're a passer. We've moved Darrell Royal to quarterback full-time and Jack Mitchell over to halfback. Jack's a fine running back, but he has an old shoulder injury that keeps him from passing for distance. He's all right on short passes but he just can't get the ball down the field. If Royal comes through, then we'll be okay. If he doesn't—then we'll have to start all over.

As the Sooners prepared to open the season against Santa Clara at San Francisco, Wilkinson was discouraged. He did not like the way his team was shaping up. He was visibly disturbed.

As the Sooners wound up preseason practice, he said:

I just don't know what we do have. They've looked all right in scrimmage but I don't know how they will react under game conditions. I'll be glad when this one is over. Win, lose, or draw, at least we'll know where we stand, what we've got to work with this season, and what holes to plug. There are no particular spots I'm worrying about. We have good overall balance. If we don't come up to par, it won't be just one position, it will be the entire squad.

The game marked the second time Oklahoma had played Santa Clara on the West Coast. In 1940, UO ran up a 13–0 lead, then went cold and finally lost, 33–13. History was about to repeat itself. Dick Friendlich, covering the game for the *San Francisco Chronicle*, wrote:

Both All-America quarterback Jack Mitchell and his wife, Jeanne, majored in psychology at the University of Oklahoma. During the 1948 season, Mrs. Mitchell helped sharpen her husband for games by rehearsing him on all his plays against the various Big Seven defenses.

SANTA CLARA SLIPS PAST OKLAHOMA, 20–17
Bronc Passes Erase Sooners' Early Margin

KEZAR STADIUM.—Sept. 25—Oklahoma was sooner, but Santa Clara was later here today as the Broncos, paced by volatile little Billy Sheridan, wiped out a 17–7 halftime deficit to defeat their favored foes from the Big Seven Conference, 20–17.

A small gathering of 7,000 saw Sheridan, 155-pound quarterback from San Francisco's Lowell High, race 15 yards around left end on a perfectly-executed bootleg play in the third quarter, then hurl a touchdown pass to Hall Haynes, 56 yards in all, for the winning points in the fourth period. It was also Sheridan who passed to Monty Osborn for a TD from 18 yards out in the second quarter after the dangerous Sooners had jumped into a 10–0 lead in the first 18 minutes.

It was a smashing comeback for Len Casanova's Broncos from their 41–19 mauling at the hands of California last week. It was not, however, distinguished by smooth, well-knit play, but rather by the individual brilliance of Sheridan, plus an aroused spirit which shattered Oklahoma's offense in the second half. There was no resemblance between the Sooner attack in the first half, which pierced the Bronco defense early and often, and the attack in the second half, which couldn't cross midfield against Santa Clara's savage mass tackling.

Oklahoma showed a quartet of very good backs, indeed, in George Thomas, Jack Mitchell, Darrell Royal and George Brewer, but in

A backfield star in high school, Oklahoma's All-America end Jim Owens, 6 feet 3 inches and 200 pounds, ran like a halfback once he got the ball. This photo shows Kansas State fullback Howard Kelly nailing Owens after a 7-yard gain as the Sooners devastated the Wildcats, 42–0, early in the 1948 season.

the clutch they had no defense for Sheridan's lightning strikes. Three times little Billy was inserted into the game to call the play and three times the very next went for a touchdown.

At no time, however, did Santa Clara put together anything resembling a sustained attack and only once, early in the second half, did the Broncos put two first downs together. The tackling, particularly in the first half, was sloppy and the blocking on the Bronco wide sweeps was simply atrocious. Still they got that big victory under their belts the hard way against a team that will make nothing but trouble for future opponents.

After losing to Santa Clara, the Sooners got their act together. They smashed on to win the Big Seven championship impressively—41–7 over Missouri, 41–14 over Nebraska, 60–7 over Kansas, for example—and then took North Carolina apart in the Sugar Bowl, 14–6, before a record crowd of 85,000 in New Orleans. The Tar Heels went into the game ranked No. 3 in the polls; Oklahoma was No. 5.

Meanwhile, Missouri was losing to Clemson, 24–23, in the Gator Bowl.

In the Oklahoma locker room, Wilkinson climbed to a bench, smiled broadly at his players, and told them after the game: "It was a fine win, but only the first of many more. We're going to get better."

How true. From 1949 until midseason of 1959, when they lost to Nebraska, 25–21, the Sooners would win sixty-one straight conference games. Oklahoma won so often that by 1960, when Oklahoma State joined the conference to make it the Big Eight, wags had started calling it "Oklahoma and the Seven Dwarfs."

The Sooners put their big UO brand on just about everybody. During the years 1948 through 1960, their league record was 75–1–1, and 125–11–2 overall. For Missouri, Nebraska, and the others, it was a humiliation hard to live with. What did it all mean? There was a growing notion that Oklahoma had a whammy over the universe.

By now, Bud Wilkinson, thirty-three, had become a fact of life. On June 1, 1949, the Associated Press reported from Chicago that he had been named to succeed Notre Dame's Frank Leahy as head coach of the College All-Stars against the Philadelphia Eagles, National Football League champions. That made Wilkinson the youngest man ever to coach the All-Stars. The AP stated:

Wilkinson, whose two-year record at Oklahoma is 17–3–1, will be the first former All-Star player to return to the big show in the role of top man. He quarterbacked the collegians in 1937 when they defeated the Green Bay Packers, 6–0. It was the All-Stars' first victory over the pros. His appointment was announced by Arch Ward, sports editor of *The Chicago Tribune,* sponsor of the game. Wilkinson is one of the few coaches in the country who combines the best features of the single wingback and T-formation to a highly successful degree. His offense is built around the quarterback who must also be a running back, unlike most T-formation generals. The quarterback handles the handoffs along the line of scrimmage, sweeps the ends, does cutbacks, spinners and half spinners. Guards pull out to run interference. All is accomplished without benefit of a shift which most coaches employ when they spice the two formations.

Briefly, the 1949 All-Stars did not live up to their build-up. Before a crowd of 93,780 at Chicago's Soldier Field, they fell flat on their faces, 38–0. It was the biggest margin of victory by the pros in the sixteen years the game had been played.

"Now Wilkinson knows how Jim Bowie must have felt at the Alamo," cracked one of

On New Year's Day, 1949, Oklahoma defeated North Carolina in the Sugar Bowl, 14–6, at New Orleans, then gave their No. 1 booster, university president Dr. George L. Cross, a victory ride to the locker room.

In the old days, only a few thousand fans attended football games at Owen Field in Norman. By 1949, Oklahoma football had grown so big it was necessary to expand the stadium to 40,000 seats. Here Dr. George L. Cross, University of Oklahoma president, shows the expansion to quarterback Darrell Royal. The stadium was later expanded to a capacity of more than 71,000.

The celebrated 1949 Oklahoma line: Bobby Goad, Wade Walker, Stan West, Charley Dowell, Dee Andros, Leon Manley, and Jim Owens.

the Eagles. All was not lost, however. Former Sooners Jack Mitchell, Buddy Burris, and Myrle Greathouse were singled out for their hustle.

For Wilkinson, better things were to come. In fact, Grantland Rice and *Look* Magazine tagged Oklahoma as the No. 1 college team in the nation as the major powers got ready to open the season in September. Rice wrote:

I hate to stick my neck out by saying any team is better than the rest this early. But if I were surrounded by king cobras and forced to make a selection, I would nominate Bud Wilkinson's big, fast, deep, aggressive Oklahoma squad. For one thing, it has Darrell Royal to replace Jack Mitchell at quarter. It also has such stars as Lindell Pearson and George Thomas, backs; Jim Owens, end; Wade Walker, tackle, and Norman McNabb and Stan West, guards. The Sooners are almost as good as the Broadway musical.

Behind Oklahoma, Granny Rice rated the rest of his Top Ten in this order:

Michigan
Vanderbilt
Cornell
Southern Methodist
Notre Dame
Army
Minnesota
Michigan State
Tulane

Just about everybody in the Midlands, from Big Seven coaches to sportswriters, agreed that Oklahoma was going to win the 1949 conference championship without working up a sweat. Missouri was picked a distant second.

Not wanting to make liars out of the ex-

Wade Walker, 6 feet and 203 pounds, was a first-team Associated Press All-America tackle on the undefeated (11–0–0) Oklahoma Sooners team in 1949. Teammate Darrell Royal observed: "Wade's the best tackle in the country and certainly the smartest. He gets the maximum benefit out of the splits on our offense. He keeps the right side of the line straight."

On New Year's Day, 1950, Coach Bud Wilkinson depended heavily on quarterback Darrell Royal to run the show on the field and to protect Oklahoma's victory string. The Sooners ripped apart Louisiana State, 35–0, in the Sugar Bowl for their twenty-first win in a row.

Though he was caught relaxing here, there was nothing lazy about 1949 All-America guard Stan West. Six feet 2 inches and 236 pounds, the Oklahoma lineman was durable enough to stand out on one of the nation's most rugged teams. He had another virtue—consistency—which included no bad games.

The 1949 Oklahoma Sooners—Big Six and Sugar Bowl Champions. FRONT ROW: Brewer, Dowell, McGugan, Andros, Moore, Bodenhamer, Anderson, Gray, West, Thomas, Bradley, Lockett, Carnahan, Smith, Murphy, Ricks. MIDDLE ROW: Heape, Owens, McNabb, Goad, Trips, Silva, Hoofnagle, Arnold,

The 1949 Texas–Oklahoma game set a new attendance record at Dallas's enlarged Cotton Bowl (80,000) as the Sooners won, 20–14, to extend their string of victories to thirteen in a row.

Cole, Manley, Weatherall, Clark, Heatly, Carney, Royal, Jones.   BACK ROW:
Ewbank, Seibert, Kidd, Cunningham, Price, Needs, Jones, Lambeth, Marcum,
Horkey, Mays, Clark, Beckman, Covin, Greenburg, Leguenec, Pearson, Lisak,
French, Mayes, Lang, Heath, Davis, Rowland, Pace, Walker, Cotton, Hoopes,
Parker.

The 1949 Gator Bowl–bound Missouri Tigers represented the first Missouri
football team to travel by airplane. Maryland brought the players back down to
earth again, 20–7.

perts, Oklahoma went around demolishing everybody, Saturday after Saturday, and in its own way looked absolutely unbeatable. It was a team with five All-Americans, a team that broke or tied thirty-three school records. Oklahoma was the complete team, coupling a balanced attack of passing and rushing with an iron defense. By the time it came to the end of the regular season, its record was incredibly imposing. It had pushed aside ten straight opponents, enough to frighten the Russians:

46	Boston College	0
33	Texas Aggies	13
20	Texas	14
48	Kansas	26
48	Nebraska	0
34	Iowa State	7
39	Kansas State	0
27	Missouri	7
28	Santa Clara	21
41	Oklahoma Aggies	0

Oklahoma thought of itself as a team without stars, but stars had emerged. At the close of the regular season, five Sooners snagged places on eleven All-America selections. Wade Walker, senior tackle, led the parade with four selections (AP, Football Writers Association for *Look* Magazine, *Collier's,* and NEA Service). Guard Stan West was on three teams, halfback George Thomas on two, and Jim Owens and quarterback Darrell Royal were on one each.

The 1949 Sooners went out in a blaze of glory. Ranked No. 2 in the national polls, behind Notre Dame, they accepted another invitation to the Sugar Bowl, where they made a joke out of Louisiana State, 35–0. Bill Keefe of the *New Orleans Times-Picayune* said it all:

Sparked and steered by slight, but rugged, Darrell Royal and showing brilliant precision and superb coaching, the big but fast Sooners ripped LSU defenses to shreds, stopped everything the Tigers threw in desperation against them and convinced every last fan among the 83,500 that the "Cinderella" team of Louisiana State had lost its silver slipper, and that the Bayou Bengal had taken in too much territory in going too far out of his domain to try to conquer all Dixie. Excepting in punting, the Tigers were outclassed in every department of football—even in spirit. Oklahoma bewildered them with tricky reverses, laterals and forwards thrown from laterals and so completely outplayed LSU in the line that Sooner after Sooner literally walked through wide avenues right through the Tigers. On the other hand, the Oklahoma defensive wall so outplayed the LSU offense that most of the Bengal ball carriers would, at times, find themselves piling into a mass of four or five Red and White uniforms with nary a Purple and Gold suit around.

The victory over LSU extended the Oklahoma winning streak to twenty-one. As a reward for his team's 11–0–0 record in 1949, Bud Wilkinson was voted Coach of the Year by America's college football coaches. Lynn "Pappy" Waldorf of unbeaten California and Frank "The Master" Leahy, with thirty-eight victories in a row at Notre Dame, were second and third, respectively. The Scripps-Howard newspapers, in conjunction with the American Football Coaches Association, sponsored the nationwide poll. Wrote Joe Williams, famous Scripps-Howard sports editor:

Does the coach make the team or vice versa? Bud Wilkinson, 34, personable, agile of mind and forceful of character, scored another touchdown for the younger school of coaching in the 15th annual coach-of-the-year derby. A head coach for only three years, all at Oklahoma, he goes along with the modern concept of the game which accents speed and deception, platoons on the field and endless hours of clinical work off the field. "The first thing I discovered about coaching," he said, "was that you need more than a couple of funny stories." Col. Earl "Red" Blaik of Army says the same thing in a different way: "There are fewer characters and more teachers in the profession today."

Here at Scripps-Howard, we feel the coach-of-the-year award is something extra special in the category of sports acclaim. First, who is better equipped to evaluate the performance of a coach than a fellow who is in the coaching business himself? Second, the fact that the vote is secret invites a frank, forthright, unrestricted appraisal, and therefore a completely honest one. Thus, when 102 of the top college coaches from coast to coast sit down and write the chairman of the Scripps-Howard board that Wilkinson did the best coaching job of the year and proceed to state their reasons for so believing, with the explicit understanding their choice and comments are not to be disclosed, the result takes on a significance and a substance that are not always associated with this sort of thing.

In spite of his youth and limited service, Wilkinson is not exactly an overnight development. A year ago he hulked sufficiently large to tie for seventh with Bob Higgins of Penn State and Leahy in the voting. And this year, with a perfect season, no losses, no ties in 11 starts, a defeatless string that extended to 21, he became a commanding figure in football. How could he miss? It is a pleasure to join the coaches of America in their salute to young Bud Wilkinson.

Another standard by which the success of the Wilkinson program could be judged was the number of his players who became coaches at major universities. From the 1949

All–Big Seven guard and cocaptain of the Kansas Jayhawks, Dick Tomlinson played four seasons of varsity football and in 1949 had everything going for him—speed, agility, endurance, team spirit, and a killer instinct.

Sooners, alone, came these: Jim Owens, who brought respectability to West Coast football, when he coached the Washington Huskies to back-to-back Rose Bowl triumphs over the Big Ten in 1960–1961; Dee Andros, Oregon State; Bert Clark, Washington State; Wade Walker, Mississippi State; and Darrell Royal, Washington and Texas, where he was Coach of the Year in 1963.

Royal

Owens

Walker

Andros

Five lettermen from the 1949 Oklahoma champions went on to become head coaches at major universities: Darrell Royal, Washington and Texas; Jim Owens, Washington; Wade Walker, Mississippi State; Dee Andros, Oregon State; and Bert Clark, Washington State.

Clark

Dynasty, Sooner Style

By now, on the early edge of the 1950s, the T formation craze had caught on across the country, and virtually every single-wing coach had switched to it. Princeton's Charley Caldwell had experimented with it, too, but when the chips were down he decided that the single wing was what he was most comfortable with and was the most reliable. Based on sheer power, with two-on-one blocking in the line to force short but sure gains, Caldwell's single wing was set up like a massed infantry attack. "Let the others stampede to the T," he said. "They're giving me an advantage. They will spend so much time learning how to defense against the different forms of the T, that they'll lack the *feel* when it comes time to tackling our single wing."

I once asked Caldwell for his opinion of all those second-guessers who contended that single-wing football was a thing of the past when pitted alongside the versatile modern T. He told me:

It depends upon whose single wing or T it is. My version of the single wing is a complex and elaborate system involving power, deception, perfect timing, and multiple threats from different sides. It is still geared to the power block, but the whole attack is more like an armored spearhead, which concentrates its full weight for short spurts but always threatens to go the whole distance to the goal line.

With twenty-four intricate offensive formations and thirty-six defensive spreads and shifts, Caldwell felt that agility was more important than size. During his unbeaten seasons of 1950 and 1951 his biggest regular lineman on defense weighed no more than 198 pounds. Caldwell said a slow reactor couldn't play for him. What he looked for in a player was speed first and intelligence second. Dumb football players sat on the bench.

In the single wing, it was all specialists. A coach had to have a center who could snap the ball unerringly while upside down. He needed a quarterback who was a vicious blocker, yet fast enough to stay ahead of his backs. He needed a fullback who could spin and pivot like a ballet dancer but had power enough to rip a line to shreds. The tailback, of course, was the core of the team. He had to run, pass, kick, and even block, and he had to be durable enough to stand up under game-to-game pounding. But the hardest man to find was probably the wingback. He needed the speed of a fifty-yard-dash man, the deftness of a broken-field runner, and the tenacity and strength to block an end or halfback who tipped the scales between 200 and 220 pounds.

Caldwell had a theory of why modern coaches had abandoned the single wing. He listed alumni displeasure and the reaction of the players, believing mistakenly that the single wing was old-fashioned. At schools where capacity audiences were financially necessary, coaches were loath to institute any system that might lessen attendance because of the lack of fan-pleasing, wide-open football. Caldwell said at the time:

A coach attributing his use of one system or the other to his material is utter nonsense. If you have the material for the T, you have the material for the single wing. Passing strategy also demonstrates the difference between the two systems, and here I must give the single wing another plus. The T quarterback takes the ball from center, swings back faking a

Oklahoma's halfback Billy Vessels was the first Heisman Trophy winner from the Big Eight, in 1952. The Sooners were 8–1–1 that season, won the conference championship (5–0–1), and lost only to Notre Dame, 27–21.

pitchout, and runs back farther to pass. He gets little opportunity to spot anyone except the primary receiver. On the other hand, the single wing passer is always looking forward, watching developments, and spotting secondary receivers in case the primary one is covered. He doesn't commit himself to pass until the last second, and defending backs cannot give undivided attention to potential receivers until he does. Many times the play continues as a ground attack.

Listening to Charley Caldwell, who succeeded Bud Wilkinson as Coach of the Year in 1950 as Princeton won thirty of thirty-one games over several years, I wondered why so many coaches were switching to the modern T with man-in-motion. "They had modern football at its best all the time," Caldwell said. "All they had to do was embellish it, as I have."

Unquestionably, football was growing more scientific; just how scientific was revealed to me one Saturday when I put a stopwatch on the Oklahoma Sooners. I discovered that the ball was largely in play for only 12 minutes. The other 48 minutes were spent calling signals, talking things over in the huddle, and otherwise preparing to put the ball in play. Subsequently, each team was on the move only 6 minutes. Unbelievable? Not by the calculations of Pappy Waldorf, the former Kansas State mentor who by this time was head coach at the University of California. He said:

Most teams are in possession of the ball only thirteen times during an average game. Top-flight teams, of course, are able to hold the ball longer than 6 minutes of actual play, but the mediocre teams don't exceed that total. When I was coaching at Northwestern and we played Notre Dame in 1946, the Irish held on to the ball for 12½ minutes in the second quarter. During that spell, they ran off

twenty-three plays, drove down to our 1-yard line, and yet failed to score. That's what I call ball control.

Brigadier-General Robert Neyland was another clock watcher. He demanded precision and split-second timing. The Tennessee coach was known to order a certain play to be run in practice 500 times prior to using it in a game. Before the Volunteers played Alabama in 1952, Neyland detailed one of his assistants to sit in the stands and clock the 'Bama punter in practice. The idea was to record the time it took the kicker to get off his punts. After ten kicks, the assistant found that half of them were timed in 2.2 seconds, the other half in 2.3. Armed with this information, Neyland organized a punt-blocking formation that would send one of his linemen into the Alabama punter's path at precisely 2.3 seconds. "If he takes 2.3 seconds on any kick in the game, he's a dead duck," Neyland declared. Alabama's first kick was 2.3. Tennessee defenders blocked it, setting up a touchdown, and the Vols went on to win, 20–0.

After nearly a decade of two-platooning and super-specialization, the year 1953 saw a return to one-platoon football, although in a somewhat modified form, giving rise to a new group of conference champions across the country, before and after the change-over. Football fans seemed to enjoy watching the players prove they could block as well as tackle, or vice versa, and if there was any deterioration in the quality of play, it was not visible to the untutored eye. As a matter of fact, the season was notable for its number of close, exciting games, and there were a gratifying number of upsets. Over the full course of the season, however, the strong teams established their strengths and the weak fell by the wayside. Despite fears to the contrary, the rules change did not seriously upset the natural balance of power.

Out in the Midlands, Oklahoma had entered what historians now refer to as the "Golden Age of Sooner Football." Backpedaling, from 1948 to 1955 the Sooners scuttled around and through opponents with the greatest of ease, piling up a record that compared with the most awesome success cycles in history. After taking Santa Clara too lightly (and losing) in its 1948 opener, the Sooners got themselves untracked and didn't lose again until Kentucky surprised them, 13–7, in the 1951 Sugar Bowl. In between, Oklahoma won thirty-one games in a row. In 1952, after getting burned by Notre Dame, 27–21, they reeled off another thirty-two victories in thirty-four games through 1955. On New Year's Day in 1956 they made it thirty-three by giving Maryland its comeuppance, 20–6, in the Orange Bowl.

During this period, Oklahoma won the Big Seven championship consistently. In 1950 and 1955, it was ranked No. 1 in the national polls and was awarded the O'Donnell Trophy. Four times—1949, 1950, 1954, and 1955—it rolled up a perfect season. It lost only once in 1948, lost one and tied once in both 1952 and 1953, and lost twice in 1951. In bowl games, it branded North Carolina with a big OU in the 1949 Sugar Bowl, Louisiana State in the 1950 Sugar Bowl, and Maryland twice in the Orange Bowl, 1954 and 1956. In eight seasons the Sooners' won-lost-tied total was a magnificent 77–6–2. Accentuating the positive was Bud Wilkinson's Coach of the Year honor in 1949, and halfback Billy Vessels's Heisman Trophy as 1952's Player of the Year. Significantly, Billy was the first player from his conference to have his name emblazoned on the Heisman.

Billy Vessels scored a total of 35 touchdowns in his varsity career, despite the fact

In 1950, Nebraska halfback Bobby Reynolds made All-American as a sophomore and led the nation's scorers with 157 points. Here the flashy Husker backfield star galloped to his second touchdown against Oklahoma, but it wasn't enough. Oklahoma won, 49–35.

Modern football was growing rougher all the time. Here Drake's Johnny Bright (No. 43) catches a blow from Oklahoma A. & M.'s Wilbanks Smith during their 1951 game. Bright left the game with a broken jaw, but Drake took the Cowboys, 27–14.

All-America center Tom Catlin put some spring into the 1951 Oklahoma line, and the Sooners outscored their ten opponents, 321–97.

that injuries limited his action to only four games in 1951. Fifteen of those touchdowns were made as a sophomore, and 18 more the year he won the Heisman, 1952, when he also rushed for 1,072 yards and passed for 209 more. Vessels was a snaky, slashing-type runner. His balance and acceleration were excellent and he broke a lot of tackles. He just threw people off him. He had good speed. "You've barely got your block and Billy's already by," said All-America center and cocaptain Tom Catlin. The 1952 Sooners outscored ten opponents, 407–141, for an 8–1–1 record.

One of Bud Wilkinson's most scintillating coaching jobs was performed in 1950. Except for fullback Leon Heath, he lost his entire starting team, and lacking eighteen of his first twenty-five players of the previous varsity, he nevertheless developed a squad that was ranked first in the country. Texas, which was defeated four times in 1949 by a total of only 10 points and which Wilkinson called "the best team we played in '49," once more slugged it out with the Sooners before yielding by a single point, 14–13.

The Sooners' thirty-one-game winning streak finally came to an end in the Sugar Bowl. Led by All-America quarterback Babe Parilli, Kentucky did what no other opponent of Oklahoma had been able to do since the first game of 1948. The Wildcats scored their first touchdown after tackle Walt Yowarsky recovered an Oklahoma fumble on the latter's 23-yard line in the opening quarter. On the very next play Parilli passed to Wilbur Jamerson to get on the scoreboard. Kentucky blasted for its second touchdown 25 minutes into the first half on a 51-yard pass from Parilli to Al Bruno to the Sooners' 1-foot line, where Jamerson bucked it across on the next play. That made the score 13–0, Kentucky.

In the third quarter, Oklahoma, battling for its life, drove 68 yards to the Wildcat 2, but couldn't punch the ball into the end zone. Later, Kentucky pushed to the Sooner 9-yard line after recovering an OU fumble at the 33. Tackle Bob Gain missed a field goal to stop the threat, and from there, Oklahoma launched its only touchdown drive of the game. Half-back Merrill Green scored on a 17-yard pass from Billy Vessels. Jim Weatherall's conversion was good and the Sooners were back in the fight with 7 minutes to go. But Jack Lockett fumbled Dom Fucci's 51-yard punt, and Kentucky recovered at the Oklahoma 32, from where it moved the ball down to the 13 before giving it up to OU. The game ended as a desperation pass by Vessels was intercepted at midfield.

Sports editor Earl Ruby of the *Louisville Courier-Journal* called it Kentucky's "greatest football triumph since it took up football in 1881."

Jim Weatherall and Leon Heath both were All-America selections in 1950, and Wilkinson received the third-largest number of votes in the annual Coach of the Year poll.

Later, Wilkinson wrote of his 1950 team: "As National Champions, we had tremendous morale and as much heart as I have ever seen. We were behind going into the fourth quarter in three of the ten games and yet always managed to win."

The 1951 Sooners lost two games, to Texas A. & M. and Texas. Although tied by Colorado in the opening game and beaten by Notre Dame, the 1952 team was one of Wilkinson's best, even superior to the 1950 edition. "Bud's 1952 team was by far his slickest offensive aggregation," said Harold Keith, Oklahoma's director of sports publicity at the time. "It averaged 40.7 points per game to lead the nation in scoring. It scored a full touchdown per game higher than any other team."

Dick Cullum, of the *Minneapolis Morning Tribune,* added:

Jim Weatherall was an All-America tackle at Oklahoma in both 1950 and 1951.

Cocaptain Eddie Crowder, who went on to coach at Colorado for eleven seasons, quarterbacked the mighty Oklahoma offense (an average of 40 points per game) in 1952.

Beyond a doubt the 1952 Sooners had the best offensive platoon of the season and, so far as I know, the best ever. Yes, this is a ground-gaining machine probably unsurpassed in football history, and it was all brought up to the peak of excellence by the superb ball handling and quarterbacking of Eddie Crowder. When Buddy Leake, the right halfback, was healthy, the Oklahoma backfield of Crowder, Leake, Billy Vessels, and Buck McPhail was the best balanced and most versatile I have ever seen. Each of them was at the All-America level. So were offensive center Tom Catlin and offensive tackle Ed Rowland. As a matter of fact, Oklahoma has class in every position. Which brings us to the most interesting of Oklahoma's stars—slim, scholarly Eddie Crowder. This man must surely be the season's best quarterback. Most of the national experts picked Maryland's quarterback John Scarbath as their Back of the Year on a preseason guess. However, having seen both this fall, I have to cast a most emphatic vote for Crowder.

Dick Cullum's judgment was upheld when all four players—Vessels, Catlin, Crowder, and McPhail—were named on All-America teams and Vessels won the Heisman Trophy.

The 1953 Sooners for the second straight year finished with an 8–1–1 record and ranked No. 4 in the AP poll. They lost again to Notre Dame, by almost identically the same score, 28–21, and were tied by Pittsburgh, 7–7. These were the first two games of the season, after which OU rolled over everyone else on its schedule. Its greatest victory was in the Orange Bowl, when it proved to be No. 1 Maryland's undoing, 7–0.

After nearly a decade of two-platooning and specialization, the year 1953 saw the change in the substitution rule that eliminated the use of platoons. This did away with offensive and defensive teams. Consequently, Wilkinson made a couple of experiments in his lineup. Max Boydston was shifted from end to fullback and then went back to end. Defensive safety Larry Grigg was moved to right half, and Buddy Leake, a halfback for two seasons, spelled off Gene Calame at quarter. Cocaptain Roger Nelson underwent a bone-spur operation, but recovered in time to play at right tackle. J. D. Roberts anchored the line at right guard, and Merrill Green was another holdover in the backfield with Leake, Grigg, and Jack Ging. Wilkinson recalled recently:

At the start of the 1953 season we were a somewhat ordinary ball club. We had lost most of the "class" players from 1952, and we lacked the finesse and deception of the preceding bunch. Our opening game against Notre Dame was played on a day very favorable to our team. The temperature was about 105 degrees down on the playing surface, and the Irish were not able to generate enough energy because of the heat. Yet they controlled the game at all times. The following week we played Pitt and we were very fortunate to tie them, 7–7. Our entire season hinged on the Texas game at Dallas. Following the first two games we made switches in personnel which helped us a great deal. We improved steadily after these changes but we were not a well-balanced team. Neither the kicking nor the passing was more than ordinary, but the team had superb spirit and a terrific will to win. It had two lines of about equal ability, which kept a steady pressure on opponents, and this pressure was a vital factor in our victories. Our victory over Maryland in the Orange Bowl was our ninth in a row since

Bill Rowekamp, 6 feet 1 inch and 190 pounds, transferred from West Point, where he played end, to Missouri. He played fullback at Missouri in 1952 and came through with flying colors as the Tigers finished second in the Big Seven standings.

Pittsburgh tied us, and we would now go through the 1954 and 1955 seasons without a loss or a tie.

Returning from the 1953 squad as the backbone of the 1954 team were Kurt Burris, center and linebacker; Max Boydston and Carl Allison, crack pair of ends; guard Bo Bolinger; tackle Don Brown; Gene Calame and Buddy Harris at quarterback; Buddy Leake at left half; and Bob Burris and Wray Littlejohn at fullback. Others were halfbacks Bob Herndon and Pat O'Neal; center Gene Mears; and end Joe Mobra. Two promising prospects in the backfield were Tommy McDonald and Billy Pricer. Wilkinson commented:

The strength of our 1954 team differed considerably from that of former years. Until then we had relied mainly on a squad ability. Games were won on the basis of superior depth or slightly better than average personnel rather than the play of a few outstanding stars. The 1954 team lacked this squad depth of sound all-around football players. To offset this we were fortunate in having far more truly outstanding individuals than we had ever had on one team before. Kurt Burris at center, Boydston and Allison at end, Calame at quarterback, and Leake at halfback were truly outstanding college football players—as good as any men we have ever had at Oklahoma. The superior ability of these individuals carried a team which was somewhat lacking in overall depth. Defensively, we were sound. Our basic weakness was a lack of offensive explosiveness. In our entire ten-game schedule, we scored only two break-away touchdowns from offensive scrimmage. The rest of our 304 total points were the result of long, sustained drives. The basic asset of the team, as in former years, was excellent overall team spirit and morale.

All-America guard J. D. Roberts, 5 feet 10 inches and 230 pounds, played for Oklahoma's 1953 Big Seven and Orange Bowl championship team.

Oklahoma's slick quarterback Eddie Crowder (later head coach at Colorado, 1963–1973) slithered through the Kansas line in their 1953 contest for a Sooner victory, 45–0.

Oklahoma end Max Boydston models his 1953 All-America sweater.

Few experts expected much from Kansas State in 1953. After all, the Wildcats hadn't won a single conference game the year before. But with their best line in three years and with 185-pound halfback Veryl Switzer here, they tied Missouri for second place.

Another reason for Kansas State's surprising second-place finish in 1953 was cocaptain and halfback Corky Taylor, an All-Conference pick.

Oklahoma moved machinelike through its 1954 schedule. "The Sooners stride through the Big Seven like some colossus," commented Herman Hickman, the former Yale coach. They had won the conference championship with such monotonous regularity for seven years that people suspected the league should have been renamed the Big One. Big Seven rules that season did not allow Oklahoma to return to the Orange Bowl on New Year's Day. So runner-up Nebraska (4–2 in the league, 6–4 overall) got to go. The Huskers were matched against Duke. Both Nebraska and the Blue Devils used the split T. Both were primarily running teams. Duke had been unbeatable in the south, but Army and Navy took them in 1954, and they were tied by Purdue. Nebraska unexpectedly finished second in the Big Seven as Coach Biff Glassford hushed his critics. Spiritually, a lot of people liked the Cornhuskers—but, realistically, the smart money was on Duke.

All in all, the Orange Bowl saw a spirited game in which Duke was the superior team. The Blue Devils were bigger, faster, had a much better passing attack, and benefited from the intelligent quarterbacking of Captain Jerry Barger. Barger recognized the weak points of Nebraska's defense and kept steady pressure on those failings. Duke took advantage of them by using pitchouts to the halfbacks and the optional run or pass to receivers in the flat. With the threat of these wide plays always hanging over their heads, the Nebraska line was vulnerable for quick-opening plays.

An 18-yard pass to Sonny Sorrell, left end, and brilliant running by Bob Pascal, the left halfback, carried Duke to its first touchdown. Then, with only 35 seconds to go in the half and the ball on the Huskers' 2-yard line, Jerry Barger passed to end Jerry Kocourek, in the end zone, for Duke's second score. After that,

Duke hardly looked back. The final score was 34–7, Blue Devils.

In the final rankings, Oklahoma was No. 3, behind Ohio State and UCLA. End Max Boydston and center Kurt Burris were consensus All-Americans. There was quite a human-interest story behind Burris. Runner-up to Wisconsin's Alan Ameche for the Heisman Trophy, he was one of six football-minded brothers from Muskogee, Oklahoma. His brother Paul ("Buddy") Burris was All-America guard in 1948 at Norman. After Kurt graduated in June 1955, brother Bob Burris would still be on hand to play halfback the next fall. Meanwhile, seventeen-year-old twins Lynn and Lyle Burris were seniors on the Muskogee High School football team and talking about playing for Wilkinson. Lynn was a guard, Lyle a pile-driving fullback. Another Burris, Don, also starred for Muskogee, but a broken arm restricted his college contribution at Oklahoma to a year of jayvee football.

In addition to the six brothers, there were also five sisters in the family, all ardent Sooner boosters. And lest Coach Wilkinson have any worries about a scarcity of Burrises, there were five grandsons already eyeing football careers at the University of Oklahoma.

That winter, verbiage spewed forth nonstop against several aspects of the game. Biggie Munn, the athletic director and former head coach of Michigan State, was outraged over the one-platoon rule. He claimed the edict was chasing the "good little man" out of college football. That was the only conclusion possible, he said, after watching college games in 1954:

One-platoon rules have forced a return to the big man, the 220-pound behemoths who can withstand the pounding of two-way football. The average guard or tackle just can't

Oklahoma ranked No. 3 in the 1954 national polls, thanks to the All-America play of center-linebacker Kurt Burris.

absorb the punishment of both offensive and defensive play and retain the quickness which earned him a place in the two-platoon game. Size is the first consideration. We're headed back to a college game reserved for only a comparative few big men of exceptional physical qualities. The finest days of my coaching life came here at Michigan State when we developed the platoon system to a degree that allowed the use of small linemen. It was a pleasure to watch 175-pound guards and tackles play big-college football by using speed, quickness and desire to overcome the natural advantages of the 220-pound opponent. By using these small guards and tackles —in effect we were playing four guards—we were able to develop our version of multiple offense, a system of attack that stressed deception and maneuverability. We played the "big game" on offense, the all-out game that presented exciting football to the fans. We were able to use the little man on defense, too—the 175-pounders who loved combat and fought like tigers against bigger opponents. In some games we were able to play as many as sixty boys. This year, 1954, against Notre Dame, we used only twenty-five and Notre Dame played only nineteen. We were able to award forty-nine letters in 1952. That number will be cut in half in another year or so. I'm afraid we are headed back to slow-motion football. More than ever the school with the big horses will dominate. In contrast, two-platoon football was an intriguing game of new ideas and developments. It was a game of imagination. But now—fans are going to be forced to watch pro football for new ideas, for action, for the "big game."

Football equipment was also subjected to criticism. Researchers, armed with facts, described the typical helmet of 1954 as "too hard, made of ironlike plastic, and fails to protect the wearer's own head." They labeled the face guard as "legalized murder, capable of breaking an opponent's nose and jaw." Detractors pointed to the thousands of knee injuries yearly as proof that knee pads were poorly designed. "They're built to protect the *other guy,* but our studies show that a half-inch pad is not thick enough to keep the bony joint from being used as a weapon," said one expert. Shoe cleats bore the brunt of the criticism. It was found that they were a major cause of injury. Besides gouging an opponent, they locked a player's foot to the ground, and when he tried to pivot or was forcibly hit, the torque wrenched or tore the ankle and the knee joints.

In 1954, shortly before he died, I asked the legendary Pudge Heffelfinger what he thought of the modern uniforms. Pudge bridged the gap. He was All-American on Yale's Walter Camp teams of 1889, 1890, and 1891. He was still playing football fifty years later. Think of it, fifty years! So when I asked him about modern football armor, he grunted, "You wouldn't get me to wear it. Why, it causes more damage than it prevents." Well, what, for example, did the old-timers wear for headgear in his day? "We didn't wear helmets," Pudge said. "We just let our hair grow long and pulled it through a turtleneck sweater."

Dr. Lewis W. Jones, the president of Rutgers, stirred up a hornets' nest in 1954 when he suggested that football coaches sit in the stands during games and leave the strategy to the players.

"Excellent," agreed New York District Attorney Frank Hogan, past president of the Columbia Alumni Association, after watching Coach Lou Little's Lions lose Saturday after Saturday. "I don't think Lou should even sit in the stands. He should take the day off."

The chief characteristic of Oklahoma's national champions of 1955, who defeated all ten opponents and then repeated their Orange Bowl victory of two years before over Maryland for their thirtieth successive triumph, was their speed. This was not quite so rugged a team as the 1949 champions, nor did it have the depth of that team. The 1955 Sooners also did not have the slick dexterity and the wildly exciting finesse in ball handling that the 1952 backfield boasted. But the 1955 champions were practically in a class unto themselves when it came to speed. As a matter of fact, those close to the team were unanimous in the opinion that this was Wilkinson's fastest team of all.

In early November, matchmakers attempted to make a lot of the Oklahoma–Missouri game before the kickoff, but Herman Hickman, writing in *Sports Illustrated,* was having none of it: "The same old story. Missouri will fight hard but the Sooners will make it 26 wins in a row." Oklahoma won, 20–0, making Hickman look like a genuine expert. By now, guard Bo Bolinger was gaining national attention. Gomer Jones, a great center himself in his playing days at Ohio State, was Wilkinson's line coach now and he told a New York reporter:

Bo is very quick and tough. He's never been hurt. He's tireless, agile, reacts well, and is an excellent blocker. Bo gets down under punts expertly, plays very well against traps, is a good pursuer, a sure tackler, and a real leader.

Late in the season, all that stood between Oklahoma and another Big Seven championship was Nebraska. The Huskers were the "comeback" team of the Midlands. After losing all their nonconference games—to Hawaii, Ohio State, Texas A. & M., and Pittsburgh—they then dished out some ferocious licks of their own, taking it out on league competition. They defeated Kansas State, 16–0; Missouri, 18–12; Kansas, 19–14; Iowa State, 10–7; and Colorado, 37–20. That tied them with Oklahoma for the conference lead, going into the last Saturday of league play.

"On paper this sounds like a natural, but the Sooners write another language," wrote Herman Hickman. Again, he was right. Oklahoma was the winner in a breeze, 41–0.

The Sooners were not finished. They still had to play nonconference Oklahoma A. & M., winner of only two of nine games. The Cowboys would just as soon forget the game totals. Oklahoma, playing under wraps but flashing usual power to protect its No. 1 ranking (10–0–0), crushed A. & M., 53–0, at Norman for its twenty-ninth victory in a row, then sat back to await an Orange Bowl date with unbeaten Maryland.

In mid-December, the Sooners were voted the nation's No. 1 college team with 3,581 points in the final AP poll. They easily outdistanced runner-up Michigan State (8–1–0). Maryland, ranked No. 3, had a won-lost-tied record of 10–0–0, until Oklahoma stuck a pin in its bubble, 20–6, in the Orange Bowl.

The victory over the Terrapins was especially satisfying, because Maryland had what many regarded as the most powerful defense against rushing in the country, led by mighty Bob Pellegrini, center and linebacker and Lineman of the Year.

When it came time to hand out All-America awards, Tommy McDonald made the first-team backfield, with TCU's Jim Swink, Michigan State's Earl Morrall, and Ohio State's Howard ("Hopalong") Cassady, winner of the Heisman and Maxwell trophies.

In a little-noticed demonstration of what Bud Wilkinson had coming along for the future, the 1955 Oklahoma frosh ran over the Air Force Academy, 48–12.

The eyes of Texas were upon Oklahoma's All-America halfback Tommy McDonald in 1955 as he exploded for a touchdown before 76,000 fans in a 20–0 victory over the Longhorns.

In 1955, on a team hit hard by graduation, Rex Fisher shifted from halfback to quarterback as Nebraska bounced back to finish runner-up to Oklahoma in the conference race. The Sooners (11–0–0) were the national champions.

In the Colorado–Nebraska contest of 1955, Colorado fullback John Bayuk gained 55 yards on this end sweep, but Nebraska still won the game, 37–20.

In its first 1956 outing, Oklahoma stopped North Carolina, 36–0, for its thirty-first straight win since 1953. The following week, the Sooners used five full teams and several sixth-team players while setting a new modern college victory string of thirty-two with a lopsided win over Kansas State, 66–0. Then came Texas, in what was always the most frenetic football weekend in the Southwest. The Oklahoma–Texas game lured some 50,000 out-of-towners to Dallas by air, rail, and highway. In the face of this human tidal wave Dallas surrendered. Hotels and plane hangars were jammed. Cab drivers worked hectic double shifts. Special "Longhorn" and "Sooner" menus—with their jacked-up prices—appeared beside the napkins at the city's less scrupulous restaurants. Merchants moistened their thumbs, for some $2 million was spent on clothes, souvenirs, nightclubbing, food, and drink. As for game tickets, they were next to impossible to come by: the Cotton Bowl was sold out months in advance.

The overpowering charge of the big red-shirted Oklahoma line ahead of adroit quarterback Jimmy Harris was just one of the reasons why the 1956 Sooners were provoking so much purple prose. Typical newspaper coverage sounded like it was coming out of a Hollywood press agent's typewriter: "Oklahoma may be the greatest college football team of all time." Coach Wilkinson's skillful veterans had still to lose a game in their entire college careers. Playing against what was in the beginning an adequate, reasonably capable Texas football team, they showed why as they won, 45–0. They showed it in the sudden, lifting charge of a line that moved all of a piece, like a lawnmower mowing down blades of grass. They showed it in meticulous, precise play patterns. And they showed it in the running of halfback Tommy McDonald and the linebacking of Jerry Tubbs. Against running

and passing, the OU defense was impeccable.

Texas was not surprised by the Oklahoma strength. For the long week before the game, Longhorn coaches had told their players that Oklahoma was, man for man, a better team. "But the better team does not always win," head coach Ed Price told them. "Figure that if everything goes right for us and the breaks go against them, we have a good chance to upset them. They have to lose sometime."

Simply winning a football game was no longer enough for the 1956 Sooners. Now they felt that the only way they could give meaning to their long string of victories over weak teams was to punish them as impressively as possible. As cocaptain Tubbs said:

Everybody is watching us. All we need is one bad Saturday—not even lose, just look bad—and they'll jump all over us. We go out to win, first. But then, in the back of our minds, we know what they're all saying about OU, and we hit a little bit harder so that at least the team we're playing against will know we're the best.

Waiting in the wings for Oklahoma was Notre Dame. Apple-cheeked, twenty-eight-year-old Terry Brennan, the child prodigy of football coaches, was concerned. "Oklahoma may not be the greatest team in the history of college football," the Notre Dame coach said, "but then again it may. And they'll be out to prove it against us. Unfortunately, we have to play 'em with sophomores."

Brennan's scouting report on Oklahoma was awesome: good run, good block, good pass, good kick, good defense. "They may have a weakness," said Brennan, "but we can't figure out what it is. Oklahoma is in a funny position. If they lose or just barely squeak by, you'll hear that old story: 'Oklahoma builds its record against medicore teams.' So they'll be out to beat us by ten touchdowns."

For the lean and lethal Sooners, it was win No. 35 in a row. The fact that they won the game, 40–0, was only incidental. What mattered most was how they did it—coolly, methodically, dispassionately. The tip-off came on the very first play from scrimmage. Jimmy Harris, the string-bean quarterback, started right off with the Sooners' bread-and-butter play, a pitchout from himself to halfback Tommy McDonald. The play was run with a reckless nonchalance. The pitchout wobbled softly through the air, end over end. McDonald grabbed it, half-heartedly faked a pass, and ran—for 18 yards. The pattern was established then and there.

The Oklahoma defense operated with the same heartless vigor as the offense. Irish runners, spotting an inviting hole in the Oklahoma line, would sprint eagerly forward, only to find themselves bombed to earth by OU tacklers. Oklahoma's pursuit, as Notre Dame quarterback Paul Hornung observed later, was "frightening." Hornung explained: "It isn't that they're big; they're not. But they're always there."

Underneath the Sooners' workmanlike attitude was a merciless desire to prove themselves college football's No. 1 team. All across the nation the following week, kind words of tender solicitude were spoken on behalf of five teams: Colorado, Iowa State, Missouri, Nebraska, and Oklahoma A. & M. What did they all have in common? They were the unfortunates who still had to play Oklahoma, an assignment that later proved a fruitless one.

Oklahoma met Colorado the Saturday after the Notre Dame game. For a long time that afternoon, Colorado was a great football team. But for 25 minutes Oklahoma demonstrated how nearly perfect a college football team could be, and that was enough to beat the

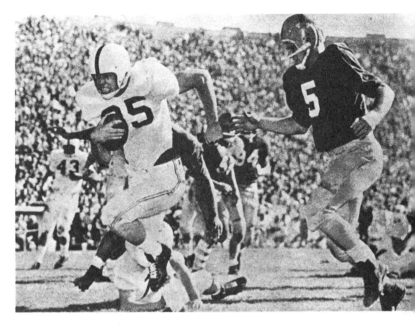

Clendon Thomas, Oklahoma's great halfback, whizzed by Notre Dame's Paul Hornung at South Bend as the Sooners routed the Irish, 40–0, in 1956.

Buffs, 27–19. The game divided neatly into two segments—a fantastic Colorado effort during the first half against nearly impossible odds, then the equally fantastic response of the Sooners to the demands of a situation beyond the capabilities of an ordinarily good team.

The game was played in the climate of an upset. After an all-out effort against Notre Dame, the Sooners were flat and ragged in workouts the following week. In contrast, Colorado players were sky-high, and by Saturday morning they were wound up tight and dangerous. And for the first half, they rammed the power of Coach Dallas Ward's single wing right down Oklahoma throats. They blocked an Oklahoma quick kick for a touchdown, and they battered aside the Oklahoma defenses on two marches. When they were into close scoring territory, they fooled the defenses smartly for touchdowns, once on a quick pitchout from T formation; again on a daring, well-executed double reverse. At the half, it was 19–6 for Colorado.

Oklahoma took the kickoff to open the third period, and, splitting its linemen somewhat wider to loosen the defense and using a delayed pitchout for the first time all season, drove 80 yards in fourteen plays with methodical precision. Almost at once everybody among the 47,000 people on hand knew that the upset was not to be. When the Colorado defense pinched in to cut off the Oklahoma power up the middle, the delayed pitchouts to halfbacks Tommy McDonald or Clendon Thomas swung outside. At the end of the third quarter, Oklahoma had the lead, 20–19. The Sooners were in command, plainly and permanently. In the Colorado dressing room after the game, center Jim Uhlir summed up the feelings of all the Buffs: "We've never enjoyed playing a football game more than today. We're only sorry we didn't win."

Battling for a shot at the Orange Bowl,

Colorado and Missouri met a week later. The Tigers jumped to an early 14–0 lead and seemed victory bound, until a pair of untimely fumbles in the third quarter changed the picture. The consequent 14–14 tie virtually insured the Buffs of a New Year's Day trip to Miami as the Big Seven representative. (Oklahoma, having represented the conference the season before, was not eligible.)

Colorado finished its regular schedule with victories over Utah, 21–7, and Arizona, 38–7, while Oklahoma demonstrated to everybody why it was No. 1 in the country with wins over Iowa State, 44–0; Missouri, 67–14; Nebraska, 54–6; and the Oklahoma Aggies, 53–0. The 656 net yards they ran up against the Nebraska Huskers was the most awesome display of power by the Sooners in three overpowering seasons.

At the end of the season, Don Faurot made an announcement. After twenty-eight years, he had coached his last game.

Colorado's opponent in the Orange Bowl on New Year's Day was Clemson, The scouting report on Coach Frank Howard's Tigers was that they were a slow, ball-control team. They depended for a steady accumulation of short yardage on the power bursts of fullback Rudy Hayes straight up the middle and the off-tackle running of halfback Joel Wells. Their passing attack, which came off roll outs by quarterback Charlie Bussey, was only fair. Clemson was not deep in talent, but it was a sound and determined team.

The Buffaloes, of course, were representing the Big Seven by default, since a league rule prevented perennial-champion Oklahoma from going to the Orange Bowl in successive years. Even though they were a second-place team, they had both style and power. Offensively, they employed both the unbalanced single wing and some split Ts. They stressed speed off both formations. Colorado was basi-

Colorado halfback Bob Stransky averaged 6.6 yards per carry in 1956 while leading the 1956 Buffs to a second-place conference standing and the Orange Bowl.

Dallas Ward's eleven-year (1948–1958) record at Colorado was 63–41–6, and he was the school's first football coach in the Big Seven Conference. Ward developed twenty-four All-Conference selections, and his 1956 team (8–2–1) defeated Clemson in the Orange Bowl, 27–21.

cally a running team, but, under pressure, it had used the pass very well. Bob Stransky, the left halfback, did most of the passing. So when the team wanted to pass, it went into single wing with Stransky at the tailback post. John Bayuk was the best fullback in the Big Seven, possibly in the country, and was very strong on that part of the fullback spin series where he kept and powered off guard. The defense was adequate.

Colorado, led by Bayuk, scored three times within five minutes in the second quarter to build up a 20–0 lead. Frank Howard told his players at halftime: "I'm going to resign my job and leave Clemson right after the ball game if you guys don't do better in the second half. I'll be damned if I'll mess around with the kind of players you've been today." The brimstone rhetoric had its effect. Clemson swarmed back with three touchdowns and were headed for a fourth when a desperation pass was intercepted. Colorado held on to win, 27–21. Coach Howard did not resign.

Going into the 1957 Notre Dame game in mid-November, Oklahoma had won ninety-four games, lost only six, and tied two since 1947. It had won sixty conference games, lost none, and tied only two. It had played in five bowl games, winning four and losing one. It had scored in 123 straight games, which was a national record, and it had won forty-seven games in a row, again a national record. It had won three national titles, 1950, 1955, and 1956. Such consistent success was not an accident.

An enthusiasm for football, which had become endemic in the state of Oklahoma, was fostered by a group called the Touchdown Club, which had members in all the small towns in the state. This gave OU a network of people interested in furthering the football program at Norman. The network spread over into Texas, too, so that OU alumni could keep their alma mater informed on the bright prospects in the vast complex of Texas high schools. Although the Oklahoma coaching staff discouraged any alumnus from contacting a high-school player, it obviously did no harm to have someone on hand to remind the youngster quietly of the advantages of education on the red clay flats of Norman.

Once a youngster had decided to enroll at Oklahoma, he was caught up in the kind of unabashed college spirit that characterized American campus life in the 1920s. At OU, a fifth-team guard was a hero on the campus, an idol in his home town, and a celebrity wherever he went. The stars of the Oklahoma teams were accorded all the adulation football heroes once received in the less-sophisticated glory days of the game, something that was true not only on the campus but all over the state. Much of this campus hero-worship was due to the fact that the Oklahoma athletes were a homogeneous part of the student body. They talked with the same western accent, wore the same faded blue jeans, and joined the same fraternities as did the nonathletic members of the OU student body. The Sooners were affectionately known as the Big Red, and Big Red was a favorite name for Oklahoma small businesses—Big Red hamburger stands, Big Red cleaning and pressing establishments, grocery stores, and furniture stores.

One merry by-product of football success in Oklahoma was that it had finally cured the state of a bad inferiority complex stemming from the Great Depression days of the Dust Bowl, when so many Oklahomans were forced off their farms and had to move west to California, where they subsisted as migratory farm laborers. The "Okie" label of those days, immortalized in John Steinbeck's *The Grapes of Wrath*, was a long time going away. Now with the Sooners blasting football foes far and wide, the state's newspapers had little trouble popularizing the slogan "I'm an Okie and I'm proud of it!" It could also have been the slogan of the Oklahoma football team, for the coaches had little trouble getting the Sooners psychologically ready Saturday after Saturday. All-America halfback candidate Clendon Thomas waxed philosophical on this point one day:

You can't pinpoint it. The guys way back started it. Then it rubs off on you. We go out to win and we play to win. None of us wants to be on the team that ends this long winning streak. I guess no matter what else you ever did, people would remember you were on the football team that lost the game that ended the streak.

The decisive factor in Oklahoma's success was the tall, soft-spoken, transplanted Minnesotan, Bud Wilkinson. By 1956 he could probably have been elected governor of the state, had he so desired. Patty Berg, one of America's greatest lady golfers in those days, had known Bud for a quarter of a century. They had grown up together on the same block back in Minneapolis and had played on the same neighborhood football team, when he was thirteen and she was eleven. Patty once recalled:

The 50th-Street Tigers were my team when we were kids. I played quarterback, Bud was right tackle, and his older brother Bill was left tackle. Once, after he had reached the top of the coaching profession, I visited Bud at Norman and he drove me out to watch the Sooners practice at Owen Field. He gathered them around and said: "This is the kind old lady who taught me how to play football. She did it merely by running right-tackle slants so often I had to learn to block opponents to keep her from trampling me."

Wilkinson organized Oklahoma football as carefully as a general would prepare an invasion—from recruiting to game preparation to public relations. He had a coldly brilliant, inventive football mind. I once asked him why his teams won so many games. He was forty-one years old at the time, and his hair was prematurely gray. He said:

There's nothing as good for a team as winning. I don't mean that the way it sounds. What I mean is the people who come into the pattern mold themselves to fit it. If it is a winning pattern, they fit that. You need good moral character, and we look for that in the boys we recruit. It's not hard to find around here. Most of the small-town people in Oklahoma and Texas, our chief hunting grounds, are good church people and the kids we get are church kids. Then the juniors and seniors set a pattern of behavior for the youngsters coming in. We try to create the atmosphere that the last boy on our squad is as important as the No. 1 boy. That's very important. That's why we spend so much time with the boys who play on the lower units.

It takes four hours of preparation by the coaches for one hour of practice. We ask the players to give a lot, but we never ask them to make any more sacrifice than the coaches. We divide preparation into two phases. First, establish the foundation of football you're going to play—fundamentals, offense and defense, and setting players in their position. While we're establishing this fundamental soundness, we come up with the twenty-two best football players on the squad, regardless of position, and we fit them into the positions we figure they can play best. We find that good football players are good at any position. This phase is extremely difficult for both players and coaches, and it makes lots of hard physical work. Then you get into the season when most of the work is mental and that's hard, too, but in a different way.

Wilkinson's preparation for any game was meticulous to the point of being finicky. It began on Sunday morning when the assistant who had scouted Oklahoma's next opponent reported to the fieldhouse and dictated his report to a stenographer. Sunday afternoon the whole coaching staff got together to study the report, and late Sunday afternoon the team heard it. At 6:30 Monday morning the staff met again, and each coach diagrammed the offense he felt would work against the upcoming opponent.

If Wilkinson and his staff agreed fairly substantially, the proposed game plan was adopted. Otherwise, they kicked it around until they did agree. On Tuesday morning, the coaches went through the same cycle with the defense. Once the offense and defense were set, the plans were typed up and each Sooner was given his assignments on a separate sheet. They got this on Wednesday at lunch and were expected to digest the information by practice time, which began at 4:15. More detailed instruction sheets were made up for offensive and defensive quarterbacks. The habits of opposing players were charted to develop patterns of play, and Oklahoma often went into a game knowing as much about the opposing team's style as its own coach.

If the Sooners had a weakness, Wilkinson confessed, it was that they didn't adjust too well during a game:

We know how we want to play a game and we play it that way. We feel that any adjustments you might make to an unfamiliar offense or defense would cost you more in efficient execution than you would gain. We also try to scout ourselves, so we don't develop any bad habits as a team. I've got three or four boys as graduate assistants who played here, and they will look at films of our games and scout Oklahoma. When you're too close to the team, you tend to lose objectivity.

Wilkinson had gained a reputation as one of football's hardest-working coaches. He had certainly given his best to football, and football, in return, had been extremely kind to him. Sample: When the University of Texas started searching around for a new head coach, after Ed Price was let out in 1956, well-heeled Texas alumni cast longing eyes toward Wilkinson. They knew he would come high. They finally gave up on him after they learned how much he was making at Norman. The Texas people had it on reliable authority that Wilkinson paid income taxes on $102,000 in 1954. (A good deal of his income came from a television series he had made, and his football salary was only a fraction of his total income.)

Oklahoma opened the 1957 season by putting a big OU brand on Pittsburgh, 26–0. It was a bruising, painstaking work of art that clearly established the superiority of the Oklahoma line and its backs. For the first 30 minutes of their next game, however, the Sooners sputtered and stumbled, before remembering their No. 1 ranking in time to teach the facts of football life to a game but outmanned Iowa State, winning 40–14 and extending the nation's longest major college victory streak to forty-two. The unbroken string was extended to 44 at the expense of Texas (21–7) and Kansas (47–0). And then for the fourth time since that long winning streak began, Colorado scared the daylights out of Oklahoma and came the closest of anyone in losing, 13–14. The Sooners' heroes were halfback Clendon Thomas, who scored the tying touchdown in the fourth quarter; quarterback Carl Dodd, who kicked the winning point; and guard Bill Krishner, who blocked the second Colorado conversion attempt.

Triumphs over Kansas State (13–0) and Missouri (39–14) lengthened Oklahoma's record string to forty-seven. The cry around Norman was "Bring on the Irish." Notre Dame was next on the Oklahoma schedule. The game was played at Norman. All week on the Notre Dame campus Irish supporters had been thinking about an upset. By proclamation of the student council, it was Beat Oklahoma Week. Students straggled across the campus through the Indiana rain and gathered 400 to 500 strong every day to watch the Irish practice and to cheer them. Spontaneous pep rallies broke out every day, and the students sang and chanted Notre Dame fight songs over and over again. Fresh in their memory was the 1956 humiliating 40–0 blasting by Oklahoma.

Before the game, Coach Terry Brennan told Bobby Williams, his quarterback: "We won't win playing cautious football. We have to gamble and do things when they least expect them."

In the first half, the Irish had to roll with the Oklahoma punch. They could get only one first down in the first quarter, but they stopped Oklahoma when they had to. The Notre Dame attack picked up steam in the second quarter, before a bad break stalled it. The Irish had reached the Sooner 6, when a pass by Williams strayed into the hands of OU's David Baker, and Oklahoma was out of trouble. The half ended, 0–0.

At halftime, Brennan told his team, "Just slant, gap, and blow. Forget the several bad breaks and bear down for the next 30 minutes. Change the plays and keep mixing them up. This is the big half."

The Irish went back onto the field confident this was the day—November 16—that Oklahoma was going to lose. And as the second half

All good things must come to an end. In 1957 it was Oklahoma's forty-seven-game victory string, still an all-time record. The headline in the *New York Herald-Tribune* told the story.

opened, Notre Dame appeared to be in clear control of the game. Brennan, thoroughly familiar with Oklahoma's tactics, made minor adjustments at the intermission and the Irish took over. Brennan was to say after the game:

We knew that Oklahoma might use an unbalanced line and flankers and even some single wing. But we knew, too, that whenever they started to move they went back to their regular split T, balanced-line offense. So we didn't do anything too different on defense. We took our basic defense and adjusted it to fit. We played the gaps in their line to close up the splits between their linemen, and we sent the linebackers in to put pressure on the quarterback a lot. We gave them the flat zone for passes that way, if they could take advantage of it, but we figured we could put on enough pressure so that they couldn't. They didn't use anything we weren't expecting.

As the Oklahoma attack stalled in the face of the intelligent, determined Notre Dame defense, the Irish offense began to move the ball.

Quarterback Williams, wholeheartedly taking Brennan's advice about shooting the works, surprised everybody, including his own coach and the Sooners, by going to the air in the last 4 minutes of the game. One big play in particular won the game for Notre Dame. On the scoring play, the Sooners positioned themselves in tight, real tight, waiting for Williams to give the ball to Nick Pietrosante, but he crossed up everybody by tossing out to Dick Lynch, faking to Nick into the line, and that was the ball game.

With the guts of a riverboat gambler, Williams again surprised everybody in the last 2 minutes of the contest by attempting two passes while his team was protecting its precarious 7–0 lead. Brennan said after the game he wasn't too much surprised at the first pass.

He considered it a smart call. He said he could read Williams's mind. Brennan explained:

Bobby was gambling on catching them by surprise and picking up a first down and making sure we would have time to run out the clock. But I must admit I was pretty mystified when Bobby threw on fourth down with 14 yards to go. Luckily, even that worked out all right.

What happened was that Williams had looked over to the sidelines to see how many yards he had to go for a first down and mistook the first pole on the chain for the second. He thought it was fourth and 4, not fourth and 14. Brennan said:

But Bobby called a great game all the way. He called all the plays in our touchdown march, and, now that it is over, I'll say I would have called the same play he called for the touchdown.

In the Oklahoma dressing room immediately after the game, Wilkinson talked to the Sooners briefly: "You played a good game and I'm proud of all of you. We couldn't go on winning forever." But his players sat in deep dejection and wept quietly. Doyle Jennings, one of the Sooners' starting tackles, summed up his teammates' feelings best. "Losing to Notre Dame today is just like death." Ken Northcutt, a guard from Texas who had sobbed loudly as he walked off the field, turned to Jennings and said, "Well, the party was fun while it lasted. I saw all forty-seven of those victories. You can't win 'em all."

Unquestionably the Notre Dame defeat hurt, but the Sooners regrouped admirably and manhandled Nebraska, 32–7, and Oklahoma State, 53–6, to set themselves up for a date with Duke in the Orange Bowl, on January 1. Coach Bill Murray said of his Blue Devils: "We telegraph our plays and dare you to stop us. We use a split T and play for the short yardage, aiming for ball control and eventually wearing down the opposition. This year we have the big, tough players to make our attack work."

On the debit side, those who watched the 1957 Blue Devils felt that they lacked fire and played only as hard as needed. That was to prove fatal against Oklahoma, a team with lots of zip and whose first and second units seldom eased up the pressure.

Surprisingly, the Blue Devils riddled the touted Oklahoma line as though they owned it. The Big Red was outgained by Duke, suffered 150 yards in penalties, but caught fire in the fourth quarter to score three touchdowns in 7 minutes and finally overwhelmed the Blue Devils, 48–21.

Oklahoma cocaptain Bob Harrison (No. 54), All-America center, broke through to throw Duke quarterback Bob Brohead for a 14-yard loss in the 1957 Orange Bowl. The Sooners won, 48–21.

In their very first game of the 1958 season, the Sooners helped to confirm the speculation that Bud Wilkinson had another solid football team. Operating from a weird and wonderful assortment of formations with chronometer-like precision, OU completely humbled West Virginia, 47–14. Putting aside their patented ball-control game, the Sooners stabbed quickly and assuredly from the conventional and split T, moved their ends in close, and split wide and made use of a widely unbalanced line as they threw the ball frequently and accurately. Quarterback Dave Baker and Bobby Boyd led the attack. Boyd spelled Baker, the regular quarterback, and completed five of nine passes for two touchdowns.

The 1958 Sooners added a dozen new formations to their spread and flanker offenses but found themselves choked off by defense-minded Oregon on the second Saturday of the season and were hard-pressed to win, 6–0. The

Ducks found the answer to the OU magic, shooting their linebackers into the gap to smother the passers while the ends stacked up the wide stuff.

T formation quarterbacks occupied a great deal of the football attention in 1958. In a season when Neanderthal-type fullbacks were conspicuous chiefly by their absence and most of the 9.6 halfbacks seemed to be busy elsewhere, the country was alive with good T quarterbacks. Two of the good ones were Dave Baker and Bobby Boyd. They possessed all the qualities desired in a model college T formation quarterback.

Contemporary football writers devoted a great deal of space to the T formation. They made it sound as though the tricky, wide-open offense was new. Actually, it dated from sometime around 1888 and even the modern T, with its flankers and man-in-motion, was bouncing around the brainpans of several coaches long before Clark Shaughnessy unleashed Frankie Albert and fellow Stanford Indians in 1940.

The T formation had gone through a number of major changes down through the years and been exposed to countless variations. The original Stanford T was followed by the split T, which in turn ran through a number of phases. Then there was the wing T and the slot T and the double-wing T and then the triple-wing T. Sometimes the quarterback was primarily a passer, sometimes a runner, but the good ones always possessed at least a few of those qualities that Frankie Albert had in such abundance: imagination, leadership, coolness under fire, and the guts of a pickpocket. The T formation, like any formation, could not get along without fullbacks who ran over people and halfbacks who ran around them, but, until someone invented the dismembered T, the quarterback was the star of the show.

It was hardly surprising, therefore, that kids grew up in the 1950s wanting to be T quarterbacks, just as they grew up for decades wanting to be the pitcher on the baseball team. Thus it wasn't surprising that there were so many good ones around in 1958.

The era of domination by Oklahoma, Notre Dame, Army, and Ohio State, so prevalent since the war years, finally came to an end. After six agonizing years of Oklahoma mistreatment, Texas got vengeance in 1958. The Longhorns beat the Sooners, 15–14, thereby righting all the injustices of the recent past.

It was no big secret that football was more than a mere game in Texas; it was a way of life. The humiliation that Oklahoma had been piling on Texas was particularly galling, because OU was beating Texas with Texans. Until Bud Wilkinson came along with the winning formula, this rugged old Southwestern rivalry had been a mighty one-sided affair. Until 1952 Texas had won thirty games and lost only fourteen against the rivals from across the Red River. From the Texas victory in 1951, however, until 1958, Oklahoma won sixty-eight of its seventy-two games and defeated the Longhorns without serious difficulty. One way the Sooners accomplished all this was by recruiting some of the slickest football talent this side of the Alamo. On the 1958 Oklahoma roster, for example, twenty-one players were from Texas, eight of them members of the first two teams. Texas football fans did not appreciate Oklahoma raids on their sons.

Only a week before, when Oregon scared the living daylights out of the Sooners, there were indications that perhaps OU's reign was ending. No longer would it take a great team to beat the Sooners, only a good one playing reasonably inspired football, and in Dallas that was just what happened. The 1958 Longhorns were hardly a great football team. They were, however, a very good one and plenty tough.

On the eve of the game, Darrell Royal said that his team didn't have the speed to be spectacular. "But my kids sure like to play football," he added. "They'll tee off against anybody." Although the former Oklahoma quarterback had arrived in Austin from the University of Washington only a little over a year before, his Longhorns were already characterized by toughness and determination and a liking for knocking people down. Against Oklahoma, they simply started knocking down Sooners at the kickoff and didn't quit until the final gun told them it was time to go home.

While the whole Texas line smashed Oklahoma's vaunted speed with jarring tackling that sent ear-shattering noises all the way back to Norman, the Longhorns probed and punched and felt their own way. Then, despite the inspired play of Texan Bob Harrison, Oklahoma's ubiquitous center, they pounded to a first-half touchdown. It took them only six plays to cover 52 yards. Southpaw halfback Rene Ramirez topped off the drive by throwing a running pass to George Blanch for the score. Then fullback Don Allen went over left tackle for the two extra points, and Texas had the lead, 8–0. In all that time the Sooners' famed attack had been held to a net gain of 39 yards rushing.

But in the third quarter the Sooners, who up until then had been acting as if the ball had a load of bricks in it, suddenly got that old itchy look, and they began to move. They blasted to the 5—and the Longhorns stopped them. Back they came again and this time they were not to be denied. Dick Carpenter, from Breckenridge, Texas, swung around left end from the 4 and fell into the end zone. But Texas still led, 8–6, after the conversion attempt by pass failed. So back stormed the Sooners once

more, that hungry look in their eyes bigger than ever. This time Texas held them on the 24.

But anyone who relaxed, even for a moment, against the boys in the blood-red jerseys was toying with disaster. On the next play, guard Jim Davis (Tyler, Texas) broke through the Longhorn line, got his paws on a handoff between Bobby Lackey, the Texas quarterback, and fullback Mike Dowdle, and raced to the goal. This time Bobby Boyd (Garland, Texas) passed to Jerry Tillery for the conversion, and the score was 14–8, Oklahoma, with most of the fourth quarter still to be played.

As much as two-touchdown underdogs in pregame betting circles, the Longhorns were expected by a lot of people to fold. But that wasn't why Darrell Royal had made the trip from Austin to Dallas—to see his team lose. He decided to put some muscle into his passing attack.

"Matthews," he called to substitute quarterback Vince Matthews, "here's your chance. Go in for Lackey."

Vince Matthews was the best passer Texas had, but he had missed most of two years with a knee injury. Consequently, the Longhorns had not gone to the air much; matter of fact, in three previous games they had completed only eight passes in twenty-six tries, for a sorry 93 yards.

Matthews cranked up his pitching arm and started firing bull's-eyes in the last quarter. He hit eight out of ten for 123 yards. Six of his completions triggered a 74-yard march by Texas to Oklahoma's 7. There Coach Royal pulled Matthews out of the game and sent Lackey back in with one play. The strategy paid off. Lackey hit end Bob Bryant on a quick jump pass, and the game was tied. Then Lackey placekicked the winning point.

The riot was on. Lackey nearly had the breath squeezed out of him by teammates

Old No. 69, John Wooten, stood 6 feet 2 inches and weighed 230 pounds. The hard-charging Colorado guard made All-American in 1958 and played in the College All-Star Game in Chicago.

Despite Iowa State's lowly finish in 1958, All-Conference tailback Dwight Nichols rushed and passed for a total of 1,172 yards. Only 164 pounds, he played practically every minute of every game.

gone crazy. Everybody tried to congratulate him at once, shaking his hand and smothering him with bear hugs. Later, in the Texas locker room, Darrell Royal sat amidst a wild scene of jubilation and talked about what the victory meant to him.

"Maybe now," he said, "Oklahoma coaches will have a little more trouble coming down here and talking our kids into crossing that river."

Until the Texas game, it had looked as if Bud Wilkinson was going to open up his offense, but after the loss to the Longhorns he went back to the grind-'em-out split T with fullback Prentice Gautt, Oklahoma's first black player, carrying most of the load up the middle.

Late in the season, Missouri coach Dan Devine, who had heard plenty about Oklahoma's snake-pit stadium, took his multiple offense into Norman with hopes for victory, but he soon discovered the bitter facts of life. The Sooners belted his Tigers, 39–0, for their seventieth straight conference victory and stuffed one foot inside the Orange Bowl door (the Big Eight finally eliminated the old rule prohibiting a member from going to the Orange Bowl two years in a row).

A week later, Oklahoma rolled over Nebraska, 40–7, for its thirteenth straight league championship and an automatic Orange Bowl bid. First-string quarterback Dave Baker was dropped from college after the close of the regular season but was ably replaced by sophomore Bob Cornell and junior Bob Boyd.

Oklahoma's opponent at Miami was Syracuse (8–1–0). Power and depth were the qualities that characterized Coach Ben Schwartzwalder's Orangemen. It was a team that liked to move straight ahead and concentrated on ball control from a straight T with unbalanced line. The Syracuse defense was rugged, having shut out Cornell, Nebraska, Bos-ton University, and West Virginia. It had held Penn State to 6 points. No one had had much success moving through its line, what with its size and strength and three-deep supply of good replacements.

Oklahoma was not intimidated by the Orangemen's credentials. On the very first play from scrimmage, the Sooners unleashed a new play, a fullback sweep, sending Prentice Gautt wide for 10 yards. On second down he ran the opposite side for 42 yards and a touchdown.

On their next possession, the Sooners got the ball on their own 21. Wilkinson remembered the scouting report he had on Syracuse: "It lacks speed on defense; it can be run around and thrown over." Wilkinson called for a pass. Halfback Brewster Hobby started to his right as if to sweep around end, then suddenly flipped the ball to end Ross Coyle, who, with the help of perfect downfield blocking from his teammates, helter-skeltered 79 yards to score. That made it 14–0.

Early in the third quarter, Hobby returned a punt 40 yards to make it 21–0. Syracuse surged back 69 yards for its only touchdown, with halfback Mark Weber bolting the final 15 yards on his only carry of the game.

Oklahoma's 21–6 victory left the Sooners No. 5 in the final polls, behind Louisiana State, Iowa, Army, and Auburn.

Oklahoma's first game of the season in 1959 was at Northwestern. This was the Sooners' first encounter with a Big Ten team since it had defeated the Northwestern Wildcats in 1939, 23–0. Forty players made the trip. On the eve of the game, thirty-eight of them traveled together from their hotel near the Northwestern campus at Evanston to Chicago's plush Chez Paree nightclub for dinner and the early show. This was to be routine pregame relaxation. Wilkinson was not there. He was dining with old friends. The two missing players, fullback Prentice Gautt and starting left end Ed ("Wahoo") McDaniel, had stayed behind at the hotel to get some extra sleep.

The team arrived at the Chez Paree about 7:15 and began eating the meal ordered in advance by the Oklahoma athletic business manager, Ken Farris: fruit cup, tossed salad, mashed potatoes, steak, rolls and butter, ice cream. The morning newspapers told the story: twelve Oklahoma players had fallen violently ill from food poisoning during the night, but no one was prepared to say exactly how it happened. The result was inevitable. That Saturday, millions of people, watching television, saw Northwestern, a team that had lost thirteen football games in the last two seasons, dazzle, stun, and finally bury the Sooners, 45–13. Bluntly, it was the worst defeat of Wilkinson's career. The Wildcats scored twice in the first quarter, twice in the second quarter, and three more times in the last half. When they weren't scoring, they were backing Oklahoma to the wall with marvelous punts; one rolled dead on the 2-yard line. The Sooners sloppily treated Northwestern to five fumbles, two of which led the home team to touchdowns, and the Wildcats treated themselves to touchdowns after blocking an Oklahoma quick kick, intercepting a pitchout, and holding OU for downs deep in its own territory.

After the game, Ara Parseghian, the Northwestern coach, said, "This is the type of game you get every so often. Everything goes right for you and everything goes wrong for them. Every time they made a mistake—bang, we took advantage of it."

In the silence of the Oklahoma dressing room, Bud Wilkinson wasn't making any excuses. He said he "wouldn't even want to make a guess" as to the effect of the food poisoning. "We just got beat," he said. "That's all you can say."

Brewster Hobby was more basic. Asked if the food poisoning had hurt his performance, he replied: "Naw. We just got our butts kicked."

Oklahoma also dropped games to Texas, 19–12, and to Nebraska, 25–21. The Sooners won another Big Eight title with a 5–1 record, a full game ahead of runner-up Missouri. But it was the Tigers who were going to the Orange Bowl in Miami to play Georgia. They had lost to Oklahoma, 23–0, but came on strong at the end of the season with triumphs over Air Force, 13–0; Kansas State, 26–0; and Kansas, 13–9.

Missouri was a multiple-offense team, which suited them fine. When they broke from a huddle and trotted up to the line of scrimmage, there was no telling what formation they'd be using: regular T, split T, wing T, or slot T. On occasion they even ran from the single wing. The Missouri line was not easily run through, but it could be passed over and around. Because they were a slow team, their pass defense was poor.

Unfortunately, Georgia had a strong passing attack. Any time, any place, no matter what the score, the amazing Bulldogs (9–1, including a 17–3 win over Alabama) were expected to pass. Never mind the quick kick or the third-down punt. Just give them that football and they'd throw. Coach Wally Butts had devised an intricate array of pass patterns, and he was fortunate to have two men who were adept at hitting the zigzagging receivers. One was Fran Tarkenton, a junior with the professional habit of waiting until a receiver was open before throwing. Although Tarkenton tossed a long one now and then, he was better at the short pass. Charley Britt took care of the long-distance numbers.

The Orange Bowl, then, brought together an interesting combination: a team that had had trouble stopping passes and a team that could pass. The professional gamblers had their money on Georgia.

Playing in front of 75,280 fans, Missouri

won the battle of statistics, but Georgia won the game, 14–0. Three times the Tigers drove deep into Bulldog territory—to the 15, 10, and 10—but they couldn't get into the end zone.

Outrushed on the ground, 260 yards to 216, Georgia struck from the air to win the game. Tarkenton, noted as a quick, short passer, crossed up the Tigers by pulling the trigger on touchdown pitches of 29 and 33 yards. Halfback Bill McKenny caught the first one, and end Aaron Box snagged the second.

For the Big Eight, it was a tough way to close out the decade.

Halfback Donnie Smith was one good reason why Missouri went to the Orange Bowl in 1959.

College Football Opens Up: 1959-1960

College football's bursting vitality in 1959 continued on into the next decade. There were great teams, great players, blazing competition, large crowds, and several significant rule changes. The "wild card" substitute rule of 1959, for instance, was liberalized to allow each team to make one free substitution between successive downs, even when the clock was running. This helped the coaches get specialists into action, pull out quarterbacks for consultation, and shuttle in plays to suit the situation.

The greater freedom in the exploitation of specialists stimulated additional offensive enterprise, along the lines of the various flanker formations inspired by the 1959 success of Red Blaik's "lonely end" formation at Army. It also allowed limited platooning of offensive and defensive units, without lowering the bars totally to flat-out two-platooning, which remained distasteful to many devotees of college football.

The collegians, sharply aware of pro football's growing popularity, also widened their goalposts in 1959 from 18 feet, 6 inches to 23 feet, 4 inches to encourage field-goal kicking. The major college placekickers responded by booting the unprecedented total of 192 field goals of 380 attempted, including one of 52 yards by Texas A. & M.'s Randy Sims, the longest by a collegian since 1941. In 1960 a record total of 224 field goals were converted in major games, and 38 of them decided the outcome.

It was not just an accident that the coaches were thinking in terms of quarterbacks. For the first time, good quarterbacks were coming out of high schools and prep schools in quantity. Where passers were once rare, almost every team now had at least one, and some had two or three. They knew what to do with a ball, too, and they knew how to take charge of a team. So, to get the most out of their quarterbacks and to open up an attack, many coaches were changing to the wing T. What attracted them most was its versatility. It enabled a team to use a power offense from a tight wing T, and it also permitted the team to split a back or end wide. Either variation could be used without having to change basic blocking patterns and assignments. Some coaches were going in for the slot wing T, which split one end wide and put a halfback in the slot between that end and tackle. Others were adopting a multiple offense, which combined fragments of the T, wing T, or split T. Regardless of what you called the formations, 1960 was to be a season of a lot of splits, flankers, lonely ends, and spreads.

To defend against all this wide-open style of play (the wing T, for example), coaches started turning to something called the three-deep defense. Eight men, rather than nine, were placed fairly close to the line. Three players were stationed deep to pick up the three receivers who could go down for the long passes from the wing T.

More and more coaches were also resorting to unbalanced lines and the man-in-motion. The wider goalposts, of course, invited more field goals, and punting was being emphasized and improved. The two-point try after touchdown was well received by fans.

Players were getting bigger than ever. Members of the first All-America team in 1889 averaged 162 pounds and just under 5 feet 10 inches. Seventy-one years later, the average was 208 pounds and 6 feet 1¼ inches.

There were more college men trying out for positions than ever before. This was because the number of high-school players was stead-

Raised in Lawrence, John Hadl, 6 feet 1 inch and 205 pounds, didn't have far to go to get to college. The two-time All-America Kansas quarterback was the leading college punter in 1959 with a 45.6-yard average.

ily increasing, while the number of college teams remained relatively stable. The added competition and the fact that many of the boys wanted to go into pro football after college had them all working harder. As a result they were better players, as a group, than they used to be.

One facet of the game that hadn't changed all that much was the coaches. "It is my conviction, based on long and intimate friendship with many football coaches and painstaking study of their tribal customs, that all members of that curious craft are mental cases, more or less advanced," quipped Red Smith at the time. "They worship idols; they practice voodoo; they do not live in this world."

Smith was reminded of a football game between Villanova and Loyola of Los Angeles, years ago. Ray Stoviak, Villanova's right halfback, started to his left from the Notre Dame box on an orthodox off-tackle run. The quarterback missed his block on the defensive end and Stoviak, seeing himself trapped, faded and began searching for a pass receiver. Walt Novak, an alert right end, saw what had happened and shook himself free. He was across the line of scrimmage, running laterally toward the left sideline, when Stoviak spotted him and connected with a pass.

John Mellus, left tackle, had been riding his man out of Stoviak's path. When he saw Novak start downfield with the ball, he dropped his man and followed, hoping to block for the runner. He didn't get there soon enough for that, but came lumbering along just as Novak was tackled. So Novak lateraled to him, and John trundled the rest of the way for his only college touchdown.

Afterward, Stoviak apologized to Clipper Smith, the coach: "Sorry I had to coin a play."

"Huh?" Clipper said.

He thought he had designed it.

Sophomore quarterback Gale Weidner scored six touchdowns and passed for seven more as he paced the 1959 Colorado attack.

The Big Eight Comes of Age: The 1960s

Since 1948 the Sooners had been almost unbeatable against the rest of the nation. They had been hanging up championship banners as regularly as doing the Monday wash. It was no secret that rival coaches made each game against Oklahoma a holy crusade and the standard by which they judged the success of their programs.

In 1960 Northwestern was the first to test the Sooners. The game was played at Norman, and for the Wildcats it was a most interesting challenge. They were still thinking how easily they had won over Oklahoma the year before at Evanston, 45–13, but a lot of the glory was rubbed off because of the Sooners' food-poisoning problems on the eve of the contest. There were many who thought that the outcome might otherwise have been reversed. So a week before Northwestern left home, Ara Parseghian needled his players about their questionable victory. He posted inflammatory newspaper articles on the dressing-room bulletin board and snidely told his players, "No one really believes you licked them." That was all he had to do. Psychology did the rest.

Northwestern licked Oklahoma, 19–3. The loss was only the Sooners' fourth at home in thirteen years. What especially pleased Coach Parseghian was the strength of his line. From tackle to tackle the Wildcats had only one player who had ever started. He knew, he explained after the game, that if his interior line held up, he would have a good team. They proved they were some group. After checking his first-stringers, Parseghian played everyone he could.

While Oklahoma was losing to Northwestern, its cross-state rival, Oklahoma State, was making its conference debut. Missouri spoiled the occasion, 28–7.

Two weeks later, Kansas shared the national spotlight with No. 1 Syracuse in Lawrence. The Jayhawks had already defeated Texas Christian, 21–7, and Kansas State, 41–0, and they were thinking upset. "We got some good boys," drawled Jack Mitchell, the folksy, handsome Kansas coach, as he talked about his team earlier in the week. "But you don't beat Syracuse with just good boys. They're too much football team for the likes of us. Our little fellas in the line just can't handle that size of team."

Although Mitchell no doubt was practicing a negative brand of positive thinking on his Jayhawks, the size of the Orangemen was considerable. Their line outweighed Kansas 19 pounds per man. And in the backfield were 215-pound fullback Art Baker and 205-pound halfback Ernie Davis, two of the most formidable runners in collegiate football.

Despite the obvious odds stacked against them, three plays after the Jays kicked off they recovered a fumble deep in Syracuse territory, and, less than a minute after that, on an end sweep by elusive Bert Coan, the TCU transfer, Kansas had a touchdown and the lead.

The rest of the game was like watching a soldier trying to hold off a tank with a bayonet. And yet Kansas left the field at halftime with a 7–0 lead, thanks to a few breaks and the matchless long punts of quarterback John Hadl.

But in the third quarter Syracuse finally got on the scoreboard with a touchdown, and with 10 minutes left in the game they scored another to take the lead, 14–7. At that point the Orangemen had run seventy-eight plays, Kansas only twenty. Syracuse had made twenty-three first downs, Kansas one. Undaunted by these statistics suggesting that Syracuse was

All-America Bobby Douglass, 6 feet 3 inches and 195 pounds, was a southpaw quarterback who passed Coach Pepper Rodgers's 1968 cochampion Kansas Jayhawks (9–2) right into the Orange Bowl, where they lost to Penn State, 15–14, in the unforgettable "twelfth man" game.

For three seasons (1959, 1960, and 1961), All-America guard Joe Romig was in on nearly half of all Colorado tackles. A physics major, Romig was graduated with a 3.87 grade average.

the superior team, Kansas fought back and launched one last effort. Switching from defensive tactics to offense, the Jays began a series of desperate razzle-dazzle maneuvers. Ten plays later they were in the Syracuse end zone with what appeared to be a touchdown and what could have been one of the biggest upsets in years. However, a penalty was called against Kansas and the threat ended. Syracuse hung on for their lives and finally a tough game was history.

Afterward, Coach Ben Schwartzwalder told the press:

I thought Kansas was as good a team as we ever played. I never saw such a grim team as they were before the game. I went over by their dressing room to talk to the officials and the Kansas players were all so quiet. I don't know why everyone has to get so worked up about beating us all the time.

While Kansas was bowing to Syracuse, Oklahoma upheld Big Eight prestige by turning back Pittsburgh, 15–14. The Sooners' alternates took over in the fourth quarter, blocked a kick, scored a touchdown, and won the game when quarterback Bennett Watts ran for two extra points.

Meanwhile, Iowa State flexed its muscles and finally pulled out a 10–7 heart-stopper with Nebraska on Larry Schreiber's 39-yard field goal.

A week later, it was already nearing showdown time in the conference. Kansas struck for 14 points in the first 10 minutes, then fought off Iowa State and its crashing fullback, Tom Watkins, to win, 28–14, as quarterback John Hadl scored twice, and passed for a third touchdown.

"Next week," predicted Coach Jack Mitchell, "we are going to be the first Kansas team in fourteen years to beat Oklahoma."

The Jayhawks came close, but with 24 seconds to play, John Suder's field-goal attempt from the 9-yard line failed, and Kansas had to settle for a frustrating 13–13 tie.

Elsewhere around the league, Colorado, playing without ailing passer Gale Weidner, marched over Iowa State, 21–6; Missouri, starting to look like a genuine contender, smashed Kansas State, 45–0; and Pat Fischer brought Nebraska from behind to beat Army, 14–9, with a touchdown plunge and a 57-yard pass to Bennie Dillard.

The Big Eight was building up to a climactic game between Missouri and Colorado as the Tigers trimmed Nebraska, 28–0, and Colorado made a second-quarter touchdown stand up for a 7–0 victory over Oklahoma. The win marked the Buffaloes' first over the Sooners in fourteen years.

Eight weeks into the season, Oklahoma's collapse as the league's perennial leader was almost complete. As Missouri moved closer to the title, the faltering Sooners lost to Iowa State, 10–6, the first time that had happened since 1931. By now, the only thing certain in the Big Eight was that the ultimate champion of the vastly improved conference would be an awfully good team. Missouri seemed like the best bet after beating Colorado, 16–6, to maintain the Big Eight lead. The victory was the Tigers' eighth of the season, with two more—Oklahoma and Kansas—still ahead.

All season long it had been apparent that Oklahoma's days of dominance in the Big Eight were at an end. Now there was no doubt about it. Unbeaten Missouri (8–0) demonstrated that even the once-dreaded "Norman snake pit" (Owen Field), where the Sooners had not lost a conference game in eighteen years, was no longer inviolable. Pushing their attack up the middle instead of to the outside, as expected, the Tigers shot through halfback Donnie Smith for two touchdowns, then

turned to the flanks and swept loose halfback Norris Stevenson for TD runs of 77 and 60 yards. Oklahoma battled back tenaciously, but Missouri pounded the Sooners, 41–19, for the first time in fifteen years. Coach Dan Devine, who had earlier described the Tigers as a bunch of "little ol' humpty dumpties who aren't very impressive looking," had to admit his kids were something special. "This is wonderful," he beamed. "We kept our poise. We beat a good, fired-up team."

But Missouri still had to beat Kansas for the title. The Jays tuned up for the Tigers by trouncing Colorado, 34–6.

The national polls now had Missouri ranked No. 1, ahead of Syracuse, Iowa, and Minnesota. The townspeople and students of Columbia, Missouri, had worked themselves into a frenzy as the big game with Kansas approached. Every day was like New Year's Eve. A local radio station reminded listeners every fifteen minutes that Missouri was the No. 1 team in the nation. Large gold buttons with a black numeral 1 were on lapels everywhere. Signs appeared in store windows urging the annihilation of Kansas and predicting an Orange Bowl invitation for the Tigers. For weeks, the contest had been a total sellout; scalpers were getting $50 a ticket. Even Coach Devine was surprised at his team's lofty status. "Of course," he said, "you go into every game expecting to win. But, frankly, I just hoped at the outset we could win half of our ten games."

Dan Devine, thirty-five, had come to Missouri three years before after a successful term at Arizona State. He was a small, trim man, with smooth dark hair, wide brown eyes, and a youthful appearance. Sitting behind a desk, wearing glasses, he looked like a man whose total football experience had been limited to touch football. More than half of his 1960 squad hailed from Missouri, and many other players were from what were discreetly called "area schools," out-of-state schools near the Missouri border. The university freely admitted it had intensified its recruiting program but was quick to stress that the school had high academic standards.

Missouri spent most of its practice time before the Kansas game working on its two best maneuvers, the criss-cross punt return and its swift end sweeps. Seven times during the season such plays had broken loose fleet Norris Stevenson, Donnie Smith, and Norm Beal for touchdown runs of 50 yards or more. The team was directed by quarterback Ron Taylor, who didn't do anything particularly well, but he was the spark who kept the team moving. His specialty was short passes.

On Saturday, a record crowd of 43,000, more than the population of Columbia, filled Missouri's Memorial Stadium. The day was perfect for football.

It took a while for people to figure out which of the teams was better. Kansas was strong. It had been getting better every week. Its only fault was that it had lost games to teams ranked No. 1—Syracuse, 7–14; Iowa, 7–21. Now it was faced with the challenge of dismantling the current No. 1.

By the third quarter everybody knew which was the better team on that day. Twice Missouri fumbled the ball in the second quarter, something it seldom did. The Tigers looked tense and expectant. They escaped from the first half with a scoreless tie, thanks to a stiff defense that twice stopped the Jayhawks deep in their own territory.

Even in the third quarter, it looked as if Missouri had stopped another Kansas threat, until senior Roger Hill stepped up and booted the first field goal of his career, a 47-yarder. That seemed to break the Tiger spirit. Bert Coan, the high-stepping halfback, caught a pass for one touchdown and ran for another.

Kansas won the 1960 conference title, then abdicated when the league ruled it had used an ineligible player in two games it had won—Colorado (34–6) and Missouri (23–7). Starring in the trenches for the Jayhawks was All-Conference guard Elvin Basham.

Suddenly Kansas was ahead, 17–0, and Missouri was headed for its only loss of the season. The Tigers did not score until late in the game; then Kansas got another touchdown to make the final score 23–7.

Defeat always hurts, but when it finally came to Missouri it brought tears. What had started out to be the most glorious day in the history of Missouri football—a victory over traditional rival Kansas, the completion of the school's first undefeated, untied season and its first national championship—ended as a black day. Although the loss cost the Tigers the national championship, they still took the conference crown. Instead of sharing the title with Colorado with a 6–1 record in the final league standings, Missouri backed into the conference championship after the Big Eight belatedly—and enigmatically—declared the Jayhawks' Bert Coan, the TCU transfer, ineligible. His suspension forced Kansas to forfeit games to Missouri and Colorado, giving Missouri a 7–0 record and the conference title. This entitled the Tigers, not Kansas, to go to the Orange Bowl.

Missouri's opponent at Miami was Navy. The midshipmen were not large and they were not exceptionally fast, but they did have a gung-ho team spirit that could cause trouble. And they also had a squirmy little fellow named Joe Bellino, around whom Coach Wayne Hardin built what he whimsically called the "jackpot T" offense. All-America halfback Bellino never really had a bad game all season. The squat, shifty runner, with the peculiar churning gait and the best fake in college football, ran wide, sifted inside the tackles, or barreled through the middle with equal effectiveness. Missouri couldn't afford to overload to stop him. If that happened, quarterbacks Hal Spooner and Harry Dietz would pick the vulnerable Tigers apart with short passes, and fullback Joe Matalavage

would crash up the center. Defensively, however, the Navy line could be dented. It gave up 1,394 yards rushing, mostly to major opponents, and that was no sort of record to throw at Missouri's power.

On the other hand, Missouri's line was quick and aggressive, with All-America end Danny LaRose, a bruising 221-pounder, the most spectacular defender. More consistent defense gave the edge to the Tigers—but only if they could contain Joe Bellino.

So with dedicated regard for Bellino, the Tigers ground out an old-fashioned, workmanlike victory over Navy, 21–14, before more than 70,000 people, including President-elect John Kennedy. Missouri had done its homework well: the crowd saw just a flash of Bellino late in the contest when he made a fantastic, acrobatic catch of a pass for a touchdown. Apart from that, little Joe, surrounded by sinister Missouri tacklers as he was, gained only 4 yards on the ground all day. Meanwhile, Missouri's talented backs danced merrily around and through the Navy line, making good use of the four-lane highways the hefty Tiger blockers opened up for traffic. Missouri pounded out 296 yards rushing, 111 of them by Mel West, who frequently out-Bellinoed Mr. Bellino.

The scene in the Missouri locker room after the game was one of hysterical joy. Coach Dan Devine and his assistants were carried into the showers with their clothes on; none of them cared. The legendary Joe Bellino had been stopped cold, Navy had been defeated, and Missouri, after six losses, had finally won a bowl game.

The 1960 football season made history. A new era of hope was here. Oklahoma's 3–6–1 record was the worst at Norman in thirty-seven years. It had taken a long time, but Big Eight rivals had finally caught up with the Sooners. They had successfully neutralized

UNIVERSITY OF MISSOURI 1960

Missouri's undefeated Big Eight and Orange Bowl champions of 1960. The Tigers ranked No. 4 in the national polls that season.

All-America end Danny LaRose (No. 87) cut ball carriers down in their tracks. He typified the crisp tackling and blocking of the 1960 Missouri Tigers, 21–14 winners over Navy in the Orange Bowl.

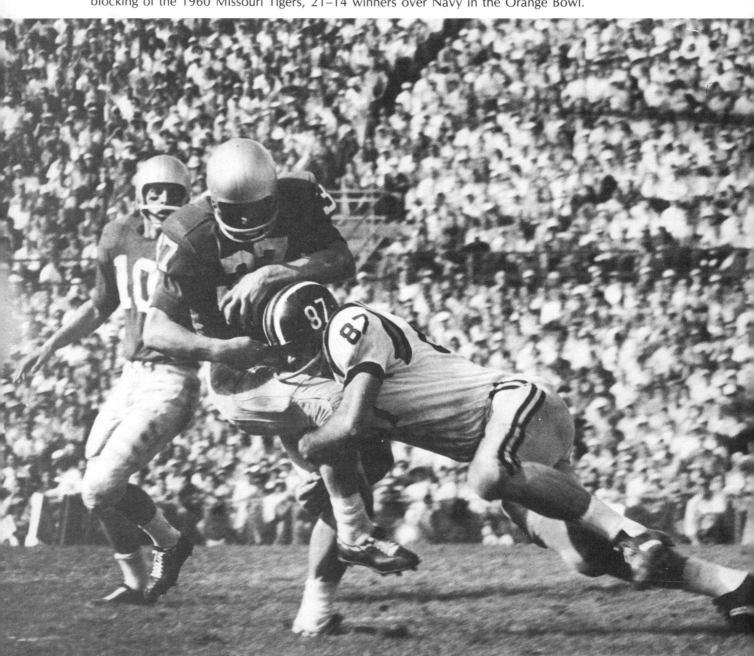

Norm Beal (No. 21) returned an intercepted pass 90 yards against Navy in the Orange Bowl on New Year's Day, 1961, for Missouri's first post–World War II bowl victory.

the Oklahoma myth. The day had passed when the Sooners could walk onto the field and defeat a good opponent just by showing up.

It would be a disservice to Oklahoma to call the 1961 Sooners a comeback team. Perhaps they would have come back from their 3–6–1 record of the previous season, but what Oklahomans had learned to call a good season was still a schedule or two away. The residue of several cautious recruiting years, when the Sooners were under NCAA probation for being too generous with some of their players, remained to plague Coach Bud Wilkinson. It was to the sophomores and freshmen of 1961 that Oklahoma was looking, and this was a pleasant look. Although sophomores made up most of the injury-riddled second team in the opening game against Notre Dame, the same sophomores were undefeated as freshmen in 1960 and would be returning for two more seasons—much healthier, it was hoped. As for the members of 1961's freshman crop, five days after reporting for practice they scored four touchdowns against the varsity in a scrimmage.

Against Notre Dame, Oklahoma didn't have a chance. The Fighting Irish won the ball game, 19–6, and if the luck of the Irish hadn't called a brief time out, figuring perhaps that it had accomplished enough for one afternoon, the score could have gone much higher. This just wasn't going to be the Sooners' year.

It was a good victory for Notre Dame, even over an Oklahoma team that had its second unit decimated by injuries in the weeks of practice leading up to the opener and was therefore ill equipped to cope with Notre Dame's superior size and depth.

The Big Eight's first big showdown in 1961 came in early October, between Kansas and Colorado. For three quarters Kansas played like the team it was supposed to be. Its front line outcharged the larger Colorado forwards, and All-America John Hadl and Curt McClinton passed and ran the Jays to a 19–0 lead. Then the Buffaloes' Gale Weidner took over. He hurriedly threw touchdowns of 58, 47, and 17 yards to ends Ken Blair and Jerry Hillebrand, and Colorado won, 20–19.

However, the Big Eight lost some national prestige that Saturday at Columbia, where defending conference champion Missouri was lucky to get a 14–14 tie with California.

By as late as October 23, there was speculation that the Big Eight might yet turn out to be a three-team race between Colorado, Kansas, and Missouri. But even after Kansas beat Oklahoma, 10–0, Colorado and Missouri were believed to still hold the aces in the league. By now the Buffaloes and Tigers were on a collision course. Week after week they moved cautiously toward their big battle at Boulder, but always looking over their shoulders to see what improved Kansas was doing. On the way to their showdown, the Buffs had to come from behind on the line-crashing of fullback Loren Schweininger in the last period to beat Oklahoma, 22–14, while Missouri, bogged down by fumbles, finally overcame Nebraska, 10–0. Meanwhile, John Hadl was directing and passing Kansas to a 42–8 victory over Oklahoma State.

The following Saturday, Colorado (5–0–0) was still in the fight for the national championship. But barely. Against Missouri, its closest contender for the Big Eight title and a trip to the Orange Bowl, the Buffaloes scored on a 21-yard pass only seconds before the clock ran out on the first half to lead, 7–0.

Missouri was held scoreless until the fourth quarter, when it got into the end zone to make it 7–6. The Tigers decided to gamble on a 2-point conversion. Mike Hunter lobbed a pass

Dick Scesniak lettered at Iowa State for three years (1959, 1960, and 1961) and is now an assistant coach to University of Washington's Don James, 1977 Coach of the Year. James is a former assistant coach at Kansas and Colorado.

Iowa State tailback Dave Hoppman was the lone Cyclone to make All-Conference in 1962. In 1961 he established a school single-game rushing record with 271 yards (against Kansas State) and led the nation in total offense (1,638 yards). He received All-America recognition in both 1961 and 1962.

The big Colorado line moved in to stop Oklahoma halfback Gary Wylie and keep their 1961 conference record spotless on their way to a 22–14 victory and the conference championship.

across the goal line, which Colorado's Reed Johnson barely deflected with his fingertips. Colorado rooters heaved a great big sigh of relief that could be heard in Miami, home of the Orange Bowl. Although Colorado's victory gave it a firm hold on the league championship, second-place Kansas looked better than ever as it beat up Nebraska, 28–6.

There was even some consolation for Bud Wilkinson, whose Sooners rallied to beat Kansas State, 17–6, to end a five-game losing streak.

Late in November, the scramble for bowl recognition was almost over. Colorado (6–0 in conference standings) was in the lead, with Kansas (5–1) and Missouri (4–2) close behind, yet rumors were strangely flying that the Orange Bowl selection committee intended to bypass the Tigers for the exciting, what-the-hell Jayhawks. So the Buffaloes got down to business and thrashed Iowa State, 34–0. That did it. The hoped-for invitation from Miami came through. Then Missouri, with no bowl ambitions of its own, gained great satisfaction in bumping Bluebonnet-bound Kansas, 10–7. That tied the Tigers with the Jays for second place in the final standings. Colorado then polished off its regular schedule with a nice workout against the Air Force Academy, winning 29–12. After the game, Coach Ben Martin of the Air Force looked at the ponderous Buffs, and said, "Boy, would I love to have beef on the hoof like that."

A final note: After five straight defeats, Oklahoma turned things around and won its last five games, including a 14–8 victory over Army at Yankee Stadium in New York City. There were moments when the Sooners looked like the Sooner teams of old. They were definitely a team to watch in the near future.

Colorado's opponent at Miami was Louisiana State, which was famous for using three teams—the starting White team, the offensive

Go team, and the defensive Chinese Bandits. Coach Paul Dietzel tried to divide the playing time evenly, so LSU's depth could be a factor. Louisiana State (9–1) were especially strong. Two of their backs, Dwight Robinson and Tommy Neck, tied for the Southeastern Conference leadership in pass interceptions, which meant trouble for Colorado's aerial attack. Louisiana State's offense was conservative, with fads and fancy stuff kept to a minimum. Using what amounted to a slot T, the team relied on counterplays and traps designed to slip its fast backs, Wendell Harris and Jerry Stovall, inside the tackles. Its strategy would be to play a cautious game, wait for Colorado to make a mistake, and then move in.

Colorado had a balanced team. Its passing attack, with quarterback Gale Weidner throwing primarily to end Jerry Hillebrand, could break open a game. Weidner was especially effective on the roll out, which Coach Sonny Grandelius called "the action pass." The Buffaloes also had a good running team, making it difficult to defend against. The team used the standard sweeps, counters, and traps, with halfbacks Teddy Woods and "Buffalo" Bill Harris doing most of the carrying. All-America middle linebacker Joe Romig led the Colorado defense. A physics major with a three-year grade average of 3.87, he was the most intellectual of athletes. "Joe does not care to be known only as a great football player," said Coach Grandelius. "He would much prefer to be recognized as an outstanding science student. Whether it's football, science, or anything else, Joe approaches it all the same way—totally full out."

Romig's peculiar talent was throwing ball carriers for losses. He was the roving linebacker who got to smother the runner going wide, or spear the scrambling pass receiver, or hit the barging plunger head-on. He was the man who got to drop off occasionally and intercept passes, and then run in such wild-boar fashion that Coach Grandelius was hard pressed to explain at the Monday boosters' luncheon why he wasn't using Joe at fullback. Romig had intuition. He was a natural at jamming up the middle against running plays. He was amazingly fast. He got to the play action because he wanted to. He loved football. He lived for contact.

Contact to Romig was really only one thing: the moment of impact with the runner. All of that other business, such as people bumping into him, foolishly trying to block him, he ignored. He hurried to the fun, which consisted of getting a good measure on a guy and stripping him down. Joe was the heart and soul of the Colorado defense. He prowled up and down the line behind his tackles and guards, anticipating where the daylight might occur so he could close it off. His job was to secure all hatches. He went full out on every play. As captain of the team, he was acclaimed its most valuable player for two straight years.

The experts predicted that the LSU–Colorado contest would probably be a chessman's game—cautious, strategic, perhaps even dull. They made Louisiana State the favorite, remembering its 42–0 pasting of Southern California earlier in the season and its overall 9–1 record.

Making its third bowl appearance, during Sonny Grandelius's third year as head coach, Colorado lost to LSU as rain, first in the Orange Bowl's twenty-eight-year history, held the crowd to 62,391. The Buffaloes led early in the contest, 7–5, when fullback Loren Schweininger intercepted a pass and ran it back 59 yards to score. The Louisianans struck back by converting two blocked punts into a touchdown and a safety, and then picked up another TD after a Colorado punt traveled only 18 yards.

Meanwhile, LSU's hard-charging line limited the Buffs to a paltry 24 yards net rushing, so quarterback Gale Weidner was forced to take to the air thirty-nine times. Surprisingly, Colorado trailed by only 4 points, 11–7, at halftime. But Louisiana State came out with fire in their eyes in the third quarter. Starting on the Colorado 42, after another poor punt, LSU required only six plays to widen its lead to 18–7. A few minutes later they put the game on ice when end Gene Sykes crashed through to block Chuck McBride's punt at the 5-yard line and pounce on it in the end zone. The final score was 25–7.

The contest marked the finale for both Paul Dietzel and Grandelius at their respective schools. Dietzel turned in his resignation to become head coach at Army, and Grandelius was sacked by the Colorado Board of Regents for overzealous recruiting. The Buffs were placed on probation for two years by the NCAA, and nine players were ruled ineligible by the Big Eight.

It was a costly way to build a football program.

On the first Saturday of the 1962 season, Syracuse pounded away at Oklahoma's snapping-quick linemen for almost 58 minutes. Bill Schoonover and Gus Giardi, a pair of elusive halfbacks, and fullback Jim Nance got the Orangemen close enough for Tom Mingo to kick a 35-yard field goal in the second quarter, but fumbles spoiled three other opportunities. Then, with only 2:07 left to play in the game and Syracuse nervously holding on to its 3–0 lead, the Sooners exploded from their 40-yard line. Joe Don Looney, a swift 207-pound third-string fullback from Fort Worth who shuttled in and out of colleges (TCU, Texas, Cameron Junior College), took a short pitch over the left side, slid away from four grasp-

All-Conference end Jerry Hillebrand gave defenders many a slip as 7–0–0 Colorado won the conference championship and an Orange Bowl invitation in 1961. The Buffs ranked No. 7 in the national polls.

Runner-up to Colorado in the 1961 Big Eight race, Kansas (6–3–1 during the regular schedule) smothered Rice, 33–7, in the Bluebonnet Bowl. All-America quarterback John Hadl wound up his college career in that game.

ing Syracuse linemen, cut sharply to his left, and raced all the way across the goal line. The final score: Oklahoma 7, Syracuse 3. "Maybe sometimes it's better to be lucky than good," quipped Coach Bud Wilkinson in the dressing room afterward. As painful as it was, Ben Schwartzwalder had to agree.

On the same day, Kansas was less fortunate. Despite the fact that they spent much of the afternoon inside Texas Christian's 20-yard line, four times the Jayhawkers were repelled by the Frogs' linemen. The fifth time, they had to settle for a 26-yard field goal by sophomore Gary Duff for a 3–0 lead. Then Sonny Gibbs, the TCU quarterback whose deep passing had been discouraged by the alertness of Kansas's corner defense men, suddenly got the Frogs jumping. He moved them 60 yards to the Jays' 12-yard line, from where Gibbs passed to Tom Magoffin for a touchdown. That made the score 6–3 in the second period. It eventually held up and TCU got the win.

A week later, the Big Eight had the Big Ten writhing in defeat and humiliation. Nebraska shocked favored Michigan, 25–13, and Missouri held touted Minnesota to a scoreless tie in Minneapolis. At Ann Arbor, fullback Thunder Thornton hammered his way to two touchdowns, and quarterback Dennis Claridge ran for another. But most of the credit for the big upset belonged to the huge Huskers line. The Missouri line was just as heroic at Minneapolis. Twice the Gophers got to the Tigers' goal line, but each time they were stopped, once at the 2 and again at the 1.

Three weeks into the season, 75,504 people were on hand to watch an overanxious Oklahoma team fumble away a possible upset victory over nationally ranked, heavily favored Texas. It was the fifty-seventh game of a series that started in 1900. The Longhorns won, 9–6, in a fierce contest that climaxed in a near riot with both benches swarming angrily onto the field. So what else was new? "Sure, it's important to us," explained one of the two dozen Texans on the Oklahoma roster, "but especially for those of us who played high school ball in Texas. It's up to us to show our folks and friends back home that we made the right choice."

This was not the day for transplanted Texans in Sooner clothing. Everything they did was wrong. In the second quarter, Oklahoma quarterback Monte Deere, from Amarillo in the panhandle, shuttled a sloppy lateral that was pounced on by Texas on the Sooner 27, setting up its first score—a fourth-down field goal by barefooted Tony Crosby from the 16-yard line. Shortly thereafter, the Longhorns got on the scoreboard again, this time when Oklahoma's halfback Paul Lea, a native of Terrell, Texas, fumbled a bad pitchout from Deere behind his own goal line, and center Perry McWilliams slashed through and fell on it for a Texas touchdown. That made the score Texas 9, Oklahoma Texans 0. The Sooners scored just before the end of the half but never seriously threatened again as halfback Ernie Koy, whose father, Ernie Sr., helped Texas defeat Oklahoma thirty years earlier, kept the Sooners bogged down in their own territory with skillful punting. Having won in each of the last five years, undefeated Texas now led the series, 35–20–2.

Undaunted by its 1–2 record after three weeks, Oklahoma opened conference play against Kansas. "I'd be surprised if we can hold them to two touchdowns, and I just don't see how we can score as many as two," said Coach Jack Mitchell before the game. He hit the nail on the head. On a halfback trap Joe Don Looney broke loose for 61 yards to score Oklahoma's first touchdown, and then Monte Deere made it 13–7 on a 3-yard sweep to end the fireworks for the day. In other Big Eight contests that weekend, Nebraska (5–0 overall) overpowered Kansas State, 26–6; Missouri alternated its famed power sweeps with lunges up the middle to beat Oklahoma State, 23–6; and Iowa State, going for a 5–5 season, clobbered Colorado, 57–19.

Moving on to the first Saturday in November, there was undefeated Nebraska, ranked high in the polls. And there was Missouri, unbeaten, and also listed among the top teams in the country. And then they met. All over the Nebraska campus at Lincoln were stickers that read: "We have not scored on Missouri in four years—let's get a bunch." After it was all over, Missouri could contemplate an even higher rating and a January bowl invitation; Nebraska, a 16–7 loser, could only ponder its mistakes and dream of what might have been.

After a couple of years of enforced servitude, Oklahoma was back in first place in the Big Eight. The Sooners caught Missouri off-balance and struck on a 42-yard screen pass on the second play of the game; then, on the fifth play, Joe Don Looney drove over from the 3. After that, the Tigers never had a chance. Oklahoma won, 13–0. But Nebraska, a 14–0 winner over Oklahoma State, was waiting to challenge the Sooners for the championship and a place in the Orange Bowl. It was the last game of the season on the Huskers' regular schedule.

Bud Wilkinson was a coach who liked his football hard and crunchy, like peanut butter, and that was the kind of game Bob Devaney, in his first season at Lincoln, was prepared to defend against. But Devaney was in for a surprise—and a 34–6 licking. Quarterback Monte Deere—when he wasn't steering sophomore fullback Jim Grisham through the middle on trap plays—passed over the puzzled Cornhuskers for three touchdowns, and Oklahoma won the Big Eight title and the trip to Miami on New Year's Day. "And we were concerned with their running game," groaned Devaney. "We should have shot the air out of the football."

In three trips to Miami, Bud Wilkinson's Sooners had never lost in the Orange Bowl. Now they had Alabama to beat. The two teams had never met before in football. The Sooners' strong point was its ground game; Alabama's strong point was stopping a ground game. Somehow, somewhere, something had to give.

After losing two of its first three games, Oklahoma wrecked its next seven opponents, 247 points to 19, and during that span it developed a solid passing attack, which was seldom used by previous Wilkinson-coached teams.

Paul ("Bear") Bryant's Alabamans had stood fast for twenty-four games without allowing an opponent more than one touchdown. Linebacker Lee Roy Jordan was the most valuable player on the team, although slotman Joe Namath had been getting more newspaper space. Namath had completed 52 percent of his passes and commanded the offense, which utilized the man-in-motion on almost every play.

As predicted by the experts, linebacker Jordan was the star of the game. He recorded an incredible thirty-three solo tackles as 'Bama shut down the Oklahoma attack to win, 17–0. The lone bright spot for the Sooners was Jim Grisham, the game's leading rusher, with 107 yards in twenty-eight carries. Unfortunately, Grisham twice fumbled the ball at the Crimson Tide's 6-yard line, ending touchdown threats that could have kept his team in the running.

Namath, nineteen, the rookie quarterback, provided the rest of the incentive for Alabama. He completed nine of seventeen passes for 86 yards and a touchdown, and set up the second.

President John F. Kennedy was among the

73,380 who watched Bear Bryant beat Bud Wilkinson for the second time in a row in bowl competition.

In other bowl games featuring the Big Eight, Missouri defeated Georgia Tech, 14–10, in the Bluebonnet Bowl at Houston, and Nebraska ran its record to 9–2 with a 36–34 victory over Miami of Florida in New York's Gotham Bowl.

In 1963, Nebraska finally gave its fans something to cheer about, for the year heralded the return of the Cornhuskers as a football power. There was a time when NU was a big bear in college football. Between 1928, when the league was born with six members, and 1940, the team won nine conference titles, six of them under Dana X. Bible. But then the war began. Whereas other campuses had naval training programs that provided a steady flow of healthy athletes, Nebraska had none. It began to lose, and when the war ended the losing habit was hard to shed. The superior high-school players, the blue-chippers, favored current winners. Since Nebraska was so sparsely populated, the Huskers had always relied heavily on athletes from out of state. The 1963 team, for example, included players from San Francisco, Chicago, and Cleveland, as well as Nebraska's own Eagle, Valentine, and Broken Bow. As the Cornhuskers continued to lose, it became increasingly difficult to attract out-of-state players. Thus, more losses.

When Nebraska finished its 1961 season with a 3–6–1 record, its sixth straight losing season and seventeenth since 1940, the university released its coach of the previous five years, Bill Jennings, and replaced him with a forty-seven-year-old Irishman named Bob Devaney. He was not precisely the very model of the modern major football coach—that electric, fiery go-getter with the military bearing,

the perfect smile, and the glad hand. Devaney's pants were baggy, his coat rumpled. He wore an old pearl stickpin in his tie. His eyes were puffy and flecks of dandruff dotted his shoulders.

Bob Devaney had been an obscure but successful high-school coach in Michigan for fourteen years, when, in 1953, Michigan State University hired him as an assistant to Biggie Munn and then Duffy Daugherty. "He was a genius at picking out what was going wrong during a game," recalled an associate. "No discredit to Duffy, but the record showed that the Spartans were not the same immediately after Devaney left." It was Duffy himself who suggested to the University of Wyoming that Devaney would make a crackerjack head coach. Wyoming agreed and in 1957 Devaney went west. There, in his first five seasons, he won four Skyline Conference titles. Everyone was pleased and the university's only worry was how to hang on to its coach. In 1961 the Wyoming board of trustees and the administration sat down with Devaney and talked things over. Devaney wanted a five-year contract. He got it. He also got the house in which the president of the university used to live. And he got an estimated salary of $16,000 and off-the-record assurance that his contract was really good forever. Everybody was happy—Devaney, the university, and the state of Wyoming.

Six months later Devaney suddenly announced he was leaving to take the coaching job at Nebraska in the higher-prestige Big Eight Conference. Howls of anger came from all over Wyoming. One state senator, Richard Jones, tried to hold Devaney to the full five years of his contract. Senator Jones did not have his way, and Devaney moved on to Lincoln the following February.

What Devaney accomplished after that was regarded by NU fans as something of a mira-

Bob Devaney, yesterday and today. His 1962–1972 football coaching record at Nebraska was 101–20–2, including eight Big Eight championships and a 6–3 bowl record. In 1970–1971 he was named national coach of the year by *Football News*. He now serves as director of athletics at Nebraska.

cle. Everyone agreed that the coaching staff (Devaney brought most of his assistants from Laramie) was the best organized they had ever seen.

Devaney was popular. He had a warm sense of humor. He clung to the almost obsolete belief that there was room for laughter in football. In his last season at Wyoming, on the morning of a tough game against Kansas, he had a magician entertain the team to relieve the tension. A two-touchdown underdog, the Cowboys held Kansas to a 6–6 tie. So in his first season at Nebraska, the sound of laughter ringing across the practice fields was not unusual. Devaney believed in short workouts and no scrimmaging. "The boys get hit hard enough on Saturdays," he said. "Why break them up during the week?"

I knew one Midwest coach who was always rattling his linemen to hit harder. "Kill, kill, kill!" he'd storm at them. One big tackle, a powerful 255-pounder, eased up in practice one afternoon. The coach was furious. Why hadn't the lineman flattened the ball carrier?

"I thought this was only supposed to be dummy scrimmage," the youth said. "I didn't want to hurt him."

"I don't care if you *kill* him," screamed the coach. "Next time you hit him. He's *expendable!*"

That night, the boy turned in his suit and transferred to another school. "I didn't want to play for a coach like that," the youngster told me later. "He took all the fun out of football."

Under Bob Devaney, there were no problems like that at Nebraska.

In 1963, the season came down to November 22. Out in the midlands, it was a historic date for two reasons: President Kennedy was assassinated, and the Big Eight title was decided on the outcome of the Nebraska–Oklahoma game. Both teams were undefeated in conference competition.

On what should have been the last full day of the college football season most college presidents, reacting quickly and decisively to the president's death, postponed or canceled scheduled games. A few colleges decided to play anyway. Nebraska and Oklahoma elected to play. Bud Wilkinson probably wished that they had not. His team was pounded, 29–20. Bob Devaney played it straight, no player shifts, no trick plays. He decided that this was no time to get fancy. He simply pitted strength against strength—his big, tough line against the Sooners' fast, shifty forwards—and his strategy paid off. The Husker line was magnificent. From tackle to tackle they jarred the Sooners loose from five fumbles and gave up only 98 yards rushing. Meanwhile, Nebraska's 269-pound guard Bob Brown and 245-pound tackle Lloyd Voss mounted a violent charge that led Rudy Johnson, Dennis Claridge, Kent McCloughan, and Fred Duda to touchdowns. Only when Nebraska was safely in front, 29–7, did Devaney start sending in his second- and third-stringers. Then Oklahoma's Wes Skidgel scored twice, on a 23-yard run and a 25-yard pass from Tommy Pannell, to make the final score appear closer than it really was. Devaney did not mind at all. He just said, "This is the biggest win of my coaching career."

The 1964 New Year's Day Orange Bowl lined up as a battle between two gifted quarterbacks, Auburn's Jimmy Sidle and Nebraska's Dennis Claridge. Claridge, 6 feet 4 inches, 222 pounds, was a long-striding power runner who telegraphed his destinations but got there anyhow. Nebraska's game was to control the ball, and no one controlled it better than Claridge.

For all its brute strength, Nebraska had weaknesses, a fact of which Devaney was only too aware. Its ends could be circled, and its defensive secondary could be pierced by good passing. As a matter of fact, a long pass was what beat the Huskers against Air Force, 17–13, for their only loss of the season.

Auburn pinned its dreams on junior Jimmy Sidle, a sensational option runner who lost the national rushing championship by 10 yards. Moreover, he was a sharp passer, with a record of 53 completions of 136 passes for 706 yards and 5 touchdowns. Auburn's season included triumphs over mortal enemies Alabama, 10–8, and Georgia Tech, 29–21. There was one last warning to Nebraska: coming from the tough Southeastern Conference, Auburn also played defense.

In Miami, Dennis Claridge was decisive. He was also in a hurry. Only a minute into the game, he popped through the right side of the line and scuttled 68 yards for the longest gain anywhere on New Year's Day and the touchdown that sealed the coffin on Auburn then and there. When the demoralized Tigers finally pulled themselves together and Jimmy Sidle shot off some dazzling running and passing fireworks in the second half, it was too late. The 13 points that the Huskers nailed on the scoreboard in the first two periods sufficed as Auburn was able to get only 7.

Nobody knew it before the game, but Nebraska's appearance in Miami concluded the Big Eight's exclusive tie-up with the Orange Bowl. The Huskers' victory left the conference with a 6–4 record over opponents there.

There was also another major announcement within the Big Eight family at the end of the season: Bud Wilkinson, master of the longest winning streak in college football history, was walking away from the head coaching job at Oklahoma to run for the U.S. Senate. "It just seems like the thing to do," he said. Gomer Jones, an assistant, was named to take his place.

A new era was under way at Oklahoma in

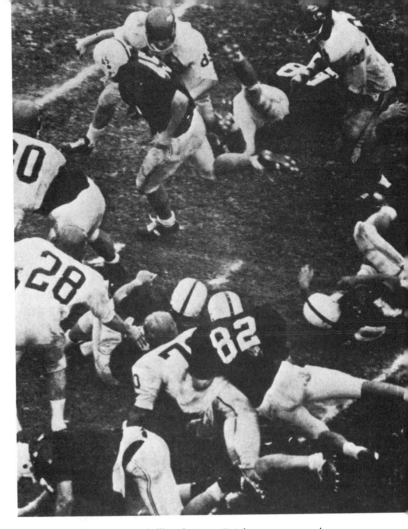

In 1963 All-America fullback Jim Grisham zoomed for 16 yards to set up the game-winning touchdown for Oklahoma in their 21–18 victory over Kansas. Grisham gained 1,572 yards on the ground in 1962–63 to top all previous Sooner fullbacks.

On the second play of the game in the 1964 Orange Bowl, Nebraska quarterback Dennis Claridge (No. 14) romped 68 yards for a touchdown. The final score: Nebraska 13, Auburn 7.

1964. Seldom had a coach started with such a legacy. Only five of the previous season's top twenty-two Sooners were gone. Among the missing, however, was Joe Don Looney. You never could tell about Joe Don. Looked at from Bud Wilkinson's standpoint, the fact that the Oklahoma coaching staff had tolerated Looney's unorthodox and unpredictable antics for several years was irrefutable testimony to Joe Don's prowess as a football player. After all, it would have been inconceivable to put up with Joe Don unless he were something really out of the ordinary. In 1962 he proved just how good he could be by leading the nation in punting, with an average of 43.4 yards, and then against Alabama in Miami he established an Oklahoma bowl record by returning four kickoffs for a total of 95 yards. A lot of the All-America teams named him on their first selections.

Joe Don was the New York Giants' No. 1 pick in the 1964 college draft. At training camp that summer he was rumored to have thrown a piano out of his hotel balcony window on a bet. The Giants unloaded him to Baltimore before the season started. At the end of the 1965 season, the Colts traded him to the Detroit Lions for middle linebacker Dennis Gaubatz.

Looney didn't last long with the Lions. Early in the 1966 season he was traded to the Redskins. Like Bud Wilkinson, professional coaches bore up with Joe Don Looney all those years because of his obvious talent, always praying that he would finally shape up. Sadly, their prayers were never answered.

Oklahoma was a heavy favorite to win the Big Eight championship in 1964. Some forecasters even went so far as to spot them among the top five teams in the country in the preseason polls. But gilt-edged as the Sooners were, there were also four other teams within the conference considered strong enough to stir up a lot of trouble: Missouri, Kansas, Nebraska, and Iowa State.

All the top teams were improved. Competition was going to be fierce. Just how fierce was underscored by Coach Clay Stapleton, who called his Iowa State team the best in seven years. "I could have won the title with this bunch six years ago," he said. "Now, I'll be fighting just to stay in the first division."

Big Eight prosperity was obvious by another fact. There were three authentic All-America backs returning—Oklahoma's Jim Grisham, Kansas's Gale Sayers, and Iowa State's Tom Vaughn. Missouri's Johnny Roland, who missed the 1963 season, was in the same category. The three linemen most prominently mentioned for All-America honors were Oklahoma's Ralph Neely, Nebraska's Larry Kramer, and Kansas's Brian Schweda.

Kansas was pinning its hopes on senior Gale Sayers, 200 pounds of thunder and lightning. In 1963 he became the first junior to rush for 2,000 yards in the Big Eight, ranking third in the nation. A native of Omaha, Sayers already held five Kansas records, including a 99-yard run from scrimmage in the 1963 Nebraska game. Before ending his college career, he would gain enough yards to rank third on KU's all-time career rushing chart (2,675 yards) and fourth in total offense (2,778 yards). Today he is listed as "the greatest football player in Kansas history." He is a member of both the college and professional football halls of fame.

Don Baker, the Kansas sports-information director, thinks Sayers's greatest game as a collegian was against Oklahoma State in 1962, when he was only a sophomore. Baker recalled:

Sayers rolled up a record 283 yards in twenty-one carries, one a 96-yarder for a touchdown. At halftime we trailed by 17 to 7. Then Gale took over. The final score was Kansas 36, Oklahoma State 17. He really lit a fire

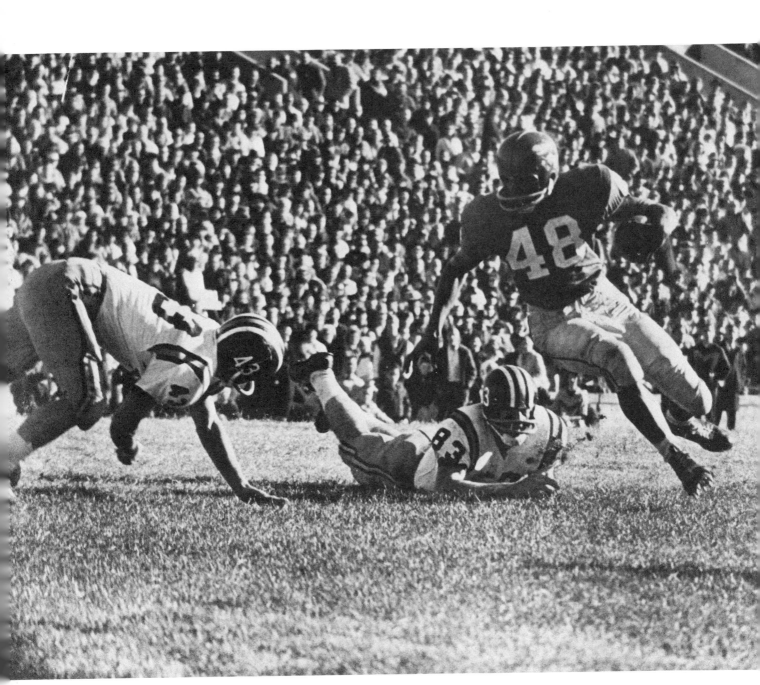

Two-time All-America (1963, 1964) Gale Sayers was devastating with a football under his arm. The Kansas halfback, 6 feet tall and 190 pounds, ran himself right into the National Football Hall of Fame.

under our kids. Gale was one of those knockdown, tackle-breaking, change-direction, aggressive runners that later became his trademark with the Chicago Bears. He was a unanimous All-America in both 1963 and 1964.

Dick Scesniak, who was just ending his career at Iowa State when Sayers was starting his at Kansas, testified that Gale did not become a "phantom-type" runner until he joined the pros. Scesniak said:

But he was a whale of a runner. You knew that if you didn't nail him at the line of scrimmage, or if he ever turned a corner on you, bye-bye ball game. Once in the clear, there just wasn't any way he was going to be caught. We simply had to contain him. Our only hope was to spread out and attempt to box him into the center. We tried to build a perimeter around him; once he broke it, it was all over. Sayers was an outstanding football player in college, but he was even superior as a professional. He really came of age as soon as he joined the Bears. Then it was a different game for him. Pro football was tailor-made for Gale Sayers.

For most of the season, Oklahoma, the preseason favorite, floundered and fumbled itself into oblivion, leaving behind enough horrendous mistakes for several seasons. They opened promisingly enough—Oklahoma 13, Maryland 3—but then lost to Southern California, 40–14; Texas, 28–7; and Kansas, 15–14. Later they were tied by Missouri, 14–14. But then they met undefeated Nebraska and put it all together. This time the Sooners held on to the ball and beat the Cornhuskers at their own system. Oklahoma pounded away diligently at Nebraska's defense, marching 88

Eddie Crowder, All-America quarterback at Oklahoma in 1952, was head coach at Colorado from 1963 to 1973. His record with the Buffs was 67–49–2 (.571 percent), and his best season was 1971 (10–2 and No. 3 in the national polls). Under Crowder the Buffs played in five bowl games—twice in the Bluebonnet, twice in the Liberty, and once in the Gator—and won three of them.

yards to go ahead, 10–7, in the last quarter. Then a substitute halfback went 48 yards on a run that gave Oklahoma the game, 17–7.

The Oklahoma victory was a case of too much, too late. Nebraska, 6–1–0, was crowned conference champion, while the Sooners, 5–1–1, had to satisfy themselves with being runner-up. The difference showed up in the bowl invitations. Nebraska was going to the Cotton Bowl, Oklahoma to the Gator.

The experts sized up the two games this way:

In the Cotton Bowl, Arkansas, which dethroned national champion Texas and shut out its opponents in five succeeding games, is a team with a hidden weapon: Ken Hatfield, who led the nation in punt returns three straight years. There are also passing and a rugged ground defense. Nebraska has speed in the backfield but a less imaginative offense. It also played a weaker schedule. The winner will be Arkansas.

In the Gator Bowl, Oklahoma's opponent was Florida State, 8–1–1. Everybody liked Oklahoma's chances.

Florida State, inching toward the big time for years, has at last arrived. Waiting there, however, is Oklahoma, which is more than anxious to atone for a disappointing season. State will discover that the Sooners' manpower is too much for either Steve Tensi's passes or Fred Biletnikoff's amazing catches and that Jim Grisham and Lance Rentzel are tough to stop.

At Dallas, Arkansas convinced some 75,504 spectators that it was the most persevering college football team in America—and proba-

One of Eddie Crowder's chief assistants at Colorado was Don James, formerly an assistant at Kansas. In 1977 James led Washington to the Rose Bowl and was named national Coach of the Year.

After seventeen golden seasons under Bud Wilkinson, Oklahoma got a new head football coach in 1964—longtime line coach Gomer Jones, shown here with All-America tackle Ralph Neely.

No Big Eight team was damaged as much by graduation in 1964 as Nebraska, the defending champion, but with players like halfback Kent McClougham, 6 feet 2 inches and 196 pounds, around, Coach Devaney was able to win another league title and go to the Cotton Bowl.

bly the best. Coach Frank Broyles's alert platoons, winners of the Southwest Conference title, moved speedily to a 3–0 lead over stunned and outraged Nebraska and seemed capable throughout the first quarter of making life miserable for the Huskers on any given play. But the slow-starting Cornhuskers began to draw inspiration from the Razorbacks' offensive errors and the open-field running of Harry Wilson, their sophomore halfback. During the regular season, Arkansas had had a reputation for flawless execution, but in the first 51 minutes against the Huskers, it was frustrated by two fumbles, an interception, a clipping penalty, and two offsides penalties. Only 9 minutes remained in the last period, with Nebraska ahead, 7–3, when the Razorbacks began doing everything right. There was still enough time on the clock to mount a winning charge. Quarterback Freddy Marshall got hot. He completed five big passes —halfback Jim Lindsey was on the end of the two most important ones—to carry his team 80 precious yards to a touchdown.

The 10–7 victory over Nebraska left the Razorbacks undefeated and untied through eleven games and a serious candidate for the mythical national championship. Among the leading teams in contention, Arkansas had the only perfect record. It had defeated not only the Big Eight champion, but Texas, conqueror of Alabama, and Tulsa, the Bluebonnet Bowl winner, as well. "I certainly consider us No. 1," said Coach Frank Broyles. The Associated Press and United Press International did not agree. In their final polls, No. 1 went to Alabama. The Razorbacks had to settle for runner-up. Nebraska finished No. 6. As for Oklahoma, a 36–19 loser to Florida State in the Gator Bowl, the Sooners failed to make even the top twenty.

In 1965, after Nebraska had won five games

in a row, and then smashed a good Colorado team, 38–13, Eddie Crowder, the Buffs' coach, said, "A good team. About three touchdowns better than last year." In six games, the Huskers had outscored opponents by a total of 221 points to 44.

The Big Eight championship came down to Nebraska versus Missouri at Columbia on the seventh Saturday of the season. The Cornhuskers went into the game as the nation's leading scorers and with the loftiest total offense average in the country, but they had not yet been tested by a team as good as Missouri. Moreover, no team had forced them to come from behind. Suddenly, against the Tigers, they were trailing, 14–0, further behind than any team coached by Bob Devaney had been in seven years. Missouri, the underdog, made it look so easy that you figured the uniforms must have been switched. Not only was MU's offense rolling early in the game, but its defense was making the Huskers look inept every time they got the ball.

But the Nebraska team was big, mobile, deep, patient, studiously unemotional, methodical, and confident. Nebraska's size was so awesome that one scout commented: "They dwarf the field. They're so big they can't use a seven-man line—they have to use a five-man line." Their uniforms were ugly, with skinny numerals, and their socks slipped down, and they stood around a lot at times, but there were moments when the ball was snapped that fantastic things happened. Gradually, Nebraska came back. It scored two touchdowns, but was still behind, 13–14, because Larry Wachholtz, the placekicker, was too deliberate on the second conversion try, and did something rare for him. His attempt was wide. That's the way the score stood until there were just 11 minutes left in the game, and Nebraska was 60 yards away from doing anything about it. Now was the time to make a move.

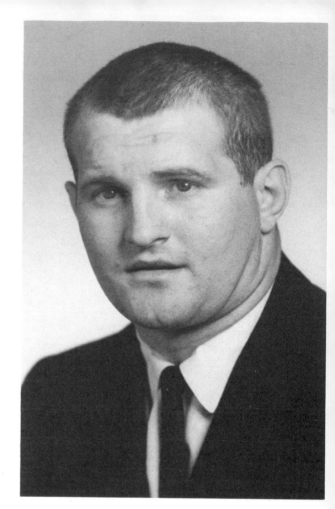

During the years 1963 through 1966, Nebraska consistently ranked among the top six teams in the national polls. All told, the Cornhuskers had a four-year record of 26–2–1 in conference competition and 38–6–0 overall. They captured four straight Big Eight championships and played in the Orange Bowl (twice), the Cotton Bowl, and the Sugar Bowl. Eight Huskers were chosen All-Americans during those years, including (FROM LEFT TO RIGHT) guard Bob Brown, tackle Larry Kramer, tackle Walt Barnes, end Tony Jeter, and middle guard Wayne Meylan.

Ron Kirkland plunged for 5 yards, Harry Wilson added 3 more, and Fred Duda ran a keeper for 8. Chuck Winters picked up another 5, and Pete Tatman smashed for 4. Sheer power. But it was fourth and 1 at the Missouri 35 now, and right there Missouri pulled a boner. What happened was that Winters carried straight ahead to the 32-yard line for first and 10, but a Missouri lineman was caught cussing and penalized 15 yards. The penalty was tacked on the end of Winters's run, and now Nebraska had the ball on the 17. The Huskers stuck to their ground game, crunching on to the 9. There Wachholtz got a chance to redeem himself. With fourth down and 2 at the 9 and only 5:56 showing on the clock, Coach Devaney played percentages. This time Wachholtz, kicking from the Missouri 26-yard line, didn't miss. Over on the sidelines a couple of Nebraska players were actually seen jumping up and down.

Upstairs in the press box, Nebraska sports-information director Don Bryant smiled. "Look," he said, "they almost look like students."

Down in the Missouri locker room, Dan Devine looked like a condemned man on death row. He leaned against a table in the silent gloom, a towel draped around his neck, a paper cup filled with water in one hand, his face drained of all emotion, and his large brown eyes fixed vacantly on a lot of things that could have happened to change the final score. He talked softly and very, very slowly. "I don't think . . . I can remember a . . . team of ours ever playing this well . . . and losing."

The only explanation seemed to be that Nebraska was overwhelming. Clumsy, but overwhelming.

The victory was probably the finest of Bob Devaney's sparkling career, the most crucial, the sweetest comeback, all of that. It all but insured him of his first perfect (10–0) record,

a goal he had come very close to but never quite realized.

Walt Barnes, Nebraska's talented middle guard, summed up the whole thing—the strength of both teams and the fierce game that it was—when he said, "Missouri almost blew us off the field all day. It's too bad a team like that has to lose."

The closest thing to an actual playoff for the national championship on New Year's Day was the Orange Bowl, where Nebraska and Alabama would decide between themselves which should be considered the country's best. The Associated Press announced it would hold off its final vote until after the bowl games. No amount of needling was able to alter the fact that in 1964 its poll had closed early, and that Alabama—though a loser to Texas, 21–17, in the Orange Bowl—was still ranked No. 1. Thus the change in AP policy. The UPI, however, continued to cast its final ballots before the bowls were played.

Nebraska, Michigan State, and Arkansas, the three unbeaten teams, were the favorites in the wire-service polls; Alabama, once beaten, was ranked fourth. Coach Paul Bryant didn't have to talk to his players about incentives. No one had to remind them how they came into the same Orange Bowl, undefeated and already voted No. 1, and were embarrassed by the Longhorns. But that was history. A victory over Nebraska would give them a legitimate claim to the national title.

It happened just that astonishingly, too. On a perfect night for football, the Crimson Tide had more fun than a weevil in a cracker barrel. Once the first lick was made, it was clear that the Southeastern Conference champions were in for a glorious hour of football. They won in the pits. They won in the air. From opening kickoff to the final gun, Alabama put on a bruising, painstaking work of art that clearly established the superiority of its line and its backs.

"The Alabama offense was probably the best I have ever seen," conceded Bob Devaney.

In the second quarter, the Tide poured into the crannies of Nebraska's pass defense as quarterback Steve Sloan riddled it to shreds. The result was 17 points for Alabama that left the Huskers forever in a rut. When it was all over, Alabama had run up 512 yards and 39 points. Normally, Nebraska's 28 points would have been enough to blow out any bowl contender, but it was the Huskers' misfortune to have met a red-hot Tide, bent on winding up at the top of the polls.

"I don't know how you'll end up in the polls, but with me you're definitely No. 1," Bear Bryant told his team after the game.

As it turned out, Nebraska scored more points on Alabama than had any team in the eight years Coach Bryant had been at the university. For a team that was not supposed to have an aerial attack, Nebraska scored three touchdowns by passing. "We pass just enough to amuse the student body," Devaney once pointed out. But against Alabama's stunting defenders, the only consistent means of moving the ball was quarterback Bob Churchich's passes. In all, the Cornhuskers compiled a total of 378 yards.

"But what's the use of scoring twenty-eight points when Alabama scores thirty-nine?" Devaney wanted to know.

Steve Sloan was outstanding. Almost deferentially he wiped out Joe Namath's Alabama passing records. Against Nebraska, he completed twenty passes for 296 yards, despite having to throw in the face of a crushing Husker rush and despite playing from the second period on with torn cartilages in his right side. Unable to follow through smoothly, he was forced to loft his passes, but when he did so, the amazingly quick Alabama receivers

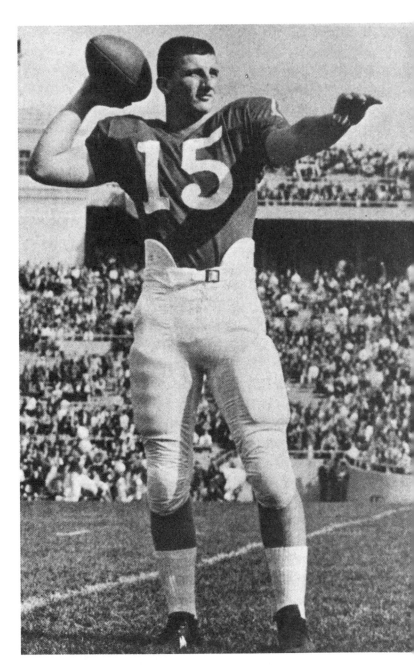

Quarterback Bob Churchich led Nebraska to another Big Eight championship in 1966 and an invitation to play Alabama in the Sugar Bowl.

Only 5 feet 8 inches tall, Missouri's amazing runner, halfback Charlie Brown, beat out Oklahoma State's Walt Garrison for Big Eight rushing honors in 1965 with a 5.39-yard average. While conference champion Nebraska was losing to Alabama in the Orange Bowl, 39–28, on New Year's Day, 1966, runner-up Missouri was beating Florida, 20–18, in the Sugar Bowl.

Missouri Coach Dan Devine, shown here talking to his 1965 All-America defensive back Johnny Roland, mastered the role of "giant killer" at Missouri. Before going to the Green Bay Packers and then Notre Dame, Devine coached the Tigers for thirteen seasons (1958–1970), with a 92–37–7 record. He won the conference title outright once (1960) and tied Nebraska for it in 1969. Under his leadership, the Tigers won four of six bowl games.

were almost always there, curling back or stretching out to make the catch. Sloan had no fewer than half a dozen excellent receivers, including All-America flanker back Ray Perkins. He caught ten passes against Nebraska for 159 yards, including two for touchdowns.

The final wire-service rankings? The Associated Press listed the teams in this order: No. 1, Alabama; No. 2, Michigan State; No. 3, Arkansas; No. 4, UCLA; No. 5, Nebraska; and No. 6, Missouri.

The UPI awarded Michigan State the national championship. Nebraska was No. 3, a notch above Alabama. Which obviously said something about final polls that were taken before the bowl games were played. Missouri also placed No. 6 in the UPI poll—an honor the Tigers lived up to by beating Florida in the Sugar Bowl, 20–18.

Defending champion Nebraska opened the 1966 season with six straight triumphs: Texas Christian, 14–10; Utah State, 28–7; Iowa State, 12–6; Wisconsin, 31–3; Kansas State, 21–10; and Colorado, 21–19. Except for Utah State and Wisconsin, the Huskers' early wins were merely wins, not blowouts. Unlike Bob Devaney's previous teams, the 1966 Cornhuskers were not yet bona-fide ogres. Tommy Prothro, the UCLA head coach, even went so far as to tell a Los Angeles newsman that Nebraska "ought to be ranked about forty-ninth instead of eighth." An obliging University of Nebraska alumnus airmailed the clipping to Coach Devaney, and he showed it to his players before taking the field against Missouri. In the understatement of the year, Devaney said, "It made our players sort of mad."

With a record crowd of 65,095 in attendance in Lincoln, the Huskers pulverized Missouri, 35–0. Encouraged by halfback Ben Gregory's two touchdowns, they busted through the Mizzou line for 271 yards, converted several Tiger errors into touchdowns, and, defensively, never let Missouri penetrate deeper than the Nebraska 34. After the game the Huskers did the proper thing. They voted the game ball to Mr. Prothro.

A week afterward, Nebraska had to fight for its life before subduing Kansas, 24–13. The Jayhawks weren't all that strong. As a matter of fact, a week before they barely escaped the ignominy of a defeat by winless Kansas State, tying 3–3 on Thermus Butler's 38-yard field goal with 8 seconds left. After the Nebraska game, Dick Bacon, the Jays' fullback, said, "Last year they were awesome. This year they are human." The Huskers then proved just how human by losing to Oklahoma, 10–9, on Thanksgiving Day.

The lead feet of Nebraska stuck out ominously throughout the loss to the Sooners, who finished fifth in the conference and were beaten by Notre Dame, 38–0. Nebraska particularly lacked speed where it needed it most—at fullback. In 1965, Devaney had a fast-starting fullback in 158-pound Frankie Solich. But with 220-pound Pete Tatman, a step slower, now in his place, Nebraska was not what it used to be. Its longest touchdown from scrimmage in 1966 was quarterback Bob Churchich's 27-yard run. The rest of the Nebraska runners, 219-pound Ben Gregory and 212-pound Harry Wilson, got their share of yardage through sheer strength.

Waiting for the slow Huskers in the Sugar Bowl was Alabama. The Tide had won the 1965 national championship, its third in five years, by beating Nebraska, and now the 1966 wire-service polls listed it No. 3, Nebraska No. 6. Most forecasters figured Alabama to beat the Huskers handily. "Nebraska makes too many mistakes," pointed out one expert. "And Alabama, which almost never makes an error, eats up teams that do."

Another consideration when weighing the strength of the two teams was that Coach Bryant had his players convinced that only Nebraska stood between them and another national championship. That meant that the Tide was primed to play its best game of the season.

That's exactly what it did, too. In fact, the match-up was more like a clinic than a bowl game, with Coach Bryant demonstrating for the nation what a top team was supposed to look like. The Sugar Bowl bore the only resemblance to a contest of importance. Alabama went into the game wanting to show the nation it was as good as, or better than, either Notre Dame or Michigan State by convincingly whipping a big, talented Nebraska team. It made its point, 34–7. Had Bryant not substituted liberally with second- and third-stringers, the score might have been much more lopsided.

There was little doubt that 'Bama would remain the only unbeaten, untied major team in America (11–0) after the first play of the game. Quarterback Kenny Stabler, a junior and everybody's choice as the best player of all the major bowls, faked, rose up, waited, then fired away like a bazooka to end Ray Perkins 45 yards downfield, and the rout was under way. No less than a dozen different Alabama backs participated in the killing. Anytime they needed a first down they got it; darting, slithering, scuttling through and around Nebraska's huge but outrun and outmaneuvered line.

For the Cornhuskers, it was a long trip home.

An old familiar name was back on top of the Big Eight in 1967—Oklahoma. The Sooners had a new coach, Chuck Fairbanks, not one to play cat-and-mouse games. He went right for the jugular. In his first five seasons at Norman, the Sooners' record was 41–14–1.

Coach Bob Devaney called Wayne Meyland "one of the finest linemen I have ever seen." Nebraska's 239-pound middle guard was All-American in 1966 and 1967.

In 1967, Oklahoma figured to be a sound team, but not an Orange Bowl entry, if only because the shocking death of their popular young head coach, Jim Mackenzie, was certain to have an upsetting effect. In Mackenzie's only term at OU the team was 6–4–0, and building. In his place now was Chuck Fairbanks.

With quarterback Bob Warmack, a frail-looking junior, performing admirably, Oklahoma won its first two games, shutting out both Washington State, 21–0, and Maryland, 35–0. Then, with archrival Texas coming up, a flu epidemic leveled the squad. Sick or not, the Sooners shoved the Longhorns all over the Cotton Bowl for a half before finally giving in to their queasiness, 9–7. "That was the game we came of age," said Fairbanks. "It really mattered. It indicated to us that we could play well against good football teams."

From then on it was just one victory after another—they didn't lose again—as Oklahoma's quick defense matured, blanking both rugged Missouri and highly touted Colorado. Over the season the Sooners gave up an average of only 6.8 points a game, making it the leading defensive team in the nation. All-America middle guard Granville Liggins and linebacker Don Pfrimmer were terrors. It was a thrill to hit people, they said; they loved collisions.

Oklahoma's opponent in the Orange Bowl was Tennessee, always tough. When Coach Doug Dickey was asked about the game, his answer did not exactly shake up headline writers. "It should be a good game," was all he said.

Despite a lot of patching up because of injuries, Dickey was reasonably sure that his Volunteers were of bowl caliber. He was certain of it after Tennessee beat Louisiana State, 17–14. In any event, the Orange Bowl was being heralded as "probably the textbook game of New Year's Day." Both teams were well balanced, perfectly drilled, and profoundly unflappable. Both had efficient, executive-style coaching staffs.

The Tennessee coach was asked if he thought the Orange Bowl might push his team to a new emotional high. His reply was typical Doug Dickey: "A bowl game is a big event for a football player. Everyone will be playing his best." Tennessee's best was expected to be just a little bit better than Oklahoma's. The Vols were ranked No. 2 in the polls.

A record crowd of 77,993 saw one of the most exciting bowl games in modern history. The blocking was crisp, the tackling fierce. There was a storybook climax, too—wild, unpredictable, breathtaking. The Sooners started fast, knocking the Volunteers dizzy in the first half, 19–0. It looked like a runaway. Bobby Warmack operated at quarterback with the skill of a magician. In the first half he piled up a total of 188 yards of total offense and had a big hand in three touchdowns. Warmack scored the first one himself, coming on a 7-yard bootleg play, his pet maneuver. A 21-yard pass from Warmack to Eddie Hinton scored the second touchdown. Steve Owens high-dived across from the 1-yard line to score the third Oklahoma TD, and a pass interception by Bob Stephenson in the fourth quarter accounted for the fourth, after Tennessee drew within 2 points (19–17) of the Sooners.

With only 4:05 left on the clock, the Vols scored again. Now it was 26–24, Oklahoma. The Sooners resorted to their ball-control ground game, eating up time. Then Oklahoma gambled on fourth down and a foot to go on the Tennessee 43. Steve Owens, who had played a whale of a game, got the call. The Tennessee line stiffened, held. Tennessee carried the ball back to the Oklahoma 40, but time was running out. Only 7 seconds remained. A strong breeze hit the Tennessee

All-Conference fullback and the league's top scorer in 1966, Colorado's Wilmer Cooks cracked the Kansas State line to pave the way for a 10–0 victory for the Buffs, but they finished second in the Big Eight.

Colorado's Bob Anderson got some excellent blocking as he swung out on a touchdown run in a 41–27 victory over Oklahoma in 1968. The Colorado upset enabled Kansas to tie Oklahoma for the Big Eight championship. During his collegiate career, Anderson made All-American as both a defensive back and a quarterback.

placekicker in the face. That was the difference. The field goal attempt fell just inches short of the crossbar. The victory left Oklahoma No. 3 in the national polls—one notch behind Tennessee!

While Oklahoma was winning in the Orange Bowl, Colorado, behind the brilliant performance of quarterback Bob Anderson, twice fought from behind to upset Miami, 31–21, in the Bluebonnet Bowl. Anderson totaled 159 yards in offense to surpass older brother Dick, the Buffs' All-America defensive halfback, in the balloting as the game's most outstanding back. There was nothing like keeping the honors in the family.

The Sooners managed to stay atop the Big Eight in 1968, only this time around they had to share the championship with Pepper Rodgers's Kansas Jayhawks. In the showdown between the old rivals, Oklahoma outshot KU, 27–23, after losing to Colorado two weeks earlier, 41–27, in a modern version of the gunfight at the O.K. Corral. While Colorado was the only conference member to beat Oklahoma, the Sooners were also blitzed by Notre Dame, 45–21; Texas, 26–20; and Southern Methodist, 28–27, in the Astro-Bluebonnet Bowl.

Operating from a new formation Coach Darrell Royal called the wishbone T, the 1968 Longhorns were the highest-scoring Texas team in fifty years, averaging 34.4 points per game. The man who made it all work was James Street, who replaced Bill Bradley at quarterback for the first time in the Oklahoma game. A baseball pitcher, Street started making the scoreboard blink with his passing and running. The change from Bradley to Street wasn't in time to save the Longhorns from a tie and a loss in their first two games, but it was in time for Street to lead Texas to its hard-fought victory over Oklahoma and go on to an 8–1–1 season and the cochampionship in the

Southwest Conference, gradually fighting its way up to No. 5 in the nation. On the Monday after Texas beat Oklahoma, Street, a handsome athlete with mod sideburns, came strolling onto the practice field as Royal and his defensive coach, Mike Campbell, sat nearby.

"I guess," said Royal, "we'd better say something to James about getting a haircut."

"Yeah," replied Campbell. "Either that or let ours grow out like his."

The University of Washington's Don James, who was Coach of the Year in 1977, was an assistant to Eddie Crowder at Colorado in the late 1960s. He talked to me recently about the comparative toughness of Big Eight football.

Before joining Crowder's staff, I coached at Kansas, Florida State, and Michigan. Because of its location, the Big Ten Conference was the most visible—but from top to bottom, not the best-balanced league. I felt the Southeastern and Big Eight leagues were stronger. Obviously, Michigan, Ohio State, and Michigan State had some great teams, but after those the caliber of the Big Ten dropped off sharply. From the standpoint of total league strength, the Southeastern and Big Eight were far superior. In the case of the latter, for example, the top teams get on TV, they get national exposure, and there are always several of them going to bowl games. The Big Eight plays really tough football. I remember 1970 and Vince Gibson had his best season at Kansas State, with Lynn Dickey, Mike Kuhn, Ron Yankowski, Oscar Gibson, Clarence Scott, and all that bunch. That year, they followed us, Colorado, through the schedule. We'd play a team on Saturday and then Kansas State played them the next week. Afterward, Vince Gibson said, thinking of the Wildcats' 5–2 conference record and a second-place tie with Oklahoma, "We'd love to play teams after

One of the country's top offensive tackles in 1968 was Colorado's All-America Mike Montler. He wound up his college career playing in the College All-Star Game, the Senior Bowl, the Hula Bowl, and the Coaches All-American Game.

An All–Big Eight linebacker in 1968 and All-Conference middle guard in 1969, Ken Geddes was one of many Nebraska starters to make the grade in pro football (Los Angeles Rams and Seattle Seahawks).

Colorado finishes with them," in reference to the manner in which we usually softened up an opponent. We even went so far as to make a study and, sure enough, the teams we played often lost the next week, because of the poor physical shape we left them in. That was also true of Nebraska and Oklahoma. It takes great depth to compete in the Big Eight. One reason some conference members don't finish higher in the polls is because they spend so much time knocking each other off.

As Nebraska's head coach, Bob Devaney had a great reputation. He was exceedingly popular with his assistants. He always went to bat for them. He paid them well; they were among the highest paid in the league. Whenever we played the Huskers, we knew we were playing one of the top two or three teams in the country—every year. We had trouble with Nebraska. While I was at Boulder, we never beat them. Eddie [Crowder] had a tough time with Devaney's teams. They'd come into your place and completely overwhelm you. It was like sending a bull terrier in against a lion and saying, "Sic 'em!"

Typical of the hard-nosed football players who graduated from the Big Eight into professional ball was Kansas State's halfback Larry Brown. In 1969 the Washington Redskins drafted him in the eighth round, and he immediately became the leading rookie rusher in the NFL. Brown was a bit of serendipity for the Redskins. Oddly enough, he had been noticed originally at Kansas State because of his blocking ability, rather than as a runner. His virtue was that he had been drafted low enough to be what was known as "a hungry ball player," someone who knew from the start he would have to go full tilt to make the Redskins. He was a serious young man, and a bit astounded with the fame and attention being showered on him around the NFL. After

all, the Big Eight publicity people hardly noticed him during the two years (1967–1968) he lettered at KSU.

Tom Dowling, author of the excellent *Coach: A Season with Lombardi,* asked Brown how the Redskins got wind of him. Brown said he didn't know. He told Dowling:

I used to get letters in college, sometimes from Dallas, the Rams, and the Colts, but that's all. Dallas stayed in real close touch. I was really looking forward to playing for the Cowboys. Why, once they even tracked me down to my uncle's house in Columbus, Ohio. I don't know how they found it, 'cause I live in Pittsburgh, and was just visiting in Columbus. I remember the first few days of the college draft in 1969, I was waiting for the call to come from the Cowboys, and then the phone rings and a voice says, "Congratulations, man, you've just been drafted by the Washington Redskins, and we're looking forward to meeting you and having you in our training camp." I thought, the Redskins? Where the hell did they come in from? So the man hung up, and I started to do some reading and find out about what kind of running backs the Redskins had. Then a few weeks later, a guy at school came up to me and said, "Man, your head coach is now Vince Lombardi." I thought, kee-ripes! Nothing has ever come easy for me. Sure enough, I catch all the hell. I had read all the articles about Coach Lombardi and I was really scared. I really didn't want to be tested by that man. I figured he sounded too severe for me. I figured Lombardi was a real mean son of a gun. And he was, but not as bad as I'd read about.

Being a rookie, I was lucky in a way, because I wasn't noticed so much at first; like, I was down on the fifth team and I was able to know a little something by the time I worked my way up to Lombardi's attention. But by the time I got up to the second team, suddenly every mistake I made seemed like he saw it. I was confronted by The Man. This was along about the third or fourth week of training camp. He was on my back all the time, and I began to have this resentment of him. "Larry," he'd shout, "you're running in the wrong damn hole, you'd better learn your assignments." Boy, he could really yell. And I'd think to myself, "If he'd just give me time, time, more time. I'm just a damn rookie fresh from Kansas State." And I'd have my head hung down and then suddenly after a while I began to notice he'd be saying, "Larry, you're a good boy," or, "Keep up the good work, Larry."

Larry Brown reported to the Redskins as a halfback, but it was his blocking that caught Lombardi's eye. One day Brown walked into the Redskins' lunchroom. The rookies were supposed to stand up at their table, introduce themselves, announce where they went to college and what their position was, and sing their school song. So Brown stood up and said, "I'm Larry Brown from Kansas State and I'm a halfback and now I'm going to sing you my school song." And as he caught his breath to start singing, from the back of the room rose this husky voice: "You aren't a halfback anymore, Brown; you're a fullback now." It was Coach Lombardi and he surprised Larry. In fact, he shook up Larry so much he didn't sing the Kansas State song very well.

"Fullback?" Brown told himself. "Hell, that kinda worries me. I don't go that big. A 195-pound fullback? I'd rather be a halfback, 'cause they carry the ball more. The fullback gets those hard-nosed inside plays and is the key blocker."

It all turned out very well for Larry Brown. He developed into one of the best fullbacks in the NFL.

Missouri was 8–3 in 1968, including a big 35–10 victory over Alabama in the Gator Bowl. Defensive back Roger Wehrli, All-American, established a Tiger season record of seven interceptions that fall.

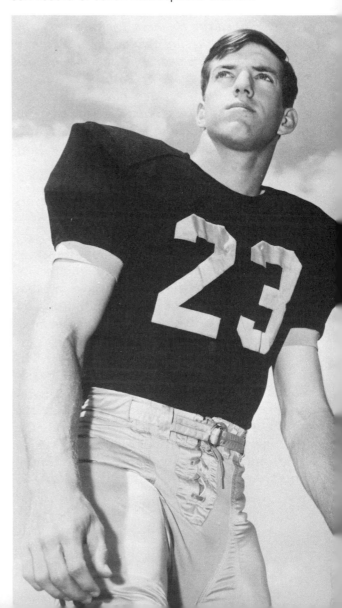

The scoreboard told it all on New Year's Day, 1969: Missouri's 35–10 victory over Alabama in the Gator Bowl.

The first three teams in the 1968 Big Eight race—Kansas (6–1–0), Oklahoma (6–1–0), and Missouri (5–2–0)—all were invited to bowls. Oklahoma lost to Southern Methodist, 28–27, in the Astro-Bluebonnet Bowl, but Missouri gave Alabama its comeuppance in the Gator Bowl, 35–10.

Because of its better overall record (9–1–0), Kansas was chosen to oppose Penn State in the Orange Bowl, the most tumultuous of all the bowl games that season. The last 80 seconds of the contest were pure madness, utter confusion. Kansas was ahead, 14–7, and was conducting an inspired goal-line stand by using twelve players against Penn State's standard eleven. Twice the twelve-man defense stopped the Lions. Then Chuck Burkhart, the Penn State quarterback, baffled everybody, including himself, by ignoring the play he had called and dashing away all by himself at the last split second to score. That made the score 14–13, with just 15 seconds left. At that point, Coach Joe Paterno, who always went for broke, decided to try for 2 points. If the Lions couldn't win, they'd lose, Paterno said afterward. It looked like "lose" when Burkhart's pass to halfback Bob Campbell was batted down by a flock of Jayhawks. But then Foster Grose, the umpire in the five-man team of officials, noticed there were lots of dark-blue Kansas helmets on the field—like a dozen or so. He later said he knew before the ball was ever snapped that he would have to call a foul on the Big Eight cochampions.

Umpire Grose's red handkerchief fluttered to the ground, alerting the Jayhawks that they might not have won the Orange Bowl after all. The penalty was marched off. Penn State went for the two-point conversion again. This time Kansas, playing now with only the regulation eleven men, was unable to stop an end sweep by Campbell. The result was the 15–14 victory, an undefeated season for Penn State, and a

No. 2 national ranking in the AP poll.

Afterward, Pepper Rodgers explained why the Jayhawks had too many players on the field when Penn State geared up its last offensive thrust with a minute left:

With first and goal to go on our 3, Penn State took time out. Paterno called Burkhart to the sidelines and outlined the next three plays. While that was going on we sent in our defensive goal-line team. And through a misunderstanding among our players on the field—two went in, only one came out.

The first two runs against Kansas failed, and Burkhart then obediently called the play Paterno had ordered up—a handoff into the line to halfback Charlie Pittman. But once the action began, Burkhart changed his mind. Instead of giving the ball to the startled Pittman, he did something he'd never done before. He kept the ball, slipped it behind his hip, and ran a bootleg around left end for the touchdown, his first in college football. Even Kansas's twelve-man defense couldn't stop that sort of deception. Then followed the two conversion attempts.

The halftime score was 7–7. In the second half, Don Shanklin, the Kansas halfback, returned a Penn State punt 47 yards to the Lions' 7-yard line to set up the go-ahead touchdown. But that was all Kansas got.

After the game, the Kansas dressing room was shrouded in gloom. Through clenched teeth, Pepper Rodgers said: "Let's just say that it was great TV fare—we turned what would've been dull entertainment into an exciting victory for Penn State."

Joe Paterno felt there was enough glory in the game for *both* teams. "No one should be ashamed," he said. "We were both great teams tonight."

In 1969, as college football marked its one-hundredth anniversary and began a new century, the mechanics of the game were pretty much the same over the entire country. That is, everybody was throwing the ball, everybody was catching it, and everybody was running with such amazing success that scoreboards had taken on the appearance of a neon sign in Times Square.

Those in charge of the rules probably hadn't intended this when they gradually resurrected free substitution and, in 1968, added more plays per game by stopping the clock after every first down, but that was what they got. The fall of 1968 had produced so much offense that even the pros looked stodgy. The average number of points scored in a game jumped to 42.4, the average total offense per game leaped to 657 yards, the average passing yardage climbed to 315.4, and the number of total-offense plays reached a peak of 150.1.

Just about every team had somebody trying to be a passer, it seemed, and a record sixteen ball carriers, headed by Southern California's O. J. Simpson, gained more than 1,000 yards apiece. The paranoia that beset coaches who thought they taught good defense was best exemplified by Frank Broyles of Arkansas, whose Razorbacks led Southern Methodist into the fourth quarter by 35 points, yet barely held on to win, 35–29. "A 35-point lead just isn't safe anymore," Broyles said afterward.

In an effort to try to keep the ball with a strong ground attack, Coach Darrell Royal of Texas developed a formation, the wishbone T, that a lot of college coaches were copying in 1969. Basically, it was a straight T formation utilizing the triple-option play of the quarterback, but a receiver was split wide and the fullback was moved a step closer to the line of scrimmage. Thus, in 1969 nearly all the major powers started trotting out their versions of the wishbone T, just as everybody had gone to the I formation of USC's John McKay several years earlier.

In the Big Eight, almost everybody was picking Dan Devine's Missouri Tigers to finish atop the standings. A few liked Oklahoma, and several voted for Colorado. Nobody mentioned Nebraska. So what happened? Missouri and Nebraska tied for the championship (6–1–0) and Colorado finished third (5–2–0).

Oklahoma opened its schedule fast, defeating Wisconsin, 48–21, and Pittsburgh, 37–8, before losing to Texas, 27–17. Then the Sooners beat Colorado, 42–30, were humbled by Kansas State, 59–21, and bounced back to blitz Iowa State, 37–14. That brought the Sooners up to the Missouri game, and the chant in Oklahoma's locker room was, "Bring on the Tigers." The victory over Iowa State had left them feeling giddy. They beat the Cyclones in so many ways that it was almost embarrassing. In the air, Oklahoma quarterback Jack Mildren hit thirteen of eighteen, but even that was peanuts compared to what Heisman candidate Steve Owens did. He carried fifty-three times for 248 yards (both Oklahoma records), scored four touchdowns, and, just for the hell of it, completed his only pass. Naturally, the press wanted to know if Steve was a little tired. "I could have carried twenty-five more times," said Owens, cheerfully.

While Oklahoma was having all that fun, Missouri was getting a stiff dose of Kansas State's Lynn Dickey and not liking it very much. He passed for 394 yards, breaking an assortment of Big Eight records along the way, and even Missouri's 41–38 victory didn't placate Dan Devine, who asked, "What happened to defense?"

On the same day, Colorado coach Eddie

Missouri tied Nebraska for the Big Eight championship in 1969 by beating the Cornhuskers 17–7. Here John Brown (No. 89), the Tiger defensive end, jars the ball loose from Nebraska quarterback Jerry Tagge.

Two-time All-America and 1969 Heisman Trophy winner Steve Owens was the workhorse of the 1967–1969 Oklahoma backfield. Ball carrier, blocker, game breaker, "Stout Steve" stands ready to ward off Kansas tacklers as Oklahoma quarterback Bobby Warmack (No. 11) gets off a pass that beat the Jayhawks, 27–23, in 1968.

Crowder decided to use Bobby Anderson as a decoy, which was just fine with Nebraska. The Cornhuskers won, 20–7, as Anderson carried only twelve times for 42 yards. Crowder invited a cat-calling Nebraska fan to come out of the stands, then muttered "no comment" when asked about Anderson. Nebraska coach Bob Devaney was more talkative: "We're as good as anybody now."

Coming down to the final weekend of the regular season, Missouri and Nebraska were all tied up in the battle for the Big Eight title. Earlier, the Tigers defeated the Huskers, 17–7, but then lost to Colorado, 31–24, to make the scramble for first place as snarled as rush-hour traffic.

As was his style, Dan Devine expressed concern on the eve of the season's wrap-up against Kansas. A loss could cost Missouri the conference championship, or at least a piece of it. So he tried some psychology on his players. He posted signs in the red and blue Kansas colors, which reminded the Tigers of their 1967 and 1968 defeats. "Kansas," said Devine of a team that ranked last in the Big Eight in rushing defense, "has better defensive personnel than Michigan." Kansas's Pepper Rodgers tried manfully to preserve his reputation as a humorist. "We are not taking Missouri lightly," he cracked. "About all we had to laugh at this week is the build-up the Missouri staff has been giving us." Whether Coach Rodgers was still chuckling after the Jayhawks' 69–21 defeat was doubtful. Terry McMillan threw for four touchdowns and ran for two more.

Rodgers was humiliated. He resented Dan Devine for running up the score. Ill feelings surfaced between them. Rodgers later was quoted as saying that Devine couldn't win the big games; Pepper, however, said he was misquoted. Then, during a banquet speech,

Rodgers told a story about that 69–21 drubbing. "During the game," Rodgers recalled, "I flashed the peace sign to Devine, and he gave half of it back to me."

While Missouri was blasting Kansas, Nebraska had an easy time, 44–14, against Steve Owens and the Oklahoma Sooners. The Huskers allowed Owens just 70 yards in 21 carries and ended his streak of 17 straight 100-yard games.

A week later, however, Steve was his old self. In his last game for Oklahoma, against Oklahoma State, he plowed up and down the field. But he and his teammates still found themselves in deep trouble with only 1:15 to go. The Cowboys had just scored on quarterback Bob Cutburth's pass to split end Hermann Eben, reducing the Sooners' lead to 28–27, and now they were lined up to go for a 2-point conversion. Suddenly, one of the game officials blew his whistle. Oklahoma State was marched back to its 8-yard line for delay of game. Even so, State gamely went for the win. Cutburth, finding no receivers open, was hit by Sooner end Albert Qualls and fumbled away his team's last chance.

"I'm eighty years older," sighed Chuck Fairbanks, the winning coach.

Two of the leading candidates for the Heisman Trophy were Oklahoma's Steve Owens and Kansas State's Lynn Dickey. Pacing the surprise team in the country (5–5–0), Dickey proved he could throw with the best. Against the Sooners, he piloted 535 yards in total offense on the way to that stunning 59–21 upset, and then there were those 394 yards against Missouri. He set conference records with sixty-one attempts and 439 yards gained through the air against Colorado. Still, the Buffs won, 45–32, as quarterback Jimmy Bratten threw for 251 yards and five touchdowns to send them into the Liberty Bowl, where they bounced Alabama, 47–33, on the strength of a brilliant performance by All-America Bob Anderson.

When all the Heisman Trophy votes were counted, the winner came up Steve Owens. His team lost four games, but there was no rule that said a Heisman winner had to go unbeaten. Owens's big claim to the award as the country's best college player was his three-year total of 3,867 yards rushing. He also scored 56 touchdowns for 336 points. All told, he carried the ball 905 times at Oklahoma, still a school record. His record of 55 carries against Oklahoma State in 1969 is also still in the books. Owens's 56 touchdowns destroyed Army's Glenn Davis's three-year mark of 51, and his rushing figures wiped out Gale Sayers's Big Eight records. Before the 1969 season even started, Owens's teammates were saying "Steve deserves the Heisman," and they went to work and helped him win it.

In the Orange Bowl, exceptional Missouri defensive play and wild kick returns by the Tigers' Jon Staggers weren't quite enough to topple tough Penn State, the No. 2 team in the country. The final score was 10–3. It was a strange sort of game. Although MU's blazing speed posed a constant threat to the Lions, fumbles and interceptions were the Tigers' downfall. All of Penn State's points came within a 21-second span late in the first quarter. Missouri outrushed the Pennsylvanians, 189 yards to 57, but Penn State had the larger numbers where they counted most—on the scoreboard.

The third Big Eight representative to play in a bowl game was Nebraska, and the Huskers embarrassed Georgia, 45–6, in the Sun Bowl. Paul Rogers kicked a record four field goals. Nebraska's six pass interceptions and two fumble recoveries were other reasons for the poor showing by the Bulldogs.

With two out of three bowl victories, the Big Eight was dreaming big dreams as it moved into the new decade.

The Decade of the Big Two: The 1970s

College football began a new decade in an atmosphere of new heroes and new promises. But it was also a decade of new fears. There was much speculation that campus disturbances might spill over onto the gridiron. Administrators and students alike wondered what issues would dominate campus life in the autumn of 1970: war and peace, the election, racism, ROTC—what? Some campus leaders felt the key issue would be something different—whether or not to abolish football. "Football is too expensive," one of them complained. "We must decide whether that's the best way of using our money, especially with rising tuition."

One major football power estimated that it cost $12,000 per player annually to budget its football program. Recruiting costs were skyrocketing (not always legally). Nebraska's Coach Tom Osborne remembers a case where a prospect was offered $10,000 to play football for a certain university. "The most exorbitant illegal offer I ever heard of," Osborne said. "I've heard of athletes being offered cars and real estate deals—but ten thousand dollars cold cash? There are a lot of devious people out there."

Terry Donahue, the UCLA coach, said he could top that. "I once heard a story of a prospect who reputedly got a total package worth about thirty thousand dollars," Donahue said. "That included land, farm equipment, tractors, and livestock. I know an assistant coach who'll swear that it happened."

College coaches were also concerned about the mood of young people and how it might affect their game. There were so many problems of a complex and sophisticated nature that some alarmists wondered aloud if college football would ever be the same again. Penn State's Joe Paterno pointed out that a coach was now faced with a new kind of nightmare. "All I know is, you can't talk to players like you once could," Paterno said. "You can't sit on them. They're exposed to too many things. They're too smart, too aware. If they're not convinced that self-discipline is for their own good, they're not going to play well."

While some students became vigilantes and others politicians, and some schools became coed (Yale), college football plunged on. Each season the competition was getting stiffer because, more and more, there was an increasing number of teams capable of beating any rival on any given day. Under the stimulus of this leveling competition on an ever-widening scale, the college game's officially reported attendance rose approximately 35 percent over the previous decade, from 20,403,409 in 1960 to a high of 27,626,160 in 1969. Continued gains were in prospect for the 1970s.

Fortunately, the NCAA Rules Committee left the football code alone again. Aside from minor technical corrections and language clarification, there were no significant rule changes in 1970, so all was set for the new decade's kickoff.

When the preseason polls came out, Nebraska was picked No. 5, Missouri No. 11, Colorado No. 13, and—surprise—Kansas State No. 18.

In his eight seasons at Nebraska, Bob Devaney's successes had been abundant—six bowl games, five Big Eight championships, and never a team with fewer than six victories. The Huskers in 1970, Devaney readily admitted, "will be one of my best." His Irish optimism could be attributed to split end Guy Ingles and flanker Johnny Rodgers, his talented pass catchers. Ingles, a senior, was

All-America and Heisman Trophy candidate Jack Thompson of Washington State threw strikes against Kansas at Lawrence in 1977, but it wasn't enough—the Jayhawks won, 14–12. The Kansas defense, which held WSU to four field goals, was the key to victory. The KU win came right after WSU had upset Nebraska and Michigan State.

The 1970 Nebraska coaching staff. FRONT ROW: Jim Ross, Carl Selmer, Bob Devaney, John Melton, Cletus Fischer. BACK ROW: Bill Thornton, Paul Schneider (trainer), Mike Corgan, Tom Osborne (now head coach at Nebraska), Warren Powers (now head coach at Missouri), George Sullivan (therapist), Monte Kiffin.

passed over by most college scouts when he attended Omaha Westside High School because he weighed only 140 pounds. But two Nebraska coaches happened to be in the stands when he scored four touchdowns and rushed for 170 yards against Omaha Tech, and they invited him to try out for the Cornhuskers. "Actually," Ingles recalled, "they were at the game to look at guys on the other team. If I hadn't had a good day it was likely I never would have played college ball."

Rodgers, a 1970 sophomore, also grew up in Omaha; a kid from the ghetto who learned his football in the streets "dodging trash cans and telephone poles." At Tech High he became a football celebrity, making the high school All-America team twice. Banquets were held in his honor and he accumulated thirty trophies. But when he had worked his way up to the Nebraska varsity, he said, "Now I'll have to prove myself all over again. Trophies and newspaper clippings don't count. Ain't nobody who knows what Johnny Rodgers has done." The Big Eight was soon to learn about him. Together with Ingles and a cluster of proven running backs, he was destined to become an important part of the league's most devastating offense.

Football fever ran high in Lincoln. Pep rallies were still being held on Friday evenings, and Dr. Joseph Soshnik, the president of the University of Nebraska, visited the locker room after the games. The Corncobs, a student organization, contributed $1,500 for athletic scholarships. In the spring of 1970, 3,500 Nebraska students demonstrated against the war in Vietnam, while the annual intrasquad varsity football game, held the same afternoon, drew nearly 14,000.

This enthusiasm for football was not limited to the students. On Saturdays some sixty thousand Nebraskans of all ages, decked out in red, drove to Lincoln from towns named Aurora, Beatrice, and Wahoo and streamed into Memorial Stadium to watch their Huskers play football. Typical of them were four farmers from the village of Shelby who hadn't missed a home game since 1962, Bob Devaney's first season. One Saturday their car caught fire on the way to Lincoln, so they abandoned it at the side of the road and hitchhiked to town.

"We are fortunate," said Devaney at the time. "Enthusiasm goes with football, and the atmosphere of the university and the state is largely responsible for the success of our program."

Nebraska opened the 1970 season beating Wake Forest, 36–12, then tied Southern California, 21–21. Meanwhile, rugged, physical, head-hunting Colorado shocked the nation by burying Penn State, 41–13. Coach Joe Paterno's Nittany Lions, seeking their twenty-fourth straight victory, had not known what it was like to lose since 1967. The Buffs of Eddie Crowder simply took the streak and crushed it like an avalanche coming down on a Rocky Mountain mine shack. Colorado started beating the Easterners on the first play of the afternoon with an interception and did not stop beating them until the final gun. The game was the biggest thing that ever happened to Colorado football. It was the big chance; national television, national press, and highly rated Penn State. Boulder had not known such moments of football glory since Whizzer White took the Buffaloes to the Cotton Bowl on New Year's Day, 1938. So there were the Colorado fans doing something they had never before had occasion to do. They were chanting, "We're No. 1!" Just like the folks at Ohio State and Texas and Southern California and Nebraska.

And there was Joe Paterno, gracious and honest in his new role as the loser of a football game. "We were outcoached, outplayed, out-

Bob Newton was All-America tackle on Nebraska's 1970 national championship team. In 1978 he played an important role in the success of the Seattle Seahawks, the top expansion team in NFL history.

hit, and outscored," he told reporters after the game. "It's as simple as that."

The Buffs couldn't stand prosperity. The very next Saturday, Kansas State, the surprise team of the Big Eight, brought them back down to earth, 21–20. The Wildcats fought on to tie Oklahoma for second place in the final conference standings, with 5–2 records. Much of the credit for K State's amazing rebirth of Purple Pride went to Coach Vince Gibson and Lynn Dickey, the quarterback who wore white football shoes just as Joe Namath did. In two seasons he had broken just about every Big Eight passing record.

Dickey grew up in Osawatomie, Kansas, where his father worked as a brakeman-conductor for the Missouri-Pacific Railroad. Osawatomie, a community of fewer than five thousand residents, claims historic significance as the place where John Brown started out. There is still a statue of him, a lookout north of town named after him, and a restored cabin where he once lived. As a small boy Dickey played touch-tackle football in John Brown Park. "Sports was all there was to do in town," Dickey said. "I was the Joe Athlete type in high school. I never had a beer until after the season of my senior year."

Coach Gibson drove over to Osawatomie in search of a star to transform his Purple Pride theme into reality. "The first thing I noticed about Coach Gibson was that he was so down to earth," Dickey recalled. "I was impressed by that, and by his enthusiasm."

Once Gibson signed Dickey, the rest of his football team fell into place. The word soon got around to other prospects. One kid called another and the whole thing mushroomed. For the first time in years, Kansas State had a genuine contender.

Down at Norman, Chuck Fairbanks felt he not only had a contender, but a bowl winner. The feeling didn't linger for long, however.

Shortly after Oklahoma's third game, Fairbanks pondered his team's 2–1 record, squirmed nervously when he thought about his sputtering offense, became downright uncomfortable when he looked ahead to Texas, Colorado, Kansas State, and Nebraska—and decided to shoot craps. Until then he had tried to parlay an inexperienced offensive line, a group of quick receivers and runners, and the cool of quarterback Jack Mildren into a pass-oriented offense.

For Mildren, 1969 had been a very long season. He had been looked upon as the hero to lead Oklahoma to a Big Eight title and national ranking, a super quarterback who, somehow, got out of Texas and away from Darrell Royal. And yet his adventure ended with innumerable handoffs to Heisman winner Steve Owens and a mediocre 6–4 record.

"When we got into the 1970 season," Fairbanks said later, "we found ourselves too dependent on the passing game. We had to get run-oriented, and the best way to do it was with the wishbone."

So right there Chuck Fairbanks started all over again. There was a team meeting, some grumbling, more explaining, and then a quick roll of the dice. Oklahoma picked a heck of a time to introduce its version of the wishbone offense. That was against Texas, the master of the wishbone, and the result was a 41–9 embarrassment. But after that, the Sooners lost only in the last seconds to Kansas State, 19–14, and by a touchdown to national champion Nebraska, 28–21.

Not until cornerback Jimmy Anderson intercepted a Mildren pass in the end zone were the Huskers' victory over Oklahoma and an undefeated season secure. Nebraska's winning touchdown came in the fourth quarter after a super third-and-14 pass from Jerry Tagge to fullback Dan Schneiss. "In our offense the fullback doesn't get to carry the ball very much, so I have to take advantage of the opportunities I have," said Schneiss. He snared a 24-yard pass amid three defenders, putting Nebraska on the Oklahoma 3. Tagge took it in from there.

"The coaches told us, watch the short passes, don't give Mildren any running room, and keep them out of the end zone," said Eddie Periard, the Huskers' 5 feet 9 inch, 201-pound middle guard. "We did all three."

Despite their loss to Nebraska, the Sooners maintained a positive attitude. They wound up their schedule by crushing Oklahoma State, 66–6. They performed flawlessly. "I'm proud of the way we progressed from the first of the season to now, when we had our best game," Fairbanks said. As usual, Oklahoma won on the ground, rushing eighty-four times for 519 yards. Speedy Greg Pruitt gained 116 yards, and classmate Joe Wylie was right behind him with 105. Both were only sophomores. Oklahoma State's Dick Graham said Oklahoma was the fastest team the Cowboys had played all year. "And they don't make mistakes," he added. The future appeared bright for the Sooners.

The question of who was No. 1 in the nation boiled down to New Year's Day, 1971. After the regular season, unbeaten but once-tied Nebraska had wound up No. 3 in the polls, behind Texas and Ohio State. But then quarterback Joe Theismann and Notre Dame hooked the Texas Horns in the Cotton Bowl, 24–11, and Jim Plunkett, a better passer than Ohio State had ever seen, led Stanford past the Buckeyes in the Rose Bowl, 27–17. Thus, in the daffy space of only 6 hours, the national championship was all there for Nebraska to take. "It's all yours," Bob Devaney told his players just before they dashed onto the field to oppose Louisiana State in the Orange Bowl. "All you have to do now is go out and win it." So instead of playing for No. 3, the Cornhuskers suddenly found themselves playing for No. 1 against the LSU Fighting Tigers.

Unlike the big games earlier in the day, the night-time Orange Bowl was not endowed with major personalities. Both squads were relatively young. Their best players were coming back the following season. Louisiana State's all-around star was handsome Tommy Casanova. He could do it all on offense or defense—either as a runner or a defensive back, depending on the urgency of the moment. The pride of LSU was its defense, where most of the athletes were.

Nebraska had a more polished, dazzling attack, with breakaway runners Joe Orduna and Johnny Rodgers and the dual quarterbacks Jerry Tagge and Van Brownson. Nebraska plunged, reversed, and passed, and only Texas outscored Nebraska on the season. But Coach Devaney also had a tough defense, featuring tackle Dave Walline. The way the experts had it figured, Nebraska had as much muscle and more imagination than LSU,

"The Huskers will go out there and outscore stodgy LSU for sure," predicted one network commentator. "Nebraska deserved to be No. 1 right along."

That's exactly what Nebraska did. Late in the game, just when it appeared that the Cornhuskers were about to choke, they suddenly steamed up a drive behind Jerry Tagge and went on to win, 17–12. The difference of those 5 points was all that it took to show all those magazine and network guys and all of those guys who voted in the polls who really was No. 1. The victory over LSU hoisted Nebraska all the way to the top of most major polls.

After Nebraska finished first in the 1970 rankings, there were no more of those "meet the rubes" anecdotes by big-city folk about the Cornhuskers. A stranger finding himself in Lincoln didn't have to ask who was No. 1 in

Nebraska's Jerry Tagge tumbles into the end zone, giving the Huskers a 17–12 Orange Bowl victory over Louisiana State and the 1970 national championship.

The 1970 national champions—the Nebraska Cornhuskers.

college football. I was on an extensive lecture tour throughout Big Eight country in the fall of 1971, and everywhere I traveled in Nebraska there was evidence of Husker fever. The whole state had broken out in a rash not only of bumper stickers and buttons but of such esoterica as wooden No. 1 statues, clocks with Big Eight symbols around a "Nebraska No. 1" center, and Nebraska helmets with the number *1* on them made into table lamps. Coach Bob Devaney finally felt obliged to declare an official back-to-earth day.

But overconfidence was not going to be a hazard for the Huskers in 1971. The players reaffirmed their down-to-earthness earlier in the year by chipping in to buy flowers for all the cafeteria helpers on Mother's Day. That was about the team's only real weakness—sentimentality.

The 1971 defending national champions' most obvious excess was at quarterback—not one, not two, but *three* excellent operators. Jerry Tagge, who grew up in Green Bay, Wisconsin, would be starting again. On the way to completing 61 percent of his passes in his first two varsity seasons, he now held nearly all Nebraska passing records. He was also a strong runner. Spelling him off were Van Brownson and sophomore David Humm, both flamboyant passers and runners.

In the backfield, slotback Johnny Rodgers appeared slipperier than ever. One thing that set him apart was his size, 5 feet 9 inches and 173 pounds, and his versatility. His specialty was a thing the NCAA records bureau called "all-purpose running"—returning kicks, catching passes, and, whenever possible, running from scrimmage. Leaping, tumbling, weaving, and wriggling, Rodgers was rapidly becoming the super-gnat of college football.

Up front, there was an oversupply of talent: stalwarts like Rich Glover, Monte Johnson, Bob Pabis, Joe Duffy, John Peterson, et cetera,

et cetera. Safety Bill Kosch and cornerbacks Joe Blahak and Jim Anderson gave the Huskers the best defensive backfield in the nation. No doubt about it, teams like Minnesota, Utah State, Hawaii, and the rest would be finding out what 1970's opponents had discovered as Nebraska powered itself to the top.

It's all in the record book. The 1971 Cornhuskers were bruising, efficient, regular sod busters. In thirteen games, including a 38–6 romp over Alabama in the Orange Bowl, they outscored their opponents, 507 to 104. Devaney found out that his 1971 team was probably the best he had had, among a lot of good ones. Except for the Oklahoma (35–31) game, which was described earlier in this book, Nebraska simply manhandled opponents in a methodical, physical way. Defensive tackle Larry Jacobson summed up the Huskers' attitude this way: "There was never a doubt in our minds that we'd win every time we put on our uniforms." As for the team's nonstar system, Jerry Tagge explained: "It's almost become a tradition under Coach Devaney that we don't have any stars on the team. We just have a lot of good football players who concentrate and carry out their assignments."

Off the field, the Cornhuskers were not all that close. They did not pal around with each other much. The lineup consisted of married men, fraternity men, and independents, and they lived all over town. Tagge's roommate, for example, wasn't even on the team. "We see each other mostly at practice and then we go off to do other things," Tagge said. "I think our success—two national championships in a row—can be attributed to the fact that we just have a lot of good players and good coaches and great fans."

Just how good were the 1971 Huskers? Perhaps Coach Bear Bryant said it best after they demolished Alabama on New Year's Day in Miami. The count of 38–6 was the worst loss of

Nebraska's 1971 team brought the national championship to the Huskers for a second year in a row.

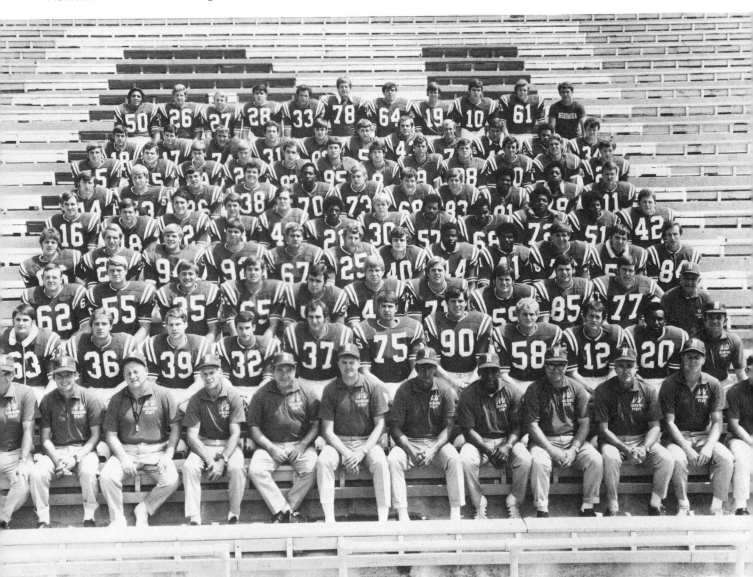

his Alabama career and equal to the worst of his entire life.

"We were beaten soundly by a far superior team," Bryant said honestly. "I wouldn't have minded our bunch playing lousy if we could have lucked out and won. But they toyed with us most of the time. Nebraska might have been the greatest college team I've ever seen."

Bob Devaney, the coach, was a mild, cordial man. He seldom talked about himself or his triumphs. Whenever a reporter pressured him for the true story of his remarkable climb to the top of the coaching profession, Devaney invariably left out all the lightning strokes of genius. According to his version of the Bob Devaney Story, Bob Devaney was just a li'l ol' country boy from upstate Michigan who lucked out. It was his style to remind listeners that in the first game he played for tiny Alma (Michigan) College in 1936, he had three teeth knocked out, cleanly, and that he never intended to become a coach at all. As a matter of fact, he was an economics major. To get through college, he waited tables, pumped gas, and swept the gym floor. He left Alma owing the school $350.

For the next fourteen years, he taught and coached in high schools in Michigan. At Big Beaver High in Birmingham, his first stop after college, he coached football and basketball and taught six subjects a day—civics, history, biology, and such. He once figured that on the basis of a sixty- to seventy-hour week, he made fifty cents an hour and deserved every penny.

"At least at Big Beaver I found out how little I knew about football coaching," Devaney said. "I discovered there was more to it than you block that man and you block this one."

After that he moved around Michigan, to Saginaw, to Keego Harbor, logging coaching years, and wound up at Alpena High, hard by Lake Huron, where he won an amazing fifty-two of sixty-one football games and an offer from head coach Duffy Daugherty to join the Michigan State coaching staff. "That's where my real life began," Devaney remembers. "I was thirty-seven. I had made up my mind that if a break didn't come before I was forty I was going to go back and get my Master's and take a boring administrative job someplace."

Eventually, Devaney got another offer. This time it was from the University of Wyoming. The Cowboys wanted him to be their head football coach. He accepted. He was forty-one.

The Devaney tradition of building winning teams continued. The grateful folk of Laramie lauded and loved him and gave him a "lifetime contract." Despite a 35–10–5 record in five years, Devaney declared his life over at Wyoming in 1962 and accepted the challenge at Nebraska. By now he was forty-six years old, but as one rival coach pointed out, "Devaney's young, no matter how old he is." Devaney took his own coaching staff with him to Lincoln. Among the hired help was Jim Walden, who had been his star quarterback at Wyoming. Now the head coach at Washington State, Walden testifies that Devaney was something special when it came to recruiting:

We recruited heavily within the state. Coach Devaney believed fiercely in homegrown athletes. He was that way when I played for him at Wyoming—and he continued the tradition at Nebraska. He learned that a kid plays better in a state where he's known. At Lincoln, he built his strength around the in-state youngsters. He made Nebraska football a national institution. A smart, exceptionally quick-witted man, he could talk crop rotation with farmers and profit and loss with financiers—if their sons were football players. He said he found recruiting very educational. One night he sat in this farmhouse listening to the mother of a hot prospect play church songs on the family organ. After a while, he even jumped in and sang hymns with her.

Did the boy go to Nebraska? Here's Devaney's version: "No, the boy enrolled at Missouri." Pause. Then, "It was the *mother* who came to Nebraska."

Devaney took his very first team of Cornhuskers to an 8–2 record and the Gotham Bowl in New York, where Miami's George Mira passed them silly for 320 yards. Yet Nebraska won, 36–34. After the game, Devaney told his players that they had made him famous. "I've received lots of offers to lecture on defense," he said.

The fact slipped up on a lot of people, but Devaney, by 1971, had become the winningest coach in college football. Which was to say that among those with at least ten years' experience, he had won with greater regularity than anyone else. Out of the depths of seventeen losing seasons in the previous twenty-one under his predecessors, the Huskers had soared to 10 straight winning seasons under Devaney. In those previous twenty-one years they had gone to one bowl game; Devaney had taken them to eight. Counting 1971, they had three times had undefeated regular seasons; before that, the last unbeaten Nebraska team was in 1915. They had won or shared seven Big Eight championships, and Devaney was named conference Coach of the Year five times. Big Ten teams used to travel to Lincoln to give the Cornhuskers lessons in football fundamentals; now they had lost ten out of ten in games with Devaney's teams, and by such scores as 42–14 and 37–0.

Boiled down, the key to Devaney's success was his ability to get along with his staff and players. Jim Walden thought so much of him that in 1971, after Devaney had won his sec-

Middle Guard Rich Glover, 1971–1972 All-American from Nebraska, won the Outland Award in his senior year as the nation's best interior lineman. (Larry Jacobson won it the year before, giving Nebraska an unprecedented double.) Glover went on to play in the NFL, with the New York Giants and the Philadelphia Eagles.

ond straight national championship, Walden quit the American College Football Coaches Association because the membership failed to name Devaney Coach of the Year. "I was ashamed of them," Walden said.

Nebraska players had the same sort of loyalty toward their head coach. Devaney's ability with them seemed to be a matter of caring. He *cared* that his athletes graduated, and 75 percent did, an impressive number. Bob Newton, All-America tackle on the 1970 national champions, told me recently that as a Cornhusker he had thought a lot of Devaney:

He was a great organizer, and he knew football, but that wasn't what impressed me most about him. What impressed me was his concern for his players. When he was recruiting me, he said, "I'm more interested in your education." I'd heard other players talk about coaches saying the same thing to them, and when they got to the college they discovered it was just a pot of bull, but after I enrolled at Nebraska I found Devaney had been telling me the truth. He was not only genuinely interested in my education, but everybody's education. I saw times when he went to recruits and told them he'd have to cut them. He and his staff had overestimated their ability. "But you still get to keep your football scholarship," he told them. "You still get your education. And if you need a fifth year, you get that, too." That was Bob Devaney.

A 1969 Nebraska teammate of Newton's, guard Ken Geddes, recalled that Coach Devaney was known to carry certain substitutes on traveling rosters just because the game was being played in their home town. Geddes told me:

Speaking for most Nebraska players, we'd have died for Devaney. I recall a very moving

experience at a luncheon in El Paso in 1969, before we beat Georgia in the Sun Bowl. Coach Devaney was introduced and received a three-minute standing ovation—from our own players.

Coach Devaney was a positive kind of coach. He was a man unafraid to take a chance. When I was a senior, Kansas had us by 3 points, 17–14, only 2 minutes to play, and us with fourth down and 13 on our own 20. Most coaches would have punted and hoped for a break. Not Coach Devaney. Tagge ran all around and finally threw an incomplete pass. Interference was called and Kansas got an additional 15-yard penalty for protesting, and when it was over we had a first down on their 12. We scored—and Kansas lost, 21–17.

Ironically, when I was a senior at Boys Town, Nebraska, I had no thought of playing for the Huskers. I remember still the University of Colorado phoning me and wanting to know what colleges had contacted me. "Has Nebraska contacted you?" they asked. I said no. "Well," they said, "what if they do?" And I said, "That's the last place I want to play football." Actually, I had nothing against the University of Nebraska; it's a great university. But the fact was we had a kid go down to Lincoln from Boys Town and screw up. He had all the tools to be a great football player, but he messed up and was dismissed from the university. To put it bluntly, he was kicked out of school. In my mind, that was a black mark on Boys Town—on all of us. I thought to myself, "If I go to Nebraska, they're going to say, ah, Ken Geddes. He's from Boys Town, he's probably like the last guy. We'll have to keep a close eye on him." Under the circumstances, I didn't want to go to Nebraska. My No. 1 choice was Missouri. I always wanted to play for the Tigers. But the Tigers didn't want me. I had football offers from every school in the Big Eight—except Missouri. Call it reverse psychology, call it anything, but the more Missouri ignored me, the more I wanted to play for them. They never did contact me. Now, here's the punch line. In my three varsity years at Nebraska—1967, 1968, 1969—not once did we beat Missouri in football.

Ken Geddes, who came from a family of seventeen children, remembers the Bob Devaney and the Dan Devine of 1971 as an interesting example of contrasting personalities. The Missouri players called Devine The Man, a term that indicated their respect for him and the fact that he was, on a personal level, complex and mysterious. "None of us really know him," lamented one of his players. "We're not scared of him, but when you go into his office you do have a funny feeling."

The Missouri players also had to wonder about Devine at practice one day. Rain started pouring down on the field, and Devine, his face lined with frustration, looked up at the dark sky and blew his whistle to call practice to an end. As soon as the whistle sounded, the rain stopped and the sky cleared.

"You have to respect a coach like that," Geddes recalled.

Devaney? Well, everybody respected him not only for his winning record, but for his warm humor as well. A typical Devaney anecdote: "Once I inadvertently sent twelve players onto the field. My quarterback told the other guys, 'I don't think the referee sees it yet, so I'll call an end run over near our bench and one of you dummies drop out.' After the play, we had five guys left on the field."

Another pure Devaney story? John McKay's USC Trojans were playing Nebraska at Lincoln. In the first half, Southern Cal was penalized four times for pass interference. Though ahead, McKay was livid. Muttering to himself as the teams broke for the locker rooms, McKay suddenly found himself walking alongside Devaney, who was wearing a sheepish grin. "Well, John," McKay claims Devaney told him, "how do you like my brother's officiating?"

In the Big Eight all the great runners in 1971 were not at Oklahoma and Nebraska. Colorado's Charlie Davis gained 342 yards in 34 carries—breaking Greg Pruitt's conference record set earlier in the fall and falling just eight yards short of Eric Allen's NCAA mark —as the Buffs stampeded Oklahoma State, 40–6. That gave Davis a total of 1,190 yards for the season, topping the school record set by Whizzer White in 1937.

In many ways, the Sugar Bowl was even more of a rout than Nebraska's annihilation of Alabama in the Orange Bowl. The total was Oklahoma 19, Auburn 0 after the first quarter, 31–0 at halftime, and, finally, 40–22. The 1971 Sooners were without doubt faster, bigger, smarter, more deceptive, and more varied than any other team in the nation except Nebraska. Those two stood alone—and then came No. 3 Colorado, beaten only by Nebraska and Oklahoma. The Buffs ended the season with a 29–17 victory over Houston in the Astro-Bluebonnet Bowl.

If Nebraska, which in 1971 crushed thirteen opponents by an average score of 39–8, could do it again, Bob Devaney, in his last season before turning his job over to Tom Osborne to become full-time athletic director, would join a fairly select list of coaches who had won three national championships in a row. As far as the AP poll was concerned, no team had ever finished No. 1 three years running. The Cornhuskers and Devaney had a shot, but considering the caliber of the Big Eight, it wasn't going to be easy.

"Our players haven't given up the thought that a third championship, while improbable, is not impossible," Devaney said. "Our

Another Texan who brought All-America fame (1971–1972) to Oklahoma was back Greg Pruitt from Houston. His biggest game net rushing was against Kansas State in 1971, with 294 yards. He averaged more than 9 yards per carry that season.

coaches have not thrown up their hands at the idea. And the fans figure it's a certainty."

They did indeed. The state was very much the Big Red. If it rained in Lincoln, the merchants sold ponchos—all red. People continued to dress their baby pet animals in red sweaters. Husker boosters went on driving red jalopies. A delegate at a national political convention stood up and his voice rang out: "The state of Nebraska, as proud of its ticket as it is of its *No. 1 football team,* proudly casts all twenty-four of its ballots for the next vice-president of . . . " In terms of zany hats, vests, jackets, and ladies' suits, the state of Nebraska was one mass spray of red.

Since Nebraska, Oklahoma, Colorado, and Iowa State figured to have the Big Eight prairie pretty much to themselves in 1972, the league was divided into the Big Four and the Little Four. At least, that was the way the pundits sized it up in September.

Historically, Oklahoma was opened to the law-abiding public by the land run of 1889. "It's no wonder we've produced so many good halfbacks," cracked a Sooner fan. "The great land rush is not over yet." Greg Pruitt and Joe Wylie, halfbacks, and fullback Leon Crosswhite were back, the mainstays of Coach Chuck Fairbanks's cruel attack. Wylie, a nice guy off the field, was asked how he could stand being so mean on it. "I wouldn't hurt anyone out on the street," he said. "I mean, really run some guy down into the ground. But in a game, if I'm fifty points ahead, I'd just as soon roll it up to one hundred." The 1972 Sooners were quite capable of doing just that. Except for quarterback Jack Mildren, who was gone, the backfield was the same that had set national records in 1971 for most yards rushing, most first downs rushing, and most total offense per game. The new quarterback was slick Dave Robertson.

At Boulder, Eddie Crowder still talked about "humble hunger," but he now had a team efficient enough that he could admit: "We're trying to build a consistent national powerhouse. We're acquiring the feeling we should be in that throne room."

Iowa State's image was changing. In 1971 the Cyclones finished the regular season with a 7–4 record, which represented the most wins in sixty-five years and produced the team's first bowl invitation (the Sun Bowl—LSU 33, Iowa State 15) and top twenty recognition. There was even a sellout at Williams Field in Ames, only the second there since the stadium was enlarged in 1964. "Iowa State was fifty years behind times when I came here in 1968," said Coach John Majors. "There were poor facilities, no alumni support, a defeatist attitude, and very little tradition. We've still got a way to go but we've caught up by about ten years." Majors's success did not go unnoticed. He heard from five college and professional teams who wanted him to be their coach.

Oklahoma proved just how cruel it could be as it opened the 1972 season with four straight wins. The Sooners scored 49 points against Utah State, 68 against Oregon, 52 against Clemson, and 27 against Texas. The defense gave up a total of only 6 points. It had switched to a five-man front largely because Lucious Selmon was such a perfect noseguard. "He may very well be the strongest man in Oklahoma," said Coach Chuck Fairbanks. One reason he was so powerful was that his family still used mules and hand plows on its farm in Eufaula. Linebacker Rod Shoate and safety Randy Hughes, both sophomores, were two more big reasons why the Oklahoma defense was so highly touted.

Then came the Colorado game—and strange things were happening at Boulder. Football, which had always lost out to the mountains as recreation at CU, had suddenly become a mania. Now the student body looked

One of professional football's most controversial coaches in 1978 was Chuck Fairbanks, who spent six seasons (1967–1972) at Oklahoma. His record was 49–18–1. He won the Big Eight title in 1967, tied for it with Kansas in 1968, and led the Sooners to a 3–1–1 record in bowl competition. In 1979 he rejoined the Big Eight when he became Colorado's coach.

In 1972, Heisman Trophy voting boiled down to the Big Eight, with Nebraska's All-America wingback Johnny Rodgers beating out Greg Pruitt of Oklahoma. Rodgers is shown here scoring one of his four touchdowns against Notre Dame in the 1973 Orange Bowl triumph, 40–6.

to the Buffs to lift their spirits. Once grim pessimists, now they wanted to be happier. And what better way to pick them up than an upset victory over powerful Oklahoma? Talk about the odds. The Oklahoma defense had yet to permit a touchdown, and its offense had beaten everybody so far by an average score of 49 to 1.5. Colorado, meanwhile, had lost to Oklahoma State, 31–6, and was only sixth in the conference in both defense and offense. Okay. So what happened? Well, Colorado came up with some off-the-wall factors and won, 20–14. You figure it. Anyway, that left Nebraska, Oklahoma, and Colorado, the Big Three of the Big Eight, each with a defeat (the Huskers earlier lost to UCLA, 20–17). Nebraska still had to play Oklahoma and Colorado, and both Nebraska and Oklahoma had to play Iowa State (4–1).

Oklahoma was not the only team to get its comeuppance that weekend. Notre Dame fans glumly witnessed an even greater miracle: Missouri 30, Notre Dame 26. Stomped 62–0 by Nebraska seven days before, shut out by so-so Baylor before that 27–0, poor ol' Mizzou was off the board. But the Tigers played almost errorless ball and scored three touchdowns and three field goals on fourth-down plays.

On the ninth weekend of the season, Iowa State came within an extra point of beating Nebraska, but had to settle for a 23–23 tie when Tom Goedjen's kick went wide. With 23 seconds left, the Cyclones scored what appeared to be the winner after four passes by quarterback George Amundson carried them 74 yards in 35 seconds. Amundson guided Iowa State to the biggest production of the year against the Huskers, 356 yards. None of this set too well with Bob Devaney. "I've never been so disgusted with a team," he said of the bumbling that led to eight turnovers. Then he upset the entire Nebraska agricultural population by comparing his players to "a bunch of farmers standing around at a picnic." That tie and the earlier loss to UCLA rankled, but then the Cornhuskers crushed Kansas State, 59–7, and in an attempt to make amends, Devaney told the press, "We looked like a bunch of farmers with a harvest to bring in who did their typically expert job."

Johnny Rodgers caught five passes and scored two touchdowns, one on his seventh all-the-way punt return of the season to tie the NCAA record. Vince Gibson, the K State coach, reckoned that Rodgers "just might be the greatest college player of all time."

Greg Pruitt, running neck and neck with Rodgers in the race for the Heisman Trophy, had his biggest day for Oklahoma with 195 yards on 27 carries in a 17–6 conquest of Missouri. The Tigers became only the second team to score a touchdown against the Sooners.

The battle for the Heisman boiled down to the Oklahoma–Nebraska confrontation at Lincoln on Thanksgiving Day. Big Eight promoters billed it as the "Rematch of the Game of the Century" and "Pick the Heisman Trophy Winner," and while the teams lived up to their part of the hoopla, the Heisman candidates did not. Consider the facts: an injured Greg Pruitt ran the ball twice for only 7 yards, and did not catch a pass, return a punt, or throw a block. All told, Oklahoma gained only 141 yards on the ground and lost four fumbles. Johnny Rodgers? He ran four times for 5 yards, caught three passes for 41 yards, and returned one punt for 7 yards. And Nebraska lost three fumbles, had three passes intercepted, and gained 77 yards rushing. The result: Oklahoma came from behind to win, 17–14, and the stars of the contest were Ken Pope and Tinker Owens.

Before the season began, it was said that this game would be for all the marbles—the national title. It wasn't. Nebraska's loss to

UCLA and its tie against Iowa State knocked the Cornhuskers off the top rung, and the Sooners' chances started failing when they were dumped by Colorado and had to struggle to beat Missouri. Anyway, as far as Oklahoma was concerned, the worst news was yet to come. After they climaxed the season with a 14–0 victory over Penn State in the Sugar Bowl, the Sooners learned that they had been playing with an ineligible player. The conference ruled they would have to forfeit the Utah State, Oregon, Clemson, Texas, Missouri, Kansas, and Oklahoma State games. It seems that the high-school transcript of Kerry Jackson, star quarterback heir apparent, had been tampered with; thus Jackson was declared ineligible, and Oklahoma forfeited all those games. Then the Big Eight zapped the Sooners with a two-year probation that would keep them out of bowl play in 1973 and 1974 and off national television in 1974 and 1975.

Despite the mess, Oklahoma placed No. 2 in the final AP and UPI polls; Nebraska finished No. 9.

On New Year's Day, 1973, the Cornhuskers, resembling the great team they had been on most Saturdays, gave the retiring Bob Devaney a going-away gift: an easy (40–6) victory over Notre Dame. It was 40–0 halfway through the third quarter, the most embarrassed a Notre Dame team under Ara Parseghian had ever been. At that point, Johnny Rodgers had very clearly demonstrated why he deserved the Heisman Trophy. Closing out a superb career, in which he topped 5,000 yards for his three varsity years of mischief, he scored three times from scrimmage against the Irish and whirled himself 50 yards for another touchdown on a sideline pass, thus setting an Orange Bowl scoring record. When the Heisman ballots were tabulated, the vote was unanimous: Johnny Rodgers, Nebraska. As a pro scout said, "Everywhere they put him

—at slot, wing, flanker, anywhere—you could see the defense lean a little." Johnny Rodgers was that kind of player.

In 1973 there was a new look at Lincoln, Nebraska. Gone was Johnny Rodgers, the Heisman winner. Gone was Rich Glover, the Outland Trophy winner. Gone to the athletic director's chair was Bob Devaney. But the Huskers were far from goners. There to keep them from backsliding was a new head coach, Tom Osborne, who taught Sunday school; a left-handed quarterback, Dave Humm, from Las Vegas; and a monster named Wonderful Monds.

Tom Osborne, thirty-four, was a tall, handsome nonsmoker, nondrinker who had been serving as Devaney's offensive coach. He had been an assistant for eleven years. At the outset he received no salary but was allowed to sit at the training table and eat all he could hold.

Despite the losses from 1972, Osborne was optimistic about his offensive line: "It may be as good as any we've ever had." Darrell White, 6 feet 4 inches and 247 pounds, was the best of those linemen. Defensively, 6 feet 7 inch, 248-pound tackle John Dutton was not easily pushed around, while Terry Rogers and Wonderful Monds displayed multiple talents spelling each other off at playing monster. In the backfield, junior Dave Humm, who completed 153 passes in 1972, I-back slot Tony Davis, and fullback Maury Damkro were expected to strengthen Nebraska's run–pass balance.

There was also a new look down at Norman, Oklahoma. Greg Pruitt was gone. Chuck Fairbanks was gone (to the pros). Kerry Jackson was gone (almost before the ink was even dry on his doctored high-school transcript). New coach Barry Switzer, who had been building the formidable Oklahoma offense and recruiting program for five years as an assistant, had a lot of pieces to pick up. But he had a strong nucleus of quality players with which to debut. Redshirt Steve Davis provided experience and running versatility at quarterback. Senior fullback Tim Welch and junior halfback Grant Burget both averaged more than 5 yards a carry in 1972, and sophomore Joe Washington boasted jet speed at the other running spot. Tinker Owens at split end and the brothers Selmon on defense were other prime reasons why Switzer was thinking conference championship in his rookie season.

The Cornhuskers appeared twice on national television in 1973, averaged 76,000 in attendance at six home games, beat Texas, 19–3, in the Cotton Bowl to cap a 9–2–1 season, and finished seventh in the final AP poll. A lot of football-minded schools would have exchanged an English professor, two vice-chancellors, and the team mascot for that kind of success. Not the Huskers. A tie with Kansas for second place in the league and another loss (27–0) to Oklahoma provoked almost as much dismay as a corn blight.

This defeat by Oklahoma on the last Saturday of the regular season gave Nebraskans all winter to ponder it. On defense the Sooners were particularly stingy. They allowed the Huskers to cross the 50-yard line only once—and that on a 33-yard pass play that ended with a fumble recovered by OU. That was the first time Nebraska had been blanked since the Sooners did it back in 1968 (47–0). In stretching its unbeaten string to seventeen, longest in the country, Oklahoma was impressive both defensively and offensively. While the Selmon brothers controlled traffic in the pits, quarterback Steve Davis gained 114 yards and scored three touchdowns (fifteen for the season). Halfback Joe Washington ran for 107 yards, prompting Coach Switzer to label him the most versatile back in college football. The future was bright for Oklahoma

football—with or without the TV cameras—for both Davis and Washington were only sophomores. The Okies were 10–0–1 in 1973, the tie being a 7–7 squeaker against No. 8 Southern California. Oklahoma finished No. 3 in the final AP poll.

With a second-place tie in the final Big Eight standings hinging on the outcome, Kansas was a classic example of ineptitude for nearly 45 minutes against Missouri. A victory assured the Jayhawks a trip to the Liberty Bowl, yet they played like a team going nowhere. The Tigers were no better. In one sequence of four plays near the end of the first half, Missouri fumbled, Kansas recovered, mishandled two snaps from center, and fumbled the ball back to Missouri. Then late in the third quarter the two teams suddenly got their acts together and turned the contest into a rousing finish. With less than 2 minutes to go, David Jaynes passed to Emmett Edwards to win it for Kansas, 14–13. The 1-point difference was a missed point after touchdown by Greg Hill, ironically the best field-goal kicker in MU history and a man who had made twenty conversions in a row in 1973.

Kansas coach Don Fambrough, remembering that his team had been picked for seventh place in the Big Eight by sportswriters, instead of a tie for second with Nebraska, called the victory over Missouri "a great win for our seniors. They hadn't had much good happen to them during their careers." Well, not much good happened to them in the Liberty Bowl, where they lost to North Carolina State, 31–18.

Not much good happened to Coach Eddie Crowder, either. Picked as high as No. 9 in the preseason polls, ahead of even Oklahoma and Nebraska, Colorado could do no better than 5–6–0 in the season. Buffalo fans expressed their feelings by peppering Crowder with snowballs as inept Colorado lost to Kansas State, 17–14, in the season's finale.

Quarterback Dave Jaynes, 1973 All-American, smashed Kansas passing and total offense records (4,857 career yards in 1971–1973). He topped off his college career by playing in the College All-Star Game at Chicago, the East–West Game at San Francisco, the Senior Bowl at Mobile, and the Hula Bowl at Honolulu.

The brothers Selmon from Eufaula, Oklahoma. Lucious Selmon was chosen All-America noseguard in 1973.

Tackle Leroy Selmon made All-American in 1974 and 1975,

and the last of the family, Dewey Selmon, was an All-America lineman in 1975.

Though they were still on probation—banned from TV and from the bowls—there were no tears shed for Oklahoma in 1974. The boomer Sooners made their presence felt the same compelling way that Red China did when it was barred from the United Nations—they kept menacing people. With swift and punishing linemen like All-America Rod Shoate and the double-trouble brothers, LeRoy and Dewey Selmon, tossing opponents around like King Kong, Oklahoma did not exactly tackle runners. They avalanched them.

"They can keep us off television and ban us from the bowls," said Coach Barry Switzer, "but nobody said that we couldn't have a little fun."

Switzer's idea of a little fun was scores like this: Oklahoma 63, Kansas State 0; Oklahoma 72, Utah State 3; Oklahoma 63, Wake Forest 0; Oklahoma 49, Colorado 14; Oklahoma 37, Missouri 0; Oklahoma 45, Kansas 14; Oklahoma 44, Oklahoma State 13. In a nutshell, the Sooners, 11–0–0, won the Associated Press version of the national championship. From the perspective of the wire service's sixty-three media representatives, the postseason bowl results proved nothing. It was a dandy way for the newspaper, radio, and television guys to show they were more liberal than the coaches who made up the United Press International panel. Oklahoma, of course, had been stricken from the UPI poll because the coaches had elected to exclude teams on NCAA probation from consideration for the national championship.

Quarterback Steve Davis, an ordained Baptist minister, showed no mercy in the ruthlessly efficient way he ran Oklahoma's vaunted wishbone offense. And Joe Washington, the country's leading all-purpose runner, displayed his exasperating flip-flop moves as he ran for 100-plus yards week after week. "Anybody who tries to cut with him," said Switzer, "who tries to go all directions with

him at the same time, will break both knees and ankles."

After Oklahoma left Kansas State sprawled all over the field to run its unbeaten streak to twenty-four, the longest in the nation, Switzer put into words what everybody was thinking: "We gotta be the nation's No. 1 unranked team." In some perversely positive way, Oklahoma's troubles with the NCAA seemed to inspire the young Sooners to play far above their potential. Coach Switzer said that was the only explanation he had for the success of his 1974 juggernaut. "Something else besides talent and coaching snuck in there," he said.

In some quarters it was felt that the AP should have followed the UPI line and not included Oklahoma in its 1974 poll. "We're not in the business of policing college football," was the AP view. "As long as Oklahoma continues to field a deserving team, we'll rank it."

Bill Mallory, who replaced retiring Eddie Crowder at Colorado in 1974, typified the reaction of some coaches. "I feel Oklahoma should be rated in the polls," he said: "They are considered eligible for the Big Eight conference race, and they are not required to forfeit any games. The penalty of ineligibility for bowl games and exclusion from TV is enough."

Had the probation had any effect on recruiting at Oklahoma? "None," said Switzer, "because a lot of schools we recruit against are on permanent probation. They're never going to any bowls."

Coach Switzer knew pretty well where he was going in the immediate future: into a $5.3-million stadium expansion program and, very probably, a second straight national championship. "I'm a fighter!" exclaimed Switzer. "I'm a competitor! I'm a winner! Nothing is going to stop us—not even probation!"

If 1975 was any criterion, the Big Eight could make a good argument that it played the

In the 1972–1975 seasons, Oklahoma halfback Joe Washington scored forty-three touchdowns, established rushing records (3,995 yards in four varsity seasons), and was All-American in 1974 and 1975.

The Big Eight Conference gained more prestige as Nebraska beat Texas on New Year's Day, 1974, in the Cotton Bowl, 19–3. Here Tony Davis is stopped on the Longhorn 1-yard line by Wade Johnston (No. 35) of Texas on the last play of the first half, with the teams tied, 3–3.

Playing in their second bowl game in three years, the 1975 Kansas Jayhawks (7–4 in the regular season) lost to Pittsburgh in the Sun Bowl, 33–19. Earlier the Jays upset national champions Oklahoma, 23–3. Quarterback Nolan Cromwell, defensive tackle Mike Butler, and safety Kurt Knoff were All–Big Eight selections.

best college football in the country. Four teams ended up in bowl games—Nebraska, Kansas, Colorado, and, yes, national champion Oklahoma (the bowl ban was lifted)—and the fact that three of them lost only led Big Eight enthusiasts to argue that they had other teams at home that might have won. Missouri, for example, which had lost five games in 1975, four to other Big Eight teams, was the only school to beat Sugar Bowl champion Alabama. Kansas was defeated in the Sun Bowl (by Pittsburgh, 33–19), but was the only team to beat Oklahoma (23–3), which beat touted Michigan in the Orange Bowl (14–6)—and Kansas was beaten (35–19) by 7–4–0 Oklahoma State, another nonbowl Big Eight team. Oklahoma State beat Arkansas (20–13), the Southwest Conference cochampion and Cotton Bowl winner, but lost, on something of a fluke, to Nebraska (28–20) and—to get back to the beginning, was thrashed by Missouri (41–14).

This wildly competitive round robin—six Big Eight teams had winning records in 1975—got so fired up and intense that Bud Moore, Kansas's rookie head coach, tried bribing his players—with food. The good guys could eat steak and lobster in a private room. The bad guys, those who failed to produce on the field, had to push trays in the cafeteria. After the Jayhawks beat Oklahoma, 23–3, Coach Moore was named Big Eight Coach of the Year—and his players ate like kings. It marked the Sooners' first loss in thirty-eight games and the first time in 103 games that they failed to score a touchdown.

As for All-America types in 1975, consider the performance of Kansas's Nolan Cromwell, who held the Texas Relays 400-meter hurdles record. He was shifted by Coach Moore from defensive back to wishbone quarterback, and in his very first game he ran for 294 yards to break the Kansas single-game record set by Gale Sayers. Cromwell went on to lead the Big Eight in running with 1,124 yards and was offensive Player of the Year in a conference loaded with All-Americans.

Yet the best teams in the Big Eight in 1975 were, as usual, Oklahoma and Nebraska, which tied for the conference championship, 6–1–0. Colorado, 5–2–0, which missed joining them at the top only because it lost to national champion Oklahoma, 21–20, was close behind. The two bottom teams, Kansas State and Iowa State, each lost only one game outside the Big Eight—but seven and six, respectively, within it.

The 1975 national title boiled down to Ohio State and Oklahoma. When the Buckeyes gambled with passes and lost to UCLA, 23–10, in the Rose Bowl, rendering Woody Hayes speechless, the door was open for the Sooners to cash in. The game at Pasadena immediately preceded the Oklahoma–Michigan game in Miami's Orange Bowl and set the stage for Switzer to pepper his troops with a pregame fight talk. For the first time in several years the Sooners were back on television, big as life in redressed red and newly cleansed white; back in the bowls and polls—both polls, not just the AP's. And back to the top as national champions for the second straight year—if they beat Michigan.

"I knew NBC-TV would be selling our game that night as the national championship," said Switzer. "So in my pregame pep talk to my players that's what I did, too. But, heck, they already knew it."

The next evening, twenty-four hours after Oklahoma had defeated the Wolverines, Switzer got the word: Oklahoma in a twin landslide (AP and UPI). Arizona State, the only major unbeaten team left at season's end and a surprise 17–14 victor over No. 9 Nebraska in the Fiesta Bowl, was runner-up in both polls.

At a press conference in Miami, Barry Switzer was candid. As he talked about the future at Norman, he said the football program would be falling off a little. They were losing some important talent—the brothers Selmon, Davis, Owens, and Elrod, to name a few. The next three years, Switzer said, were not going to be what the last three were.

"Talk about irony," Switzer said. "Now we'll be on TV and everybody will see us—and we won't be as good."

Spoiled was the only word to describe Oklahoma fans in 1976. After all, their beloved Sooners gave them only nine wins to shout about—the fewest in Coach Barry Switzer's four years at Norman—and instead of a trip to Miami and the Orange Bowl, there was only a 41–7 victory over outmanned Wyoming in a wishbone versus wishbone Fiesta Bowl.

A series of unexpected hurts and bruises in the secondary, the necessity of starting an inexperienced quarterback, and the unusual absence of a genuine superstar contributed to the Sooners' 9–2–1 record, which included back-to-back losses to Oklahoma State (31–24) and Colorado (42–31). This dropped Switzer's record at Oklahoma to 41–3–2. How dreadful.

Sharing the 1976 Big Eight championship with Oklahoma were Colorado and Oklahoma State. The Buffs got to go to the Orange Bowl because they beat both the Sooners (42–31) and the Cowboys (20–10). But 1976 was not a typical year in the Big Eight. Since the conference went from the Big Seven to the Big Eight in 1960, Oklahoma and Nebraska, the two powerhouses, had won or tied for the league championship fifteen times between them. Like Michigan and Ohio State in the Big Ten Conference, they had become the Big Two of the midlands. But in 1976 Oklahoma lost two

games, Nebraska three. Colorado was picked to finish sixth in the preseason poll but wound up with a third share of the championship, largely on the play of quarterback Jeff Knapple, a transfer from UCLA, where he had spent a dismal freshman year. On the way to leading the Buffaloes to an 8–3 record during the regular season, sophomore Knapple engineered five touchdowns in five possessions as Colorado whipped Drake, 45–24. He led his team to 265 yards total offense in one quarter as the Buffs thrashed a good (8–3–0) Iowa State team, 33–14, and he piled up 286 more yards during a furious comeback against Oklahoma that produced the most points scored against the Sooners (42) since 1969. In eight games the 6-foot-2-inch, 202-pound Knapple passed for 904 yards and averaged nearly 4 yards a carry. Unfortunately, this momentum did not carry into the Orange Bowl, where the Buffs lost to Ohio State, 27–10.

By December, Terry Miller was a household word around Oklahoma State. A 6-foot, 196-pound halfback from Colorado Springs, Miller attracted enough national attention when he rushed for 1,541 yards to finish fourth in the Heisman balloting. He rushed for more than 100 yards eight times, twice topped the 200-yard mark, and added 173 yards and four touchdowns in OSU's 49–21 rout of Brigham Young in the Tangerine Bowl. Miller was also a big reason why the Cowboys won a piece of the Big Eight title for the first time since they began playing a conference schedule in 1960. All told, Miller scored twenty-three touchdowns.

Taking some of the shine off Oklahoma State's success, however, was the rumor that the NCAA was about to slap State with some sort of probation for recruiting violations.

Down at Missouri, the Tigers seemed to

Split end Billy Brooks of Oklahoma's 1975 national championship team was yet another Texan who chose the Sooners over the Longhorns. Oklahoma recruiters snapped up All-American Billy (who came from Austin) from the University of Texas.

play winning football everywhere but at home. Among their victims were Southern California (46–25), Ohio State (22–21), and Nebraska (34–24), a remarkable toll. But when the season was over Missouri's record was 6–5; they'd lost at home to such teams as Illinois and Kansas, which nearly cost Coach Al Onofrio his job. Quarterback Pete Woods was a superb runner who also completed a 98-yard pass to slotback Joe Stewart to overcome Nebraska. Stewart also flagged down forty-four other passes during the season for a total of 834 yards.

Meanwhile, Iowa State, thanks to halfback Dexter Green's 1,074 yards, was 8–3 in 1976 and finished second to Michigan nationally in total offense—and still wasn't rewarded with a bowl bid.

Nebraska? Although Tom Osborne's Cornhuskers had always finished in the Top Ten in the year-end polls in the four years since he succeeded Bob Devaney as head coach, the rap against him was that he was too conservative, especially at crucial moments in a game. Nebraska was 9–3–1 in 1976, and all three of its defeats were within the conference, which told you something about the well-balanced power of the Big Eight. In losses to Missouri (34–24) and Iowa State (37–28), the Huskers' legendary bend-but-never-break defense cracked wide open, but outside the league it was a different story: Nebraska 45, Indiana 13; Nebraska 64, TCU 10; Nebraska 68, Hawaii 3. The Cornhuskers closed out the season with a 27–24 defeat over Texas Tech in the Astro-Bluebonnet Bowl for their seventh bowl victory in the past eight seasons.

The 1976 Nebraska-Oklahoma finale at Lincoln was typical of the long rivalry. With only 3 minutes left to play, the Sooners had grown desperate. They had exhausted almost all of their X's and O's and a lot of their muscle and still trailed, 17–13. So, with a strong wind

at their back and the ball on their own 15-yard line, they abandoned their patented ground game and took to the air. This despite the cold fact that they had not completed a pass in nearly four weeks.

Woodie Shepard, a sophomore reserve halfback, started the fireworks when he took a pitchout and tossed the first pass of his college career far downfield to split end Steve Rhodes. The razzle-dazzle was good for a gain of 47 yards. On the next two plays, the Sooners lost 10 yards. That made it third and 20 at the Huskers' 34-yard line. The clock ticked away, only 44 seconds remaining. Oklahoma tried another pass, this time from quarterback Dean Blevins to Rhodes for 10 more yards. That, though, was not the end of the play, for Rhodes lateraled the ball to halfback Elvis Peacock, who gained another 22 yards down to the Husker two. Then, 6 seconds later, Peacock scored his third touchdown of the afternoon to win the game for Oklahoma, 20–17. The victory was the fifth straight for Oklahoma over Nebraska. It was enough to give the Cornhuskers a complex.

There was no Leroy Selmon left, and there darn sure was no Joe Washington around, but the 1977 Sooners shaped up in preseason reports as so talent-laden that even the loss of those two wasn't going to keep them out of the battle with Notre Dame, Michigan, Alabama, and Southern California for the national championship. A ground attack based on the speed of Elvis Peacock, Kenny King, and Billy Ray Sims and a defense braced with the strength of nine starters back from 1976 again was the norm at Norman. At quarterback, Coach Switzer was confident he could count on a Lott—junior Thomas Lott, who had been starter Dean Blevins's backup in 1976 until Blevins was hurt. Lott went on to average 5.5 yards per carry as the leading rusher for the

All–Big Eight linebacker Terry Beeson was the heart and soul of the 1976 Kansas defense. He completed his college career competing in the East–West Game, the Blue–Gray Game, and the Senior Bowl. Today he stars for the Seattle Seahawks.

team whose rushing average (328.9 yards) was to lead the nation in 1977. Switzer called Lott "the best wishbone quarterback ever to play at Oklahoma."

The Sooners would get a clue as to how good they were in late September, when they played Ohio State for the first time—in Columbus. No doubt they were looking ahead to the Buckeyes when they opened the season against tiny Vanderbilt. Vandy was only supposed to be a warmup, a punching bag to show to the rest of the universe just how good Oklahoma was. But eleven fumbles, an OU record, 104 yards in penalties, and enough amateur performances nearly floored Oklahoma. Behind 15–0 in the second quarter, the Sooners were forced to come from behind to win, 25–23. Coach Barry Switzer called it "the worst exhibition of Oklahoma football I've ever seen."

At Lincoln, Nebraska also opened the season with troubles. Behind the sharp passing of quarterback Jack Thompson, Washington State knocked the Cornhuskers right out of the national polls, 19–10. The following week, Nebraska, junking its conservative offense, took its frustration out on Alabama, 31–24, on national television. The last time anyone scored more than 30 points against the Crimson Tide was in the 1972 Orange Bowl—*Nebraska* 38, Alabama 6.

After bombing Utah, 62–24, Oklahoma was 2–0 going into the Ohio State game. It had already established itself in the minds of rival coaches as a team that fumbled a lot, passed poorly, played defense irregularly, but usually won.

Against Ohio State, the Sooners finally put it all together. Except for six turnovers, they played an almost flawless game; a bruising, helmet-rattling, blockbusting performance, filled with moments of inspiring imagination. Ohio State played similarly. It was too bad someone had to lose.

Trailing 20–28 with 6 minutes-plus to play, when fumbles meant death and could no longer be afforded, Oklahoma held on to the ball. When key passing was a must, the Sooners' passes were on the mark. And when the Oklahoma defense positively had no other alternative, it met the challenge brilliantly.

In the last quarter Oklahoma had a strong wind to its back. On the last, breathtaking drive, Dean Blevins, who had replaced the injured Thomas Lott, was at quarterback. After middle guard Reggie Kinlaw pounced on an Ohio State fumble at the Buckeye 43, Blevins, who had been booed to tears in the Vanderbilt game, got the Sooners moving. It required only twelve plays to move the ball into the end zone. Elvis Peacock scored on a fourth-down option from the 1½-yard line. That made the score 28–26. Oklahoma went for the 2-point conversion, Peacock with the ball, but he couldn't get in. The Sooners still trailed by 2.

Uwe von Schamann, nicknamed "Von Foot" by his teammates, then executed an onside kick perfectly. He sliced the ball hard off a Buckeye in the front line. It caromed free just over the 50-yard line, and Oklahoma's Mike Babb threw his body on top of it.

On first down Blevins got man-to-man coverage on split end Steve Rhodes and hit him for 18 yards to the Ohio State 32. From there he worked carefully on the inside legs of the option, deliberately keeping to the middle of the field and working the clock down. With 6 seconds to go, the ball rested on the 23, and von Schamann was rushed into the game. He was the last chance the Sooners had.

As "Von Foot" got ready for the kick attempt on the Ohio State 41, the 88,119 spectators, mostly Buckeye fans, invoked their wrath on him. "Block that kick! Block that kick!" they screamed. Von Schamann looked over the crowd coolly. If they were getting on his nerves, he certainly didn't show it.

"What the hell are we doing in this profession?" Coach Switzer asked his assistants over on the Oklahoma sideline. It didn't take him long to find out. With one soccer-style swipe of the ball, Von Schamann put it perfectly between the goal posts, winning the game for Oklahoma with 3 seconds to spare. Switzer was seen to kiss his ace placekicker as he ran off the field.

After the game, in the Oklahoma locker room, Switzer faced the facts: "Twenty-four fumbles in three games, and we lost seventeen of them," he said, shaking his head. "And still we're 3–0. It's unbelievable."

Oklahoma's streak rose to four after a 24–9 defeat of Kansas. That's the way the Sooners stood as they traveled to the Cotton Bowl to face Texas in the battle of the unbeatens. But everyone knew that Oklahoma was more unbeaten than Texas, for the latter counted among its victims such competition as Virginia. Besides, Oklahoma was considered a leading contender for No. 1 in the nation; and Texas wasn't considered No. 1 even in its own conference.

"We're not ready at this point to be a contender," said Fred Akers, who had replaced retiring Darrell Royal as head coach. "We are so young we still hold hands going onto the field." The last time Texas had whipped Oklahoma in football was 1970.

So what happened? Common sense suggested an Oklahoma victory. So—Texas won, 13–6. Spare the details.

The rest of the Oklahoma schedule showed how the Sooners reacted to the upset by the Longhorns:

21	Missouri	17
35	Iowa State	16
42	Kansas State	7
61	Oklahoma State	28
52	Colorado	14
38	Nebraska	7

While the Sooners made a shambles of the Big Eight, the talk around the league was Oklahoma State's Terry Miller, a prime candidate for the Heisman Trophy. In losing causes, he romped for 120 yards and three touchdowns against Oklahoma, and he got 116 more against Nebraska. The Huskers won, 31–14, but the game marked the sixteenth time in a row that Miller had gained more than 100 yards rushing. He also became the fourth major-college player ever to rush for 4,000 career yards. As the Big Eight's all-time rushing leader, he was now the first runner in conference history to gain 1,000 yards in three straight seasons.

Barry Switzer said his 1977 edition was the best team he'd ever had at Oklahoma. It was ranked No. 2 nationally, despite the wide attention it received by losing thirty fumbles during the regular season. There was a logical chance the Sooners would be voted the national championship—their third in four years—if they made a strong showing against No. 6 Arkansas in the Orange Bowl.

A week before the game, Arkansas Coach Lou Holtz, late of the New York Jets, virtually eliminated any chance of winning by dropping the cogs of his offense. Just before Christmas, he announced that three key black stars—running back Ben Cowins, top receiver Donny Bobo, and second-team running back Michael Forrest—would be left off the traveling squad as punishment over an incident involving a white coed in a dorm room at Fayetteville. Then a lawyer stepped in on the players' behalf, a boycott by the team's blacks was threatened, and Razorback morale was somewhere between awful and rotten. Two days before the game, Holtz was asked how he was holding up, and he said he was one step short of suicide.

But once the game was under way, death was the furthest thing from his mind. His best weapon turned out to be the Oklahoma fumble. Less than 2 minutes after the opening kickoff Arkansas recovered a fumble by Billy Sims on the OU 9-yard line. Two plays later Roland Sales, a sophomore from Fort Worth, ripped through the vaunted Sooner defense to score. Later in the first period, Oklahoma's Kenny King fumbled, the Hogs got it again, and Sales promptly ho-hummed 38 yards to the Oklahoma 3. Quarterback Ron Calcagni carried the ball into the end zone to make the score 14–0 at halftime. Now it was the Sooners, 18-point favorites coming into the game, who wore the look of death.

In the third quarter, Arkansas kicker Steve Little widened his team's lead with a 32-yard field goal. Now Roland Sales took over. The next time the Hogs got the ball he went crazy, gaining 12 yards, then 38, then slipping through for 4 more and the touchdown that put Arkansas ahead, 24–0. Oklahoma fumbled again—but that was where we came in.

For Sales, it was a night to remember. In addition to the two touchdowns he scored, he gained 205 yards, an Orange Bowl record and only 25 yards less than the whole Oklahoma team, the No. 1 rushing team in the nation, managed to total. Sales also topped the game's pass catchers with four receptions good for 52 yards.

After the game, Sales was hugged by his mother. "Aw, gee, Mom," he shrugged, "it wasn't anything at all." Then he thought about the 31–6 rout. "Yes," he grinned. "Yes, it was."

The year 1977 had also been a long season for Missouri. After the Tigers lost five of their first six games, Coach Al Onofrio was on the hot seat. Fans shouted at him, "Impeach Onofrio," and, "A.O. must go." A "Help Wanted—Coach" advertisement appeared in a local newspaper. That winter, Al Onofrio

was gone. In his place came Warren Powers, who wanted the Missouri coaching job so badly he was willing to pay Washington State $55,000 in three cash installments to let him out of his contract.

For a while in 1978, the Big Eight Commissioner's office in Kansas City resembled a police blotter. Judged by some member schools' off-field ethics, it looked as if the conference had redshirted morality. Oklahoma State was plastered all over the pages of *Sports Illustrated* after being accused by one of its own alumni of having a slush fund; two of its players pleaded guilty to burglary charges; and it received two years' NCAA probation for recruiting violations. Kansas State, 1–10 in 1977, making its all-time record of 271–417–38 the worst of any major college, was put on indefinite probation by the conference for exceeding scholarship limitations by twenty; two varsity players were accused and later convicted of raping a coed in the athletic dorm. In December, Jim Dickey, an assistant at North Carolina, became the new football coach at K State after Ellis Rainsberger resigned under pressure. Meanwhile, down at Norman, strife was rife among Oklahoma coaches, culminating in the resignation of three of Barry Switzer's assistants.

In any case, the Big Eight season was another—ho-hum—struggle between Oklahoma and—guess who?—Nebraska for the league championship. In the preseason national polls, the Sooners were ranked No. 4, the Cornhuskers No. 10.

By the time Oklahoma traveled to Lincoln for the showdown, Nebraska, loser only to Alabama in the opening game, had moved up to No. 4 in the polls. Rankled by five consecutive losses to Oklahoma and the ensuing succession of bowls less juicy than the Orange, Tom

---

In 1977, Coach Warren Powers was working on the Washington State side of the field at Lincoln, Nebraska, as the Cougars defeated the Huskers, 19–10, in one of the major upsets of the season. That winter Powers created a furor in the Pacific Northwest by buying up his contract ($55,000) to accept the head football job at Missouri.

Osborne detected that the string was about to break. Nothing would give him more pleasure than to knock Oklahoma out of its No. 1 ranking.

As it turned out, for Nebraskans it was very definitely a Saturday made in heaven. The No. 4 Huskers, a good but not great football team, went out and whipped No. 1 Oklahoma, 17–14, putting them in the driver's seat to win the Big Eight outright for the first time since 1972. The only thing standing between Nebraska and the title, an Orange Bowl bid, and maybe even another national championship was Missouri. The Huskers' record was now 9–1, the same as Oklahoma's, and had moved up to No. 2 in the polls.

The way Nebraska fans had it figured out, their No. 2 Cornhuskers would stomp No. 18 Missouri and thereby lure No. 1 Penn State to the Orange Bowl and a one-on-one clash for the national title. It was a beautiful plan, except nobody talked to Missouri about it. The Tigers, 6–4, including a big upset of mighty Notre Dame, smelled Liberty Bowl. They had been averaging almost 32 points a game to rank sixth in the nation in scoring; they also were tenth in total offense.

On the game's very first play from scrimmage, Rick Berns broke into the clear and rumbled 82 yards to score for Nebraska. The contest had opened according to the Nebraska script. But as in all dramas, it's the final scene that counts. Late in the third quarter, Missouri actually went ahead, 28–24, on a 4-yard run by Jim Wilder. Then Nebraska recaptured the lead, 31–28, when Tim Hager burst across the goal line from the 4-yard line. The Tigers fought back to the Nebraska 4-yard line, only to lose the ball on a fumble. Still they kept the pressure on. With 3:42 left, they started at their own 26-yard line and drove 74 yards for the winning touchdown. Wilder's 7-yard run capped the drive.

Berns set Nebraska records with 36 carries and 255 yards rushing. In all, the two teams gained a total of 993 yards, 517 by the Huskers.

After the game, a Cotton Bowl representative called a press conference to announce that Oklahoma would play in Dallas, but at the last minute the Sooners changed their minds. They decided they wanted to try to avenge the previous week's loss to Nebraska by meeting the Huskers in the first-ever all-Big Eight Orange Bowl. The Sooners had ended the regular season by amassing 692 yards in total offense while stampeding Oklahoma State, 62–7. Billy Sims demonstrated his Heisman Trophy credentials as he ran for 209 yards and scored three touchdowns. That gave him twenty touchdowns and a Big Eight single-season rushing record of 1,762 yards, 82 more than Terry Miller had for Oklahoma State in 1977.

The Cornhuskers were infuriated that Oklahoma was chosen as their opponent in Miami. The complaint was that they beat the Sooners once and shouldn't have to do it again. Tom Osborne said it was a raw deal. Nebraska Athletic Director Bob Devaney said it wasn't fair to the team. The only comment the odds-makers had was to make Oklahoma the favorite by as much as 10 points.

In Nebraska's 17–14 victory over the Sooners in November, Oklahoma had fumbled the ball away six times. Heisman winner Billy Sims, whose fumble at the Nebraska 3-yard line with 3:27 to play in the game was crucial in the loss, promised it wouldn't happen again. In the rematch, he said, he was going to run like a crazy man. "We're going to throw everything at them," he vowed.

And that was just what the No. 4 Sooners

did in their 31–24 victory. Spotting Nebraska an opening-drive touchdown on a 21-yard pass from Tom Sorley to split end Tim Smith, Oklahoma went nowhere the first time they had the ball. After that, it was as if Nebraska had given them an open-door policy. Sims, quarterback Thomas Lott, and teammates went pretty much anywhere they wanted.

After the game, Barry Switzer told the press he felt his Sooners were as good as anybody. He confessed he didn't know who deserved to be ranked No. 1—Oklahoma, Alabama, or USC. Then, remembering that his team was the top scoring team in the nation with an average of 40 points per game, he added: "But we're the best offensive team in the country."

The Big Eight wound up the bowl season with a split: Missouri hung on for a 20–15 victory over Louisiana State in the Liberty Bowl, and Iowa State lost to Texas A. & M., 28–12, in the Hall of Fame Bowl.

And Heisman winner Billy Sims? Billy, along with Oklahoma roommate Greg Roberts, winner of the 1978 Outland Trophy as the nation's outstanding lineman, joined the Have Tuxedo, Will Travel circuit. In Seattle, where he was presented with the *Seattle Times* Gold Helmet Award as College Player of the Year, he shared the spotlight with Arkansas Coach Lou Holtz, who noted in his speech that Billy still had another season to play at Oklahoma.

"I've been trying to talk Billy into transferring to Arkansas," Lou told the audience. "I told him we could offer him room, board, books, tuition, and laundry. I figured his laundry would run about $1,200 a month."

Good old Lou Holtz.

And good old Chuck Fairbanks, who returned to the Big Eight in 1979 by way of the University of Colorado. Like Warren Powers

the year before, the forty-five-year-old Fairbanks wanted back into the league so much he was willing to buy his way back.

For the record, the former Oklahoma coach, who in three seasons had turned the New England Patriots from the bumblers of the NFL into a playoff team, still had four years left on his Patriots contract. But that didn't stop him—or the Flatirons, Colorado's affluent booster club. Granted, there were some red faces around Boulder when the Patriots asked the courts to hold Fairbanks to his contract, but the indefatigable Flatirons four months later dissolved the legal tug of war by agreeing to pay $200,000 to the Patriots in exchange for dropping the suit. And what enticed Fairbanks to give up his $150,000 salary with New England? The Flatirons put together a package that reportedly included a $45,000 salary, frequent TV appearances and football clinics worth an estimated $100,000 annually, a $250,000 paid-up life-insurance policy, and a chance to play golf and give "motivational talks" to businessmen at $3,000 a shot.

When the terms of the agreement leaked out, Colorado students and professors (average salary, $23,100) were bitterly resentful. After all, the school was fighting a budget-saving move by the state legislature that would cut back enrollment, slice millions from the UC budget, and drop 202 faculty members. "The priorities are way off," editorialized the *Colorado Daily*, the student newspaper, "but it shows where the interests lie in the state of Colorado."

It also showed what a well-heeled booster club will do after hungering year after year for the championship of football's tough Big Eight conference.

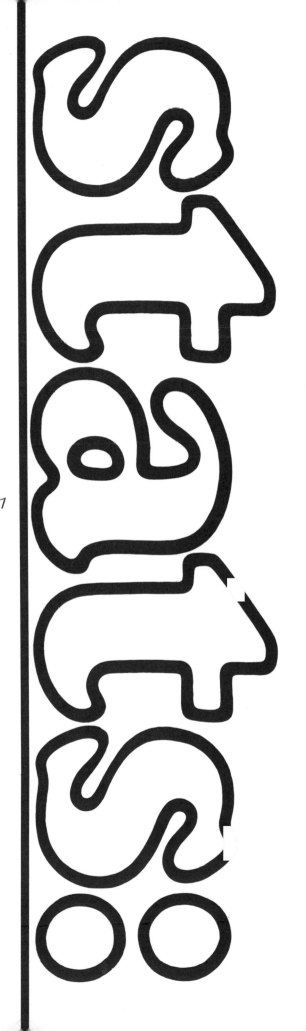

Statistics

National Football Rankings Associated Press

(Writers' Poll, 1936–1978)

1936

1. Minnesota
2. Louisiana State
3. Pittsburgh
4. Alabama
5. Washington
6. Santa Clara
7. Northwestern
8. Notre Dame
9. NEBRASKA
10. Pennsylvania

1937

1. Pittsburgh
2. California
3. Fordham
4. Alabama
5. Minnesota
6. Villanova
7. Dartmouth
8. Louisiana State
9. Notre Dame
10. Santa Clara

1938

1. Texas Christian
2. Tennessee
3. Duke
4. OKLAHOMA
5. Notre Dame
6. Carnegie Tech
7. Southern California
8. Pittsburgh
9. Holy Cross
10. Minnesota

1939

1. Texas A. & M.
2. Tennessee
3. Southern California
4. Cornell
5. Tulane
6. MISSOURI
7. UCLA
8. Duke
9. Iowa
10. Duquesne

1940

1. Minnesota
2. Stanford
3. Michigan
4. Tennessee
5. Boston College
6. Texas A. & M.
7. Northwestern
8. NEBRASKA
9. Mississippi State
10. Washington

1941

1. Minnesota
2. Duke
3. Notre Dame
4. Texas
5. Michigan
6. Fordham
7. MISSOURI
8. Duquesne
9. Texas A. & M.
10. Navy

1942

1. Ohio State
2. Georgia
3. Wisconsin
4. Tulsa
5. Georgia Tech
6. Notre Dame
7. Tennessee
8. Boston College
9. Michigan
10. Alabama

1943

1. Notre Dame
2. Iowa Pre-Flight
3. Michigan
4. Navy
5. Purdue
6. Great Lakes
7. Duke
8. Del Monte P.
9. Northwestern
10. March Field

1944

1. Army
2. Ohio State
3. Randolph Field
4. Navy
5. Bainbridge
6. Iowa Pre-Flight
7. Southern California
8. Michigan
9. Notre Dame
10. 4th AAF

1945

1. Army
2. Alabama
3. Navy
4. Indiana
5. OKLAHOMA STATE
6. Michigan
7. St. Mary's
8. Pennsylvania
9. Notre Dame
10. Texas

1946

1. Notre Dame
2. Army
3. Georgia
4. UCLA
5. Illinois
6. Michigan
7. Tennessee
8. Louisiana State
9. North Carolina
10. Rice

1947

1. Notre Dame
2. Michigan
3. Southern Methodist
4. Penn State
5. Texas
6. Alabama
7. Pennsylvania
8. Southern California
9. North Carolina
10. Georgia Tech

1948

1. Michigan
2. Notre Dame
3. North Carolina
4. California
5. OKLAHOMA
6. Army
7. Northwestern
8. Georgia
9. Oregon
10. Southern Methodist

1949

1. Notre Dame
2. OKLAHOMA
3. California
4. Army
5. Rice
6. Ohio State
7. Michigan
8. Minnesota
9. Louisiana State
10. College Pacific

1950

1. OKLAHOMA
2. Army
3. Texas
4. Tennessee
5. California
6. Princeton
7. Kentucky
8. Michigan State
9. Michigan
10. Clemson

1951

1. Tennessee
2. Michigan State
3. Maryland
4. Illinois
5. Georgia Tech
6. Princeton
7. Stanford
8. Wisconsin
9. Baylor
10. OKLAHOMA

1952

1. Michigan State
2. Georgia Tech
3. Notre Dame
4. OKLAHOMA
5. Southern California
6. UCLA
7. Mississippi
8. Tennessee
9. Alabama
10. Texas

1953

1. Maryland
2. Notre Dame
3. Michigan State
4. OKLAHOMA
5. UCLA
6. Rice
7. Illinois
8. Georgia Tech
9. Iowa
10. West Virginia

1954

1. Ohio State
2. UCLA
3. OKLAHOMA
4. Notre Dame
5. Navy
6. Mississippi
7. Army
8. Maryland
9. Wisconsin
10. Arkansas

1955

1. OKLAHOMA
2. Michigan State
3. Maryland
4. UCLA
5. Texas Christian
6. Ohio State
7. Georgia Tech
8. Notre Dame
9. Mississippi
10. Auburn

1956

1. OKLAHOMA
2. Tennessee
3. Iowa
4. Georgia Tech
5. Texas A. & M.
6. Miami
7. Michigan
8. Syracuse
9. Michigan State
10. Oregon State

1957

1. Auburn
2. Ohio State
3. Michigan State
4. OKLAHOMA
5. Navy
6. Iowa
7. Mississippi
8. Rice
9. Texas A. & M.
10. Notre Dame

1958

1. Louisiana State
2. Iowa
3. Army
4. Auburn
5. OKLAHOMA
6. Air Force
7. Wisconsin
8. Ohio State
9. Syracuse
10. Texas Christian

1959

1. Syracuse
2. Mississippi
3. Louisiana State
4. Texas
5. Georgia
6. Wisconsin
7. Texas Christian
8. Washington
9. Arkansas
10. Alabama

1960

1. Minnesota
2. Mississippi
3. Iowa
4. Navy
5. MISSOURI
6. Washington
7. Arkansas
8. Ohio State
9. Alabama
10. Duke

1961

1. Alabama
2. Ohio State
3. Texas
4. Louisiana State
5. Mississippi
6. Minnesota
7. COLORADO
8. Michigan State
9. Arkansas
10. Utah State

1962

1. Southern California
2. Wisconsin
3. Mississippi
4. Texas
5. Alabama
6. Arkansas
7. Louisiana State
8. OKLAHOMA
9. Penn State
10. Minnesota

1963

1. Texas
2. Navy
3. Illinois
4. Pittsburgh
5. Auburn
6. NEBRASKA
7. Mississippi
8. Alabama
9. Michigan State
10. OKLAHOMA

1964

1. Alabama
2. Arkansas
3. Notre Dame
4. Michigan
5. Texas
6. NEBRASKA
7. Louisiana State
8. Oregon State
9. Ohio State
10. Southern California

1965

1. Alabama
2. Michigan State
3. Arkansas
4. UCLA
5. NEBRASKA
6. MISSOURI
7. Tennessee
8. Louisiana State
9. Notre Dame
10. Southern California

1966

1. Notre Dame
2. Michigan State
3. Alabama
4. Georgia
5. UCLA
6. NEBRASKA
7. Purdue
8. Georgia Tech
9. Miami
10. Southern Methodist

1967

1. Southern California
2. Tennessee
3. OKLAHOMA
4. Indiana
5. Notre Dame
6. Wyoming
7. Oregon State
8. Alabama
9. Purdue
10. Penn State

1968

1. Ohio State
2. Penn State
3. Texas
4. Southern California
5. Notre Dame
6. Arkansas
7. KANSAS
8. Georgia
9. MISSOURI
10. Purdue

1969

1. Texas
2. Penn State
3. Southern California
4. Ohio State
5. Notre Dame
6. MISSOURI
7. Arkansas
8. Mississippi
9. Michigan
10. Louisiana State

1970

1. NEBRASKA
2. Notre Dame
3. Texas
4. Tennessee
5. Ohio State
6. Arizona State
7. Louisiana State
8. Stanford
9. Michigan
10. Auburn

1971

1. NEBRASKA
2. OKLAHOMA
3. COLORADO
4. Alabama
5. Penn State
6. Michigan
7. Georgia
8. Arizona State
9. Tennessee
10. Stanford

1972

1. Southern California
2. OKLAHOMA
3. Ohio State
4. Alabama
5. Penn State
6. Auburn
7. Texas
8. Michigan
9. NEBRASKA
10. Louisiana State

1973

1. Notre Dame
2. Ohio State
3. OKLAHOMA
4. Alabama
5. Penn State
6. Michigan
7. NEBRASKA
8. Southern California
9. Arizona State, Houston[1]

1974

1. OKLAHOMA
2. Southern California
3. Michigan
4. Ohio State
5. Alabama
6. Notre Dame
7. Penn State
8. Auburn
9. NEBRASKA
10. Miami (Ohio)

1975

1. OKLAHOMA
2. Arizona State
3. Alabama
4. Ohio State
5. UCLA
6. Texas
7. Arkansas
8. Michigan
9. NEBRASKA
10. Penn State

1976

1. Pittsburgh
2. Southern California
3. Michigan
4. Houston
5. OKLAHOMA
6. Ohio State
7. Texas A. & M.
8. Maryland
9. NEBRASKA
10. Georgia

1977

1. Notre Dame
2. Alabama
3. Arkansas
4. Texas
5. Penn State
6. Kentucky
7. OKLAHOMA
8. Pittsburgh
9. Michigan
10. Washington

1978

1. Alabama
2. Southern California
3. OKLAHOMA
4. Penn State
5. Michigan
6. Clemson
7. Notre Dame
8. Nebraska
9. Texas
10. Houston

National Football Rankings United Press International

(Coaches' Poll, 1950–1978)

1950

1. OKLAHOMA
2. Texas
3. Tennessee
4. California
5. Army
6. Michigan
7. Kentucky
8. Princeton
9. Michigan State
10. Ohio State

1951

1. Tennessee
2. Michigan State
3. Illinois
4. Maryland
5. Georgia Tech
6. Princeton
7. Stanford
8. Wisconsin
9. Baylor
10. Texas Christian

1952

1. Michigan State
2. Georgia Tech
3. Notre Dame
4. OKLAHOMA, Southern California[2]
6. UCLA
7. Mississippi
8. Tennessee
9. Alabama
10. Wisconsin

1953

1. Maryland
2. Notre Dame
3. Michigan State
4. UCLA
5. OKLAHOMA
6. Rice
7. Illinois
8. Texas
9. Georgia Tech
10. Iowa

1954

1. UCLA
2. Ohio State
3. OKLAHOMA
4. Notre Dame
5. Navy
6. Mississippi
7. Army
8. Arkansas
9. Miami
10. Wisconsin

1955

1. OKLAHOMA
2. Michigan State
3. Maryland
4. UCLA
5. Ohio State
6. Texas Christian
7. Georgia Tech
8. Auburn
9. Notre Dame
10. Mississippi

1956

1. OKLAHOMA
2. Tennessee
3. Iowa
4. Georgia Tech
5. Texas A. & M.
6. Miami
7. Michigan
8. Syracuse
9. Minnesota
10. Michigan State

1957

1. Ohio State
2. Auburn
3. Michigan State
4. OKLAHOMA
5. Iowa
6. Navy
7. Rice
8. Mississippi
9. Notre Dame
10. Texas A. & M.

1958

1. Louisiana State
2. Iowa
3. Army
4. Auburn
5. OKLAHOMA
6. Wisconsin
7. Ohio State
8. Air Force
9. Texas Christian
10. Syracuse

1959

1. Syracuse
2. Mississippi
3. Louisiana State
4. Texas
5. Georgia
6. Wisconsin
7. Washington
8. Texas Christian
9. Arkansas
10. Penn State

1960

1. Minnesota
2. Iowa
3. Mississippi
4. MISSOURI
5. Washington
6. Navy
7. Arkansas
8. Ohio State
9. KANSAS, Alabama[3]

1961

1. Alabama
2. Ohio State
3. Louisiana State
4. Texas
5. Mississippi
6. Minnesota
7. COLORADO
8. Arkansas
9. Michigan State
10. Utah State

1962

1. Southern California
2. Wisconsin
3. Mississippi
4. Texas, Alabama[4]
6. Arkansas
7. OKLAHOMA
8. Louisiana State
9. Penn State
10. Minnesota

1963

1. Texas
2. Navy
3. Pittsburgh
4. Illinois
5. NEBRASKA
6. Auburn
7. Mississippi
8. OKLAHOMA
9. Alabama
10. Michigan

1964

1. Alabama
2. Arkansas
3. Notre Dame
4. Michigan
5. Texas
6. NEBRASKA
7. Louisiana State
8. Oregon State
9. Ohio State
10. Southern California

1965

1. Michigan State
2. Arkansas
3. NEBRASKA
4. Alabama
5. UCLA
6. MISSOURI
7. Tennessee
8. Notre Dame
9. Southern California
10. Texas Tech

1966

1. Notre Dame
2. Michigan State
3. Alabama
4. Georgia
5. UCLA
6. Purdue
7. NEBRASKA
8. Georgia Tech
9. Southern Methodist
10. Miami

1967

1. Southern California
2. Tennessee
3. OKLAHOMA
4. Notre Dame
5. Wyoming
6. Indiana
7. Alabama
8. Oregon State
9. Purdue
10. UCLA

1968

1. Ohio State
2. Southern California
3. Penn State
4. Georgia
5. Texas
6. KANSAS
7. Tennessee
8. Notre Dame
9. Arkansas
10. OKLAHOMA

1969

1. Texas
2. Penn State
3. Arkansas
4. Southern California
5. Ohio State
6. MISSOURI
7. Louisiana State
8. Michigan
9. Notre Dame
10. UCLA

1970

1. Texas
2. Ohio State
3. NEBRASKA
4. Tennessee
5. Notre Dame
6. Louisiana State
7. Michigan
8. Arizona State
9. Auburn
10. Stanford

1971

1. NEBRASKA
2. Alabama
3. OKLAHOMA
4. Michigan
5. Auburn
6. Arizona State
7. COLORADO
8. Georgia
9. Tennessee
10. Louisiana State

1972

1. Southern California
2. OKLAHOMA
3. Ohio State
4. Alabama
5. Texas
6. Michigan
7. Auburn
8. Penn State
9. NEBRASKA
10. Louisiana State

1973

1. Alabama
2. OKLAHOMA
3. Ohio State
4. Notre Dame
5. Penn State
6. Michigan
7. Southern California
8. Texas
9. UCLA
10. Arizona State

1974[5]

1. Southern California
2. Alabama

3. Ohio State
4. Notre Dame
5. Michigan
6. Auburn
7. Penn State
8. NEBRASKA
9. North Carolina State
10. Miami (Ohio)

1975

1. OKLAHOMA
2. Arizona State
3. Alabama
4. Ohio State
5. UCLA
6. Arkansas
7. Texas
8. Michigan
9. NEBRASKA
10. Penn State

1976

1. Pittsburgh
2. Southern California
3. Michigan
4. Houston
5. Ohio State
6. OKLAHOMA

7. NEBRASKA
8. Texas A. & M.
9. Alabama
10. Georgia

1977

1. Notre Dame
2. Alabama
3. Arkansas
4. Penn State
5. Texas
6. OKLAHOMA
7. Pittsburgh
8. Michigan
9. Washington
10. NEBRASKA

1978

1. Southern California
2. Alabama
3. OKLAHOMA
4. Penn State
5. Michigan
6. Clemson, Notre Dame[6]
8. NEBRASKA
9. Texas
10. Arkansas

NOTES

[1] Arizona State and Houston tied for ninth place; therefore, no team was selected for the No. 10 slot.

[2] Oklahoma and Southern California tied·for fourth place; therefore, no team was selected for the No. 5 slot.

[3] Kansas and Alabama tied for ninth place; therefore, no team was selected for the No. 10 slot.

[4] Texas and Alabama tied for fourth place; therefore, no team was selected for the No. 5 slot.

[5] UPI refused to rank undefeated Oklahoma because of its probationary status.

[6] Clemson and Notre Dame tied for sixth place; therefore, no team was selected for the No. 7 slot.

Conference Champions

BIG SIX

| Year | Team | CONFERENCE GAMES | | | | ALL GAMES | | | | Coach |
		W	L	T	Pct.	W	L	T	Pct.	
1928	Nebraska	5	0	0	1.000	7	1	1	.875	Ernie Bearg
1929	Nebraska	3	0	2	1.000	4	1	3	.800	D. X. Bible
1930	Kansas	4	1	0	.800	6	2	0	.750	H. W. Hargiss
1931	Nebraska	5	0	0	1.000	8	2	0	.800	D. X. Bible
1932	Nebraska	5	0	0	1.000	7	1	1	.833	D. X. Bible
1933	Nebraska	5	0	0	1.000	8	1	0	.888	D. X. Bible
1934	Kansas State	5	0	0	1.000	7	2	1	.750	Lynn Waldorf
1935	Nebraska	4	0	0	1.000	6	2	1	.722	D. X. Bible
1936	Nebraska	5	0	0	1.000	7	2	0	.778	D. X. Bible
1937	Nebraska	3	0	2	.800	6	1	2	.778	Biff Jones
1938	Oklahoma	5	0	0	1.000	10	1	0	.909	Tom Stidham
1939	Missouri	5	0	0	1.000	8	2	0	.800	Don Faurot
1940	Nebraska	5	0	0	1.000	8	2	0	.800	Biff Jones
1941	Missouri	5	0	0	1.000	8	2	0	.800	Don Faurot
1942	Missouri	4	0	1	.900	8	3	1	.708	Don Faurot
1943	Oklahoma	5	0	0	1.000	7	2	0	.778	Dewey Luster
1944	Oklahoma	4	0	1	.900	6	3	1	.650	Dewey Luster
1945	Missouri	5	0	0	1.000	6	4	0	.600	Chauncey Simpson
1946	Kansas	4	1	0	.800	7	2	1	.750	George Sauer
	Oklahoma	4	1	0	.800	8	3	0	.727	Jim Tatum
1947	Kansas	4	0	1	.900	8	1	2	.818	George Sauer
	Oklahoma	4	0	1	.900	7	2	1	.750	Bud Wilkinson

BIG SEVEN

Year	Team	W	L	T	Pct.	W	L	T	Pct.	Coach
1948	Oklahoma	5	0	0	1.000	10	1	0	.909	Bud Wilkinson
1949	Oklahoma	5	0	0	1.000	11	0	0	1.000	Bud Wilkinson
1950	Oklahoma	6	0	0	1.000	10	1	0	.909	Bud Wilkinson
1951	Oklahoma	6	0	0	1.000	8	2	0	.800	Bud Wilkinson
1952	Oklahoma	5	0	1	.916	8	1	1	.850	Bud Wilkinson
1953	Oklahoma	6	0	0	1.000	9	1	1	.863	Bud Wilkinson
1954	Oklahoma	6	0	0	1.000	10	0	0	1.000	Bud Wilkinson
1955	Oklahoma	6	0	0	1.000	11	0	0	1.000	Bud Wilkinson
1956	Oklahoma	6	0	0	1.000	10	0	0	1.000	Bud Wilkinson
1957	Oklahoma	6	0	0	1.000	10	1	0	.909	Bud Wilkinson

BIG EIGHT

| Year | Team | CONFERENCE GAMES | | | | ALL GAMES | | | | Coach |
		W	L	T	Pct.	W	L	T	Pct.	
1958	Oklahoma	6	0	0	1.000	10	1	0	.909	Bud Wilkinson
1959	Oklahoma	5	1	0	.833	7	3	0	.700	Bud Wilkinson
1960	Missouri	7	0	0	1.000	11	0	0	1.000	Dan Devine
1961	Colorado	7	0	0	1.000	9	2	0	.818	Sonny Grandelius
1962	Oklahoma	7	0	0	1.000	8	3	0	.727	Bud Wilkinson
1963	Nebraska	7	0	0	1.000	10	1	0	.909	Bob Devaney
1964	Nebraska	6	1	0	.857	9	2	0	.818	Bob Devaney
1965	Nebraska	7	0	0	1.000	10	1	0	.909	Bob Devaney
1966	Nebraska	6	1	0	.857	9	2	0	.818	Bob Devaney
1967	Oklahoma	7	0	0	1.000	10	1	0	.909	Chuck Fairbanks
1968	Kansas	6	1	0	.857	9	2	0	.818	Pepper Rodgers
	Oklahoma	6	1	0	.857	7	4	0	.636	Chuck Fairbanks
1969	Missouri	6	1	0	.857	9	2	0	.818	Dan Devine
	Nebraska	6	1	0	.857	9	2	0	.818	Bob Devaney
1970	Nebraska	7	0	0	1.000	11	0	1	.959	Bob Devaney
1971	Nebraska	7	0	0	1.000	13	0	0	1.000	Bob Devaney
1972	Nebraska	5	1	1	.786	10	1	1	.875	Bob Devaney
1973	Oklahoma	7	0	0	1.000	10	0	1	.955	Barry Switzer
1974	Oklahoma	7	0	0	1.000	11	0	0	1.000	Barry Switzer
1975	Nebraska	6	1	0	.857	10	2	0	.833	Tom Osborne
	Oklahoma	6	1	0	.857	11	1	0	.916	Barry Switzer
1976	Oklahoma State	5	2	0	.714	9	3	0	.750	Jim Stanley
	Colorado	5	2	0	.714	8	4	0	.667	Bill Mallory
	Oklahoma	5	2	0	.714	9	2	1	.792	Barry Switzer
1977	Oklahoma	7	0	0	1.000	10	2	0	.833	Barry Switzer
1978	Nebraska	6	1	0	.857	9	2	0	.818	Tom Osborne
	Oklahoma	6	1	0	.857	10	1	0	.909	Barry Switzer

Big Eight Win-Loss Standings

1928

CONFERENCE GAMES

	W	L	T	Pct.	Pts.	Opp. Pts.
Nebraska	5	0	0	1.000	108	6
Missouri	3	2	0	.600	72	69
Oklahoma	3	2	0	.600	60	78
Iowa State	2	2	1	.500	39	40
Kansas	1	3	1	.250	13	52
Kansas State	0	5	0	.000	27	74

FULL SEASON

	W	L	T	Pct.	Pts.	Opp. Pts.
Nebraska	7	1	1	.875	144	31
Missouri	4	4	0	.500	138	102
Oklahoma	5	3	0	.625	120	88
Iowa State	2	5	1	.286	39	67
Kansas	2	4	2	.333	34	73
Kansas State	3	5	0	.375	94	94

1929

CONFERENCE GAMES

	W	L	T	Pct.	Pts.	Opp. Pts.
Nebraska	3	0	2	1.000	73	44
Missouri	3	1	1	.750	52	14
Kansas State	3	2	0	.600	35	32
Oklahoma	2	2	1	.500	48	53
Kansas	2	3	0	.400	46	25
Iowa State	0	5	0	.000	21	107

FULL SEASON

	W	L	T	Pct.	Pts.	Opp. Pts.
Nebraska	4	1	3	.800	93	62
Missouri	5	2	1	.714	78	28
Kansas State	3	5	0	.375	55	102
Oklahoma	3	3	2	.500	81	81
Kansas	4	4	0	.500	97	50
Iowa State	1	7	0	.125	54	135

1930

CONFERENCE GAMES

	W	L	T	Pct.	Pts.	Opp. Pts.
Kansas	4	1	0	.800	79	22
Oklahoma	3	1	1	.700	46	33
Kansas State	3	2	0	.600	43	43
Nebraska	2	2	1	.500	46	42
Missouri	1	2	2	.400	27	52
Iowa State	0	5	0	.000	31	80

FULL SEASON

	W	L	T	Pct.	Pts.	Opp. Pts.
Kansas	6	2	0	.750	144	50
Oklahoma	4	3	1	.563	100	57
Kansas State	5	3	0	.625	91	66
Nebraska	4	3	2	.556	119	61
Missouri	2	5	2	.333	41	132
Iowa State	0	9	0	.000	64	134

1931

CONFERENCE GAMES

	W	L	T	Pct.	Pts.	Opp. Pts.
Nebraska	5	0	0	1.000	58	10
Iowa State	3	1	0	.750	40	41
Kansas State	3	2	0	.600	56	20
Kansas	1	3	0	.250	14	29
Missouri	1	4	0	.200	21	64
Oklahoma	1	4	0	.200	22	47

FULL SEASON

	W	L	T	Pct.	Pts.	Opp. Pts.
Nebraska	8	2	0	.800	136	82
Iowa State	5	3	0	.625	72	74
Kansas State	8	2	0	.800	164	39
Kansas	5	5	0	.500	112	54
Missouri	2	8	0	.200	72	183
Oklahoma	4	7	1	.375	88	108

1932

CONFERENCE GAMES

	W	L	T	Pct.	Pts.	Opp. Pts.
Nebraska	5	0	0	1.000	64	18
Kansas	3	2	0	.600	64	41
Oklahoma	3	2	0	.600	66	50
Kansas State	2	3	0	.400	69	45
Missouri	1	3	1	.300	20	59
Iowa State	0	4	1	.100	18	88

FULL SEASON

	W	L	T	Pct.	Pts.	Opp. Pts.
Nebraska	7	1	1	.833	105	52
Kansas	5	3	0	.625	89	77
Oklahoma	4	4	1	.500	90	81
Kansas State	4	4	0	.500	160	80
Missouri	1	7	1	.167	32	184
Iowa State	3	4	1	.438	105	101

1933

CONFERENCE GAMES

	W	L	T	Pct.	Pts.	Opp. Pts.
Nebraska	5	0	0	1.000	83	7
Kansas State	4	1	0	.800	60	9
Oklahoma	3	2	0	.600	67	37
Kansas	2	3	0	.400	47	44
Iowa State	1	4	0	.200	27	73
Missouri	0	5	0	.000	7	121

FULL SEASON

	W	L	T	Pct.	Pts.	Opp. Pts.
Nebraska	8	1	0	.888	138	19
Kansas State	6	2	1	.722	105	29
Oklahoma	4	4	1	.500	83	70
Kansas	5	4	1	.550	102	51
Iowa State	3	5	1	.388	73	120
Missouri	1	8	0	.111	58	193

1934

CONFERENCE GAMES

	W	L	T	Pct.	Pts.	Opp. Pts.
Kansas State	5	0	0	1.000	89	14
Nebraska	4	1	0	.800	36	31
Oklahoma	2	2	1	.500	57	21
Kansas	1	2	2	.400	27	23
Iowa State	1	3	1	.300	19	39
Missouri	0	5	0	.000	6	106

FULL SEASON

	W	L	T	Pct.	Pts.	Opp. Pts.
Kansas State	7	2	1	.750	149	81
Nebraska	6	3	0	.667	106	89
Oklahoma	3	4	2	.333	64	43
Kansas	3	4	3	.450	74	48
Iowa State	5	3	1	.611	132	66
Missouri	0	8	1	.055	25	172

1935

CONFERENCE GAMES

	W	L	T	Pct.	Pts.	Opp. Pts.
Nebraska	4	0	1	.900	77	26
Oklahoma	3	2	0	.600	39	32
Kansas	2	2	1	.500	41	42
Kansas State	1	2	2	.400	15	19
Iowa State	1	3	1	.300	34	60
Missouri	0	2	3	.300	25	52

FULL SEASON

	W	L	T	Pct.	Pts.	Opp. Pts.
Nebraska	6	2	1	.722	138	71
Oklahoma	6	3	0	.667	99	44
Kansas	4	4	1	.500	102	118
Kansas State	2	4	3	.389	40	49
Iowa State	2	4	3	.389	82	101
Missouri	3	3	3	.500	97	77

1936

CONFERENCE GAMES

	W	L	T	Pct.	Pts.	Opp. Pts.
Nebraska	5	0	0	1.000	134	0
Missouri	3	1	1	.700	57	44
Kansas State	2	1	2	.600	86	66
Oklahoma	1	2	2	.400	41	48
Iowa State	1	3	1	.300	35	105
Kansas	0	5	0	.000	16	106

FULL SEASON

	W	L	T	Pct.	Pts.	Opp. Pts.
Nebraska	7	2	0	.778	185	49
Missouri	6	2	1	.722	107	74
Kansas State	4	3	2	.556	137	89
Oklahoma	3	3	3	.500	84	67
Iowa State	3	3	2	.500	94	112
Kansas	1	6	1	.188	35	153

1937

CONFERENCE GAMES

	W	L	T	Pct.	Pts.	Opp. Pts.
Nebraska	3	0	2	.800	43	20
Oklahoma	3	1	1	.700	62	13
Kansas	2	1	2	.600	33	29
Missouri	2	2	1	.500	26	21
Iowa State	1	4	0	.200	33	86
Kansas State	1	4	0	.200	21	49

FULL SEASON

	W	L	T	Pct.	Pts.	Opp. Pts.
Nebraska	6	1	2	.778	99	42
Oklahoma	5	2	2	.667	98	39
Kansas	3	4	2	.444	72	74
Missouri	3	6	1	.350	42	64
Iowa State	3	6	0	.333	50	161
Kansas State	4	5	0	.444	76	84

1938

CONFERENCE GAMES

	W	L	T	Pct.	Pts.	Opp. Pts.
Oklahoma	5	0	0	1.000	90	0
Iowa State	3	1	1	.700	58	50
Missouri	2	3	0	.400	52	75
Nebraska	2	3	0	.400	47	49
Kansas State	1	3	1	.300	48	93
Kansas	1	4	0	.200	48	76

FULL SEASON

	W	L	T	Pct.	Pts.	Opp. Pts.
Oklahoma	10	1	0	.909	185	29
Iowa State	7	1	1	.833	125	64
Missouri	6	3	0	.667	111	82
Nebraska	3	5	1	.389	68	84
Kansas State	4	4	1	.500	108	134
Kansas	3	6	0	.333	132	169

1939

CONFERENCE GAMES

	W	L	T	Pct.	Pts.	Opp. Pts.
Missouri	5	0	0	1.000	84	32
Nebraska	4	1	0	.800	68	50
Oklahoma	3	2	0	.600	91	43
Kansas	1	4	0	.200	27	81
Iowa State	1	4	0	.200	29	83
Kansas State	1	4	0	.200	53	63

FULL SEASON

	W	L	T	Pct.	Pts.	Opp. Pts.
Missouri	8	2	0	.800	155	79
Nebraska	7	1	1	.833	115	70
Oklahoma	6	2	1	.722	186	62
Kansas	2	6	0	.250	47	107
Iowa State	2	7	0	.222	50	117
Kansas State	4	5	0	.444	117	108

1940

CONFERENCE GAMES

	W	L	T	Pct.	Pts.	Opp. Pts.
Nebraska	5	0	0	1.000	127	21
Oklahoma	4	1	0	.800	54	20
Missouri	3	2	0	.600	106	74
Iowa State	2	3	0	.400	52	71
Kansas State	1	4	0	.200	33	70
Kansas	0	5	0	.000	22	138

FULL SEASON

	W	L	T	Pct.	Pts.	Opp. Pts.
Nebraska	8	2	0	.800	183	75
Oklahoma	6	3	0	.667	121	105
Missouri	6	3	0	.667	213	125
Iowa State	4	5	0	.444	118	132
Kansas State	2	7	0	.222	73	145
Kansas	2	7	0	.222	75	183

1941

CONFERENCE GAMES

	W	L	T	Pct.	Pts.	Opp. Pts.
Missouri	5	0	0	1.000	153	19
Nebraska	3	2	0	.600	59	24
Oklahoma	3	2	0	.600	115	35
Kansas	2	3	0	.400	39	131
Kansas State	1	3	1	.300	40	89
Iowa State	0	4	1	.100	25	133

FULL SEASON

	W	L	T	Pct.	Pts.	Opp. Pts.
Missouri	8	2	0	.800	226	39
Nebraska	4	5	0	.444	93	81
Oklahoma	6	3	0	.667	218	95
Kansas	3	6	0	.333	74	222
Kansas State	2	5	2	.333	67	168
Iowa State	2	6	1	.278	85	181

1942

CONFERENCE GAMES

	W	L	T	Pct.	Pts.	Opp. Pts.
Missouri	4	0	1	.900	165	33
Oklahoma	3	1	1	.700	121	20
Nebraska	3	2	0	.600	53	52
Kansas State	2	3	0	.400	35	147
Iowa State	1	4	0	.200	39	105
Kansas	1	4	0	.200	52	108

FULL SEASON

	W	L	T	Pct.	Pts.	Opp. Pts.
Missouri	8	3	1	.708	288	107
Oklahoma	3	5	2	.400	135	78
Nebraska	3	7	0	.300	55	158
Kansas State	3	8	0	.272	79	334
Iowa State	3	6	0	.333	94	177
Kansas	2	8	0	.200	77	248

1943

CONFERENCE GAMES

	W	L	T	Pct.	Pts.	Opp. Pts.
Oklahoma	5	0	0	1.000	130	40
Missouri	3	2	0	.600	145	68
Iowa State	3	2	0	.600	102	58
Kansas	2	3	0	.400	57	54
Nebraska	2	3	0	.400	53	120
Kansas State	0	5	0	.000	23	170

FULL SEASON

	W	L	T	Pct.	Pts.	Opp. Pts.
Oklahoma	7	2	0	.778	187	92
Missouri	3	5	0	.375	170	142
Iowa State	4	4	0	.500	147	104
Kansas	4	5	1	.450	96	107
Nebraska	2	6	0	.250	79	261
Kansas State	1	7	0	.125	48	209

1944

CONFERENCE GAMES

	W	L	T	Pct.	Pts.	Opp. Pts.
Oklahoma	4	0	1	.900	152	40
Iowa State	3	1	1	.700	86	39
Missouri	2	1	2	.600	123	66
Nebraska	2	3	0	.400	77	90
Kansas	1	4	0	.200	34	91
Kansas State	1	4	0	.200	18	164

FULL SEASON

	W	L	T	Pct.	Pts.	Opp. Pts.
Oklahoma	6	3	1	.650	227	149
Iowa State	6	1	1	.725	203	39
Missouri	3	5	2	.400	176	224
Nebraska	2	6	0	.250	83	210
Kansas	3	6	1	.350	128	153
Kansas State	2	5	2	.333	45	215

1945

CONFERENCE GAMES

	W	L	T	Pct.	Pts.	Opp. Pts.
Missouri	5	0	0	1.000	120	32
Oklahoma	4	1	0	.800	120	41
Iowa State	2	2	1	.500	94	60
Nebraska	2	3	0	.400	58	79
Kansas	1	3	1	.300	72	112
Kansas State	0	5	0	.000	33	173

FULL SEASON

	W	L	T	Pct.	Pts.	Opp. Pts.
Missouri	6	4	0	.600	170	174
Oklahoma	5	5	0	.500	169	138
Iowa State	4	3	1	.562	156	97
Nebraska	4	5	0	.444	145	200
Kansas	4	5	1	.450	139	175
Kansas State	1	7	0	.125	71	268

1946

CONFERENCE GAMES

	W	L	T	Pct.	Pts.	Opp. Pts.
Kansas	4	1	0	.800	108	56
Oklahoma	4	1	0	.800	158	35
Missouri	3	2	0	.600	105	80
Nebraska	3	2	0	.600	106	62
Iowa State	1	4	0	.200	34	160
Kansas State	0	5	0	.000	14	132

FULL SEASON

	W	L	T	Pct.	Pts.	Opp. Pts.
Kansas	7	2	1	.750	157	145
Oklahoma	8	3	0	.727	309	120
Missouri	5	4	1	.550	158	166
Nebraska	3	6	0	.333	126	161
Iowa State	2	6	1	.278	77	239
Kansas State	0	9	0	.000	41	233

1947

CONFERENCE GAMES

	W	L	T	Pct.	Pts.	Opp. Pts.
Kansas	4	0	1	.900	128	41
Oklahoma	4	0	1	.900	102	60
Missouri	3	2	0	.600	146	61
Nebraska	2	3	0	.400	54	88
Iowa State	1	4	0	.200	44	94
Kansas State	0	5	0	.000	27	157

FULL SEASON

	W	L	T	Pct.	Pts.	Opp. Pts.
Kansas	8	1	2	.818	304	102
Oklahoma	7	2	1	.750	194	161
Missouri	6	4	0	.600	240	116
Nebraska	2	7	0	.222	73	191
Iowa State	3	6	0	.333	111	141
Kansas State	0	10	0	.000	71	283

1948

CONFERENCE GAMES

	W	L	T	Pct.	Pts.	Opp. Pts.
Oklahoma	5	0	0	1.000	217	34
Missouri	5	1	0	.833	186	81
Kansas	4	2	0	.667	121	116
Colorado	2	3	0	.400	97	98
Iowa State	2	4	0	.333	73	128
Nebraska	2	4	0	.333	84	135
Kansas State	0	6	0	.000	28	214

FULL SEASON

	W	L	T	Pct.	Pts.	Opp. Pts.
Oklahoma	10	1	0	.909	350	121
Missouri	8	3	0	.727	331	161
Kansas	7	3	0	.700	199	137
Colorado	3	6	0	.333	168	164
Iowa State	4	6	0	.400	116	197
Nebraska	2	8	0	.200	137	273
Kansas State	1	9	0	.100	78	323

1949

CONFERENCE GAMES

	W	L	T	Pct.	Pts.	Opp. Pts.
Oklahoma	5	0	0	1.000	196	40
Missouri	5	1	0	.883	148	115
Iowa State	3	3	0	.500	64	106
Nebraska	3	3	0	.500	78	116
Kansas	2	4	0	.333	137	127
Colorado	1	4	0	.200	59	97
Kansas State	1	5	0	.167	81	162

FULL SEASON

	W	L	T	Pct.	Pts.	Opp. Pts.
Oklahoma	11	0	0	1.000	399	88
Missouri	7	4	0	.636	264	225
Iowa State	5	3	1	.611	169	134
Nebraska	4	5	0	.444	124	172
Kansas	5	5	0	.500	259	183
Colorado	3	7	0	.300	129	184
Kansas State	2	8	0	.200	191	257

1950

CONFERENCE GAMES

	W	L	T	Pct.	Pts.	Opp. Pts.
Oklahoma	6	0	0	1.000	228	80
Nebraska	4	2	0	.667	196	171
Missouri	3	2	1	.583	130	133
Kansas	3	3	0	.500	152	135
Iowa State	2	3	1	.416	88	107
Colorado	2	4	0	.333	127	114
Kansas State	0	6	0	.000	48	229

FULL SEASON

	W	L	T	Pct.	Pts.	Opp. Pts.
Oklahoma	10	1	0	.909	352	148
Nebraska	6	2	1	.722	267	217
Missouri	4	5	1	.450	166	215
Kansas	6	4	0	.600	284	188
Iowa State	3	6	1	.350	174	200
Colorado	5	4	1	.550	227	172
Kansas State	1	9	1	.136	122	355

1951

CONFERENCE GAMES

	W	L	T	Pct.	Pts.	Opp. Pts.
Oklahoma	6	0	0	1.000	217	61
Colorado	5	1	0	.833	186	136
Kansas	5	2	0	.667	202	150
Iowa State	2	4	0	.333	139	189
Nebraska	2	4	0	.333	80	158
Missouri	2	4	0	.333	122	163
Kansas State	0	6	0	.000	47	136

FULL SEASON

	W	L	T	Pct.	Pts.	Opp. Pts.
Oklahoma	8	2	0	.800	321	97
Colorado	7	3	0	.700	289	229
Kansas	8	2	0	.800	316	208
Iowa State	4	4	1	.500	211	216
Nebraska	2	8	0	.200	121	259
Missouri	3	7	0	.300	169	292
Kansas State	0	9	0	.000	73	228

1952

CONFERENCE GAMES

	W	L	T	Pct.	Pts.	Opp. Pts.
Oklahoma	5	0	1	.916	234	67
Missouri	5	1	0	.833	109	79
Nebraska	3	2	1	.583	92	87
Colorado	2	2	2	.500	111	111
Kansas	3	3	0	.500	142	94
Iowa State	1	5	0	.166	39	140
Kansas State	0	6	0	.000	40	189

FULL SEASON

	W	L	T	Pct.	Pts.	Opp. Pts.
Oklahoma	8	1	1	.850	407	141
Missouri	5	5	0	.500	147	159
Nebraska	5	4	1	.550	173	123
Colorado	6	2	2	.700	246	158
Kansas	7	3	0	.700	214	110
Iowa State	3	6	0	.333	158	199
Kansas State	1	9	0	.100	81	255

1953

CONFERENCE GAMES

	W	L	T	Pct.	Pts.	Opp. Pts.
Oklahoma	6	0	0	1.000	197	34
Kansas State	4	2	0	.667	88	76
Missouri	4	2	0	.667	89	62
Kansas	2	4	0	.333	56	92
Colorado	2	4	0	.333	126	153
Nebraska	2	4	0	.333	60	113
Iowa State	1	5	0	.167	78	164

FULL SEASON

	W	L	T	Pct.	Pts.	Opp. Pts.
Oklahoma	9	1	1	.863	293	90
Kansas State	6	3	1	.650	198	116
Missouri	6	4	0	.600	130	116
Kansas	2	8	0	.200	83	179
Colorado	6	4	0	.600	201	194
Nebraska	3	6	1	.350	119	184
Iowa State	2	7	0	.222	120	211

1954

CONFERENCE GAMES

	W	L	T	Pct.	Pts.	Opp. Pts.
Oklahoma	6	0	0	1.000	228	26
Nebraska	4	2	0	.667	135	121
Colorado	3	2	1	.583	116	66
Missouri	3	2	1	.583	159	117
Kansas State	3	3	0	.500	68	110
Iowa State	1	5	0	.167	68	149
Kansas	0	6	0	.000	50	235

FULL SEASON

	W	L	T	Pct.	Pts.	Opp. Pts.
Oklahoma	10	0	0	1.000	304	62
Nebraska	6	5	0	.545	233	202
Colorado	7	2	1	.750	283	91
Missouri	4	5	1	.450	198	261
Kansas State	7	3	0	.700	191	154
Iowa State	3	6	0	.333	151	182
Kansas	0	10	0	.000	93	377

1955

CONFERENCE GAMES

	W	L	T	Pct.	Pts.	Opp. Pts.
Oklahoma	6	0	0	1.000	253	34
Nebraska	5	1	0	.833	100	94
Colorado	3	3	0	.500	139	126
Kansas State	3	3	0	.500	96	97
Kansas	1	4	1	.250	40	135
Iowa State	1	4	1	.250	41	132
Missouri	1	5	0	.167	53	104

FULL SEASON

	W	L	T	Pct.	Pts.	Opp. Pts.
Oklahoma	11	0	0	1.000	385	60
Nebraska	5	5	0	.500	127	176
Colorado	6	4	0	.600	203	149
Kansas State	4	6	0	.400	165	191
Kansas	3	6	1	.350	93	222
Iowa State	1	7	1	.167	69	218
Missouri	1	9	0	.100	92	192

1956

CONFERENCE GAMES

	W	L	T	Pct.	Pts.	Opp. Pts.
Oklahoma	6	0	0	1.000	292	51
Colorado	4	1	1	.750	161	66
Missouri	3	2	1	.583	111	115
Nebraska	3	3	0	.500	63	121
Kansas	2	4	0	.333	115	130
Kansas State	2	4	0	.333	63	153
Iowa State	0	6	0	.000	27	196

FULL SEASON

	W	L	T	Pct.	Pts.	Opp. Pts.
Oklahoma	10	0	0	1.000	466	51
Colorado	8	2	1	.773	294	143
Missouri	4	5	1	.450	200	183
Nebraska	4	6	0	.400	125	206
Kansas	3	6	1	.350	163	215
Kansas State	3	7	0	.300	143	259
Iowa State	2	8	0	.200	92	260

1957

CONFERENCE GAMES

	W	L	T	Pct.	Pts.	Opp. Pts.
Oklahoma	6	0	0	1.000	185	48
Kansas	4	2	0	.667	77	128
Colorado	3	3	0	.500	160	93
Missouri	3	3	0	.500	100	103
Iowa State	2	4	0	.333	92	133
Kansas State	2	4	0	.333	65	113
Nebraska	1	5	0	.167	46	107

Note: Oklahoma State did not play a conference schedule.

FULL SEASON

	W	L	T	Pct.	Pts.	Opp. Pts.
Oklahoma	10	1	0	.909	333	89
Kansas	5	4	1	.550	115	230
Colorado	6	3	1	.650	250	137
Missouri	5	4	1	.550	149	157
Iowa State	4	5	1	.450	142	160
Kansas State	3	6	1	.350	124	166
Nebraska	1	9	0	.100	67	243

1958

CONFERENCE GAMES

	W	L	T	Pct.	Pts.	Opp. Pts.
Oklahoma	6	0	0	1.000	205	20
Missouri	4	1	1	.750	123	75
Colorado	4	2	0	.667	107	75
Kansas	3	2	1	.583	70	106
Kansas State	2	4	0	.333	66	118
Nebraska	1	5	0	.167	43	156
Iowa State	0	6	0	.000	18	82

Note: Oklahoma State did not play a conference schedule.

FULL SEASON

	W	L	T	Pct.	Pts.	Opp. Pts.
Oklahoma	10	1	0	.909	300	55
Missouri	5	4	1	.550	164	141
Colorado	6	4	0	.600	207	122
Kansas	4	5	1	.450	87	175
Kansas State	3	7	0	.300	110	192
Nebraska	3	7	0	.300	71	235
Iowa State	4	6	0	.400	127	88

1959

CONFERENCE GAMES

	W	L	T	Pct.	Pts.	Opp. Pts.
Oklahoma	5	1	0	.833	164	55
Missouri	4	2	0	.667	82	53
Kansas	3	3	0	.500	79	64
Iowa State	3	3	0	.500	83	62
Colorado	3	3	0	.500	92	134
Nebraska	2	4	0	.333	62	99
Kansas State	1	5	0	.167	60	155

Note: Oklahoma State did not play a conference schedule.

FULL SEASON

	W	L	T	Pct.	Pts.	Opp. Pts.
Oklahoma	7	3	0	.700	234	146
Missouri	6	5	0	.545	125	124
Kansas	5	5	0	.500	163	134
Iowa State	7	3	0	.700	248	80
Colorado	5	5	0	.500	144	177
Nebraska	4	6	0	.400	108	160
Kansas State	2	8	0	.200	109	266

1960

CONFERENCE GAMES*

	W	L	T	Pct.	Pts.	Opp. Pts.
Missouri	7	0	0	1.000	199	63
Colorado	6	1	0	.857	99	75
Kansas	4	2	1	.642	184	47
Iowa State	4	3	0	.571	81	109
Oklahoma	2	4	1	.357	118	101
Oklahoma State	2	5	0	.285	67	98
Nebraska	2	5	0	.285	53	116
Kansas State	0	7	0	.000	35	227

FULL SEASON

	W	L	T	Pct.	Pts.	Opp. Pts.
Missouri	11	0	0	1.000	295	93
Colorado	7	3	0	.700	140	133
Kansas	5	4	1	.550	219	89
Iowa State	7	3	0	.700	185	136
Oklahoma	3	6	1	.350	136	158
Oklahoma State	3	7	0	.300	102	126
Nebraska	4	6	0	.400	95	164
Kansas State	1	9	0	.100	78	316

*KU defeated CU, 34-6, and MU, 23-7, but forfeited games when player ruled ineligible. Won-Lost column conforms to forfeited games. Team points and opponents points include all points scored on the field.

1961

CONFERENCE GAMES

	W	L	T	Pct.	Pts.	Opp. Pts.
Colorado	7	0	0	1.000	127	39
Kansas	5	2	0	.714	161	51
Missouri	5	2	0	.714	76	37
Oklahoma	4	3	0	.571	95	86
Iowa State	3	4	0	.429	93	113
Nebraska	2	5	0	.285	66	93
Oklahoma State	2	5	0	.285	87	117
Kansas State	0	7	0	.000	22	191

FULL SEASON

	W	L	T	Pct.	Pts.	Opp. Pts.
Colorado	9	2	0	.818	184	104
Kansas	7	3	1	.682	269	88
Missouri	7	2	1	.750	124	57
Oklahoma	5	5	0	.500	122	141
Iowa State	5	5	0	.500	151	133
Nebraska	3	6	1	.350	119	135
Oklahoma State	4	6	0	.400	154	166
Kansas State	2	8	0	.200	58	232

1962

CONFERENCE GAMES

	W	L	T	Pct.	Pts.	Opp. Pts.
Oklahoma	7	0	0	1.000	247	19
Missouri	5	1	1	.786	152	35
Nebraska	5	2	0	.714	160	100
Kansas	4	2	1	.643	164	89
Iowa State	3	4	0	.428	155	167
Oklahoma State	2	5	0	.285	102	166
Colorado	1	6	0	.142	55	278
Kansas State	0	7	0	.000	26	207

FULL SEASON

	W	L	T	Pct.	Pts.	Opp. Pts.
Oklahoma	8	3	0	.727	267	61
Missouri	8	1	2	.818	204	62
Nebraska	9	2	0	.818	293	161
Kansas	6	3	1	.650	214	116
Iowa State	5	5	0	.500	235	235
Oklahoma State	4	6	0	.400	138	214
Colorado	2	8	0	.200	122	346
Kansas State	0	10	0	.000	39	283

1963

CONFERENCE GAMES

	W	L	T	Pct.	Pts.	Opp. Pts.
Nebraska	7	0	0	1.000	175	76
Oklahoma	6	1	0	.858	181	83
Missouri	5	2	0	.714	108	57
Kansas	3	4	0	.428	166	91
Iowa State	3	4	0	.428	100	122
Colorado	2	5	0	.286	80	173
Kansas State	1	5	0	.166	54	148
Oklahoma State	0	6	0	.000	67	181

FULL SEASON

	W	L	T	Pct.	Pts.	Opp. Pts.
Nebraska	10	1	0	.909	273	114
Oklahoma	8	2	0	.800	236	137
Missouri	7	3	0	.700	151	86
Kansas	5	5	0	.500	207	122
Iowa State	4	5	0	.444	129	143
Colorado	2	8	0	.200	100	245
Kansas State	2	7	0	.222	91	222
Oklahoma State	1	8	0	.111	107	260

1964

CONFERENCE GAMES

	W	L	T	Pct.	Pts.	Opp. Pts.
Nebraska	6	1	0	.857	139	48
Oklahoma	5	1	1	.786	154	63
Kansas	5	2	0	.714	109	88
Missouri	4	2	1	.643	88	54
Kansas State	3	4	0	.429	40	139
Oklahoma State	3	4	0	.429	110	110
Colorado	1	6	0	.143	66	98
Iowa State	0	7	0	.000	40	146

FULL SEASON

	W	L	T	Pct.	Pts.	Opp. Pts.
Nebraska	9	2	0	.818	256	85
Oklahoma	6	4	1	.591	207	170
Kansas	6	4	0	.600	136	146
Missouri	6	3	1	.650	142	88
Kansas State	3	7	0	.300	64	186
Oklahoma State	4	6	0	.400	165	192
Colorado	2	8	0	.200	101	156
Iowa State	1	8	1	.150	72	155

1965

CONFERENCE GAMES

	W	L	T	Pct.	Pts.	Opp. Pts.
Nebraska	7	0	0	1.000	223	59
Missouri	6	1	0	.857	172	56
Colorado	4	2	1	.643	134	93
Iowa State	3	3	1	.500	110	124
Oklahoma	3	4	0	.429	97	108
Oklahoma State	2	5	0	.286	86	114
Kansas	2	5	0	.286	97	149
Kansas State	0	7	0	.000	19	235

FULL SEASON

	W	L	T	Pct.	Pts.	Opp. Pts.
Nebraska	10	1	0	.909	349	129
Missouri	8	2	1	.772	223	101
Colorado	6	2	2	.700	163	106
Iowa State	5	4	1	.550	178	147
Oklahoma	3	7	0	.300	106	150
Oklahoma State	3	7	0	.300	131	173
Kansas	2	8	0	.200	119	215
Kansas State	0	10	0	.000	43	296

1966

CONFERENCE GAMES

	W	L	T	Pct.	Pts.	Opp. Pts.
Nebraska	6	1	0	.857	143	64
Colorado	5	2	0	.714	165	92
Oklahoma State	4	2	1	.643	77	79
Missouri	4	2	1	.643	61	78
Oklahoma	4	3	0	.571	157	75
Iowa State	2	3	2	.429	116	130
Kansas State	0	6	1	.072	38	149
Kansas	0	6	1	.072	48	138

FULL SEASON

	W	L	T	Pct.	Pts.	Opp. Pts.
Nebraska	9	2	0	.818	223	118
Colorado	7	3	0	.700	191	132
Oklahoma State	4	5	1	.450	103	138
Missouri	6	3	1	.650	121	116
Oklahoma	6	4	0	.600	192	122
Iowa State	2	6	2	.300	160	211
Kansas State	0	9	1	.050	66	226
Kansas	2	7	1	.250	106	188

1967

CONFERENCE GAMES

	W	L	T	Pct.	Pts.	Opp. Pts.
Oklahoma	7	0	0	1.000	201	59
Colorado	5	2	0	.714	137	72
Kansas	5	2	0	.714	116	77
Missouri	4	3	0	.571	83	67
Oklahoma State	3	4	0	.429	116	115
Nebraska	3	4	0	.429	74	76
Iowa State	1	6	0	.143	66	177
Kansas State	0	7	0	.000	63	213

FULL SEASON

	W	L	T	Pct.	Pts.	Opp. Pts.
Oklahoma	10	1	0	.909	290	92
Colorado	9	2	0	.818	245	113
Kansas	5	5	0	.500	166	146
Missouri	7	3	0	.700	134	76
Oklahoma State	4	5	1	.450	123	140
Nebraska	6	4	0	.600	127	83
Iowa State	2	8	0	.200	86	275
Kansas State	1	9	0	.100	90	263

1968

CONFERENCE GAMES

	W	L	T	Pct.	Pts.	Opp. Pts.
Kansas	6	1	0	.857	227	141
Oklahoma	6	1	0	.857	241	112
Missouri	5	2	0	.714	216	111
Colorado	3	4	0	.429	157	169
Nebraska	3	4	0	.429	94	131
Kansas State	2	5	0	.286	130	203
Oklahoma State	2	5	0	.286	132	208
Iowa State	1	6	0	.143	110	222

FULL SEASON

	W	L	T	Pct.	Pts.	Opp. Pts.
Kansas	9	2	0	.818	394	190
Oklahoma	7	4	0	.636	343	225
Missouri	8	3	0	.727	308	136
Colorado	4	6	0	.400	220	244
Nebraska	6	4	0	.600	155	161
Kansas State	4	6	0	.400	194	247
Oklahoma State	3	7	0	.300	161	288
Iowa State	3	7	0	.300	178	273

1969

CONFERENCE GAMES

	W	L	T	Pct.	Pts.	Opp. Pts.
Missouri	6	1	0	.857	266	141
Nebraska	6	1	0	.857	132	68
Colorado	5	2	0	.714	161	143
Oklahoma	4	3	0	.571	183	233
Kansas State	3	4	0	.429	215	174
Oklahoma State	3	4	0	.429	156	133
Iowa State	1	6	0	.143	81	197
Kansas	0	7	0	.000	134	236

FULL SEASON

	W	L	T	Pct.	Pts.	Opp. Pts.
Missouri	9	2	0	.818	365	191
Nebraska	9	2	0	.818	254	119
Colorado	8	3	0	.727	276	227
Oklahoma	6	4	0	.600	285	289
Kansas State	5	5	0	.500	319	233
Oklahoma State	5	5	0	.500	197	200
Iowa State	3	7	0	.300	152	231
Kansas	1	9	0	.100	176	290

1970

CONFERENCE GAMES

	W	L	T	Pct.	Pts.	Opp. Pts.
Nebraska	7	0	0	1.000	289	134
Kansas State	5	2	0	.714	130	134
Oklahoma	5	2	0	.714	209	133
Colorado	3	4	0	.429	200	148
Missouri	3	4	0	.429	150	150
Oklahoma State	2	5	0	.286	133	263
Kansas	2	5	0	.286	142	186
Iowa State	1	6	0	.143	135	240

FULL SEASON

	W	L	T	Pct.	Pts.	Opp. Pts.
Nebraska	11	0	1	.959	426	189
Kansas State	6	5	0	.545	190	218
Oklahoma	7	4	1	.583	305	239
Colorado	6	5	0	.545	309	206
Missouri	5	6	0	.455	243	223
Oklahoma State	4	7	0	.364	213	337
Kansas	5	6	0	.455	270	277
Iowa State	5	6	0	.455	248	284

1971

CONFERENCE GAMES

	W	L	T	Pct.	Pts.	Opp. Pts.
Nebraska	7	0	0	1.000	277	68
Oklahoma	6	1	0	.857	328	119
Colorado	5	2	0	.714	181	138
Iowa State	4	3	0	.571	189	145
Kansas State	2	5	0	.286	142	248
Oklahoma State	2	5	0	.286	110	254
Kansas	2	5	0	.286	104	218
Missouri	0	7	0	.000	57	200

FULL SEASON

	W	L	T	Pct.	Pts.	Opp. Pts.
Nebraska	13	0	0	1.000	507	104
Oklahoma	11	1	0	.917	535	217
Colorado	10	2	0	.834	370	220
Iowa State	8	4	0	.667	337	250
Kansas State	5	6	0	.455	219	296
Oklahoma State	4	6	1	.409	184	322
Kansas	4	7	0	.364	187	286
Missouri	1	10	0	.091	93	260

1972

CONFERENCE GAMES

	W	L	T	Pct.	Pts.	Opp. Pts.
Nebraska	5	1	1	.786	281	57
Oklahoma State	5	2	0	.714	163	135
Colorado	4	3	0	.571	158	145
Missouri	4	3	0	.571	96	140
Kansas	3	4	0	.429	83	201
Oklahoma	3	4	0	.429	289	68
Iowa State	2	4	1	.357	159	158
Kansas State	1	6	0	.143	94	271

FULL SEASON

	W	L	T	Pct.	Pts.	Opp. Pts.
Nebraska	10	1	1	.875	501	97
Oklahoma State	7	4	0	.636	259	203
Colorado	8	4	0	.667	313	206
Missouri	7	5	0	.583	219	311
Kansas	5	6	0	.455	208	305
Oklahoma	3	9	0	.250	399	74
Iowa State	5	6	1	.458	319	238
Kansas State	3	8	0	.273	169	407

1973

CONFERENCE GAMES

	W	L	T	Pct.	Pts.	Opp. Pts.
Oklahoma	7	0	0	1.000	275	79
Kansas	4	2	1	.643	117	134
Nebraska	4	2	1	.643	148	110
Oklahoma State	2	3	2	.429	132	146
Missouri	3	4	0	.429	93	107
Iowa State	2	5	0	.286	124	150
Kansas State	2	5	0	.286	107	223
Colorado	2	5	0	.286	116	163

FULL SEASON

	W	L	T	Pct.	Pts.	Opp. Pts.
Oklahoma	10	0	1	.955	400	133
Kansas	7	4	1	.625	253	220
Nebraska	9	2	1	.792	306	163
Oklahoma State	5	4	2	.545	303	186
Missouri	8	4	0	.667	219	152
Iowa State	4	7	0	.364	245	236
Kansas State	5	6	0	.455	176	260
Colorado	5	6	0	.455	240	250

1974

CONFERENCE GAMES

	W	L	T	Pct.	Pts.	Opp. Pts.
Oklahoma	7	0	0	1.000	294	65
Missouri	5	2	0	.714	147	127
Nebraska	5	2	0	.714	176	87
Oklahoma State	4	3	0	.571	134	125
Colorado	3	4	0	.429	160	186
Iowa State	2	5	0	.286	94	133
Kansas State	1	6	0	.143	91	241
Kansas	1	6	0	.143	72	204

FULL SEASON

	W	L	T	Pct.	Pts.	Opp. Pts.
Oklahoma	11	0	0	1.000	473	92
Missouri	7	4	0	.636	204	217
Nebraska	9	3	0	.750	373	132
Oklahoma State	7	5	0	.583	262	183
Colorado	5	6	0	.455	226	307
Iowa State	4	7	0	.364	186	198
Kansas State	4	7	0	.364	193	283
Kansas	4	7	0	.364	157	247

1975

CONFERENCE GAMES

	W	L	T	Pct.	Pts.	Opp. Pts.
Nebraska	6	1	0	.857	211	83
Oklahoma	6	1	0	.857	178	97
Colorado	5	2	0	.714	174	166
Kansas	4	3	0	.571	154	112
Oklahoma State	3	4	0	.429	153	142
Missouri	3	4	0	.429	198	162
Iowa State	1	6	0	.143	82	205
Kansas State	0	7	0	.000	23	206

FULL SEASON

	W	L	T	Pct.	Pts.	Opp. Pts.
Nebraska	10	2	0	.833	367	137
Oklahoma	11	1	0	.917	343	154
Colorado	9	3	0	.750	331	251
Kansas	7	5	0	.583	262	180
Oklahoma State	7	4	0	.636	285	178
Missouri	6	5	0	.545	282	241
Iowa State	4	7	0	.364	161	263
Kansas State	3	8	0	.273	89	248

1976

CONFERENCE GAMES

	W	L	T	Pct.	Pts.	Opp. Pts.
Oklahoma State	5	2	0	.714	179	133
Colorado	5	2	0	.714	189	140
Oklahoma	5	2	0	.714	203	150
Iowa State	4	3	0	.571	179	175
Nebraska	4	3	0	.571	192	96
Missouri	3	4	0	.429	175	134
Kansas	2	5	0	.286	126	179
Kansas State	0	7	0	.000	118	247

FULL SEASON

	W	L	T	Pct.	Pts.	Opp. Pts.
Oklahoma State	9	3	0	.750	329	214
Colorado	8	4	0	.667	305	221
Oklahoma	9	2	1	.792	326	192
Iowa State	8	3	0	.727	369	216
Nebraska	9	3	1	.731	419	161
Missouri	6	5	0	.545	273	214
Kansas	6	5	0	.545	260	251
Kansas State	1	10	0	.091	155	317

1977

CONFERENCE GAMES

	W	L	T	Pct.	Pts.	Opp. Pts.
Oklahoma	7	0	0	1.000	273	98
Iowa State	5	2	0	.714	138	99
Nebraska	5	2	0	.714	191	110
Colorado	3	3	1	.500	124	146
Missouri	3	4	0	.429	142	114
Kansas	2	4	1	.357	89	198
Oklahoma State	2	5	0	.286	124	197
Kansas State	0	7	0	.000	79	191

FULL SEASON

	W	L	T	Pct.	Pts.	Opp. Pts.
Oklahoma	10	2	0	.833	401	217
Iowa State	8	4	0	.667	249	178
Nebraska	9	3	0	.750	315	193
Colorado	7	3	1	.682	266	174
Missouri	4	7	0	.364	195	180
Kansas	3	7	1	.318	131	269
Oklahoma State	4	7	0	.364	235	267
Kansas State	1	10	0	.091	131	286

1978

CONFERENCE GAMES

	W	L	T	Pct.	Pts.	Opp. Pts.
Oklahoma	6	1	0	.857	256	95
Nebraska	6	1	0	.857	256	112
Iowa State	4	3	0	.571	104	121
Missouri	4	3	0	.571	235	166
Kansas State	3	4	0	.429	121	221
Oklahoma State	3	4	0	.429	123	177
Colorado	2	5	0	.286	112	178
Kansas	0	7	0	.000	78	215

FULL SEASON*

	W	L	T	Pct.	Pts.	Opp. Pts.
Oklahoma	10	1	0	.909	440	151
Nebraska	9	2	0	.818	420	185
Iowa State	8	3	0	.727	207	160
Missouri	7	4	0	.636	348	221
Kansas State	4	7	0	.364	201	342
Oklahoma State	3	8	0	.273	167	266
Colorado	6	5	0	.545	230	306
Kansas	1	10	0	.091	124	345

*Note: Full-season figures do not include the January 1, 1979, bowl games.

Big Eight Bowl Game Record

1938	Cotton Bowl	COLORADO 14, Rice 28
1939	Orange Bowl	OKLAHOMA 0, Tennessee 17
1940	Orange Bowl	MISSOURI 7, Georgia Tech 21
1941	Rose Bowl	NEBRASKA 13, Stanford 21
1942	Sugar Bowl	MISSOURI 0, Fordham 2
1945	Cotton Bowl	OKLAHOMA STATE 34, Texas Christian 9
1946	Sugar Bowl	OKLAHOMA STATE 33, St. Mary's 13
1946	Cotton Bowl	MISSOURI 27, Texas 40
1947	Gator Bowl	OKLAHOMA 34, North Carolina State 13
1948	Orange Bowl	KANSAS 14, Georgia Tech 20
1948	Delta Bowl	OKLAHOMA STATE 0, William & Mary 20
1949	Gator Bowl	MISSOURI 23, Clemson 24
1949	Sugar Bowl	OKLAHOMA 14, North Carolina 6
1950	Gator Bowl	MISSOURI 7, Maryland 20
1950	Sugar Bowl	OKLAHOMA 35, Louisiana State 0
1951	Sugar Bowl	OKLAHOMA 7, Kentucky 13
1954	Orange Bowl	OKLAHOMA 7, Maryland 0
1955	Orange Bowl	NEBRASKA 7, Duke 34
1956	Orange Bowl	OKLAHOMA 20, Maryland 6
1957	Orange Bowl	COLORADO 27, Clemson 21
1958	Bluegrass Bowl	OKLAHOMA STATE 15, Florida State 6
1958	Orange Bowl	OKLAHOMA 48, Duke 21
1959	Orange Bowl	OKLAHOMA 21, Syracuse 6
1960	Orange Bowl	MISSOURI 0, Georgia 14
1961	Orange Bowl	MISSOURI 21, Navy 14
1961	Bluebonnet Bowl	KANSAS 33, Rice 7
1962	Orange Bowl	COLORADO 7, Louisiana State 25
1962	Gotham Bowl	NEBRASKA 36, Miami, 34
1962	Bluebonnet Bowl	MISSOURI 14, Georgia Tech 10
1963	Orange Bowl	OKLAHOMA 0, Alabama 17
1964	Orange Bowl	NEBRASKA 13, Auburn 7
1965	Cotton Bowl	NEBRASKA 7, Arkansas 10
1965	Gator Bowl	OKLAHOMA 19, Florida State 36
1966	Orange Bowl	NEBRASKA 28, Alabama 39
1966	Sugar Bowl	MISSOURI 20, Florida 18
1967	Sugar Bowl	NEBRASKA 7, Alabama 34
1967	Bluebonnet Bowl	COLORADO 31, Miami, 21
1968	Orange Bowl	OKLAHOMA 26, Tennessee 24
1968	Astro–Bluebonnet Bowl	OKLAHOMA 27, Southern Methodist 28
1969	Gator Bowl	MISSOURI 35, Alabama 10

/ 249

1969	Orange Bowl	KANSAS 14, Penn State 15
1969	Liberty Bowl	COLORADO 47, Alabama 33
1969	Sun Bowl	NEBRASKA 45, Georgia 6
1970	Orange Bowl	MISSOURI 3, Penn State 10
1970	Liberty Bowl	COLORADO 3, Tulane 17
1970	Astro–Bluebonnet Bowl	OKLAHOMA 24, Alabama 24
1971	Orange Bowl	NEBRASKA 17, Louisiana State 12
1971	Sun Bowl	IOWA STATE 15, Louisiana State 33
1971	Astro–Bluebonnet Bowl	COLORADO 29, Houston 17
1972	Sugar Bowl	OKLAHOMA 40, Auburn 22
1972	Orange Bowl	NEBRASKA 38, Alabama 6
1972	Liberty Bowl	IOWA STATE 30, Georgia Tech 31
1972	Fiesta Bowl	MISSOURI 35, Arizona State 49
1973	Gator Bowl	COLORADO 3, Auburn 24
1973	Sugar Bowl	OKLAHOMA 14, Penn State 0
1973	Orange Bowl	NEBRASKA 40, Notre Dame 6
1973	Sun Bowl	MISSOURI 34, Auburn 17
1973	Liberty Bowl	KANSAS 18, North Carolina State 31
1974	Cotton Bowl	NEBRASKA 19, Texas 3
1974	Fiesta Bowl	OKLAHOMA STATE 16, Brigham Young 6
1974	Sugar Bowl	NEBRASKA 13, Florida 10
1975	Sun Bowl	KANSAS 19, Pittsburgh 33
1975	Astro–Bluebonnet Bowl	COLORADO 21, Texas 38
1975	Fiesta Bowl	NEBRASKA 14, Arizona State 17
1976	Orange Bowl	OKLAHOMA 14, Michigan 6
1977	Orange Bowl	COLORADO 10, Ohio State 27
1977	Astro–Bluebonnet Bowl	NEBRASKA 27, Texas Tech 24
1977	Tangerine Bowl	OKLAHOMA STATE 49, Brigham Young 21
1977	Fiesta Bowl	OKLAHOMA 41, Wyoming 7
1978	Orange Bowl	OKLAHOMA 6, Arkansas 31
1978	Peach Bowl	IOWA STATE 14, North Carolina State 24
1978	Liberty Bowl	NEBRASKA 21, North Carolina 17
1979	Orange Bowl	OKLAHOMA 31, NEBRASKA 24
1979	Liberty Bowl	MISSOURI 20, Louisiana State 15
1979	Hall of Fame	IOWA STATE 12, Texas A. & M. 28

All-Conference Teams

(Composite of Recognized Selections)

BIG SIX

1928

Ends—**Miller Brown (Missouri), Tom Churchill (Oklahoma)**

Tackles—**Marion Broadstone (Nebraska), Bill Smith (Missouri)**

Guards—**Dan McMullen (Nebraska), Elmer Holm (Nebraska)**

Center—**Ted James (Nebraska)**

Backs—**Bob Mehrle (Missouri), Clair Sloan (Nebraska), Paul Trauger (Iowa State), Blue Howell (Nebraska)**

1929

Ends—**Keith Hursley (Missouri), Steve Hokuf (Nebraska), Tom Churchill (Oklahoma)**

Tackles—**Orin Tackwell (Kansas State), John Schopflin (Kansas), Ray Richards (Nebraska)**

Guards—**K. C. Bauman (Kansas State), Paul Brayton (Missouri), Maynard Spear (Iowa State)**

Center—**Ray Smith (Missouri)**

Backs—**Frank Crider (Oklahoma), John Waldorf (Missouri), Clair Sloan (Nebraska), James Bausch (Kansas)**

1930

Ends—**Steve Hokuf (Nebraska), Henry Cronkite (Kansas State)**

Tackles—**Hugh Rhea (Nebraska), Earl Foy (Kansas)**

Guards—**Hilary Lee (Oklahoma), Elmer Greenberg (Nebraska), Leonard Magirl (Missouri)**

Center—**Robert Armstrong (Missouri), Charles Smoot (Kansas)**

Backs—**Buster Mills (Oklahoma), Alex Nigro (Kansas State), Frosty Cox (Kansas), James Bausch (Kansas), Herald Frahm (Nebraska), Ormand Beach (Kansas)**

1931

Ends—**Henry Cronkite (Kansas State), Charles Schiele (Missouri)**

Tackles—**Hugh Rhea (Nebraska), Otto Rost (Kansas)**

Guards—**George Koster (Nebraska), Charles Teel (Oklahoma)**

Center—**Lawrence Ely (Nebraska)**

Backs—**Roger Bowen (Iowa State), Eldon Auker (Kansas State), Richard Grefe (Iowa State), George Sauer (Nebraska), Everett Kreizinger (Nebraska)**

1932

Ends—**Steve Hokuf (Nebraska), Charles Schiele (Missouri)**

Tackles—**Corwin Hulbert (Nebraska), Pete Mehringer (Kansas)**

Guards—**George Atkeson (Kansas), Ellis Bashara (Oklahoma)**

Center—**Lawrence Ely (Nebraska)**

Backs—**Robert Dunlap (Oklahoma), Elmer Schaake (Kansas), Chris Mathis (Nebraska), George Sauer (Nebraska), Dougal Russell (Kansas State)**

1933

Ends—**Lee Penney (Nebraska), Bruce Kilbourne (Nebraska)**

Tackles—**Cassius Gentry (Oklahoma), Gail O'Brien (Nebraska), Pete Mehringer (Kansas)**

Guards—**Warren DeBus (Nebraska), Ellis Bashara (Oklahoma), Homer Hanson (Kansas State), James Stacy (Oklahoma)**

Center—**Franklin Meier (Nebraska)**

Backs—**Robert Dunlap (Oklahoma), Ralph Graham (Kansas State), Dougal Russell (Kansas State), George Sauer (Nebraska), Bernard Masterson (Nebraska), Hubert Boswell (Nebraska)**

1934

Ends—**Bernard Scherer (Nebraska), Frank Hood (Iowa State), Ralph Churchill (Kansas State), Fred Poole (Iowa State)**

Tackles—**George Maddox (Kansas State), Dub Wheeler (Oklahoma), Cassius Gentry (Oklahoma), Milo Clawson (Kansas)**

Guards—**James Stacy (Oklahoma), Richard Sklar (Kansas), Ike Hayes (Iowa State)**

Center—**Franklin Meier (Nebraska)**

1934 Continued

Backs—Leo Ayers (Kansas State), Oren Stoner (Kansas State), George Hapgood (Kansas), Maurice Elder (Kansas State), Harold Miller (Iowa State), Henry Bauer (Nebraska), Lloyd Cardwell (Nebraska), Ben Poynor (Oklahoma)

1935

Ends—Bernard Scherer (Nebraska), Rutherford Hayes (Kansas)
Tackles—Fred Shirey (Nebraska), Dub Wheeler (Oklahoma), John Catron (Iowa State), Paul Flenthrope (Kansas State), Ralph Brown (Oklahoma)
Guards—Richard Sklar (Kansas), Ike Hayes (Iowa State), Rolla Holland (Kansas State)
Center—Edwin Phelps (Kansas), Houston Betty (Missouri)
Backs—Lloyd Cardwell (Nebraska), Jerry LaNoue (Nebraska), Sam Francis (Nebraska), Leo Ayers (Kansas State), Nick Robertson (Oklahoma), John Peterson (Kansas), Bill Breeden (Oklahoma)

1936

Ends—Lester McDonald (Nebraska), Clarence Gustine (Iowa State)
Tackles—Ralph Brown (Oklahoma), Fred Shirey (Nebraska)
Guards—Rolla Holland (Kansas State), Maurice Kirk (Missouri)
Center—Red Conkright (Oklahoma)
Backs—Al Londe (Missouri), Red Elder (Kansas State), Lloyd Cardwell (Nebraska), Sam Francis (Nebraska)

1937

Ends—Pete Smith (Oklahoma), Roland Young (Oklahoma), Elmer Dohrmann (Nebraska)
Tackles—Lewis Ward (Kansas), Fred Shirey (Nebraska), Anthony Krueger (Kansas State)
Guards—Ed Bock (Iowa State), Maurice Kirk (Missouri), Robert Mehring (Nebraska)
Center—Mickey Parks (Oklahoma), Charles Brock (Nebraska)
Backs—Johnny Howell (Nebraska), Howard Cleveland (Kansas State), Jack Baer (Oklahoma), Clarence Douglass (Kansas), Everett Kischer (Iowa State), Henry Mahley (Missouri), Elmer Hackney (Kansas State)

1938

Ends—Roland Young (Oklahoma), Charles Heileman (Iowa State)
Tackles—Gilford Duggan (Oklahoma), Clyde Shugart (Iowa State), Shirley Davis (Kansas State)

Guards—Ed Bock (Iowa State), Ferrell Anderson (Kansas)
Centers—Charles Brock (Nebraska), Jack Kinnison (Missouri)
Backs—Everett Kischer (Iowa State), Hugh McCullough (Oklahoma), Paul Christman (Missouri), Elmer Hackney (Kansas State), Earl Crowder (Oklahoma)

1939

Ends—Frank Ivy (Oklahoma), Don Crumbaker (Kansas State), Robert Orf (Missouri)
Tackles—Bernard Weiner (Kansas State), Gilford Duggan (Oklahoma), Justin Bowers (Oklahoma), Melvin Wetzel (Missouri)
Guards—Warren Alfson (Nebraska), Robert Waldorf (Missouri)
Center—Jack West (Iowa State)
Backs—Paul Christman (Missouri), Beryl Clark (Oklahoma), Herman Rohrig (Nebraska), Robert Seymour (Oklahoma), Harry Hopp (Nebraska)

1940

Ends—Ray Prochaska (Nebraska), Bill Jennings (Oklahoma)
Tackles—Forrest Behm (Nebraska), Bernard Weiner (Kansas State), Roger Eason (Oklahoma)
Guards—Warren Alfson (Nebraska), Harold Lahar (Oklahoma), Ed Schwartzkopf (Nebraska)
Center—Don Pierce (Kansas), Darold Jenkins (Missouri)
Backs—Paul Christman (Missouri), Harry Hopp (Nebraska), Walter Luther (Nebraska), John Martin (Oklahoma), Roy Petsch (Nebraska)

1941

Ends—Hubert Ulrich (Kansas), Frank Barnhart (Kansas State), Fred Preston (Nebraska)
Tackles—Norville Wallach (Missouri), Roger Eason (Oklahoma)
Guards—Robert Jeffries (Missouri), George Abel (Nebraska)
Center—Darold Jenkins (Missouri)
Backs—Harry Ice (Missouri), Robert Steuber (Missouri), Dale Bradley (Nebraska), Don Reece (Missouri), Jack Jacobs (Oklahoma), Lye Wilkins (Kansas State)

1942

Ends—W. G. Lamb (Oklahoma), Marshall Shurnas (Missouri), Bert Ekern (Missouri)
Tackles—Vic Schleich (Nebraska), Ed Hodges (Missouri), Homer Simmons (Oklahoma)
Guards—Charles Duda (Nebraska), Mike Fitzgerald (Missouri), Clare Morford (Oklahoma)

1942 Continued

Center—**Jack Marsee (Oklahoma)**
Backs—**Ray Evans (Kansas), Robert Steuber (Missouri), William Campbell (Oklahoma), Paul Darling (Iowa State), Huel Hamm (Oklahoma)**

1943

Ends—**John Morton (Missouri), W. G. Wooten (Oklahoma)**
Tackles—**Alfred Anderson (Missouri), Lee Kennon (Oklahoma)**
Guards—**Gale Fulghum (Oklahoma), Frank Gruden (Kansas)**
Center—**Bob Mayfield (Oklahoma)**
Backs—**Howard Tippee (Iowa State), Bob Brumley (Oklahoma), Derald Lebow (Oklahoma), Don Reece (Missouri)**

1944

Ends—**W. G. Wooten (Oklahoma), Rex Wagner (Iowa State)**
Tackles—**James Kekeris (Missouri), John Harley (Oklahoma)**
Guards—**Jack Fathauer (Iowa State), Charles Wright (Iowa State)**
Center—**Bob Mayfield (Oklahoma)**
Backs—**Paul Collins (Missouri), Charles Moffett (Kansas), Bill Dellastatious (Missouri), Derald Lebow (Oklahoma)**

1945

Ends—**Dave Schmidt (Kansas), Omer Burgert (Oklahoma)**
Tackles—**James Kekeris (Missouri), Thomas Tallchief (Oklahoma)**
Guards—**Lester Jensen (Oklahoma), Russell Hardin (Kansas State), Robert Eigelberger (Missouri), Jack Fathauer (Iowa State)**
Center—**Ralph Stewart (Missouri), James Riding (Iowa State)**
Backs—**Leonard Brown (Missouri), Richard Howard (Iowa State), John West (Oklahoma), Jack Venable (Oklahoma), Loyd Brinkman (Missouri), Gene Phelps (Iowa State), Gerald Moore (Nebraska)**

1946

Ends—**Roland Oakes (Missouri), Marsh Shurnas (Missouri), Dave Schmidt (Kansas), Otto Schnellbacher (Kansas), Warren Geise (Oklahoma)**
Tackles—**Jim Kekeris (Missouri), Homer Paine (Oklahoma), Carl Samuelson (Nebraska), Wade Walker (Oklahoma)**

Guards—**Don Fambrough (Kansas), Buddy Burris (Oklahoma), Ralph Stewart (Missouri), Plato Andros (Oklahoma)**
Center—**John Rapacz (Oklahoma)**
Backs—**Loyd Brinkman (Missouri), Sam Vacanti (Nebraska), Lynn McNutt (Kansas), Ray Evans (Kansas), Joe Golding (Oklahoma), Tom Novak (Nebraska), Dick Hutton (Nebraska)**

1947

Ends—**Mel Sheehan (Missouri), Jim Tyree (Oklahoma), Otto Schnellbacher (Kansas)**
Tackles—**Chester Fritz (Missouri), Don Ettinger (Kansas), Carl Samuelson (Nebraska), Wade Walker (Oklahoma)**
Guards—**Don Fambrough (Kansas), Tom Novak (Nebraska), Virlie Abrams (Missouri), Buddy Burris (Oklahoma)**
Center—**John Rapacz (Oklahoma)**
Backs—**Bus Entsminger (Missouri), Jack Mitchell (Oklahoma), Ray Evans (Kansas), Dick Braznell (Missouri), Webb Halbert (Iowa State), Forrest Griffith (Kansas)**

BIG SEVEN

1948

Ends—**Mel Sheehan (Missouri), Dean Laun (Iowa State), Jim Owens (Oklahoma), Ed Pudlik (Colorado), Bryan Sperry (Kansas)**
Tackles—**Chester Fritz (Missouri), Wade Walker (Oklahoma), Homer Paine (Oklahoma)**
Guards—**Buddy Burris (Oklahoma), Dick Tomlinson (Kansas), Clair Mayes (Oklahoma)**
Center—**Tom Novak (Nebraska), Bob Fuchs (Missouri)**
Backs—**Jack Mitchell (Oklahoma), Dick Gilman (Kansas), Bus Entsminger (Missouri), Harry Narcissian (Colorado), Forrest Griffith (Kansas)**

1949

Ends—**Jim Owens (Oklahoma), Jim Doran (Iowa State), Bill Schaake (Kansas), Gene Ackerman (Missouri)**
Tackles—**Wade Walker (Oklahoma), Lowell Titus (Iowa State), Charles Toogood (Nebraska)**
Guards—**Stan West (Oklahoma), Dick Tomlinson (Kansas), Gene Pepper (Missouri)**
Center—**Tom Novak (Nebraska)**
Backs—**Bill Weeks (Iowa State), Darrell Royal (Oklahoma), John Glorioso (Missouri), George Thomas (Oklahoma), Dick Braznell (Missouri), Winfard Carter (Missouri)**

1950

Ends—Jim Doran (Iowa State), Frank Anderson (Oklahoma), Gene Ackerman (Missouri), Chuck Mosher (Colorado)

Tackles—Jim Weatherall (Oklahoma), Mike McCormack (Kansas), Charles Toogood (Nebraska)

Guards—Norman McNabb (Oklahoma), Don Strasheim (Nebraska), John Kadlec (Missouri), George Mrkonic (Kansas)

Center—Harry Moore (Oklahoma), Tom Catlin (Oklahoma), Harold Robinson (Kansas State)

Backs—Bill Weeks (Iowa State), Claude Arnold (Oklahoma), Fran Nagle (Nebraska), Bob Reynolds (Nebraska), Wade Stinson (Kansas), Billy Vessels (Oklahoma), Leon Heath (Oklahoma), Merwin Hodel (Colorado)

1951

Ends—Frank Simon (Nebraska), Bill Schabacher (Nebraska), Mal Schmidt (Iowa State), Don Branby (Colorado), Chuck Mosher (Colorado), Bill Schaake (Kansas), Orban Tice (Kansas), Dennis Emanuel (Nebraska)

Tackles—Art Janes (Oklahoma), Jim Weatherall (Oklahoma), Jack Jorgenson (Colorado), Oliver Spencer (Kansas), Jerry Minnick (Nebraska), George Mrkonic (Kansas)

Guards—George Kennard (Kansas), Roger Nelson (Oklahoma), Bert Clark (Oklahoma), Fred Smith (Oklahoma), Stan Campbell (Iowa State), Bob Hantla (Kansas), Tom O'Boyle (Kansas State)

Center—Tom Catlin (Oklahoma), Bill Fuchs (Missouri)

Backs—Eddie Crowder (Oklahoma), Larry Grigg (Oklahoma), Dick Mann (Iowa State), Veryl Switzer (Kansas State), Junior Wren (Missouri), Merwin Hodel (Colorado), Charlie Hoag (Kansas), Tom Brookshier (Colorado), Bob Brandeberry (Kansas), John Konek (Kansas), Buck McPhail (Oklahoma)

1952

Ends—Max Boydston (Oklahoma), Dennis Emanuel (Nebraska), Paul Leoni (Kansas), Don Branby (Colorado), Bill Schabacher (Nebraska)

Tackles—Oliver Spencer (Kansas), Ed Rowland (Oklahoma), Jerry Minnick (Nebraska), Don Rutter (Missouri), Paul Fuchs (Missouri), Jim Davis (Oklahoma)

Guards—Bob Castle (Missouri), Clayton Curtis (Nebraska), Bob Hantla (Kansas), Jack Lordo (Missouri), Don Boll (Nebraska), J. D. Roberts (Oklahoma), Terry Roberts (Missouri)

Center—Tom Catlin (Oklahoma)

Backs—Eddie Crowder (Oklahoma), Veryl Switzer (Kansas State), Billy Vessels (Oklahoma), Gil Reich (Kansas), Charles Hoag (Kansas), Tom Brookshier (Colorado), Zack Jordan (Colorado), Ed Merrifield (Missouri), Buck McPhail (Oklahoma), Galen Fiss (Kansas)

1953

Ends—Gary Knafelc (Colorado), Max Boydston (Oklahoma), Ed Pence (Kansas State)

Tackles—Jerry Minnick (Nebraska), Roger Nelson (Oklahoma), Ted Connor (Oklahoma)

Guards—Terry Roberts (Missouri), Tom O'Boyle (Kansas State), J. D. Roberts (Oklahoma)

Center—Kurt Burris (Oklahoma)

Backs—John Bordogna (Nebraska), Gene Calame (Oklahoma), Larry Grigg (Oklahoma), Veryl Switzer (Kansas State), Max Burkett (Iowa State), Bob Baumann (Missouri)

1954

Ends—Max Boydston (Oklahoma), Carl Allison (Oklahoma)

Tackles—Al Portney (Missouri), Ron Nerry (Kansas State), Don Glantz (Nebraska)

Guards—Bo Bolinger (Oklahoma), Ron Marciniak (Kansas State), Charles Bryant (Nebraska)

Center—Kurt Burris (Oklahoma)

Backs—Buddy Leake (Oklahoma), Gene Calame (Oklahoma), Carroll Hardy (Colorado), Frank Bernardi (Colorado), Bob Smith (Nebraska), Corky Taylor (Kansas State)

1955

Ends—Harold Burnine (Missouri), Jon McWilliams (Nebraska), Lamar Meyer (Colorado)

Tackles—Ed Gray (Oklahoma), Cal Woodworth (Oklahoma), Sam Salerno (Colorado), Laverne Torczon (Nebraska), Ron Nery (Kansas State)

Guards—Bo Bolinger (Oklahoma), Cecil Morris (Oklahoma)

Center—Jerry Tubbs (Oklahoma)

Backs—Jimmy Harris (Oklahoma), Rex Fischer (Nebraska), Tommy McDonald (Oklahoma), Willie Greenlaw (Nebraska), Bob Burris (Oklahoma), Doug Roether (Kansas State)

1956

Ends—Jerry Leahy (Colorado), John Bell (Oklahoma), Wally Merz (Colorado), Jim Letcavits (Kansas)

Tackles—Ed Gray (Oklahoma), Tom Emerson (Oklahoma), Frank Gibson (Kansas), Dick Stapp (Colorado)

1956 Continued

Guards—**Bill Krisher (Oklahoma), Laverne Torczon (Nebraska), Ellis Rainsberger (Kansas State)**
Center—**Jerry Tubbs (Oklahoma)**
Backs—**Jim Hunter (Missouri), Tommy McDonald (Oklahoma), Clendon Thomas (Oklahoma), Jerry Brown (Nebraska), John Bayuk (Colorado)**

1957

Ends—**Don Stiller (Oklahoma), Don Zadnik (Kansas State), Ross Coyle (Oklahoma), Jim Letcavits (Kansas)**
Tackles—**Jack Keelan (Kansas State), Merv Johnson (Missouri)**
Guards—**Charles Rash (Missouri), John Wooten (Colorado), Bill Krisher (Oklahoma)**
Center—**Ellis Rainsberger (Kansas State), Bob Harrison (Oklahoma)**
Backs—**Dwight Nichols (Iowa State), Bob Stransky (Colorado), Clendon Thomas (Oklahoma), Hank Kuhlmann (Missouri)**

BIG EIGHT

1958

Ends—**Ross Coyle (Oklahoma), Danny LaRose (Missouri)**
Tackles—**Mike Magac (Missouri), Jack Himelwright (Colorado), Steve Jennings (Oklahoma), John Peppercorn (Kansas), Gilmer Lewis (Oklahoma)**
Guards—**Don Chadwick (Missouri), Dick Corbitt (Oklahoma), Dave Noblitt (Kansas State), Charles Rash (Missouri)**
Center—**Bob Harrison (Oklahoma)**
Backs—**Boyd Dowler (Colorado), Dwight Nichols (Iowa State), Homer Floyd (Kansas), Prentice Gautt (Oklahoma)**

1959

Ends—**John Peppercorn (Kansas), Don Webb (Iowa State), Russ Sloan (Missouri)**
Tackles—**Mike Magac (Missouri), Jerry Thompson (Oklahoma), John Stolte (Kansas State)**
Guards—**Don Olson (Nebraska), Joe Romig (Colorado), Jerry Thompson (Oklahoma)**
Center—**Fred Hageman (Kansas), Tom Swaney (Missouri)**
Backs—**Bobby Boyd (Oklahoma), Gale Weidner (Colorado), Dwight Nichols (Iowa State), John Hadl (Kansas), Curtis McClinton (Kansas), Prentice Gautt (Oklahoma), Tom Watkins (Iowa State)**

1960

Ends—**Danny LaRose (Missouri), Jerry Hillebrand (Colorado), Don Purcell (Nebraska)**
Tackles—**Harold Beaty (Oklahoma State), Rockne Calhoun (Missouri), Billy White (Oklahoma)**
Guards—**Paul Henley (Missouri), Elvin Basham (Kansas), Joe Romig (Colorado)**
Center—**Fred Hageman (Kansas)**
Backs—**John Hadl (Kansas), Mel West (Missouri), Curtis McClinton (Kansas), Tom Watkins (Iowa State)**

1961

Ends—**Jerry Hillebrand (Colorado), Conrad Hitchler (Missouri)**
Tackles—**Ed Blaine (Missouri), Billy White (Oklahoma), Bill Wegener (Missouri)**
Guards—**Joe Romig (Colorado), Dan Celoni (Iowa State), Elvin Basham (Kansas)**
Center—**Walt Klinker (Colorado)**
Backs—**John Hadl (Kansas), Dave Hoppmann (Iowa State), Curtis McClinton (Kansas), Bill Thornton (Nebraska), Gale Weidner (Colorado)**

1962

Ends—**Conrad Hitchler (Missouri), Ken Blair (Colorado)**
Tackles—**Dennis Ward (Oklahoma), Tyrone Robertston (Nebraska), Jerry Wallach (Missouri)**
Guards—**Leon Corss (Oklahoma), Bob Brown (Nebraska), Tom Hertz (Missouri)**
Center—**Wayne Lee (Oklahoma)**
Backs—**Dave Hoppmann (Iowa State), Dennis Claridge (Nebraska), John Roland (Missouri), Gale Sayers (Kansas), Jim Grisham (Oklahoma), Joe Don Looney (Oklahoma)**

1963

Ends—**Mike Shinn (Kansas), John Flynn (Oklahoma), George Seals (Missouri)**
Tackles—**Dave Gill (Missouri), Ralph Neely (Oklahoma), Lloyd Voss (Nebraska)**
Guards—**Bob Brown (Nebraska), Newt Burton (Oklahoma)**
Center—**John Berrington (Iowa State), Pete Quatrochi (Kansas), Gene Oliver (Missouri)**
Backs—**Gary Lane (Missouri), Dennis Claridge (Nebraska), Tom Vaughn (Iowa State), Gale Sayers (Kansas), Jim Grisham (Oklahoma)**

1964

Offense

Ends—**Tony Jeter (Nebraska), Freeman White (Nebraska)**
Tackles—**Larry Kramer (Nebraska), Ralph Neely (Oklahoma)**
Guards—**Newt Burton (Oklahoma), Tom Wyrostek (Missouri), Bob Brown (Missouri)**
Center—**Lyle Sittler (Nebraska)**

1964 Continued

Backs—**Gary Lane (Missouri), Gale Sayers (Kansas), Kent McCloughan (Nebraska), Jim Grisham (Oklahoma)**

Defense

Ends—**Bill Matan (Kansas State), Jack Jacobson (Oklahoma State)**

Tackles—**John Van Sicklen (Iowa State), Butch Allison (Missouri), Brian Schweda (Kansas)**

Middle Guards—**Walt Barnes (Nebraska), Bob Mitts (Kansas State)**

Linebackers—**Carl McAdams (Oklahoma), Mike Cox (Iowa State), Gus Otto (Missouri)**

Backs—**Tom Vaughn (Iowa State), Ken Boston (Missouri), John Roland (Missouri), Gary Duff (Kansas)**

1965

Offense

Ends—**Freeman White (Nebraska), Tony Jeter (Nebraska), Eppie Barney (Iowa State)**

Tackles—**Dennis Carlson (Nebraska), Francis Peay (Missouri)**

Guards—**Dick Pratt (Kansas), LaVerne Allers (Nebraska), Mike Eader (Missouri)**

Center—**Dick Kasperek (Iowa State)**

Quarterback—**Gary Lane (Missouri)**

Halfbacks—**Charlie Brown (Missouri), Harry Wilson (Nebraska), Frank Solich (Nebraska)**

Fullback—**Walt Garrison (Oklahoma State)**

Defense

Ends—**Sam Harris (Colorado), Bill Matan (Kansas State)**

Tackles—**Walt Barnes (Nebraska), Bruce Van Dyke (Missouri)**

Guard—**Charley Harper (Oklahoma State)**

Linebackers—**Carl McAdams (Oklahoma), Mike Kennedy (Nebraska), Steve Sidwell (Colorado)**

Halfbacks—**John Roland (Missouri), Hale Irwin (Colorado), Larry Wachholtz (Nebraska)**

1966

Offense

Ends—**Eppie Barney (Iowa State), Ben Hart (Oklahoma)**

Tackles—**J. B. Christian (Oklahoma State), Bob Pickens (Nebraska), Ed Hall (Oklahoma)**

Guards—**LaVerne Allers (Nebraska), John Beard (Colorado)**

Center—**Kelly Petersen (Nebraska)**

Quarterback—**Bob Churchich (Nebraska)**

Halfbacks—**Harry Wilson (Nebraska), Cornelius Davis (Kansas State)**

Fullback—**Wilmer Cooks (Colorado)**

Defense

Ends—**Bill Fairband (Colorado), Dan Schuppan (Missouri)**

Tackles—**Dennis Randall (Oklahoma State), Carel Stith (Nebraska)**

Guard—**Wayne Meylan (Nebraska)**

Linebackers—**Mike Sweatman (Kansas), Danny Lankas (Kansas State), Eugene Ross (Oklahoma), Lynn Senkbeil (Nebraska)**

Halfbacks—**Jim Whitaker (Missouri), Hale Irwin (Colorado), Larry Wachholtz (Nebraska), Kaye Carstens (Nebraska)**

1967

Offense

Ends—**Dave Jones (Kansas State), Dennis Richnafsky (Nebraska)**

Tackles—**Bob Kalsu (Oklahoma), Mike Montler (Colorado), Russ Washington (Missouri)**

Guards—**John Greene (Kansas), Kirk Tracy (Colorado)**

Center—**Jon Kolb (Oklahoma State)**

Quarterback—**Bob Douglass (Kansas)**

Halfbacks—**Steve Owens (Oklahoma), Bob Warmack (Oklahoma)**

Fullbacks—**Dick Davis (Nebraska), Barry Lischner (Missouri)**

Defense

Ends—**John Zook (Kansas), John Koller (Oklahoma), Mike Schnitker (Colorado)**

Tackles—**Granville Liggins (Oklahoma), Frank Bosch (Colorado), Jim McCord (Nebraska)**

Guard—**Wayne Meylan (Nebraska)**

Linebackers—**Jon Douglas (Missouri), Dan Lankas (Kansas State), Mike Sweatman (Kansas)**

Halfbacks—**Dick Anderson (Colorado), Harry Cheatwood (Oklahoma State), Roger Wehrli (Missouri)**

1968

Offense

Ends—**Dave Jones (Kansas State), John Mosier (Kansas), Steve Zabel (Oklahoma)**

Tackles—**Keith Christensen (Kansas), Mike Montler (Colorado)**

Guards—**Joe Armstrong (Nebraska), Jim Anderson (Missouri), Ken Mendenhall (Oklahoma)**

Center—**Jon Kolb (Oklahoma State)**

1968 Continued

Backs—**Bob Anderson (Colorado), Bob Douglass (Kansas), Eddie Hinton (Oklahoma), Steve Owens (Oklahoma), John Riggins (Kansas)**

Defense

Ends—**Bill Schmitt (Missouri), John Zook (Kansas)**
Tackles—**George Dimitri (Iowa State), Rocky Wallace (Missouri)**
Middle Guard—**John Little (Oklahoma State)**
Linebackers—**Carl Garber (Missouri), Ken Geddes (Nebraska), Emery Hicks (Kansas), Rocky Martin (Colorado)**
Backs—**Steve Barrett (Oklahoma), Dana Stephenson (Nebraska), Roger Wehrli (Missouri)**

1969

Offense

Ends—**Mel Gray (Missouri), Jim McFarland (Nebraska), Steve Zabel (Oklahoma)**
Tackles—**Larron Jackson (Missouri), John Ward (Oklahoma State)**
Guards—**Dick Melin (Colorado), Bill Elfstrom (Oklahoma), Ken Mendenhall (Oklahoma)**
Center—**Dale Evans (Kansas)**
Backs—**Lynn Dickey (Kansas State), Bob Anderson (Colorado), Mack Herron (Kansas State), Steve Owens (Oklahoma)**

Defense

Ends—**Manuel Barrera (Kansas State), Bill Brundige (Colorado)**
Tackles—**John Little (Oklahoma State), Mark Kuhlmann (Missouri), Jerry Sherk (Oklahoma State)**
Middle Guard—**John Stucky (Kansas State)**
Linebackers—**Ken Geddes (Nebraska), Emery Hicks (Kansas), Jerry Murtaugh (Nebraska)**
Backs—**Dennis Poppe (Missouri), Dana Stephenson (Nebraska), Tony Washington (Iowa State)**

1970

Offense

Ends—**Otto Stowe (Iowa State), Hermann Eben (Oklahoma State), Johnny Rodgers (Nebraska)**
Tackles—**Larron Jackson (Missouri), Bob Newton (Nebraska)**
Guards—**Dennis Havig (Colorado), Donnie McGhee (Nebraska), Steve Lawson (Kansas)**
Center—**Don Popplewell (Colorado)**
Backs—**Lynn Dickey (Kansas State), Joe Orduna (Nebraska), John Riggins (Kansas), Joe Wylie (Oklahoma)**

Defense

Ends—**Mike Kuhn (Kansas State), Herb Orvis (Colorado)**
Tackles—**Dave Walline (Nebraska), Ron Yankowski (Kansas State)**
Middle Guard—**Ed Periard (Nebraska)**
Linebackers—**Jerry Murtaugh (Nebraska), Steve Aycock (Oklahoma), Oscar Gibson (Kansas State), Rocky Wallace (Missouri)**
Backs—**Clarence Scott (Kansas State), Tony Washington (Iowa State), Bill Kosch (Nebraska), Monty Johnson (Oklahoma)**

1971

Offense

Ends—**John Schroll (Kansas), Albert Chandler (Oklahoma), Johnny Rodgers (Nebraska)**
Tackles—**Carl Johnson (Nebraska), Marion Latimore (Kansas State), Jake Zumbach (Colorado)**
Guards—**Dick Rupert (Nebraska), Ken Jones (Oklahoma)**
Backs—**Jack Mildren (Oklahoma), Jerry Tagge (Nebraska), Jeff Kinney (Nebraska), Greg Pruitt (Oklahoma)**
Kicker—**Reggie Shoemake (Iowa State)**

Defense

Ends—**Willie Harper (Oklahoma), Raymond Hamilton (Oklahoma)**
Tackles—**Larry Jacobson (Nebraska), Herb Orvis (Colorado), Derland Moore (Oklahoma)**
Guards—**Rich Glover (Nebraska), Bud Magrum (Colorado)**
Linebackers—**Keith Schroeder (Iowa State), Steve Aycock (Oklahoma), Ken Page (Kansas)**
Backs—**Jim Anderson (Nebraska), Bill Kosch (Nebraska), John Shelly (Oklahoma), Joe Blahak (Nebraska)**

1972

Offense

Ends—**Johnny Rodgers (Nebraska), Keith Krepfle (Iowa State), J. V. Cain (Colorado)**
Tackles—**Daryl White (Nebraska), Dean Unruh (Oklahoma), Jake Zumbach (Colorado)**
Guards—**Ken Jones (Nebraska), Geary Murdock (Iowa State)**
Center—**Tom Brahaney (Oklahoma)**
Backs—**George Amundson (Iowa State), Greg Pruitt (Oklahoma), Charlie Davis (Colorado), Mike Strachan (Iowa State), Leon Crosswhite (Oklahoma)**
Kicker—**Greg Hill (Missouri)**

Defense

Ends—**Willie Harper (Nebraska), Merv Krakau (Iowa State)**

1972 Continued

Tackles—**Derland Moore (Oklahoma), Lucious Selmon (Oklahoma), Raymond Hamilton (Oklahoma)**
Guard—**Rich Glover (Nebraska)**
Linebackers—**Bud Magrum (Colorado), Eddie Sheats (Kansas), Rod Shoate (Oklahoma), Cleveland Vann (Oklahoma State)**
Backs—**Cullen Bryant (Colorado), Joe Blahak (Nebraska), Darryll Stewart (Oklahoma State), John Stearns (Colorado)**

1973

Offense

Ends—**Emmett Edwards (Kansas), Frosty Anderson (Nebraska), J. V. Cain (Colorado)**
Tackles—**Daryl White (Nebraska), Jim Schnietz (Missouri), Eddie Foster (Oklahoma)**
Guards—**Bill Brittain (Kansas State), Doug Payton (Colorado), Greg Horton (Colorado), John Roush (Oklahoma)**
Center—**Scott Anderson (Missouri)**
Backs—**Dave Jaynes (Kansas), Mike Strachan (Iowa State), Isaac Jackson (Kansas State), Joe Washington (Oklahoma)**
Kicker—**Greg Hill (Missouri)**

Defense

Ends—**Steve Manstedt (Nebraska), Dean Zook (Kansas), Gary Baccus (Oklahoma)**
Tackles—**John Dutton (Nebraska), Barry Price (Oklahoma State)**
Guard—**Lucious Selmon (Oklahoma)**
Linebackers—**Lawrence Hunt (Iowa State), Rod Shoate (Oklahoma), Cleveland Vann (Oklahoma State)**

1974

Offense

Ends—**Emmett Edwards (Kansas), Mark Miller (Missouri), Wayne Hoffman (Oklahoma), Tinker Owens (Oklahoma)**
Tackles—**Marvin Crenshaw (Nebraska), Jerry Arnold (Oklahoma)**
Guards—**Tom Wolf (Oklahoma State), John Roush (Oklahoma), Terry Webb (Oklahoma)**
Center—**Rik Bonness (Nebraska)**
Backs—**Dave Humm (Nebraska), Laverne Smith (Kansas), Tony Galbreath (Missouri), Joe Washington (Oklahoma)**
Kicker—**Tom Goedjen (Iowa State)**
Punter—**Cliff Parsley (Oklahoma State)**

Defense

Ends—**Bob Martin (Nebraska), Jimbo Elrod (Oklahoma)**

Tackles—**Phillip Dokes (Oklahoma State), Dewey Selmon (Oklahoma), Leroy Selmon (Oklahoma)**
Guards—**Mike Lemon (Kansas), Dewey Selmon (Oklahoma)**
Linebackers—**Steve Towle (Kansas), Tom Ruud (Nebraska), Rod Shoate (Oklahoma)**
Backs—**Barry Hill (Iowa State), Kurt Knoff (Kansas), Randy Hughes (Oklahoma)**

1975

Offense

Ends—**Henry Marshall (Missouri), Don Hasselbeck (Colorado)**
Tackles—**Mark Koncar (Colorado), Mike Vaughan (Oklahoma)**
Guards—**Derrel Gofourth (Oklahoma State), Terry Webb (Oklahoma)**
Center—**Rik Bonness (Nebraska)**
Backs—**Nolan Cromwell (Kansas), Terry Miller (Oklahoma State), Terry Kunz (Colorado), Laverne Smith (Kansas), Joe Washington (Oklahoma)**
Kicker—**Tony DiRienzo (Oklahoma)**
Punter—**Cliff Parsley (Oklahoma State)**

Defense

Ends—**Bob Martin (Nebraska), Jimbo Elrod (Oklahoma)**
Tackles—**Mike Fultz (Nebraska), Mike Butler (Kansas), Leroy Selmon (Oklahoma)**
Middle Guard—**Dewey Selmon (Oklahoma)**
Linebackers—**Gary Spani (Kansas State), Gary Campbell (Colorado)**
Backs—**Kurt Knoff (Kansas), Kenny Downing (Missouri), Dave Butterfield (Nebraska), Wonder Monds (Nebraska), Zac Henderson (Oklahoma)**

1976

Offense

Ends—**Luther Blue (Iowa State), Don Hasselbeck (Colorado)**
Tackles—**Bob Lingenfelter (Nebraska), Mike Vaughan (Oklahoma), Morris Towns (Missouri)**
Guards—**Dave Greenwood (Iowa State), Dan Schmidt (Nebraska)**
Center—**Derrel Gofourth (Oklahoma State)**
Backs—**Vince Ferragamo (Nebraska), Terry Miller (Oklahoma State), Tony Reed (Colorado), Joe Stewart (Missouri)**
Kicker—**Abby Daigle (Oklahoma State)**
Punter—**Cliff Parsley (Oklahoma State)**

Defense

Ends—**Daria Butler (Oklahoma State), Ray Phillips (Nebraska)**
Tackles—**Phillip Dokes (Oklahoma State), Mike Fultz (Nebraska)**

1976 Continued

Middle Guards—**Charlie Johnson (Colorado), Maynard Stensrud (Iowa State)**
Linebackers—**Clete Pillen (Nebraska), Daryl Hunt (Oklahoma), Gary Spani (Kansas State), Terry Beeson (Kansas)**
Backs—**Mike Spivey (Colorado), Dave Butterfield (Nebraska), Zac Henderson (Oklahoma), Scott Hill (Oklahoma), Tony Hawkins (Iowa State), Chris Golub (Kansas)**

AP ALL–BIG EIGHT FOOTBALL TEAM

1977

Offense

Tight End—**Kellen Winslow (Missouri)**
Tackles—**Karl Baldishwiller (Oklahoma), James Taylor (Missouri)**
Guards—**Greg Roberts (Oklahoma), Greg Jorgensen (Nebraska)**
Backs—**Terry Miller (Oklahoma State), Dexter Green (Iowa State), I. M. Hipp (Nebraska)**
Quarterback—**Thomas Lott (Oklahoma)**
Center—**Tom Davis (Nebraska)**
Wide Receiver—**Joe Stewart (Missouri)**

Defense

Ends—**Randy Westendorf (Colorado), Daria Butler (Oklahoma State)**
Tackles—**Tom Randall (Iowa State), Mike Stensrud (Iowa State)**
Noseguard—**Reggie Kinlaw (Oklahoma)**
Linebackers—**Gary Spani (Kansas State), George Cumby (Oklahoma), Daryl Hunt (Oklahoma)**
Backs—**Zac Henderson (Oklahoma), Odis McKinney (Colorado), Tom Fitch (Kansas)**

UPI ALL–BIG EIGHT FOOTBALL TEAM

1977

Offense

Tight End—**Kellen Winslow (Missouri)**
Tackles—**Karl Baldishwiller (Oklahoma), James Taylor (Missouri)**
Guards—**Greg Jorgensen (Nebraska), Leon White (Colorado)**
Center—**Tom Davis (Nebraska)**
Wide Receiver—**Joe Stewart (Missouri)**
Backs—**Terry Miller (Oklahoma State), Dexter Green (Iowa State), I. M. Hipp (Nebraska)**
Quarterback—**Thomas Lott (Oklahoma)**

Defense

Ends—**Randy Westendorf (Colorado), Daria Butler (Oklahoma State)**
Tackles—**Mike Stensrud (Iowa State), Tom Randall (Iowa State)**
Noseguard—**Reggie Kinlaw (Oklahoma)**
Linebackers—**Gary Spani (Kansas State), Daryl Hunt (Oklahoma)**
Backs—**Zac Henderson (Oklahoma), Tom Fitch (Kansas), Russ Calabrese (Missouri), Kevin Hart (Iowa State)**

AP ALL–BIG EIGHT FOOTBALL TEAM

1978

Offense

Tight End—**Junior Miller (Nebraska)**
Tackles—**Matt Miller (Colorado), Kelvin Clark (Nebraska)**
Guards—**Greg Roberts (Oklahoma), Steve Lindquist (Nebraska)**
Center—**Pete Allard (Missouri)**
Wide Receiver—**Charlie Green (Kansas State)**
Backs—**Billy Sims (Oklahoma), Richard Berns (Nebraska), Dexter Green (Iowa State)**
Quarterback—**Thomas Lott (Oklahoma)**
Kicker—**Uwe von Schamann (Oklahoma)**

Defense

Ends—**Reggie Mathis (Oklahoma), George Andrews (Nebraska)**
Tackles—**Mike Stensrud (Iowa State), Phil Tabor (Oklahoma)**
Noseguard—**Reggie Kinlaw (Oklahoma)**
Linebackers—**Daryl Hunt (Oklahoma), George Cumby (Oklahoma), John Corker (Oklahoma State)**
Backs—**Darrol Ray (Oklahoma), Mark Haynes (Colorado), Jim Pillen (Nebraska)**
Punter—**Mike Hubach (Kansas)**

UPI ALL–BIG EIGHT FOOTBALL TEAM

1978

Offense

Ends—**Charlie Green (Kansas State), Kellen Winslow (Missouri)**
Tackles—**Kelvin Clark (Nebraska), Matt Miller (Colorado)**
Guards—**Greg Roberts (Oklahoma), Steve Lindquist (Nebraska)**
Center—**Pete Allard (Missouri)**
Backs—**Thomas Lott (Oklahoma), Billy Sims (Oklahoma), Phil Bradley (Missouri), Rick Berns (Nebraska)**

1978 Continued

Kicker—**Uwe von Schamann (Oklahoma)**

Defense

Ends—**George Andrews (Nebraska), Rick White (Iowa State)**

Tackles—**Mike Stensrud (Iowa State), Rod Horn (Nebraska)**

Noseguard—**Reggie Kinlaw (Oklahoma)**

Linebackers—**John Corker (Oklahoma State), Daryl Hunt (Oklahoma), Darrol Ray (Oklahoma)**

Backs—**Darrol Ray (Oklahoma), Mark Haynes (Colorado), Russ Calabrese (Missouri), Mike Schwartz (Iowa State)**

Punter—**Mike Hubach (Kansas)**

National Football Hall Of Fame

BIG EIGHT MEMBERS

PLAYERS

Year Elected	Name	Team	Position
1951	Ed Weir	Nebraska	Tackle
1954	Jim Bausch	Kansas	Fullback
1954	George Sauer	Nebraska	Fullback
1954	Byron White	Colorado	Halfback
1961	Claude Reeds	Oklahoma	Fullback
1962	Guy Chamberlain	Nebraska	Halfback
1963	Paul Christman	Missouri	Tailback
1964	Ray Evans	Kansas	Halfback
1970	Ed Bock	Iowa State	Guard
1971	Bob Steuber	Missouri	Halfback
1973	Forest Geyer	Oklahoma	Fullback
1974	Ed Travis	Missouri	Tackle
1976	Darold Jenkins	Missouri	Quarterback
1977	Gale Sayers	Kansas	Halfback
1977	Sam Francis	Nebraska	Fullback

COACHES

Year	Name	Team
1951	Dana X. Bible	Nebraska
1951	Bennie Owen	Oklahoma
1951	Bill Roper	Missouri
1951	Glenn S. Warner	Iowa State
1951	Fielding H. Yost	Nebraska, Kansas
1954	Biff Jones	Nebraska
1955	E. N. Robinson	Nebraska
1961	Don Faurot	Missouri
1966	Lynn Waldorf	Kansas State
1969	Bud Wilkinson	Oklahoma

Big Eight Season Games

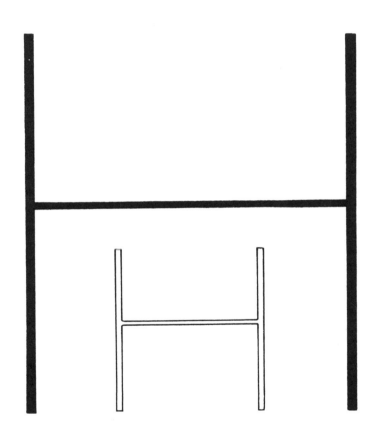

UNIVERSITY OF COLORADO

Boulder, Colorado

Founded 1876   *COLORS: Silver and Gold*   *NICKNAME: Buffaloes*

Head Coaches since 1928

Myron E. Witham	*1920–1931*	James J. Yeager	*1946–1947*
William H. Saunders	*1932–1934*	Dallas Ward	*1948–1958*
Bernard F. Oakes	*1935–1940*	Sonny Grandelius	*1959–1961*
Frank Potts	*1940*	Bud Davis	*1962*
James J. Yeager	*1941–1943*	Eddie Crowder	*1963–1973*
Frank Potts	*1944–1945*	Bill Mallory	*1974–*

1928

21	Colorado (Greeley) State	6
39	Colorado Mines	0
6	Utah	25
13	Colorado A. & M.	7
24	Colorado College	19
7	Denver	0

1929

27	Regis	13
19	Colorado (Greeley) State	0
0	Utah	40
0	Denver	0
13	Colorado Mines	9
6	Colorado A. & M.	0
13	Colorado College	7

1930

9	Missouri	0
0	Utah State	0
36	Colorado Mines	7
7	Colorado A. & M.	0
14	Colorado College	13
27	Colorado (Greeley) State	7
0	Utah	34
27	Denver	7

1931

0	Oregon State	16
27	Colorado Mines	0
9	Missouri	7
6	Colorado A. & M.	19
25	Denver	6
0	Utah	32
17	Colorado College	7
27	Arizona	7

1932

31	Colorado Mines	9
26	Utah State	7
6	Colorado A. & M.	7
0	Utah	14
0	Colorado College	12
0	Denver	6

1933

19	Nebraska (Chadron) State	0
6	Oklahoma A. & M.	0
42	Colorado Mines	0
6	Colorado A. & M.	19
40	Wyoming	12
26	Colorado College	0

6	Utah	13
24	Colorado (Greeley) State	0
14	Denver	7

1934

0	Kansas	0
0	Missouri	0
7	Colorado (Greeley) State	13
48	Brigham Young	6
27	Colorado A. & M.	9
40	Colorado Mines	6
7	Utah	6
31	Colorado College	0
7	Denver	0

1935

0	Oklahoma	3
6	Missouri	20
58	Colorado Mines	0
19	Colorado A. & M.	6
23	Colorado College	0
14	Utah	0
6	Kansas	12
0	Wyoming	6
14	Denver	0

1936

0	Oklahoma	8
33	Colorado Mines	0
9	Colorado A. & M.	7
7	Colorado College	0
31	Utah	7
13	Utah State	14
6	Denver	7

1937

14	Missouri	6
33	Utah State	0
14	Brigham Young	0
47	Colorado A. & M.	0
54	Colorado Mines	0
17	Utah	7
35	Colorado College	6
34	Denver	7
	Cotton Bowl Game	
14	Rice	28

1938

7	Missouri	14
0	Utah State	20
0	George Washington	13
31	Colorado A. & M.	6
20	Wyoming	6
0	Utah	0
8	Brigham Young	0
12	Denver	19

1939

0	Missouri	30
6	Utah State	16
0	Kansas State	20
13	Colorado A. & M.	0
27	Wyoming	7
21	Utah	14
12	Brigham Young	6
27	Denver	17

1940

7	Texas	39
7	Kansas State	6
26	Utah State	0
33	Colorado A. & M.	14
62	Wyoming	0
13	Utah	21
6	Missouri	21

25	Brigham Young	2
3	Denver	3

1941

6	Texas	34
6	Missouri	21
13	Utah State	7
26	Colorado A. & M.	13
27	Wyoming	0
6	Utah	46
13	Brigham Young	13
0	Denver	27

1942

54	Colorado Mines	0
13	Missouri	26
31	Utah State	14
12	New Mexico	0
34	Colorado A. & M.	7
28	Wyoming	7
0	Utah	13
48	Brigham Young	0
31	Denver	6

1943*

38	Fort Francis E. Warren (Wyo.)	0
19	Lowry Air Force Base (Colo.)	6
35	Utah	0
14	Salt Lake City Air Force Base	0
6	Colorado College	16
22	Utah	19
0	Colorado College	6

*No conference play because of World War II.

1944*

6	Fort Francis E. Warren (Wyo.)	7
6	Second Air Force (Colo.)	33
26	Utah	0
28	Colorado College	0
39	New Mexico	0
40	Nebraska (Peru) State V-12	12
16	Denver	14

*No conference play because of World War II.

1945

0	Fort Francis E. Warren (Wyo.)	6
13	Colorado College	0
18	Utah	13
21	Colorado A. & M.	6
31	Colorado College	0
6	New Mexico	12
14	Utah State	7
8	Denver	14

1946

13	Iowa State	7
0	Texas	76
6	Utah State	0
20	Wyoming	0
7	Brigham Young	10
14	New Mexico	13
0	Utah	7
0	Missouri	21
13	Denver	13
18	Colorado A. & M.	0

1947

7	Iowa State	0
0	Army	47
0	Missouri	21
9	Brigham Young	7
14	Colorado A. & M.	7
7	Utah	13
12	Utah State	35
21	Wyoming	6
20	Denver	26

1948*

6	New Mexico	9
7	Kansas	40
19	Nebraska	6
7	Iowa State	18
51	Kansas State	7
12	Utah	14
28	Utah State	14
13	Missouri	27
25	Colorado A. & M.	29

*Colorado's first season in the Big Seven Conference.

1949

13	Kansas	12
13	Kansas State	27

6	Iowa State	13
14	Oregon	42
20	Utah State	7
14	Utah	7
13	Missouri	20
15	New Mexico	17
14	Nebraska	25
7	Colorado A. & M.	14

1950

7	Iowa State	14
34	Kansas State	6
21	Kansas	27
28	Nebraska	19
28	Arizona	25
20	Utah	20
18	Oklahoma	27
19	Missouri	21
21	Oregon	7
31	Colorado A. & M.	6

1951

28	Colorado A. & M.	13
14	Northwestern	35
35	Kansas	27
34	Missouri	13
20	Kansas State	7
14	Oklahoma	55
47	Iowa State	20
54	Utah	0
36	Nebraska	14
7	Michigan State	45

1952

20	San Jose State	14
21	Oklahoma	21
12	Kansas	21
34	Arizona	19
21	Iowa State	12
16	Nebraska	16
20	Utah	14
7	Missouri	27
34	Kansas State	14
61	Colorado A. & M.	0

1953

21	Washington	20
20	Arizona	14
16	Missouri	27

21	Kansas	27
14	Kansas State	28
20	Oklahoma	27
41	Iowa State	34
21	Utah	0
14	Nebraska	10
13	Colorado A. & M.	7

1954

61	Drake	0
46	Colorado A. & M.	0
27	Kansas	0
40	Arizona	18
20	Iowa State	0
6	Nebraska	20
6	Oklahoma	13
19	Missouri	19
20	Utah	7
38	Kansas State	14

1955

14	Arizona	0
12	Kansas	0
13	Oregon	6
34	Kansas State	13
21	Oklahoma	56
12	Missouri	20
37	Utah	7
20	Nebraska	37
40	Iowa State	0
0	Colorado A. & M.	10

1956

0	Oregon	35
34	Kansas State	0
26	Kansas	25
47	Colorado State	7
52	Iowa State	0
16	Nebraska	0
19	Oklahoma	27
14	Missouri	14
21	Utah	7
38	Arizona	7
	Orange Bowl	
27	Clemson	21

1957

6	Washington	6
30	Utah	24

34	Kansas	35
34	Arizona	14
42	Kansas State	14
13	Oklahoma	14
6	Missouri	9
20	Colorado State	0
27	Nebraska	0
38	Iowa State	21

1958

13	Kansas State	3
31	Kansas	0
65	Arizona	12
20	Iowa State	0
27	Nebraska	16
7	Oklahoma	23
9	Missouri	33
7	Utah	0
14	Colorado State	15
14	Air Force	20

1959

12	Washington	21
7	Baylor	15
12	Oklahoma	42
20	Kansas State	17
0	Iowa State	27
18	Arizona	0
21	Missouri	20
27	Kansas	14
12	Nebraska	14
15	Air Force	7

1960

0	Baylor	26
27	Kansas State	7
35	Arizona	16
21	Iowa State	6
19	Nebraska	6
7	Oklahoma	0
6	Missouri	16
6	Kansas	34*
13	Oklahoma State	6
6	Air Force	16

*Later forfeited to Colorado because Kansas used an ineligible player.

1961

24	Oklahoma State	0
20	Kansas	19
9	Miami	7
13	Kansas State	0
22	Oklahoma	14
7	Missouri	6
12	Utah	21
7	Nebraska	0
34	Iowa State	0
29	Air Force	12
	Orange Bowl	
7	Louisiana State	25

1962

21	Utah	37
6	Kansas State	0
6	Kansas	35
16	Oklahoma State	36
19	Iowa State	57
6	Nebraska	31
0	Oklahoma	62
0	Missouri	57
12	Texas Tech	21
34	Air Force	10

1963

0	Southern California	14
6	Oregon State	41
21	Kansas State	7
25	Oklahoma State	0
7	Iowa State	19
6	Nebraska	41
0	Oklahoma	35
7	Missouri	28
14	Kansas	43
14	Air Force	17

1964

0	Southern California	21
7	Oregon State	14
14	Kansas State	16
10	Oklahoma State	14
14	Iowa State	7
3	Nebraska	21
11	Oklahoma	14
7	Missouri	16
7	Kansas	10
28	Air Force	23

1965

0	Wisconsin	0
10	Fresno State	7
36	Kansas State	0
34	Oklahoma State	11
10	Iowa State	10
13	Nebraska	38
13	Oklahoma	0
7	Missouri	20
21	Kansas	14
19	Air Force	6

1966

3	Miami	24
13	Baylor	7
10	Kansas State	0
10	Oklahoma State	11
41	Iowa State	21
19	Nebraska	21
24	Oklahoma	21
26	Missouri	0
35	Kansas	18
10	Air Force	9

1967

27	Baylor	7
17	Oregon	13
34	Iowa State	0
23	Missouri	9
21	Nebraska	16
7	Oklahoma State	10
0	Oklahoma	23
12	Kansas	8
40	Kansas State	6
33	Air Force	0
	Bluebonnet Bowl	
31	Miami	21

1968

28	Oregon	7
0	California	10
28	Iowa State	18
14	Missouri	27
37	Kansas State	14
41	Oklahoma	27
14	Kansas	27
17	Oklahoma State	34
6	Nebraska	22
35	Air Force	58

1969

35	Tulsa	14
3	Penn State	27
30	Indiana	7
14	Iowa State	0
30	Oklahoma	42
31	Missouri	24
7	Nebraska	20
17	Kansas	14
17	Oklahoma State	14
45	Kansas State	32
	Liberty Bowl	
47	Alabama	33

1970

16	Indiana	9
41	Penn State	13
20	Kansas State	21
61	Iowa State	10
15	Oklahoma	23
16	Missouri	30
13	Nebraska	29
45	Kansas	29
30	Oklahoma State	6
49	Air Force	19
	Liberty Bowl	
3	Tulane	17

1971

31	Louisiana State	21
56	Wyoming	13
20	Ohio State	14
31	Kansas State	21
24	Iowa State	14
17	Oklahoma	45
27	Missouri	7
7	Nebraska	31
35	Kansas	14
40	Oklahoma State	6
53	Air Force	17
	Astro-Bluebonnet Bowl	
29	Houston	17

1972

20	California	10
56	Cincinnati	14
38	Minnesota	6
6	Oklahoma State	31
38	Kansas State	17
34	Iowa State	22

20	Oklahoma	14
17	Missouri	20
10	Nebraska	33
33	Kansas	8
38	Air Force	7
	Gator Bowl	
3	Auburn	24

1973

6	Louisiana State	17
28	Wisconsin	25
52	Baylor	28
38	Air Force	17
23	Iowa State	16
7	Oklahoma	34
17	Missouri	13
16	Nebraska	28
15	Kansas	17
24	Oklahoma State	38
14	Kansas State	17

1974

14	Louisiana State	42
0	Michigan	31
24	Wisconsin	21
28	Air Force	27
34	Iowa State	7
14	Oklahoma	49
24	Missouri	30
15	Nebraska	31
17	Kansas	16
37	Oklahoma State	20
23	Kansas State	33

1975

34	California	27
27	Wyoming	10
52	Wichita State	0
20	Oklahoma	21
23	Miami	10
31	Missouri	20
21	Nebraska	63
28	Iowa State	27
17	Oklahoma State	7
24	Kansas	21
33	Kansas State	7
	Astro-Bluebonnet Bowl	
21	Texas	38

1976

7	Texas Tech	24
21	Washington	3
33	Miami	3
45	Drake	24
12	Nebraska	24
20	Oklahoma State	10
33	Iowa State	14
42	Oklahoma	31
7	Missouri	16
40	Kansas	17
35	Kansas State	28
	Orange Bowl	
10	Ohio State	27

1977

27	Stanford	21
42	Kent State	0
42	New Mexico	7
31	Army	0
29	Oklahoma State	13
17	Kansas	17
15	Nebraska	33
14	Missouri	24
12	Iowa State	7
14	Oklahoma	52
23	Kansas State	0

1978

24	Oregon	7
17	Miami	7
22	San Jose State	7
55	Northwestern	7
17	Kansas	7
20	Oklahoma State	24
14	Nebraska	52
28	Missouri	27
7	Oklahoma	28
10	Kansas State	20
16	Iowa State	20

IOWA STATE UNIVERSITY
Ames, Iowa

Founded 1858   COLORS: Cardinal and Gold   NICKNAME: Cyclones

Head Coaches since 1928

C. Noel Workman	*1926–1930*	Vince DiFrancesca	*1954–1956*
George F. Veenker	*1931–1936*	J. A. Myers	*1957*
James Yeager	*1936–1940*	Clay Stapleton	*1958–1967*
Ray O. Donels	*1941–1942*	John Majors	*1968–1972*
Mike Michalske	*1943–1946*	Earle Bruce	*1973–*
Abe Stuber	*1947–1953*		

1928

0	Nebraska	12
0	Grinnell	3
19	Missouri	28
0	Kansas	0
13	Oklahoma	0
7	Kansas State	0
0	Drake	18
0	Marquette	6

1929

27	Grinnell	7
0	Missouri	19
6	Marquette	14
0	Kansas	33
2	Kansas State	3
0	Drake	7
12	Nebraska	31

1930

0	Illinois	7
12	Nebraska	14
6	Kansas	20
13	Oklahoma	19
0	Missouri	14
0	Kansas State	13

19	Drake	20
7	Loyola	13
7	Rice	14

1931

6	Simpson	0
20	Morningside	6
0	Detroit	20
20	Missouri	0
13	Oklahoma	12
7	Kansas State	6
6	Drake	7
0	Nebraska "B" Team	23
6	Emmets Junior College	13
0	Central College	35
19	Drake "B" Team	26
35	Mason City Junior College	6

1932

21	Simpson	0
32	Morningside	0
6	Nebraska	12
0	Kansas	26
0	Missouri	0
0	Kansas State	31

12	Oklahoma	19
34	Drake "B" Team	13
0	Grinnell	6
14	Ft. Dodge Junior College	20
0	Drake	7

1933

14	Central College	0
18	Denver	13
0	Nebraska	20
7	Oklahoma	19
14	Missouri	7
7	Iowa	27
0	Kansas State	7
6	Kansas	20
7	Drake	7

1934

23	Luther	3
26	Grinnell	6
13	Missouri	0
31	Iowa	6
6	Nebraska	7
0	Kansas	0
0	Oklahoma	12
33	Drake	12
0	Kansas State	20

1935

6	Cornell	6
7	Nebraska	20
23	Upper Iowa	0
0	Oklahoma	16
6	Missouri	6
12	Marquette	28
0	Kansas State	6
7	Drake	7
21	Kansas	12

1936

0	Northern Iowa	0
0	Nebraska	34
21	Kansas	7
38	Cornell	0
0	Missouri	10
7	Oklahoma	7
7	Kansas State	47
21	Drake	7

1937

14	Northern Iowa	12
0	Northwestern	33
7	Nebraska	20
6	Kansas	14
0	Drake	30
0	Missouri	12
7	Oklahoma	33
3	Marquette	0
13	Kansas State	7

1938

14	Denver	7
32	Luther	7
8	Nebraska	7
16	Missouri	13
21	Kansas	7
7	Marquette	0
14	Drake	0
13	Kansas State	13
0	Oklahoma	10

1939

19	Coe	0
0	Denver	6
0	Kansas	14
7	Nebraska	10
0	Drake	7
6	Missouri	21
6	Oklahoma	38
2	Marquette	21
10	Kansas State	0

1940

27	Luther	0
7	Denver	14
7	Kansas	0
25	Marquette	41
14	Missouri	30
7	Oklahoma	20
7	Drake	6
12	Kansas State	0
12	Nebraska	21

1941

7	Denver	6
0	Nebraska	14
13	Missouri	39
0	Kansas	13
27	South Dakota	0
0	Oklahoma	55
13	Drake	14
12	Kansas State	12
13	Marquette	28

1942

7	Denver	0
0	Nebraska	26
12	Marquette	34
29	Drake	6
6	Missouri	45
7	Oklahoma	14
7	Villanova	32
20	Kansas	13
6	Kansas State	7

1943

13	Iowa Pre-Flight	33
13	Kansas	6
27	Nebraska	6
12	Ottumwa NAS	13
7	Oklahoma	21
7	Missouri	25
20	Drake	0
48	Kansas State	0

1944

49	G. Adolphus	0
59	Doane	0
25	Kansas	0
21	Missouri	21
14	Kansas State	0
7	Oklahoma	12
19	Nebraska	6
9	Drake	0

1945

6	Northwestern	18
48	Northern Iowa	13
13	Kansas	13
7	Missouri	13
27	Nebraska	7
40	Kansas State	13
7	Oklahoma	14
8	Drake	6

1946

7	Colorado	13
9	Northwestern	41
20	Northern Iowa	18
8	Kansas	24
13	Missouri	33
0	Oklahoma	63
13	Kansas State	7
7	Drake	7
0	Nebraska "B" Team	33
33	Ottumwa NAS	0
6	Nebraska	32
32	Ottumwa NAS	0
69	Drake	0

1947

31	Northern Iowa	14
0	Colorado	7
7	Kansas	27
7	Nebraska	14
0	Michigan State	20
7	Missouri	26
9	Oklahoma	27
36	Drake	6
14	Kansas State	0

1948

27	Northern Iowa	7
15	Nebraska	10
20	Kansas State	0
7	Kansas	20
18	Colorado	7
7	Missouri	49
6	Oklahoma	33
2	Drake	0
7	Michigan State	48
7	Arizona "B" Team	14
26	Burlington Junior College	0
40	Mason City Junior College	0

1949

64	Dubuque	0
20	Illinois	20
19	Kansas	6
13	Colorado	6
25	Kansas State	21
0	Missouri	32
7	Oklahoma	34
21	Drake	8
0	Nebraska	7

1950

14	Colorado	7
13	Northwestern	23
26	Northern Iowa	8
21	Kansas	33
20	Missouri	20
7	Oklahoma	20
13	Kansas State	7
21	Drake	35
13	Nebraska	20
26	Arizona	27

1951

53	Wayne	21
33	Kansas	53
6	Marquette	6
32	Kansas State	6
21	Missouri	14
13	Drake	0
20	Colorado	47
27	Nebraska	34
6	Oklahoma "B" Team	35
6	Graceland	0
13	Buena Vista	12
21	Missouri	12
22	Nebraska	19

1952

57	South Dakota State	19
7	Illinois	33
0	Nebraska	16
0	Kansas	43
12	Colorado	21
0	Missouri	10
0	Oklahoma	41
55	Drake	7
27	Kansas State "B" Team	0
30	Buena Vista	0

1953

35	South Dakota	0
0	Northwestern	35
0	Kansas	23
12	Kansas State	20
13	Missouri	6
7	Drake	12
34	Colorado	41
19	Nebraska	27
0	Oklahoma	47

1954

34	South Dakota State	6
14	Northwestern	27
14	Nebraska	39
33	Kansas	6
0	Colorado	20
14	Missouri	32
35	Drake	0
0	Oklahoma	40
7	Kansas State	12

1955

7	Denver	19
0	Illinois	40
7	Kansas	7
20	Missouri	14
7	Kansas State	9
21	Drake	27
7	Nebraska	10
0	Oklahoma	52
0	Colorado	40

1956

13	Denver	10
13	Northwestern	14
7	Nebraska	9
14	Kansas	25

0	Colorado	52
0	Missouri	34
39	Drake	14
0	Oklahoma	44
6	Kansas State	32
0	Villanova	26

1957

10	Denver	0
7	Syracuse	7
14	Oklahoma	40
21	Kansas	6
13	Missouri	35
10	Kansas State	14
0	Drake	20
13	Nebraska	0
33	South Dakota	0
21	Colorado	38

1958

33	Drake	0
14	Arizona	0
6	Nebraska	7
0	Kansas	7
0	Colorado	20
6	Missouri	14
53	South Dakota	0
0	Oklahoma	20
6	Kansas State	14
9	San Jose State	6

1959

41	Drake	0
28	Denver	12
0	Missouri	14
41	South Dakota	6
27	Colorado	0
26	Kansas State	0
0	Kansas	7
18	Nebraska	6
55	San Jose State	0
12	Oklahoma	35

1960

46	Drake	0
44	Detroit	21
10	Nebraska	7
14	Kansas	28
6	Colorado	21

8	Missouri	34
13	Oklahoma State	6
10	Oklahoma	6
20	Kansas State	7
14	University of the Pacific	6

1961

21	Drake	0
14	Oklahoma State	7
21	Oklahoma	15
7	Kansas	21
7	Missouri	13
31	Kansas State	7
10	Boston College	14
13	Nebraska	16
27	Tulsa	6
0	Colorado	34

1962

14	Drake	7
35	Oregon State	39
22	Nebraska	36
8	Kansas	29
57	Colorado	19
6	Missouri	21
34	Oklahoma State	7
0	Oklahoma	41
28	Kansas State	14
31	Ohio	22

1963

8	California	15
21	VMI	6
7	Nebraska	21
17	Kansas	14
19	Colorado	7
0	Missouri	7
33	Oklahoma State	28
14	Oklahoma	24
10	Kansas State	21

1964

25	Drake	0
14	Oklahoma State	29
7	Nebraska	14
6	Kansas	42
7	Colorado	14

0	Missouri	10
7	Army	9
0	Oklahoma	30
6	Kansas State	7
0	Arizona	0

1965

21	Drake	0
38	University of the Pacific	13
0	Nebraska	44
21	Kansas	7
10	Colorado	10
7	Missouri	23
14	Oklahoma State	10
20	Oklahoma	24
38	Kansas State	6
9	New Mexico	10

1966

10	Wisconsin	20
11	Oklahoma	33
6	Nebraska	12
24	Kansas	7
21	Colorado	41
10	Missouri	10
14	Oklahoma State	14
30	Kansas State	13
24	Arizona	27
10	Colorado State	34

1967

3	South Carolina	34
0	Texas Tech	52
17	New Mexico	12
0	Colorado	34
17	Kansas State	0
7	Missouri	23
14	Kansas	28
0	Nebraska	12
14	Oklahoma	52
14	Oklahoma State	28

1968

28	Buffalo	10
12	Arizona	21
28	Brigham Young	20
18	Colorado	28

23	Kansas State	14
7	Oklahoma	42
25	Kansas	46
13	Nebraska	24
7	Missouri	42
17	Oklahoma State	26

1969

13	Syracuse	14
10	Brigham Young	0
48	Illinois	20
0	Colorado	14
7	Kansas State	34
44	Kansas	20
14	Oklahoma	37
3	Nebraska	17
13	Missouri	40
0	Oklahoma State	35

1970

32	New Mexico	3
37	Colorado State	6
16	Utah	13
10	Colorado	61
0	Kansas State	17
10	Kansas	24
28	Oklahoma	29
29	Nebraska	54
31	Missouri	19
27	Oklahoma State	36
28	San Diego State	22

1971

24	Idaho	7
44	New Mexico	20
12	Kent State	14
14	Colorado	24
24	Kansas State	0
40	Kansas	24
12	Oklahoma	43
0	Nebraska	37
45	Missouri	17
54	Oklahoma State	0
48	San Diego State	31
	Sun Bowl	
15	Louisiana State	33

1972

41	Colorado State	0
44	Utah	22
31	New Mexico	0
22	Colorado	34
55	Kansas State	22
34	Kansas	8
6	Oklahoma	20
23	Nebraska	23
5	Missouri	6
14	Oklahoma State	45
14	San Diego State	27
	Liberty Bowl	
30	Georgia Tech	31

1973

48	Idaho	0
19	Arkansas	21
16	Colorado	23
26	Brigham Young	24
19	Kansas State	21
20	Kansas	22
17	Oklahoma	34
7	Nebraska	31
17	Missouri	7
28	Oklahoma State	12
28	San Diego State	41

1974

3	Texas Tech	24
28	Washington	31
34	Brigham Young	7
27	New Mexico	3
7	Colorado	34
23	Kansas State	18
22	Kansas	6
10	Oklahoma	28
13	Nebraska	23
7	Missouri	10
12	Oklahoma State	14

1975

21	UCLA	37
17	Air Force	12
10	Florida State	6
31	Utah	3
17	Kansas State	7

10	Kansas	21
7	Oklahoma	39
27	Colorado	28
14	Missouri	44
0	Nebraska	52
7	Oklahoma State	14

1976

58	Drake	14
41	Air Force	6
47	Kent State	7
10	Oklahoma	24
44	Utah	14
21	Missouri	17
14	Colorado	33
45	Kansas State	14
31	Kansas	17
37	Nebraska	28
21	Oklahoma State	42

1977

35	Wichita State	9
10	Iowa	12
35	Bowling Green	21
17	Dayton	13
7	Missouri	0
24	Nebraska	21
16	Oklahoma	35
41	Kansas	3
7	Colorado	12
22	Kansas State	15
21	Oklahoma State	13
	Peach Bowl	
14	North Carolina State	24

1978

23	Rice	19
14	San Diego State	13
31	Iowa	0
35	Drake	7
0	Nebraska	23
13	Missouri	26
6	Oklahoma	34
13	Kansas	7
24	Kansas State	0

28	Oklahoma State	15
20	Colorado	16
	Hall of Fame Bowl	
12	Texas A. & M.	28

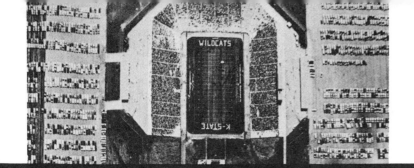

KANSAS STATE UNIVERSITY

Manhattan, Kansas

Founded 1863   COLORS: Purple and White   NICKNAME: Wildcats

Head Coaches since 1928

A. N. McMillin	*1928–1933*	Sam Francis	*1947*
Lynn O. ("Pappy") Waldorf	*1934*	Ralph Graham	*1948–1950*
Wes Fry	*1935–1939*	Bill Meek	*1951–1954*
Hobbs Adams	*1940–1941*	Bus Mertes	*1955–1959*
Ward Haylett	*1942–1944*	Doug Weaver	*1960–1966*
Lud Fiser	*1945*	Vince Gibson	*1967–1974*
Hobbs Adams	*1946*	Ellis Rainsberger	*1975–*

1928

32	Bethany	7
13	Oklahoma State	6
22	Fort Hays State	7
0	Kansas	7
21	Oklahoma	33
6	Missouri	10
0	Iowa State	7
0	Nebraska	8

1929

14	Purdue	26
0	Texas A. & M.	19
6	Kansas	0
13	Oklahoma	14
7	Missouri	6
3	Iowa State	2
6	Nebraska	10
6	Marquette	25

1930

14	Washburn	0
0	Kansas	14
0	Oklahoma	7
7	West Virginia	23
20	Missouri	13
13	Iowa State	0
27	Centre	0
10	Nebraska	9

1931

28	KSTC, Pittsburgh	7
20	Missouri	7
13	Kansas	0
14	Oklahoma	0
19	West Virginia	0
6	Iowa State	7
3	Nebraska	6
19	North Dakota State	6
22	Washburn	0
20	Wichita	6

1932

26	Wichita	0
13	Purdue	29
52	Kansas Wesleyan	6
25	Missouri	0
13	Oklahoma	20
0	Nebraska	6
31	Iowa State	0
0	Kansas	19

1933

25	Emporia State	0
20	Washington	14
33	Missouri	0
0	Nebraska	9
6	Kansas	0
0	Michigan State	0
7	Iowa State	0
14	Oklahoma	0
0	Texas Tech	6

1934

13	Fort Hays State	0
13	Manhattan	13
20	Marquette	27
13	Kansas	0
0	Tulsa	21
14	Washburn	6
29	Missouri	0
8	Oklahoma	7
20	Iowa State	0
19	Nebraska	7

1935

12	Duquesne	0
0	Fort Hays State	3
0	Marquette	14
0	Nebraska	0
2	Kansas	9
13	Tulsa	13
6	Iowa State	0
0	Oklahoma	3
7	Missouri	7

1936

13	Fort Hays State	0
31	Oklahoma State	0
7	Missouri	7
0	Marquette	13
26	Kansas	6
7	Tulsa	10
6	Oklahoma	6
47	Iowa State	7
0	Nebraska	40

1937

7	Boston	21
7	Missouri	14
13	Marquette	0
15	Creighton	7
0	Oklahoma	19
20	Washburn	7
7	Kansas	0
7	Iowa State	13
0	Nebraska	3

1938

0	Northwestern	21
21	Missouri	13
6	Marquette	0
13	Indiana	6
7	Kansas	27
0	Oklahoma	26
13	Iowa State	13
41	Washburn	14
7	Nebraska	14

1939

34	Fort Hays State	7
20	Colorado	0
3	Marquette	0
7	Missouri	9
27	Kansas	6
10	Oklahoma	13

0	Iowa State	10
7	Boston	38
9	Nebraska	25

1940

21	Emporia State	16
6	Colorado	6
13	Missouri	24
0	Oklahoma	14
20	Kansas	0
0	Michigan State	32
13	South Carolina	20
0	Iowa State	12
0	Nebraska	20

1941

0	Fort Hays State	0
3	Northwestern	51
0	Missouri	35
0	Oklahoma	16
3	South Carolina	0
16	Kansas	20
12	Iowa State	12
21	Arizona	28
12	Nebraska	6

1942

37	Kansas Wesleyan	6
0	Texas	64
7	Fort Riley	21
0	Duquesne	33
2	Missouri	46
7	Kansas	19
0	Wichita	9
0	Oklahoma	76
0	Indiana	54
7	Iowa State	6
19	Nebraska	0

1943

13	Washburn	7
14	Missouri	47
6	William Jewell	19
0	Oklahoma	37
2	Kansas	25
7	Nebraska	13
6	Washburn	13
0	Iowa State	48

1944

6	Wichita	6
0	Missouri	33
6	Michigan State	45
0	Oklahoma	68
0	Iowa State	14
15	Wichita	0
18	Kansas	14
0	Olathe NAS	0
0	Nebraska	35

1945

13	Wichita	6
12	Olathe NAS	34
13	Marquette	55
7	Missouri	41
13	Oklahoma	41
13	Iowa State	40
0	Nebraska	24
0	Kansas	27

1946

7	Hardin-Simmons	21
0	Nebraska	31
0	Missouri	26
7	Oklahoma	28
7	Iowa State	13
6	San Francisco	38
0	Kansas	34
7	New Mexico	14
7	Arizona	28

1947

0	Oklahoma State	12
6	Texas (El Paso)	20
18	New Mexico	20
13	Boston	49
7	Missouri	47
7	Nebraska	14
9	Kansas	55
13	Oklahoma	27
0	Iowa State	14
7	Florida	25

1948

0	Illinois	40
0	Iowa State	20
37	Arkansas State	6
0	Oklahoma	42
7	Colorado	51
7	Missouri	49

0	Nebraska	32
14	Kansas	20
6	Oklahoma State	42
7	Washington	21

1949

55	Fort Hays State	0
27	Colorado	13
6	Nebraska	13
21	Iowa State	25
14	Memphis State	21
0	Kansas	38
0	Oklahoma	39
14	Oklahoma State	26
27	Tulsa	48
27	Missouri	34

1950

55	Baker	0
7	Washington	33
6	Colorado	34
6	Marquette	46
7	Missouri	28
0	Oklahoma	58
7	Iowa State	13
21	Nebraska	49
7	Kansas	47
0	Oklahoma State	41
6	Wichita	6

1951

20	Cincinnati	34
0	Iowa	16
0	Nebraska	1
6	Iowa State	32
7	Colorado	20
14	Kansas	33
0	Oklahoma	33
26	Tulsa	42
0	Missouri	1

1952

21	Bradley	7
6	Cincinnati	13
0	Missouri	26
14	Nebraska	27
7	Tulsa	26
6	Oklahoma	49
6	Kansas	26
7	Wyoming	20

14	Colorado	34
0	Iowa State	27

1953

50	Drake	0
13	Colorado State	14
27	Nebraska	0
20	Iowa State	12
28	Colorado	14
21	Wichita	0
0	Oklahoma	34
7	Kansas	0
6	Missouri	16
26	Arizona	26

1954

29	Colorado State	0
21	Wyoming	13
7	Missouri	35
7	Nebraska	3
20	Tulsa	13
0	Oklahoma	21
28	Kansas	6
53	Drake	18
12	Iowa State	7
14	Colorado	38

1955

20	Wyoming	38
7	Iowa	28
0	Nebraska	16
42	Marquette	0
13	Colorado	34
9	Iowa State	7
7	Oklahoma	40
46	Kansas	0
21	Missouri	0
0	Oklahoma State	28

1956

7	Oklahoma State	27
0	Colorado	34
0	Oklahoma	66
10	Nebraska	7
6	Missouri	20
15	Wyoming	27
15	Kansas	20
41	Marquette	14

32	Iowa State	6
17	Michigan State	38

1957

7	Wyoming	12
36	Brigham Young	7
7	Nebraska	14
7	College of the Pacific	7
14	Colorado	42
14	Iowa State	10
0	Oklahoma	13
7	Kansas	13
23	Missouri	21
9	Michigan State	27

1958

17	Wyoming	14
3	Colorado	13
13	Utah State	20
23	Nebraska	6
8	Missouri	32
6	Oklahoma	40
12	Kansas	21
7	Oklahoma State	14
14	Iowa State	6
7	Michigan State	26

1959

0	Wichita	19
28	South Dakota State	12
21	Oklahoma State	27
17	Colorado	20
14	Kansas	33
0	Iowa State	26
0	Iowa	53
0	Oklahoma	36
0	Missouri	26
29	Nebraska	14

1960

20	South Dakota State	6
0	Kansas	41
7	Colorado	27
7	Nebraska	17
0	Missouri	45
7	Oklahoma	49
7	Minnesota	48
7	Oklahoma State	28
7	Iowa State	20
16	Arizona	35

1961

14	Indiana	8
14	Air Force	12
0	Nebraska	24
8	Kentucky	21
0	Colorado	13
7	Iowa State	31
6	Oklahoma	17
0	Kansas	34
9	Missouri	27
0	Oklahoma State	45

1962

0	Indiana	21
0	Colorado	6
0	Washington	41
0	Missouri	32
6	Nebraska	26
0	Oklahoma	47
0	Kansas	38
13	Arizona	14
14	Iowa State	28
6	Oklahoma State	30

1963

24	Brigham Young	7
0	San Jose State	16
7	Colorado	21
11	Missouri	21
6	Nebraska	28
9	Oklahoma	34
0	Kansas	34
13	Texas Tech	51
21	Iowa State	10

1964

7	Wisconsin	17
16	Colorado	14
0	Missouri	7
0	Nebraska	47
0	Oklahoma	44
0	Kansas	7
10	Arizona State	21
7	Iowa State	6
17	Oklahoma State	14
7	New Mexico	9

1965

7	Indiana	19
3	Brigham Young	21

0	Colorado	36
6	Missouri	28
0	Nebraska	41
0	Oklahoma	27
0	Kansas	34
14	Cincinnati	21
6	Iowa State	38
7	Oklahoma State	31

1966

6	Army	21
8	New Mexico	28
0	Colorado	10
0	Missouri	27
10	Nebraska	21
14	Cincinnati	28
3	Kansas	3
6	Oklahoma	37
13	Iowa State	30
6	Oklahoma State	21

1967

17	Colorado State	7
3	Virginia Tech	15
14	Nebraska	16
0	Iowa State	17
7	Oklahoma	46
7	Arkansas	28
16	Kansas	17
6	Missouri	28
6	Colorado	40
14	Oklahoma State	49

1968

21	Colorado State	0
9	Penn State	25
34	Virginia Tech	19
14	Colorado	37
20	Missouri	56
20	Oklahoma	35
12	Nebraska	0
29	Kansas	38
21	Oklahoma State	14

1969

48	Baylor	15
42	Arizona	27
14	Penn State	17
26	Kansas	22
34	Iowa State	7

59	Oklahoma	21
38	Missouri	41
19	Oklahoma State	28
7	Nebraska	10
32	Colorado	45

1970

37	Utah State	0
3	Kentucky	16
13	Arizona State	35
21	Colorado	20
15	Kansas	21
17	Iowa State	0
19	Oklahoma	14
17	Missouri	13
28	Oklahoma State	15
13	Nebraska	51
7	Florida State	33

1971

7	Utah State	10
19	Tulsa	10
23	Brigham Young	7
21	Colorado	31
13	Kansas	39
0	Iowa State	24
28	Oklahoma	75
28	Missouri	12
35	Oklahoma State	23
17	Nebraska	44
28	Memphis State	21

1972

21	Tulsa	13
9	Brigham Young	32
14	Arizona State	56
31	Tampa	7
17	Colorado	38
20	Kansas	19
22	Iowa State	55
0	Oklahoma	52
14	Missouri	31
14	Oklahoma State	45
7	Nebraska	59

1973

10	Florida	21
21	Tulsa	0
17	Tampa	0

21	Memphis State	16
18	Kansas	25
21	Iowa State	19
14	Oklahoma	56
7	Missouri	31
9	Oklahoma State	28
21	Nebraska	50
17	Colorado	14

1974

31	Tulsa	14
17	Wichita State	0
38	Pacific	7
16	Mississippi State	21
13	Kansas	20
18	Iowa State	23
0	Oklahoma	63
15	Missouri	52
5	Oklahoma State	29
7	Nebraska	35
33	Colorado	19

1975

17	Tulsa	16
32	Wichita State	0
17	Wake Forest	16
0	Texas A. & M.	10
7	Iowa State	17
3	Oklahoma	25
3	Missouri	35
0	Kansas	28
0	Nebraska	12
3	Oklahoma State	56
7	Colorado	33

1976

13	Brigham Young	3
14	Texas A. & M.	34
0	Wake Forest	13
10	Florida State	20
21	Missouri	28
0	Nebraska	51
14	Kansas	24
14	Iowa State	15
20	Oklahoma	49
21	Oklahoma State	45
28	Colorado	35

1977

0	Brigham Young	39
10	Florida State	18
21	Wichita State	14
21	Mississippi State*	24
9	Nebraska	26
14	Oklahoma State	21
13	Missouri	28
7	Oklahoma	42
21	Kansas	29
15	Iowa State	22
0	Colorado	23

*Victory forfeited to Kansas State.

1978

0	Arizona	31
32	Auburn	45
14	Tulsa	24
34	Air Force	21
18	Oklahoma State	7
14	Nebraska	48
14	Missouri	56
19	Oklahoma	56
0	Iowa State	24
20	Colorado	10
36	Kansas	20

UNIVERSITY OF KANSAS

Lawrence, Kansas

Founded 1866   COLORS: Crimson and Blue   NICKNAME: Jayhawks

Head Coaches since 1928

W. H. Hargiss	*1928–1931*	Chuck Mather	*1954–1957*
Ad Lindsey	*1932–1938*	Jack Mitchell	*1958–1966*
Gwinn Henry	*1939–1942*	Pepper Rodgers	*1967–1970*
Henry Shenk	*1943–1945*	Don Fambrough	*1970–1974*
George Sauer	*1946–1947*	Bud Moore	*1975–*
J. V. Sikes	*1948–1953*		

1928

14	Grinnell	0
7	Washington	7
7	Kansas State	0
0	Iowa State	0
0	Nebraska	20
0	Marquette	7
0	Oklahoma	7
6	Missouri	25

1929

0	Illinois	25
38	Emporia State	0
0	Kansas State	6
33	Iowa State	0
6	Nebraska	12
7	Oklahoma	0
13	Washington	0
0	Missouri	7

1930

26	Creighton	0
33	Haskell	7
14	Kansas State	0
20	Iowa State	6
6	Pennsylvania	21

0	Nebraska	16
13	Oklahoma	0
32	Missouri	0

1931

27	Colorado State	6
0	Haskell	6
30	James Milliken	0
0	Kansas State	13
0	Nebraska	6
7	Oklahoma State	13
0	Oklahoma	10
28	Washington	0
14	Missouri	0
6	Washburn	0

1932

13	Denver	12
6	Oklahoma	21
26	Iowa State	0
6	Nebraska	20
6	St. Louis	0
6	Notre Dame	24
7	Missouri	0
19	Kansas State	0

1933

34	Warrensburg	0
14	Creighton	0
0	Notre Dame	0
0	Tulsa	7
0	Kansas State	6
0	Oklahoma	20
0	Nebraska	12
20	Iowa State	6
27	Missouri	0
7	George Washington	0

1934

0	Colorado	0
0	Tulsa	7
34	St. Benedict's	12
0	Kansas State	13
7	Oklahoma	7
0	Iowa State	0
13	Washington	0
0	Nebraska	3
0	Michigan State	6
20	Missouri	0

1935

7	Notre Dame	28
42	St. Benedict's	0
0	Michigan State	42
9	Kansas State	2
7	Oklahoma	0
13	Nebraska	19
12	Colorado	6
12	Iowa State	21
0	Missouri	0

1936

10	Washburn	6
7	Iowa State	21
0	Oklahoma	14
6	Kansas State	26
0	Arizona	0
0	Nebraska	26
0	Michigan State	41
3	Missouri	19

1937

25	Washburn	2
7	Wichita	18
14	Iowa State	6
6	Oklahoma	3
0	Michigan State	16
13	Nebraska	13
0	Kansas State	7
7	Arizona	9
0	Missouri	0

1938

19	Texas	18
0	Notre Dame	52
58	Washburn	14
0	Oklahoma	19
7	Iowa State	21
27	Kansas State	7
7	Nebraska	16
7	George Washington	9
7	Missouri	13

1939

6	Drake	12
14	Iowa State	0
7	Colorado State	0
7	Oklahoma	27
6	Kansas State	27
0	Nebraska	7
7	George Washington	14
0	Missouri	20

1940

0	Iowa State	7
20	Drake	6
2	Nebraska	53
0	Kansas State	20
7	Villanova	33
0	Oklahoma	13
0	George Washington	6
20	Missouri	45
26	Colorado State	0

1941

9	Temple	31
19	Washington	6
0	Nebraska	32
7	Marquette	33
13	Iowa State	0
0	Oklahoma	38
0	West Virginia	21
20	Kansas State	16
6	Missouri	45

1942

0	Iowa Seahawks	61
0	Marquette	14
0	Denver	17
6	Texas Christian	41
0	Oklahoma	25
19	Kansas State	7
7	Nebraska	14
19	Washington	7
13	Iowa State	20
13	Missouri	42

1943

0	Washburn	0
6	Denver	19
6	Iowa State	13
13	Washburn	0
6	Nebraska	7
25	Kansas State	2
13	Oklahoma	26
13	Warrensburg	12
7	Missouri	6
7	Ft. Riley	22

1944

47	Washburn	0
0	Texas Christian	7
14	Denver	14
0	Tulsa	27
0	Iowa State	25
20	Nebraska	0
33	Olathe Navy	14
14	Kansas State	18
0	Oklahoma	20
0	Missouri	28

1945

0	Texas Christian	18
20	Denver	19
13	Iowa State	13
34	Washburn	0
7	Oklahoma	39
13	Wichita	0
13	Nebraska	27
0	Marquette	26
27	Kansas State	0
12	Missouri	33

1946

0	Texas Christian	0
21	Denver	13
14	Wichita	7
24	Iowa State	8
14	Nebraska	16
0	Tulsa	56
14	Oklahoma State	13
16	Oklahoma	13
34	Kansas State	0
20	Missouri	19

1947

0	Texas Christian	0
9	Denver	0
27	Iowa State	7
86	South Dakota State	6
13	Oklahoma	13
55	Kansas State	0
13	Nebraska	7
13	Oklahoma State	7
20	Missouri	14
54	Arizona	28
	Orange Bowl	
14	Georgia Tech	20

1948

13	Texas Christian	14
40	Denver	0
40	Colorado	7
20	Iowa State	7
12	George Washington	0
27	Nebraska	7
13	Oklahoma State	7
20	Kansas State	14
7	Oklahoma	60
7	Missouri	21

1949

0	Texas Christian	28
12	Colorado	13
6	Iowa State	19
21	George Washington	14
26	Oklahoma	48
55	Oklahoma State	14
38	Kansas State	0
27	Nebraska	13
28	Missouri	34
46	Arizona	0

1950

7	Texas Christian	14
46	Denver	6
27	Colorado	21
33	Iowa State	21
40	Oklahoma State	7
26	Nebraska	33
39	Utah	26
13	Oklahoma	33
47	Kansas State	7
6	Missouri	20

1951

27	Texas Christian	13
53	Iowa State	33
27	Colorado	35
26	Utah	7
21	Oklahoma	33
33	Kansas State	14
27	Nebraska	7
34	Loyola (L.A.)	26
27	Oklahoma State	12
41	Missouri	28

1952

13	Texas Christian	0
21	Santa Clara	9
21	Colorado	12
43	Iowa State	0
20	Oklahoma	42
26	Southern Methodist	0
26	Kansas State	6
13	Nebraska	14
12	Oklahoma State	7
19	Missouri	20

1953

0	Texas Christian	13
7	UCLA	19
23	Iowa State	0
27	Colorado	21
0	Oklahoma	45
6	Southern Methodist	14
0	Nebraska	9
0	Kansas State	7
14	Oklahoma State	41
6	Missouri	10

1954

6	Texas Christian	27
7	UCLA	32
0	Colorado	27
6	Iowa State	33
0	Oklahoma	65
18	Southern Methodist	36
6	Kansas State	28
20	Nebraska	41
12	Oklahoma State	47
18	Missouri	41

1955

14	Texas Christian	47
13	Washington State	0

0	Colorado	12
7	Iowa State	7
6	Oklahoma	44
14	Southern Methodist	33
14	Nebraska	19
0	Kansas State	46
12	Oklahoma State	7
13	Missouri	7

1956

0	Texas Christian	32
27	College of the Pacific	27
25	Colorado	26
25	Iowa State	14
12	Oklahoma	34
21	Oklahoma State	13
20	Kansas State	15
20	Nebraska	26
0	UCLA	13
13	Missouri	15

1957

13	Texas Christian	13
6	Oregon State	34
35	Colorado	34
6	Iowa State	21
0	Oklahoma	47
6	Miami	48
14	Nebraska	12
13	Kansas State	7
13	Oklahoma State	7
9	Missouri	7

1958

0	Texas Christian	42
0	Oregon State	12
0	Colorado	31
7	Iowa State	0
0	Oklahoma	43
14	Tulane	9
21	Kansas State	12
29	Nebraska	7
3	Oklahoma State	6
13	Missouri	13

1959

7	Texas Christian	14
21	Syracuse	35
28	Boston U.	7
10	Nebraska	3

33	Kansas State	14
6	Oklahoma	7
7	Iowa State	0
14	Colorado	27
28	Oklahoma State	14
9	Missouri	13

1960

21	Texas Christian	7
41	Kansas State	0
7	Syracuse	14
28	Iowa State	14
13	Oklahoma	13
14	Oklahoma State	7
7	Iowa	21
31	Nebraska	0
34	Colorado*	6
23	Missouri*	7

*Ordered to forfeit victories because of ineligible player.

1961

16	Texas Christian	17
6	Wyoming	6
19	Colorado	20
21	Iowa State	7
10	Oklahoma	0
42	Oklahoma State	8
28	Nebraska	6
34	Kansas State	0
53	California	7
7	Missouri	10
	Bluebonnet Bowl	
33	Rice	7

1962

3	Texas Christian	6
14	Boston U.	0
35	Colorado	8
29	Iowa State	8
7	Oklahoma	13
36	Oklahoma State	17
38	Kansas State	0
16	Nebraska	40
33	California	21
3	Missouri	3

1963

6	Texas Christian	10
10	Syracuse	0

25	Wyoming	21
14	Iowa State	17
18	Oklahoma	21
41	Oklahoma State	7
34	Kansas State	0
9	Nebraska	23
43	Colorado	14
7	Missouri	9

1964

7	Texas Christian	3
6	Syracuse	38
14	Wyoming	17
42	Iowa State	6
15	Oklahoma	14
14	Oklahoma State	13
7	Kansas State	0
7	Nebraska	14
10	Colorado	7
14	Missouri	34

1965

7	Texas Tech	26
15	Arizona	23
0	California	17
7	Iowa State	21
7	Oklahoma	21
0	Oklahoma State	0
34	Kansas State	0
6	Nebraska	42
14	Colorado	21
20	Missouri	44

1966

7	Texas Tech	23
35	Arizona	13
16	Minnesota	14
7	Iowa State	24
0	Oklahoma	35
7	Oklahoma State	10
3	Kansas State	3
13	Nebraska	24
18	Colorado	35
0	Missouri	7

1967

20	Stanford	21
15	Indiana	18

15	Ohio	30
10	Nebraska	0
26	Oklahoma State	15
28	Iowa State	14
17	Kansas State	16
8	Colorado	12
10	Oklahoma	14
17	Missouri	6

1968

47	Illinois	7
38	Indiana	20
68	New Mexico	7
23	Nebraska	13
49	Oklahoma State	14
46	Iowa State	25
27	Colorado	14
23	Oklahoma	27
38	Kansas State	29
21	Missouri	19
	Orange Bowl	
14	Penn State	15

1969

22	Texas Tech	38
13	Syracuse	0
7	New Mexico	16
22	Kansas State	26
17	Nebraska	21
20	Iowa State	44
25	Oklahoma State	28
14	Colorado	17
15	Oklahoma	31
21	Missouri	69

1970

48	Washington State	31
0	Texas Tech	23
31	Syracuse	14
49	New Mexico	23
21	Kansas State	15
20	Nebraska	41
24	Iowa State	10
7	Oklahoma State	19
29	Colorado	45
24	Oklahoma	28
17	Missouri	28

1971

34	Washington State	0
22	Baylor	0
7	Florida State	30
20	Minnesota	38
39	Kansas State	13
0	Nebraska	55
24	Iowa State	40
10	Oklahoma State	17
14	Colorado	35
10	Oklahoma	56
7	Missouri	2

1972

17	Washington State	18
52	Wyoming	14
22	Florida State	44
34	Minnesota	28
19	Kansas State	20
0	Nebraska	56
8	Iowa State	34
13	Oklahoma State	10
8	Colorado	33
7	Oklahoma	31
28	Missouri	17

1973

29	Washington State	8
28	Florida State	0
34	Minnesota	19
27	Tennessee	28
25	Kansas State	18
9	Nebraska	10
22	Iowa State	20
10	Oklahoma State	10
17	Colorado	15
20	Oklahoma	48
14	Missouri	13
	Liberty Bowl	
18	North Carolina State	31

1974

14	Washington State	7
3	Tennessee	17
40	Florida State	9
28	Texas A. & M.	10
20	Kansas State	13

0	Nebraska	56
6	Iowa State	22
13	Oklahoma State	24
16	Colorado	17
14	Oklahoma	45
3	Missouri	27

1975

14	Washington State	18
14	Kentucky	10
20	Oregon State	0
41	Wisconsin	7
0	Nebraska	16
21	Iowa State	10
19	Oklahoma State	35
28	Kansas State	0
23	Oklahoma	3
21	Colorado	24
42	Missouri	24
	Sun Bowl	
19	Pittsburgh	33

1976

28	Oregon State	16
35	Washington State	16
37	Kentucky	16
34	Wisconsin	24
14	Oklahoma State	21
10	Oklahoma	28
24	Kansas State	14
3	Nebraska	31
17	Iowa State	31
17	Colorado	40
41	Missouri	14

1977

14	Texas A. & M.	28
7	UCLA	17
14	Washington State	12
9	Oklahoma	24
7	Miami	14
17	Colorado	17
0	Oklahoma State	21
3	Iowa State	41
29	Kansas State	21
7	Nebraska	52
24	Missouri	12

1978

10	Texas A. & M.	37
2	Washington	31
28	UCLA	24
6	Miami	38
7	Colorado	17
16	Oklahoma	17
7	Oklahoma State	21
7	Iowa State	13
21	Nebraska	63
0	Missouri	48
20	Kansas State	36

UNIVERSITY OF MISSOURI

Columbia, Missouri

Founded 1839   COLORS: *Black and Gold*   NICKNAME: *Tigers*

Head Coaches Since 1928

Gwinn Henry	*1923–1931*	Frank Broyles	*1957*
Frank Carideo	*1932–1934*	Dan Devine	*1958–1970*
Don Faurot	*1935–1942*	Al Onofrio	*1971–1977*
Chauncey Simpson	*1943–1945*	Warren Powers	*1978–*
Don Faurot	*1946–1956*		

1928

60	Centre	0
28	Iowa State	19
0	Nebraska	24
0	Drake	6
19	Kansas State	6
6	New York	27
25	Kansas	6
0	Oklahoma	14

1929

19	Iowa State	0
20	Drake	0
7	Nebraska	7
6	Kansas State	7
6	Washington	0
0	New York	14
7	Kansas	0
13	Oklahoma	0

1930

0	Colorado	9
0	St. Louis	20
0	New York	38
14	Drake	13
13	Kansas State	20

14	Iowa State	0
0	Nebraska	0
0	Kansas	32
0	Oklahoma	0

1931

0	Texas	31
7	Kansas State	20
7	Colorado	9
0	Iowa State	20
7	Nebraska	10
32	Drake	20
7	Oklahoma	0
0	Kansas	14
6	Temple	38
6	St. Louis	21

1932

0	Northwestern	27
0	Texas	65
0	Kansas State	25
0	Iowa State	0
6	Washington	14
14	Oklahoma	6
6	Nebraska	21

6	St. Louis	19
0	Kansas	7

1933

31	Central College	0
6	Kirksville	26
0	Kansas State	33
7	St. Louis	13
7	Iowa State	14
0	Nebraska	26
0	Oklahoma	21
7	Washington	33
0	Kansas	27

1934

0	Colorado	0
0	Iowa State	13
0	St. Louis	7
6	Chicago	19
0	Oklahoma	31
0	Kansas State	29
13	Washington	40
6	Nebraska	13
0	Kansas	20

1935

39	William Jewell	0
7	Warrensburg	0
20	Colorado	6
6	Iowa State	6
6	Nebraska	19
6	Oklahoma	20
6	Washington	19
7	Kansas State	7
0	Kansas	0

1936

20	Cape Girardeau	0
7	Kansas State	7
0	Michigan State	13
10	Iowa State	0
0	Nebraska	20
13	St. Louis	7
21	Oklahoma	14
17	Washington	10
19	Kansas	3

1937

6	Colorado	14
14	Kansas State	7
0	Michigan State	2
0	Nebraska	7
12	Iowa State	0
7	St. Louis	14
0	Oklahoma	7
3	Washington	0
0	Kansas	0
0	UCLA	13

1938

14	Colorado	7
13	Kansas State	21
13	Iowa State	16
13	Washington	0
13	Nebraska	10
6	Michigan State	0
0	Oklahoma	21
26	St. Louis	0
13	Kansas	7

1939

30	Colorado	0
0	Ohio State	19

14	Washington	0
9	Kansas State	7
21	Iowa State	6
27	Nebraska	13
20	New York	7
7	Oklahoma	6
20	Kansas	0

1940

40	St. Louis	26
13	Pittsburgh	19
24	Kansas State	13
30	Iowa State	14
7	Nebraska	20
33	New York	0
21	Colorado	6
0	Oklahoma	7
45	Kansas	20

1941

7	Ohio State	12
12	Colorado	6
35	Kansas State	0
39	Iowa State	13
6	Nebraska	0
19	Michigan State	0
26	New York	0
28	Oklahoma	0
45	Kansas	6
	Sugar Bowl	
0	Fordham	2

1942

31	Ft. Riley	0
38	St. Louis	7
26	Colorado	13
9	Wisconsin	17
46	Kansas State	2
45	Iowa State	6
0	Great Lakes NTS	17
26	Nebraska	6
6	Oklahoma	6
12	Fordham	20
42	Kansas	13
7	Iowa Navy Pre-Flight	0

1943

13	Minnesota	26
6	Ohio State	27

47	Kansas State	14
6	Iowa Navy Pre-Flight	21
54	Nebraska	20
25	Iowa State	7
13	Oklahoma	20
6	Kansas	7

1944

6	Arkansas	7
0	Ohio State	54
33	Kansas State	0
27	Minnesota	39
21	Iowa State	21
20	Nebraska	24
13	Michigan State	7
21	Oklahoma	21
7	Iowa Navy Pre-Flight	51
28	Kansas	0

1945

0	Minnesota	34
6	Ohio State	7
10	Southern Methodist	7
13	Iowa State	7
41	Kansas State	7
19	Nebraska	0
7	Michigan State	14
14	Oklahoma	6
33	Kansas	12
	Cotton Bowl	
27	Texas	40

1946

0	Texas	42
13	Ohio State	13
19	St. Louis	14
26	Kansas State	0
33	Iowa State	13
0	Southern Methodist	17
21	Nebraska	20
21	Colorado	0
6	Oklahoma	27
19	Kansas	20

1947

19	St. Louis	0
7	Ohio State	13

19	Southern Methodist	35
21	Colorado	0
47	Kansas State	7
26	Iowa State	7
47	Nebraska	6
28	Duke	7
12	Oklahoma	21
14	Kansas	20

1948

7	Ohio State	21
60	St. Louis	7
20	Southern Methodist	14
35	Navy	14
49	Iowa State	7
49	Kansas State	7
7	Oklahoma	41
27	Colorado	13
33	Nebraska	6
21	Kansas	7
	Gator Bowl	
23	Clemson	24

1949

34	Ohio State	35
27	Southern Methodist	28
21	Oklahoma A. & M.	7
27	Illinois	20
32	Iowa State	0
21	Nebraska	20
20	Colorado	13
7	Oklahoma	27
34	Kansas	28
34	Kansas State	27
	Gator Bowl	
7	Maryland	20

1950

0	Clemson	34
0	Southern Methodist	21
28	Kansas State	7
20	Iowa State	20
27	Oklahoma A. & M.	0
34	Nebraska	40
21	Colorado	19
7	Oklahoma	41
20	Kansas	6
9	Miami	27

1951

20	Fordham	34
27	Oklahoma A. & M.	26
0	Southern Methodist	34
13	Colorado	34
14	Iowa State	21
35	Nebraska	19
0	Maryland	35
20	Oklahoma	34
12	Kansas State	14*
28	Kansas	41

*Forfeit victory for Missouri.

1952

10	Maryland	13
14	California	28
26	Kansas State	0
7	Southern Methodist	25
7	Oklahoma A. & M.	14
19	Iowa State	0
10	Nebraska	6
27	Colorado	7
7	Oklahoma	47
20	Kansas	19

1953

6	Maryland	20
14	Purdue	7
27	Colorado	16
7	Southern Methodist	20
6	Iowa State	13
23	Nebraska	7
14	Indiana	7
7	Oklahoma	14
16	Kansas State	6
10	Kansas	6

1954

0	Purdue	31
35	Kansas State	7
6	Southern Methodist	25
20	Indiana	14
32	Iowa State	14
19	Nebraska	25
19	Colorado	19
13	Oklahoma	34
41	Kansas	18
13	Maryland	74

1955

12	Maryland	13
7	Michigan	42
14	Utah	20
6	Southern Methodist	13
14	Iowa State	20
12	Nebraska	18
20	Colorado	12
0	Oklahoma	20
0	Kansas State	21
7	Kansas	13

1956

13	Oregon State	19
7	Purdue	16
27	Southern Methodist	33
42	North Dakota State	0
20	Kansas State	6
34	Iowa State	0
14	Nebraska	15
14	Colorado	14
14	Oklahoma	67
15	Kansas	13

1957

7	Vanderbilt	7
35	Arizona	13
0	Texas A. & M.	28
7	Southern Methodist	6
35	Iowa State	13
14	Nebraska	13
9	Colorado	39
14	Oklahoma	39
21	Kansas State	23
7	Kansas	9

1958

8	Vanderbilt	12
14	Idaho	10
0	Texas A. & M.	12
19	Southern Methodist	32
32	Kansas State	8
14	Iowa State	6
31	Nebraska	0
33	Colorado	9
0	Oklahoma	39
13	Kansas	13

1959

8	Penn State	19
20	Michigan	15
14	Iowa State	0
2	Southern Methodist	23
0	Oklahoma	23
9	Nebraska	0
20	Colorado	21
13	Air Force	0
26	Kansas State	0
13	Kansas	9
	Orange Bowl	
0	Georgia	14

1960

20	Southern Methodist	0
28	Oklahoma State	7
21	Penn State	8
34	Air Force	8
45	Kansas State	0
34	Iowa State	8
28	Nebraska	0
16	Colorado	6
41	Oklahoma	19
7	Kansas	23*
	Orange Bowl	
21	Navy	14

*Forfeit victory.

1961

28	Washington State	6
6	Minnesota	0
14	California	14
10	Oklahoma State	0
13	Iowa State	7
10	Nebraska	0
6	Colorado	7
0	Oklahoma	7
27	Kansas State	9
10	Kansas	7

1962

21	California	10
0	Minnesota	0
17	Arizona	7
32	Kansas State	0
23	Oklahoma State	6
21	Iowa State	6
16	Nebraska	7
57	Colorado	0
0	Oklahoma	13

3	Kansas	3
	Bluebonnet Bowl	
14	Georgia Tech	10

1963

12	Northwestern	23
7	Arkansas	6
24	Idaho	0
21	Kansas State	11
28	Oklahoma State	6
7	Iowa State	0
12	Nebraska	13
28	Colorado	7
3	Oklahoma	13
9	Kansas	7

1964

14	California	21
23	Utah	6
7	Oklahoma State	10
7	Kansas State	0
17	Air Force	7
10	Iowa State	0
0	Nebraska	9
16	Colorado	7
14	Oklahoma	14
34	Kansas	14

1965

0	Kentucky	7
13	Oklahoma State	0
17	Minnesota	6
28	Kansas State	6
14	UCLA	14
23	Iowa State	7
14	Nebraska	16
20	Colorado	7
30	Oklahoma	0
44	Kansas	20
	Sugar Bowl	
20	Florida	18

1966

24	Minnesota	0
21	Illinois	14
15	UCLA	24
27	Kansas City	0
7	Oklahoma State	0

10	Iowa State	10
0	Nebraska	35
0	Colorado	26
10	Oklahoma	7
7	Kansas	0

1967

21	Southern Methodist	0
13	Northwestern	6
17	Arizona	3
9	Colorado	23
23	Iowa State	7
0	Oklahoma	7
7	Oklahoma State	0
28	Kansas State	6
10	Nebraska	7
6	Kansas	17

1968

6	Kentucky	12
44	Illinois	0
7	Army	3
27	Colorado	14
16	Nebraska	14
56	Kansas State	20
42	Oklahoma State	7
42	Iowa State	7
14	Oklahoma	28
19	Kansas	21
	Gator Bowl	
35	Alabama	10

1969

19	Air Force	17
37	Illinois	6
40	Michigan	17
17	Nebraska	7
31	Oklahoma State	21
24	Colorado	31
41	Kansas State	38
44	Oklahoma	10
40	Iowa State	13
69	Kansas	21
	Orange Bowl	
3	Penn State	10

1970

38	Baylor	0
34	Minnesota	12

14	Air Force	37
40	Oklahoma State	20
7	Nebraska	21
7	Notre Dame	24
30	Colorado	16
13	Kansas State	17
13	Oklahoma	28
19	Iowa State	31
28	Kansas	17

1971

0	Stanford	19
6	Air Force	7
24	Southern Methodist	12
6	Army	22
0	Nebraska	36
16	Oklahoma State	37
7	Colorado	27
12	Kansas State	28
3	Oklahoma	20
17	Iowa State	45
2	Kansas	7

1972

24	Oregon	22
0	Baylor	27
34	California	27
16	Oklahoma State	17
0	Nebraska	62
30	Notre Dame	26
20	Colorado	17
31	Kansas State	14
6	Oklahoma	17
6	Iowa State	5
17	Kansas	28
	Fiesta Bowl	
35	Arizona State	49

1973

17	Mississippi	0
31	Virginia	7
27	North Carolina	14
17	Southern Methodist	7
13	Nebraska	12
13	Oklahoma State	9
13	Colorado	17
31	Kansas State	7
3	Oklahoma	31
7	Iowa State	17

13	Kansas	14
	Sun Bowl	
34	Auburn	17

1974

0	Mississippi	10
28	Baylor	21
9	Arizona State	0
20	Wisconsin	59
21	Nebraska	10
7	Oklahoma State	31
30	Colorado	24
52	Kansas State	15
0	Oklahoma	37
10	Iowa State	7
27	Kansas	3

1975

20	Alabama	7
30	Illinois	20
27	Wisconsin	21
7	Michigan	31
41	Oklahoma State	14
20	Colorado	31
35	Kansas State	3
7	Nebraska	30
44	Iowa State	14
27	Oklahoma	28
24	Kansas	4?

1976

46	Southern California	25
6	Illinois	31
22	Ohio State	21
24	North Carolina	3
28	Kansas State	21
17	Iowa State	21
34	Nebraska	24
19	Oklahoma State	20
16	Colorado	7
20	Oklahoma	27
41	Kansas	14

1977

10	Southern California	27
7	Illinois	11
21	California	28
15	Arizona State	0

0	Iowa State	7
17	Oklahoma	21
28	Kansas State	13
24	Colorado	14
10	Nebraska	21
41	Oklahoma State	14
22	Kansas	24

1978

3	Notre Dame	0
20	Alabama	38
45	Mississippi	14
23	Oklahoma	45
45	Illinois	3
26	Iowa State	13
56	Kansas State	14
27	Colorado	28
20	Oklahoma State	35
48	Kansas	0
35	Nebraska	31
	Liberty Bowl	
20	Louisiana State	15

UNIVERSITY OF NEBRASKA

Lincoln, Nebraska

Founded 1869   COLORS: *Scarlet and Cream*   NICKNAME: *Cornhuskers*

Head Coaches since 1928

E. E. Bearg	*1925–1928*	George ("Potsy") Clark	*1948*
Dana X. Bible	*1929–1936*	James W. Glassford	*1949–1955*
Lawrence McCeney ("Biff") Jones	*1937–1941*	Pete Elliott	*1956*
Glenn Presnell	*1942*	Bill Jennings	*1957–1961*
A. J. Lewandowski	*1943–1944*	Bob Devaney	*1962–1972*
George ("Potsy") Clark	*1945*	Tom Osborne	*1973–*
B. E. ("Bernie") Masterson	*1946–1947*		

1928

12	Iowa State	00
26	Montana State	6
7	Syracuse	6
24	Missouri	0
20	Kansas	0
44	Oklahoma	6
0	Pittsburgh	0
3	Army	13
8	Kansas State	0

1929

0	Southern Methodist	0
13	Syracuse	6
7	Pittsburgh	12
7	Missouri	7
12	Kansas	6
13	Oklahoma	13
10	Kansas State	6
31	Iowa State	12

1930

13	Texas A. & M.	0
7	Oklahoma	20

14	Iowa State	12
53	Montana State	7
0	Pittsburgh	0
16	Kansas	0
0	Missouri	0
7	Iowa	12
9	Kansas State	10

1931

44	South Dakota	6
7	Northwestern	19
13	Oklahoma	9
6	Kansas	0
10	Missouri	7
7	Iowa	0
6	Kansas State	3
23	Iowa State	0
0	Pittsburgh	40
20	Colorado State	7

1932

12	Iowa State	6
6	Minnesota	7

20	Kansas	6
6	Kansas State	0
14	Iowa	13
0	Pittsburgh	0
5	Oklahoma	0
21	Missouri	6
21	Southern Methodist	14

1933

26	Texas	0
20	Iowa State	0
9	Kansas State	9
16	Oklahoma	7
26	Missouri	0
12	Kansas	0
0	Pittsburgh	6
7	Iowa	6
22	Oregon State	0

1934

50	Wyoming	0
0	Minnesota	20
14	Iowa	13
6	Oklahoma	0

7	Iowa State	6
6	Pittsburgh	25
3	Kansas	0
13	Missouri	6
7	Kansas State	19

1935

28	Chicago	7
20	Iowa State	7
7	Minnesota	12
0	Kansas State	0
19	Oklahoma	0
19	Missouri	6
19	Kansas	13
0	Pittsburgh	6
26	Oregon State	20

1936

34	Iowa State	0
0	Minnesota	7
13	Indiana	9
14	Oklahoma	0
20	Missouri	0
26	Kansas	0
6	Pittsburgh	19
40	Kansas State	9
32	Oregon State	14

1937

14	Minnesota	9
20	Iowa State	7
0	Oklahoma	0
7	Missouri	0
7	Indiana	0
13	Kansas	13
7	Pittsburgh	13
28	Iowa	0
3	Kansas State	0

1938

7	Minnesota	16
7	Iowa State	8
0	Indiana	0
0	Oklahoma	14
10	Missouri	13
16	Kansas	7
0	Pittsburgh	19

14	Iowa	0
14	Kansas State	7

1939

7	Indiana	7
6	Minnesota	0
10	Iowa State	7
20	Baylor	0
25	Kansas State	9
13	Missouri	27
7	Kansas	0
14	Pittsburgh	13
13	Oklahoma	7

1940

7	Minnesota	13
13	Indiana	7
53	Kansas	2
20	Missouri	7
13	Oklahoma	0
14	Iowa	6
9	Pittsburgh	7
21	Iowa State	12
20	Kansas State	0
	Rose Bowl	
13	Stanford	21

1941

14	Iowa State	0
32	Kansas	0
13	Indiana	21
0	Missouri	6
6	Kansas State	12
0	Minnesota	9
7	Pittsburgh	14
14	Iowa	13
7	Oklahoma	6

1942

0	Iowa	27
26	Iowa State	0
0	Indiana	12
2	Minnesota	15
7	Oklahoma	0
14	Kansas	7
6	Missouri	26
0	Pittsburgh	6

0	Iowa Pre-Flight	46
0	Kansas State	19

1943

0	Minnesota	54
13	Indiana	54
6	Iowa State	27
7	Kansas	6
20	Missouri	54
13	Kansas State	7
	Pittsburgh*	
13	Iowa	33
7	Oklahoma	26

*Game cancelled.

1944

0	Minnesota	39
0	Indiana	54
0	Kansas	20
24	Missouri	20
6	Iowa	27
6	Iowa State	19
35	Kansas State	0
12	Oklahoma	31

1945

0	Oklahoma	20
7	Minnesota	61
14	Indiana	54
7	Iowa State	27
0	Missouri	19
27	Kansas	13
24	Kansas State	0
53	South Dakota	0
13	Iowa	6

1946

6	Minnesota	33
31	Kansas State	0
7	Iowa	21
16	Kansas	14
7	Indiana	27
20	Missouri	21
33	Iowa State	0
6	Oklahoma	27
0	UCLA	18

1947

0	Indiana	17
13	Minnesota	28
14	Iowa State	7
0	Notre Dame	31
14	Kansas State	7
6	Missouri	47
7	Kansas	13
13	Oklahoma	14
6	Oregon State	27

1948

19	Iowa State	15
13	Minnesota	39
6	Colorado	19
13	Notre Dame	44
7	Kansas	27
15	UCLA	27
32	Kansas State	0
14	Oklahoma	41
6	Missouri	33
12	Oregon State	28

1949

33	South Dakota	6
6	Minnesota	28
13	Kansas State	6
7	Penn State	22
0	Oklahoma	48
20	Missouri	21
13	Kansas	27
7	Iowa State	0
25	Colorado	14

1950

20	Indiana	20
32	Minnesota	26
19	Colorado	28
19	Penn State	0
33	Kansas	26
40	Missouri	34
49	Kansas State	21
20	Iowa State	13
35	Oklahoma	49

1951

7	Texas Christian	28
1	Kansas State*	0
7	Penn State	15
20	Minnesota	39
19	Missouri	35
7	Kansas	27
34	Iowa State	27
14	Colorado	36
0	Oklahoma	27
7	Miami	19

*Forfeit by Kansas State.

1952

46	South Dakota	0
28	Oregon	13
16	Iowa State	0
27	Kansas State	14
0	Penn State	10
16	Colorado	16
6	Missouri	10
14	Kansas	13
7	Minnesota	13
13	Oklahoma	34

1953

12	Oregon	20
21	Illinois	21
0	Kansas State	27
6	Pittsburgh	14
20	Miami	16
7	Missouri	23
9	Kansas	0
27	Iowa State	19
10	Colorado	14
7	Oklahoma	30

1954

7	Minnesota	19
39	Iowa State	14
3	Kansas State	7
27	Oregon State	7
20	Colorado	6
25	Missouri	19
41	Kansas	20
7	Pittsburgh	21
7	Oklahoma	55
50	Hawaii	0
	Orange Bowl	
7	Duke	34

1955

0	Hawaii	6
20	Ohio State	28
16	Kansas State	0
0	Texas A. & M.	27
7	Pittsburgh	21
18	Missouri	12
19	Kansas	14
10	Iowa State	7
37	Colorado	20
0	Oklahoma	41

1956

34	South Dakota	6
7	Ohio State	34
9	Iowa State	7
7	Kansas State	10
14	Indiana	19
0	Colorado	16
15	Missouri	14
26	Kansas	20
7	Baylor	26
6	Oklahoma	54

1957

12	Washington State	34
0	Army	42
14	Kansas State	7
0	Pittsburgh	34
9	Syracuse	26
13	Missouri	14
12	Kansas	14
0	Iowa State	13
0	Colorado	27
7	Oklahoma	32

1958

14	Penn State	7
0	Purdue	28
7	Iowa State	6
6	Kansas State	23
0	Syracuse	38
16	Colorado	27
0	Missouri	31
7	Kansas	29
14	Pittsburgh	6
7	Oklahoma	40

1959

0	Texas	20
32	Minnesota	12
7	Oregon State	6
3	Kansas	10
7	Indiana	23
0	Missouri	9
25	Oklahoma	21
6	Iowa State	18
14	Colorado	12
14	Kansas State	29

1960

14	Texas	13
14	Minnesota	26
7	Iowa State	10
17	Kansas State	7
14	Army	9
6	Colorado	19
0	Missouri	28
0	Kansas	31
6	Oklahoma State	7
17	Oklahoma	14

1961

33	North Dakota	0
14	Arizona	14
24	Kansas State	0
6	Syracuse	28
6	Oklahoma State	14
0	Missouri	10
6	Kansas	28
16	Iowa State	13
0	Colorado	7
14	Oklahoma	21

1962

53	South Dakota	0
25	Michigan	13
36	Iowa State	22
19	North Carolina State	14
26	Kansas State	6
31	Colorado	6
7	Missouri	16
40	Kansas	16
14	Oklahoma State	0
6	Oklahoma	34
	Gotham Bowl	
36	Miami	34

1963

58	South Dakota State	7
14	Minnesota	7
21	Iowa State	7
13	Air Force	17
28	Kansas State	6
41	Colorado	6
13	Missouri	12
23	Kansas	9
20	Oklahoma State	16
29	Oklahoma	20
	Orange Bowl	
13	Auburn	7

1964

56	South Dakota	0
26	Minnesota	21
14	Iowa State	7
28	South Carolina	6
47	Kansas State	0
21	Colorado	3
9	Missouri	0
14	Kansas	7
27	Oklahoma State	14
7	Oklahoma	17
	Cotton Bowl	
7	Arkansas	10

1965

34	Texas Christian	14
27	Air Force	17
44	Iowa State	0
37	Wisconsin	0
41	Kansas State	0
38	Colorado	13
16	Missouri	14
42	Kansas	6
21	Oklahoma State	17
21	Oklahoma	9
	Orange Bowl	
28	Alabama	39

1966

14	Texas Christian	10
28	Utah State	7
12	Iowa State	6
31	Wisconsin	3

21	Kansas State	10
21	Colorado	19
35	Missouri	0
24	Kansas	13
21	Oklahoma State	6
9	Oklahoma	10
	Sugar Bowl	
7	Alabama	34

1967

17	Washington	7
7	Minnesota	0
16	Kansas State	14
0	Kansas	10
16	Colorado	21
29	Texas Christian	0
12	Iowa State	0
9	Oklahoma State	0
7	Missouri	10
14	Oklahoma	21

1968

13	Wyoming	10
31	Utah	0
17	Minnesota	14
13	Kansas	23
14	Missouri	16
21	Oklahoma State	20
24	Iowa State	13
0	Kansas State	12
22	Colorado	6
0	Oklahoma	47

1969

21	Southern California	31
14	Texas A. & M.	0
42	Minnesota	14
7	Missouri	17
21	Kansas	17
13	Oklahoma State	3
20	Colorado	7
17	Iowa State	3
10	Kansas State	7
44	Oklahoma	14
	Sun Bowl	
45	Georgia	6

1970

36	Wake Forest	12
21	Southern California	21
28	Army	0
35	Minnesota	10
21	Missouri	7
41	Kansas	20
65	Oklahoma State	31
29	Colorado	13
54	Iowa State	29
51	Kansas State	13
28	Oklahoma	21
	Orange Bowl	
17	Louisiana State	12

1971

34	Oregon	7
35	Minnesota	7
34	Texas A. & M.	7
42	Utah State	6
36	Missouri	0
55	Kansas	0
41	Oklahoma State	13
31	Colorado	7
37	Iowa State	0
44	Kansas State	17
35	Oklahoma	31
45	Hawaii	3
	Orange Bowl	
38	Alabama	6

1972

17	UCLA	20
37	Texas A. & M.	7
77	Army	7
49	Minnesota	0
62	Missouri	0
56	Kansas	0
34	Oklahoma State	0
33	Colorado	10
23	Iowa State	23
59	Kansas State	7
14	Oklahoma	17
	Orange Bowl	
40	Notre Dame	6

1973

40	UCLA	13
31	North Carolina State	14
20	Wisconsin	16
48	Minnesota	7
12	Missouri	13
10	Kansas	9
17	Oklahoma State	17
28	Colorado	16
31	Iowa State	7
50	Kansas State	21
0	Oklahoma	27
	Cotton Bowl	
19	Texas	3

1974

61	Oregon	7
20	Wisconsin	21
49	Northwestern	7
54	Minnesota	0
10	Missouri	21
56	Kansas	0
7	Oklahoma State	3
31	Colorado	15
23	Iowa State	13
35	Kansas State	7
14	Oklahoma	28
	Sugar Bowl	
13	Florida	10

1975

10	Louisiana State	7
45	Indiana	0
56	Texas Christian	14
31	Miami	16
16	Kansas	0
28	Oklahoma State	20
63	Colorado	21
30	Missouri	7
12	Kansas State	0
52	Iowa State	0
10	Oklahoma	35
	Fiesta Bowl	
14	Arizona State	17

1976

6	Louisiana State	6
45	Indiana	13

64	Texas Christian	10
17	Miami	9
24	Colorado	12
51	Kansas State	0
24	Missouri	34
31	Kansas	3
28	Iowa State	37
14	Oklahoma State	10
17	Oklahoma	20
68	Hawaii	3
	Astro-Bluebonnet Bowl	
27	Texas Tech	24

1977

10	Washington State	19
31	Alabama	24
31	Baylor	10
31	Indiana	13
26	Kansas State	9
21	Iowa State	24
33	Colorado	15
31	Oklahoma State	14
21	Missouri	10
52	Kansas	7
7	Oklahoma	31
21	Memphis	17

1978

3	Alabama	20
36	California	26
56	Hawaii	10
69	Indiana	17
23	Iowa State	0
48	Kansas State	14
52	Colorado	14
22	Oklahoma State	14
63	Kansas	21
17	Oklahoma	14
31	Missouri	35
	Orange Bowl	
24	Oklahoma	31

OKLAHOMA STATE UNIVERSITY

Stillwater, Oklahoma

Founded 1890   COLORS: *Orange and Black*   NICKNAME: *Cowboys*

Head Coaches since 1928

John F. Maulbetsch	*1921–1928*	Cliff Speegle	*1955–1962*
Lynn O. ("Pappy") Waldorf	*1929–1933*	Phil Cutchin	*1963–1968*
Albert A. Exendine	*1934–1935*	Floyd Gass	*1969–1971*
Tex Cox	*1936–1938*	Dave Smith	*1972*
Jim Lookabaugh	*1939–1949*	Jim Stanley	*1973–1978*
J. B. Whitworth	*1950–1954*	Jim Johnson	*1979–*

1928

13	St. Regis	6
6	Kansas State	13
0	Creighton	37
0	Marquette	26
0	Oklahoma City	9
6	West Virginia	32
0	Oklahoma	46
0	Tulsa	31

1929

12	Northwestern	0
6	Drake	18
18	Oklahoma City	0
32	Creighton	13
6	West Virginia	9
20	Tulsa	0
0	St. Louis	0
7	Oklahoma	7
6	Arkansas	32

1930

12	Wichita	0
6	Iowa	0
7	Indiana	7
0	Oklahoma City	6
28	Washington	7
12	Haskell	13

26	Arkansas	0
7	Oklahoma	0
13	Creighton	0
13	Tulsa	7

1931

34	Bethany	9
25	Northeastern	0
0	Minnesota	20
31	Arizona	0
39	Haskell	0
0	Oklahoma City	13
13	Kansas	7
20	Creighton	0
7	Tulsa	6
14	Wichita	6
0	Oklahoma	0

1932

13	Phillips	0
0	Central State	0
33	Southwestern	3
27	Drake	7
18	Creighton	7
14	Oklahoma City	6
7	Oklahoma	0
0	Tulsa	0

6	Jefferson	12
27	Grinnell	0
13	Arizona	6
20	Texas	7

1933

20	Central State	12
0	Colorado	6
13	Oklahoma City	19
7	Southern Methodist	7
18	Haskell	0
7	Tulsa	0
21	Drake	0
33	Creighton	13
13	Oklahoma	0

1934

12	Oklahoma Baptist	0
7	Drake	0
9	Haskell	6
0	Southern Methodist	41
7	Creighton	13
19	Detroit	6
0	Duquesne	32
0	Tulsa	19
0	Oklahoma	0
0	Oklahoma City	13

1935

6	Oklahoma City	0
20	Southeastern	13
20	Haskell	0
0	Tulsa	12
7	Duquesne	20
0	Detroit	13
0	Texas Tech	14
0	Oklahoma	25
13	Washington	39
0	Creighton	16

1936

6	Oklahoma City	9
0	Kansas State	31
6	Washburn	0
0	Tulsa	13
0	Baylor	13
6	Washington	39
12	Detroit	46
0	Texas Tech	12
13	Oklahoma	35
0	Centenary	7

1937

14	Wichita	8
16	Creighton	13
13	Arizona	22
25	Washburn	3
0	Tulsa	27
6	Texas Tech	14
0	Washington	12
27	Oklahoma City	7
0	Oklahoma	16
0	Centenary	19

1938

23	Central State	12
7	Arkansas	27
6	Baylor	20
7	Creighton	16
7	Tulsa	20
0	Washburn	14
0	Washington	24
6	Wichita	14
19	Oklahoma City	12
0	Oklahoma	19

1939

0	Texas A. & M.	32
52	Northwestern	0

0	Baylor	13
9	Tulsa	7
27	Washburn	6
0	Oklahoma	41
20	New Mexico State	0
0	Washington	7
0	Wichita	0
20	Creighton	9

1940

25	Central State	6
6	Texas Tech	6
27	Oklahoma	29
26	Wichita	6
53	Washington	12
0	Arizona	24
20	Creighton	14
33	Washburn	14
14	St. Louis	7
6	Tulsa	19

1941

0	Oklahoma	19
6	Texas Tech	16
41	Washington	12
14	Detroit	20
0	Tulsa	16
13	Creighton	6
13	St. Louis	7
41	Arizona	14
33	Wichita	13

1942

0	Oklahoma	0
12	Baylor	18
9	Texas Tech	6
6	Arizona	20
40	Washington	7
20	Creighton	6
6	Tulsa	34
54	St. Louis	7
55	Drake	12
33	Detroit	6

1943

21	Texas Tech	13
13	Oklahoma	22
0	Navy Zoomers	20

0	Texas Christian	25
6	Tulsa	55
19	Arkansas	13
7	Denver	6

1944

41	West Texas	6
19	Arkansas	0
14	Texas Tech	7
33	Denver	21
46	Tulsa	40
0	Navy Zoomers	15
13	Texas	8
28	Oklahoma	6
	Cotton Bowl	
34	Texas Christian	0

1945

19	Arkansas	14
31	Denver	7
26	Southern Methodist	12
46	Utah	6
25	Texas Christian	12
12	Tulsa	6
46	Texas Tech	6
47	Oklahoma	0
	Sugar Bowl	
33	St. Mary's (Calif.)	13

1946

40	Denver	7
21	Arkansas	21
6	Texas	54
6	Southern Methodist	15
13	Georgia	33
7	Texas Christian	6
13	Kansas	14
18	Tulsa	20
7	Texas Tech	14
59	Drake	7
12	Oklahoma	73

1947

12	Kansas State	0
14	Texas Christian	7
14	Denver	26
14	Southern Methodist	21
7	Georgia	20

9	Drake	13
26	Temple	0
0	Tulsa	13
7	Kansas	13
13	Oklahoma	21

1948

27	Wichita	14
14	Texas Christian	21
27	Denver	7
27	San Francisco	20
41	Temple	7
7	Kansas	13
19	Tulsa	0
42	Kansas State	6
15	Oklahoma	19
	Delta Bowl	
0	William and Mary	20

1949

33	Texas Christian	33
48	Denver	2
7	Missouri	21
28	Drake	0
14	Kansas	55
7	Detroit	13
13	Tulsa	13
26	Kansas State	14
47	Wichita	20
0	Oklahoma	41

1950

12	Arkansas	7
13	Texas Christian	7
14	Drake	14
0	Southern Methodist	56
7	Kansas	40
0	Missouri	27
13	Tulsa	27
32	Wichita	20
13	Detroit	20
41	Kansas State	0
14	Oklahoma	41

1951

7	Arkansas	42
26	Missouri	27
13	Washington State	27
43	Wichita	0
27	Drake	14
20	Detroit	7
7	Tulsa	35
12	Kansas	27
7	Houston	31
6	Oklahoma	41

1952

20	Arkansas	22
7	Texas A. & M.	14
7	Houston	10
35	Wichita	21
14	Missouri	7
21	Detroit	6
21	Tulsa	23
7	Kansas	12
7	Washington State	9
7	Oklahoma	54

1953

20	Hardin-Simmons	0
7	Arkansas	6
13	Texas Tech	27
14	Wichita	7
14	Houston	7
14	Detroit	18
28	Tulsa	14
20	Wyoming	14
41	Kansas	14
7	Oklahoma	42

1954

14	Wyoming	6
14	Texas A. & M.	6
13	Texas Tech	13
13	Wichita	22
7	Houston	14
7	Hardin-Simmons	13
12	Tulsa	0
34	Detroit	19
47	Kansas	12
0	Oklahoma	14

1955

0	Arkansas	21
6	Texas Tech	24

7	Wichita	14
13	Houston	21
0	Detroit	7
14	Tulsa	0
13	Colorado State	20
7	Kansas	12
28	Kansas State	0
0	Oklahoma	53

1956

27	Kansas State	7
7	Arkansas	19
32	Wichita	6
14	Tulsa	14
0	Houston	13
13	Kansas	21
13	Texas Tech	13
0	Louisiana State	13
25	Detroit	7
0	Oklahoma	53

1957

0	Arkansas	12
25	North Texas State	19
26	Wichita	9
28	Tulsa	13
6	Houston	6
13	Texas Tech	0
39	Wyoming	6
7	Kansas	13
32	Hardin-Simmons	7
6	Oklahoma	53

1958

31	Denver	14
21	North Texas State	14
43	Wichita	12
16	Tulsa	24
7	Houston	0
19	Cincinnati	14
29	Air Force	33
14	Kansas State	7
6	Kansas	3
0	Oklahoma	7
	Blue Grass Bowl	
15	Florida State	6

1959

9	Cincinnati	22
7	Arkansas	13
27	Kansas State	21
26	Tulsa	0
19	Houston	12
34	Wichita	14
18	Marquette	12
20	Denver	12
14	Kansas	28
7	Oklahoma	17

1960

0	Arkansas	9
7	Missouri	28
28	Tulsa	7
7	Houston	12
7	Kansas	14
6	Iowa State	13
28	Kansas State	7
7	Nebraska	6
6	Colorado	13
6	Oklahoma	17

1961

7	Iowa State	14
0	Colorado	24
26	Tulsa	0
0	Missouri	10
14	Nebraska	6
8	Kansas	42
13	Wichita	25
28	Houston	24
45	Kansas State	0
13	Oklahoma	21

1962

7	Arkansas	34
17	Tulsa	7
36	Colorado	16
6	Missouri	23
17	Kansas	36
7	Iowa State	34
12	Army	7
0	Nebraska	14
30	Kansas State	6
6	Oklahoma	37

1963

0	Arkansas	21
7	Texas	34

0	Colorado	25
6	Missouri	28
7	Kansas	41
28	Iowa State	33
33	Tulsa	24
16	Nebraska	20
	Kansas State*	
10	Oklahoma	34

*Game cancelled.

1964

10	Arkansas	14
29	Iowa State	14
10	Missouri	7
14	Colorado	10
13	Kansas	14
14	Tulsa	61
31	Wichita	7
14	Nebraska	27
14	Kansas State	17
16	Oklahoma	21

1965

14	Arkansas	28
0	Missouri	13
17	Tulsa	14
11	Colorado	34
14	Texas Tech	17
0	Kansas	9
10	Iowa State	14
17	Nebraska	21
31	Kansas State	7
17	Oklahoma	16

1966

10	Arkansas	14
9	Houston	35
11	Colorado	10
0	Missouri	7
10	Kansas	7
14	Iowa State	14
7	Texas Tech	10
6	Nebraska	21
21	Kansas State	6
15	Oklahoma	14

1967

0	Air Force	0
7	Arkansas	6

0	Texas	19
15	Kansas	26
10	Colorado	7
0	Missouri	7
0	Nebraska	9
28	Iowa State	14
49	Kansas State	14
14	Oklahoma	38

1968

15	Arkansas	32
3	Texas	31
21	Houston	17
14	Kansas	49
20	Nebraska	21
7	Missouri	42
34	Colorado	17
26	Iowa State	17
14	Kansas State	21
7	Oklahoma	41

1969

0	Arkansas	39
24	Houston	18
17	Texas Tech	10
21	Missouri	31
3	Nebraska	13
28	Kansas	25
28	Kansas State	19
14	Colorado	17
35	Iowa State	0
27	Oklahoma	28

1970

13	Mississippi State	14
7	Arkansas	23
26	Houston	17
29	Missouri	40
34	Texas Christian	20
31	Nebraska	65
19	Kansas	7
15	Kansas State	28
6	Colorado	30
36	Iowa State	27
6	Oklahoma	66

1971

26	Mississippi State	7
10	Arkansas	31

24	Virginia Tech	16
14	Texas Christian	14
37	Missouri	16
13	Nebraska	41
17	Kansas	10
23	Kansas State	35
6	Colorado	40
0	Iowa State	54
14	Oklahoma	58

1972

21	Texas (Arlington)	3
23	Arkansas	24
31	Colorado	6
17	Missouri	16
32	Virginia Tech	34
20	Baylor	7
0	Nebraska	34
10	Kansas	13
45	Kansas State	14
45	Iowa State	14
15	Oklahoma	38

1973

56	Texas (Arlington)	7
38	Arkansas	6
70	Southern Illinois	7
7	Texas Tech	20
9	Missouri	13
17	Nebraska	17
10	Kansas	10
28	Kansas State	9
38	Colorado	24
12	Iowa State	28
18	Oklahoma	45

1974

59	Wichita State	0
26	Arkansas	7
14	Baylor	31
13	Texas Tech	14
31	Missouri	7
3	Nebraska	7
24	Kansas	13
29	Kansas State	5
20	Colorado	37
14	Iowa State	12
13	Oklahoma	44
	Fiesta Bowl	
16	Brigham Young	6

1975

34	Wichita State	0
20	Arkansas	13
61	North Texas State	7
17	Texas Tech	16
14	Missouri	41
20	Nebraska	28
35	Kansas	19
7	Oklahoma	27
7	Colorado	17
56	Kansas State	3
14	Iowa State	7

1976

33	Tulsa	21
10	Arkansas	16
16	North Texas State	10
21	Kansas	14
10	Colorado	20
31	Oklahoma	24
20	Missouri	19
10	Nebraska	14
45	Kansas State	21
42	Iowa State	21
42	Texas	13
	Tangerine Bowl	
49	Brigham Young	21

1977

34	Tulsa	17
6	Arkansas	28
54	Texas	0
17	Florida State	25
13	Colorado	29
21	Kansas State	14
21	Kansas	0
14	Nebraska	31
28	Oklahoma	61
14	Missouri	41
13	Iowa State	21

1978

10	Wichita State	20
20	Florida State	38
7	Arkansas	19
7	North Texas State	12
7	Kansas State	18
24	Colorado	20
21	Kansas	7
14	Nebraska	22
35	Missouri	20

15	Iowa State	28
7	Oklahoma	62

UNIVERSITY OF OKLAHOMA

Norman, Oklahoma

Founded 1890   COLORS: Crimson and Cream   NICKNAME: Sooners

Head Coaches since 1928

Adrian Lindsey	*1927–1931*	Bud Wilkinson	*1947–1963*
Lewis Hardage	*1932–1934*	Gomer Jones	*1964–1965*
Lawrence McCeney ("Biff") Jones	*1935–1936*	Jim Mackenzie	*1966*
Tom Stidham	*1937–1940*	Chuck Fairbanks	*1967–1972*
Dewey ("Snorter") Luster	*1941–1945*	Barry Switzer	*1973–*
Jim Tatum	*1946*		

1928

7	Indiana	10
7	Creighton	0
33	Kansas A. & M.	21
0	Iowa State	13
6	Nebraska	44
7	Kansas	0
46	Oklahoma A. & M.	0
14	Missouri	0

1929

26	Creighton	0
0	Texas	21
14	Kansas A. & M.	13
21	Iowa State	7
0	Kansas	7
13	Nebraska	13
7	Oklahoma A. & M.	7
0	Missouri	13

1930

47	New Mexico	0
20	Nebraska	7
7	Texas	17
7	Kansas A. & M.	0
19	Iowa State	13
0	Kansas	13
0	Oklahoma A. & M.	7
0	Missouri	0

1931

19	Rice	6
0	Nebraska	13
0	Texas	3
0	Kansas A. & M.	14
12	Iowa State	13
10	Kansas	0
0	Missouri	7
0	Oklahoma A. & M.	0
0	Oklahoma City	6
20	Tulsa	7
20	Honolulu Town Team	39
7	Hawaii	0

1932

7	Tulsa	0
21	Kansas	6
10	Texas	17
20	Kansas State	13
0	Oklahoma A. & M.	7
6	Missouri	14

1933

0	Vanderbilt	0
6	Tulsa	20
9	Texas	0
19	Iowa State	7
7	Nebraska	16
20	Kansas	0
21	Missouri	0
0	Kansas State	14
0	Oklahoma A. & M.	13

1934

7	Centenary	0
0	Texas	19
0	Nebraska	6
7	Kansas	7
31	Missouri	0
12	Iowa State	0
7	Kansas State	8
0	Oklahoma A. & M.	0
0	George Washington	3

(continued under 1932 column top: 19 Iowa State 12; 0 Nebraska 5; 7 George Washington 7)

1935

3	Colorado	0
25	New Mexico	0
7	Texas	12
16	Iowa State	0
0	Nebraska	19
0	Kansas	7
20	Missouri	6
3	Kansas State	0
25	Oklahoma A. & M.	0

1936

0	Tulsa	0
8	Colorado	0
0	Texas	6
14	Kansas	0
0	Nebraska	14
7	Iowa State	7
6	Kansas State	6
14	Missouri	21
35	Oklahoma A. & M.	13

1937

7	Tulsa	19
6	Rice	0
7	Texas	7
0	Nebraska	0
3	Kansas	6
19	Kansas State	0
33	Iowa State	7
7	Missouri	0
16	Oklahoma A. & M.	0

1938

7	Rice	6
13	Texas	0
19	Kansas	0
14	Nebraska	0
28	Tulsa	6
26	Kansas State	0
21	Missouri	0
10	Iowa State	0
19	Oklahoma A. & M.	0
28	Washington State	0
	Orange Bowl	
0	Tennessee	17

1939

7	Southern Methodist	7
23	Northwestern	0
24	Texas	12
27	Kansas	7
41	Oklahoma A. & M.	0
38	Iowa State	6
13	Kansas State	10
6	Missouri	7
7	Nebraska	13

1940

29	Oklahoma A. & M.	27
16	Texas	19
14	Kansas State	0
20	Iowa State	7
0	Nebraska	13
13	Kansas	0
7	Missouri	0
0	Temple	6
13	Santa Clara	33

1941

19	Oklahoma A. & M.	0
7	Texas	40
16	Kansas State	0
16	Santa Clara	6
38	Kansas	0
55	Iowa State	0
0	Missouri	28
61	Marquette	14
6	Nebraska	7

1942

0	Oklahoma A. & M.	0
0	Tulsa	23
0	Texas	7
25	Kansas	0
0	Nebraska	7
14	Iowa State	7
76	Kansas State	0
6	Missouri	6
7	Temple	14
7	William and Mary	14

1943

22	Norman NAS	6
22	Oklahoma A. & M.	13
7	Texas	13
6	Tulsa	20
37	Kansas State	0
21	Iowa State	7
26	Kansas	13
20	Missouri	13
26	Nebraska	7

1944

14	Norman NAS	28
21	Texas A. & M.	14
0	Texas	20
68	Kansas State	0
34	Texas Christian	19
12	Iowa State	7
21	Missouri	21
20	Kansas	0
6	Oklahoma A. & M.	28
31	Nebraska	12

1945

21	Hondo, Texas, AAF	6
20	Nebraska	0
14	Texas A. & M.	19
7	Texas	12
39	Kansas	7
41	Kansas State	13
7	Texas Christian	13
14	Iowa State	7
6	Missouri	14
0	Oklahoma A. & M.	47

1946

7	Army	21
10	Texas A. & M.	7
13	Texas	20
28	Kansas State	7
63	Iowa State	0
14	Texas Christian	12
13	Kansas	16
27	Missouri	6
27	Nebraska	6
73	Oklahoma A. & M.	12
	Gator Bowl	
34	North Carolina State	13

1947

24	Detroit	20
26	Texas A. & M.	14
14	Texas	34
13	Kansas	13
7	Texas Christian	20
27	Iowa State	9
27	Kansas State	13
21	Missouri	12
14	Nebraska	13
21	Oklahoma A. & M.	13

1948

17	Santa Clara	20
42	Texas A. & M.	14
20	Texas	14
42	Kansas State	0
21	Texas Christian	18
33	Iowa State	6
41	Missouri	7
41	Nebraska	14
60	Kansas	7
19	Oklahoma A. & M.	15
	Sugar Bowl	
14	North Carolina	6

1949

46	Boston College	0
33	Texas A. & M.	13
20	Texas	14
48	Kansas	26
48	Nebraska	0
34	Iowa State	7
39	Kansas State	0
27	Missouri	7
28	Santa Clara	21
41	Oklahoma A. & M.	0
	Sugar Bowl	
35	Louisiana State	0

1950

28	Boston College	0
34	Texas A. & M.	28
14	Texas	13
58	Kansas State	0
20	Iowa State	7
27	Colorado	18
33	Kansas	13
41	Missouri	7
49	Nebraska	35

41	Oklahoma A. & M.	14
	Sugar Bowl	
7	Kentucky	13

1951

49	William and Mary	7
7	Texas A. & M.	14
7	Texas	9
33	Kansas	21
55	Colorado	14
33	Kansas State	0
34	Missouri	20
35	Iowa State	6
27	Nebraska	0
41	Oklahoma A. & M.	6

1952

21	Colorado	21
49	Pittsburgh	20
49	Texas	20
42	Kansas	20
49	Kansas State	6
41	Iowa State	0
21	Notre Dame	27
47	Missouri	7
34	Nebraska	13
54	Oklahoma A. & M.	7

1953

21	Notre Dame	28
7	Pittsburgh	7
19	Texas	14
45	Kansas	0
27	Colorado	20
34	Kansas State	9
14	Missouri	7
47	Iowa State	0
30	Nebraska	7
42	Oklahoma A. & M.	7
	Orange Bowl	
7	Maryland	0

1954

27	California	13
21	Texas Christian	16
14	Texas	7
65	Kansas	0
21	Kansas State	0

13	Colorado	6
40	Iowa State	0
34	Missouri	13
55	Nebraska	7
14	Oklahoma A. & M.	0

1955

13	North Carolina	6
26	Pittsburgh	14
20	Texas	0
44	Kansas	6
56	Colorado	21
40	Kansas State	7
20	Missouri	0
52	Iowa State	0
41	Nebraska	0
53	Oklahoma A. & M.	0
	Orange Bowl	
20	Maryland	6

1956

36	North Carolina	0
66	Kansas State	0
45	Texas	0
34	Kansas	12
40	Notre Dame	0
27	Colorado	19
44	Iowa State	0
67	Missouri	14
54	Nebraska	6
53	Oklahoma A. & M.	0

1957

26	Pittsburgh	0
40	Iowa State	14
21	Texas	7
47	Kansas	0
14	Colorado	13
13	Kansas State	0
39	Missouri	14
0	Notre Dame	7
32	Nebraska	7
53	Oklahoma State	6
	Orange Bowl	
48	Duke	21

1958

47	West Virginia	14
6	Oregon	0

14	Texas	15
43	Kansas	0
40	Kansas State	6
23	Colorado	7
20	Iowa State	0
39	Missouri	0
40	Nebraska	7
7	Oklahoma State	0
	Orange Bowl	
21	Syracuse	6

1959

13	Northwestern	45
42	Colorado	12
12	Texas	19
23	Missouri	0
7	Kansas	6
21	Nebraska	25
36	Kansas State	0
28	Army	20
35	Iowa State	12
17	Oklahoma State	7

1960

3	Northwestern	19
15	Pittsburgh	14
0	Texas	24
13	Kansas	13
49	Kansas State	7
0	Colorado	7
6	Iowa State	10
19	Missouri	14
14	Nebraska	17
17	Oklahoma State	6

1961

6	Notre Dame	19
15	Iowa State	21
7	Texas	28
0	Kansas	10
14	Colorado	22
17	Kansas State	6
7	Missouri	0
14	Army	8
21	Nebraska	14
21	Oklahoma State	13

1962

7	Syracuse	3
7	Notre Dame	13

6	Texas	9
13	Kansas	7
47	Kansas State	0
62	Colorado	0
41	Iowa State	0
13	Missouri	0
34	Nebraska	6
37	Oklahoma State	6
	Orange Bowl	
0	Alabama	17

1963

31	Clemson	14
17	Southern California	12
7	Texas	28
21	Kansas	18
34	Kansas State	9
35	Colorado	0
24	Iowa State	14
13	Missouri	3
20	Nebraska	29
34	Oklahoma State	10

1964

13	Maryland	3
14	Southern California	40
7	Texas	28
14	Kansas	15
44	Kansas State	0
14	Colorado	11
30	Iowa State	0
14	Missouri	14
17	Nebraska	7
21	Oklahoma State	16
	Gator Bowl	
19	Florida State	36

1965

9	Pittsburgh	13
0	Navy	10
0	Texas	19
21	Kansas	7
27	Kansas State	0
0	Colorado	13
24	Iowa State	20
0	Missouri	30
9	Nebraska	21
16	Oklahoma State	17

1966

17	Oregon	0
33	Iowa State	11
18	Texas	9
35	Kansas	0
0	Notre Dame	38
21	Colorado	24
37	Kansas State	6
7	Missouri	10
10	Nebraska	9
14	Oklahoma State	15

1967

21	Washington State	0
35	Maryland	0
7	Texas	9
46	Kansas State	7
7	Missouri	0
23	Colorado	0
52	Iowa State	14
14	Kansas	10
21	Nebraska	14
38	Oklahoma State	14
	Orange Bowl	
26	Tennessee	24

1968

21	Notre Dame	45
28	North Carolina State	14
20	Texas	26
42	Iowa State	7
27	Colorado	41
35	Kansas State	20
27	Kansas	23
28	Missouri	14
47	Nebraska	0
41	Oklahoma State	7
	Astro-Bluebonnet Bowl	
27	Southern Methodist	28

1969

48	Wisconsin	21
37	Pittsburgh	8
17	Texas	27
42	Colorado	30
21	Kansas State	59
37	Iowa State	14
10	Missouri	44
31	Kansas	15
14	Nebraska	11
28	Oklahoma State	27

1970

28	Southern Methodist	11
21	Wisconsin	7
14	Oregon State	23
9	Texas	41
23	Colorado	15
14	Kansas State	19
29	Iowa State	28
28	Missouri	13
28	Kansas	24
21	Nebraska	28
66	Oklahoma State	6

Astro-Bluebonnet Bowl

24	Alabama	24

1971

30	Southern Methodist	0
55	Pittsburgh	29
33	Southern California	20
48	Texas	27
45	Colorado	17
75	Kansas State	28
43	Iowa State	12
20	Missouri	3
56	Kansas	10
31	Nebraska	35
58	Oklahoma State	14

Sugar Bowl

40	Auburn	22

1972

49	Utah State	0
68	Oregon	3
52	Clemson	3
27	Texas	0
14	Colorado	20
52	Kansas State	0
20	Iowa State	6
17*	Missouri	6
31*	Kansas	7
17	Nebraska	14
38*	Oklahoma State	15

Sugar Bowl

14	Penn State	0

*Oklahoma forfeited games because of an ineligible player.

1973

42	Baylor	14
7	Southern California	7

24	Miami	20
52	Texas	13
34	Colorado	7
56	Kansas State	14
34	Iowa State	17
31	Missouri	3
48	Kansas	20
27	Nebraska	0
45	Oklahoma State	18

1974

28	Baylor	11
72	Utah State	3
63	Wake Forest	0
16	Texas	13
49	Colorado	14
63	Kansas State	0
28	Iowa State	10
37	Missouri	0
45	Kansas	14
28	Nebraska	14
44	Oklahoma State	13

1975

62	Oregon	7
46	Pittsburgh	10
20	Miami	17
21	Colorado	20
24	Texas	17
25	Kansas State	3
39	Iowa State	7
27	Oklahoma State	7
3	Kansas	23
28	Missouri	27
35	Nebraska	10

Orange Bowl

14	Michigan	6

1976

24	Vanderbilt	3
28	California	17
24	Florida State	9
24	Iowa State	10
6	Texas	6
28	Kansas	10
24	Oklahoma State	31
31	Colorado	42
49	Kansas State	20
27	Missouri	20

20	Nebraska	17

Fiesta Bowl

41	Wyoming	7

1977

25	Vanderbilt	23
62	Utah	24
29	Ohio State	28
24	Kansas	9
6	Texas	13
21	Missouri	17
35	Iowa State	16
42	Kansas State	7
61	Oklahoma State	28
52	Colorado	14
38	Nebraska	7

Orange Bowl

6	Arkansas	31

1978

35	Stanford	29
52	West Virginia	10
66	Rice	7
45	Missouri	23
31	Texas	10
17	Kansas	16
34	Iowa State	6
56	Kansas State	19
28	Colorado	7
14	Nebraska	17
62	Oklahoma State	7

Orange Bowl

31	Nebraska	24

Index